HANDBOOK
OF
EQUIPMENT
LEASING

HANDBOOK OF EQUIPMENT LEASING

A Deal Maker's Guide

Richard M. Contino

amacom
American Management Association

This book is available at a special
discount when ordered in bulk quantities.
For information, contact Special Sales Department,
AMACOM, a division of American Management Association,
135 West 50th Street, New York, NY 10020.

Library of Congress Cataloging-in-Publication Data

Contino, Richard M., 1941–
    Handbook of equipment leasing : a deal maker's guide / Richard M.
    Contino.
        p.   cm.
    Includes index.
    ISBN 0-8144-5973-0
    1. Industrial equipment leases—United States—Handbooks, manuals,
    etc.   2. Lease or buy decisions—Handbooks, manuals, etc.
    I. Title.
    HD39.4.C66   1989   89–6527
    658.1'5242—dc20   CIP

Printing number

10 9 8 7 6 5

Dedication
To
May-Lynne
and
My **Father**
In The Future There Is No Past

Introduction

This book's purpose is to provide the legal, financial, accounting, and business background essential to evaluate, negotiate, and advise on successful equipment lease transactions. Equipment leasing is one of the most complex forms of financing in existence today, involving sophisticated concepts often understood only by experts. Many equipment users fail to consider this important alternative when they need equipment because of their lack of understanding of the advantages. Even those who do consider it frequently do not know how to maximize their position.

And even many of those who have participated in leasing transactions in the past now feel less secure in their understanding because of the 1986 Tax Reform Act. Changing the way equipment is to be depreciated, virtually eliminating the investment tax credit, and launching an expanded minimum tax, the 1986 TRA has caused prospective lessees and lessors, and their advisers, to re-examine whether and how to engage in leasing transactions.

This book will assist both leasing novices and those with more experience. It analyzes the equipment lease transaction from start to finish, taking the reader step-by-step through the seven most important aspects of leasing—the general marketplace, the preliminary evaluation stage, the proposal, the documents, the tax issues, the accounting treatment, and the economics. The latest and best techniques for dealing with technical issues are explained. Practical suggestions and insights are offered throughout to enable the reader to gain every advantage and avoid the many legal and financial pitfalls. It addresses, for example, issues such as:

- How does the leasing marketplace really work?
- Can leasing avoid the corporate and individual alternative minimum tax?
- Do bank leasing companies give the most aggressive rates?
- When is leasing a poor choice?
- What is the best way for a company to solicit lease bids?
- Does a proposal letter really commit a lessor?
- What should a properly written lease cover?
- How can an underwriter protect his fee?
- How good is a legal opinion on questionable issues?
- When should a leveraged lease be used?
- When will a lease meet the IRS requirements?
- Can a fixed price purchase option be used?
- What advantageous depreciation methods are now available?
- Is the investment tax credit completely gone?

- What tax and economic risks does a lessor have?
- What special risks must a leveraged lease investor consider?
- How should a lease be analyzed financially?
- What impact do the lease accounting rules have?

Many prospective lessees do not know the optimum way to assess the leasing marketplace. As a result, they do not find the most favorable deals available. Some lessors, for example, are more suited than others for particular transactions. The characteristics of the various lessors are explained, as well as the pros and cons of dealing with each.

Proposal stage. In any lease financing arrangement, the proposal stage is the critical point when the parties establish the transaction's business parameters. At this stage, the prospective lessee will be in his strongest negotiating position. If he takes advantage of some simple techniques recommended by the author, he can, for example, get a "below market" lease rent. A prospective lessor can, on the other hand, gain some valuable advantages at this time by properly structuring his offer.

Documentation. The documentation stage—where the participant's rights and obligations are defined—is another crucial step in the transaction. To be fully aware of what their risks and obligations will be, all participants must understand the transaction's basic concepts. For example, a lessor may inadvertently assume certain state tax payment obligations that can drastically reduce his profits. A lessee may also unknowingly assume burdensome obligations. This book comprehensively examines the documents to give anyone responsible for negotiating an equipment lease the essentials necessary to avoid the many traps.

Tax issues. Problems often arise because of lack of understanding of the complex tax issues. Parties spend time and money on transactions that will not be approved by the IRS. The revised alternative minimum tax is an important consideration in whether to lease or buy equipment. Understanding how it works is essential.

Accounting issues. How a lease must be accounted for should always be a foremost consideration. Improper structuring can cause undesirable accounting treatment. The Financial Accounting Standards Board has promulgated an extensive and complicated set of rules on accounting for leases. A chapter summarizes the rules and puts them into a more meaningful context.

Financial issues.   Another key consideration is the financial side of a lease decision. There are many apparent—and some not so apparent—economic advantages and disadvantages to leasing. Lease investors, for example, should be aware that incorrect equipment residual assumptions can wipe out profits. A prospective lessee can end up making the wrong financing decision by using an incorrect method of analysis. The economic advantages and disadvantages, as well as the methods of financial analysis, are explained so that a prospective lessor, lessee, lender, or investor can determine what his position is or should be.

Leveraged leasing.   An entire chapter explains the specialized field of leveraged leasing—where the lease transaction is financed largely with nonrecourse debt. One of the most sophisticated and competitive forms of leasing, leveraged leasing can produce many unique benefits. There are, however, many dangers. Some lease underwriters, for example, "low ball" rent quotations to eliminate the competition and then later raise the rates. A prospective lease investor can end up making a poor investment by relying on an unrealistic investment analysis.

Many chapters include time-saving checklists covering the critical stages and aspects of an equipment lease financing. Examples have been incorporated to illustrate many of the financial points discussed. In one chapter, all of the leasing industry's important terms and "buzz" words have been compiled and simply defined for ready access. Finally, selected sample lease documents have been supplied.

In summary, this book gives the reader a complete grasp of the legal, financial, accounting, and business considerations that are necessary to originate, evaluate, and negotiate the most favorably structured equipment leasing transaction.

Richard M. Contino

Contents

CHAPTER **1**
The Fundamentals Of Equipment Leasing

A. Overview

The concept of the lease as a property right, and the rights and duties of lessors and lessees, has been part of our legal tradition for centuries, particularly with respect to real estate. During the 1950's, leasing began to emerge as a viable alternative for acquiring equipment. Today, the equipment leasing industry plays a major role in the financial community: A user can lease virtually any type of equipment on a variety of terms. There is, however, a drawback—the legal requirements and financial considerations are extremely complex. In fact, many transactions involve concepts so sophisticated that even the most experienced people sometimes Inadvertently miss points that could cost them or their clients many thousands of dollars.

This increased interest in leasing as an alternate means of acquiring equipment has prompted a deluge of questions not only from equipment users, but also from the legal and financial community. For example:

- What are the tax advantages and disadvantages to the lessee?
- What are the tax benefits available to the lessor?
- How can you be sure a lease qualifies as a true lease for tax purposes?
- How should a lease transaction be analyzed from a financial viewpoint?
- How are leases treated for accounting purposes?

For these, and many other questions, there are no easy answers.

The rapidly changing tax laws have added new questions. Safe harbor leases have come and gone. The 1986 Tax Reform Act (1986 TRA) took away the investment tax credit (ITC) and expanded the alternative minimum tax (AMT). Both prospective lessees and lessors are now pondering whether the revised tax rules enhance or reduce leasing's attraction.

Unfortunately, because of the many variables that can be involved in a lease decision, this book cannot answer all the questions concerning the desirability of entering into a specific transaction. The criteria used by one company may be totally inappropriate for another company. This book will, however, provide the reader with a comprehensive working knowledge of the fundamental tools necessary to handle competently any lease situation from start to finish. The relevant issues will be identified, described, and explained.

This chapter sets the stage for the following chapters. After briefly reviewing the tax motivations behind leasing transactions, it describes the major players—the typical lessees and lessors—explains the types of leases commonly offered, and then sets out what equipment users should consider when deciding whether to enter the leasing arena.

B.   Leasing's Tax Motivations

1.   The General Tax Picture

While any type of equipment can be leased, the critical question to the prospective lessee is—at what cost? While the answer is complex, as a threshold matter, leasing generally is not an economical way to acquire equipment unless the lessor receives certain tax benefits. Consider the following hypothetical example.

> **Illustrative Example**—*The Tax Advantage*: Company Able wants to acquire the use of a $20,000 truck. It can borrow funds from its bank for five years at the prime rate, assumed for this example to be 10% a year. If Company Able were able to borrow 100% of the funds required, its cost to finance the truck would be the cost of the $20,000 loan.
>
> As an alternative, Company Able could lease the truck from Company Baker. Assume Company Baker also borrowed "at prime" from the same bank and that it would fund the truck purchase entirely from its bank borrowings. If there were no truck ownership tax advantages, the only way it could make a profit would be to charge a lease rate greater than its cost of funds. Thus, Company Able would have to pay something over the prime rate to Company Baker, a not very attractive arrangement.

Although the above example is admittedly oversimplified and not completely realistic, it makes the point—leasing may not make any economic sense unless there are ownership tax benefits that can be claimed by a lessor.

2. The Lessor's Tax Benefits

What tax benefits are available to the lessor? For equipment placed in service before 1986, the lessor could obtain both ITC and depreciation deductions as an equipment owner. With limited exceptions, the 1986 TRA did away with the ITC for equipment placed in service after 1985. Thus, the tax benefits for the lessor today are the depreciation deductions available under the Modified Accelerated Cost Recovery System (MACRS), introduced by the 1986 TRA.

Unders MACRS, a lessor generally can write off his equipment's cost over a period significantly shorter than its useful life and at an accelerated rate. For example, a lessor can deduct the cost of leased computer equipment over a six-year period with the percentages for each year as 20%, 32%, 19.2%, 11.52%, 11.52% and 5.76%. In a typical lease, the lessor's deductions in the early years will exceed the rental income, permitting the lessor to offset other income with those excess deductions.

▶ **A Word of Warning:** As explained in Chapter 6, if the lessor is subject to the revised corporate and individual AMTs, his depreciation deductions will be deferred significantly. Potential lessors must review their AMT exposure when pricing a leasing transaction.

3. The Lessee's Tax Consequences

Basically, a user decreases its tax benefits by becoming a lessee rather than an owner. As lessee, the user can deduct his rental payments, but those will be less than the depreciation he could have deducted in the lease's early years. Then why should leasing be considered? As explained below, there are numerous financial and business reasons for a prospective lessee to lease rather than buy. Also, leasing is particularly attractive to equipment users who cannot take timely advantage of the depreciation deductions. Two types of users basically fall into this category. First are those who have negative taxable income or carryover losses, so that they have no taxable income to offset; and second, to a lesser extent, those subject to the AMT because the AMT would reduce the value of an equipment owner's tax benefits, but will not in most cases affect deductions for rent. For those users, the rental payments charged by a lessor who is taking the ownership tax benefits into account in setting his lease rate, can be worth more than the ownership tax benefits.

4.   The Importance of Lease Structuring

When the lessor anticipates tax benefits, he will suffer an economic loss if those benefits are unavailable. Those benefits will be available only if the lessor remains the equipment owner for tax purposes. The lessor will be treated as the tax owner only if the lease is a true lease. Chapter 8 explains the true lease tax guidelines. Although, as explained in that chapter, there is the possibility of some variation from the guidelines, it is advisable to comply with the following:

- The lessor must make an economic profit, apart from the tax benefits, on the lease.
- The lessor's equity investment must be at least 20% of the equipment's cost throughout the lease term.
- The lesseee cannot, with limited exceptions, make any investment in the property, or make any loan to the lessor.
- Lessee purchase options must be at the equipment's fair market value at the time of purchase.
- The property must be usable by a party other than the lessee after the lease term's end.

Poor lease structuring can lead to disaster. If the transaction does not qualify as a true lease, the lessee will not be able to deduct the rental payments and the lessor cannot use the ownership tax benefits. For example, if the lease was classified as a loan, the lessee would be deemed the equipment owner and the lessor deemed the lender. Then, if the lessee cannot use any tax benefits and the lessor must have them for the transaction to make economic sense, everyone loses.

▶ **Observation:**   While all leases must be true leases for the lessor to obtain tax benefits, for leases where the lease term is significantly shorter than the equipment's useful life, there will be little risk that the lease will not be treated as a true lease, because the lessor's ownership status will be clear. Generally, the closer the lease term comes to matching the equipment's useful life, the more attention that must be paid to the true lease rules.

C.   Who Are the Prospective Lessees?

Any equipment user is a prospective lessee. The users can range from multi-national corporations, to sole proprietorships, to individuals using equipment for personal reasons. Whether or not the user should lease is another, more complicated question, and depends on a variety of factors that vary with each situation. Those factors are reviewed in Section F of this chapter.

D. Who Are the Potential Lessors?

In theory, any entity can be a lessor. However, unlike the scope of potential lessees, the way the leasing industry has developed permits the prospective lessors to be put into categories that have certain characteristics.

For discussion purposes, it is useful to separate the potential lessors into five categories: individuals, independent leasing companies, lease brokers, captive leasing companies, and banks. Prospective lessees may find the categories helpful in narrowing the field of potential lessors. And prospective lessors may find the categories helpful in determining their potential competition.

1. Individuals

In the past, the role of the individual as lessor was limited because of the rules limiting an individual from claiming ITCs on leased property. Now that the ITC is no longer available to lessors, wealthy individuals can enter the leasing arena more often because they can be more rate competitive. When they do, they frequently can be competitive be cause they often will take greater risks than a traditional leasing company. A few innovative equipment leasing companies and investment bankers have begun to develop interesting investment programs for individuals that will make them an increasing part of the equipment financing business. For example, some railcar lessors have set up individual investor programs that provide individuals with opportunities to invest in short-term railcar leases.

An individual considering becoming an equipment lessor must, however, now contend with the passive loss rules. An explanation of those rules is outside the scope of this book. A prospective lessee receiving a lease proposal from an individual lessor, however, need not be concerned with the passive loss rules, except to be sure that any tax indemnities do not require the lessee to reimburse the lessor for deductions lost under those rules.

▶ **A Word Of Caution:** A prospective lessee considering leasing from an individual must look at more than the rent advantage. For example, because individuals often take aggressive tax positions, they may run afoul of the IRS. The IRS may then put a lien on all the individual's property, including the leased equipment. Also, individuals can be somewhat more arbitrary to deal with when variances from the lease terms are required.

2.   Independent Leasing Companies

Independent leasing companies provide a major source of equipment lease financing. Because leasing is their principal source of revenue, they have to be extremely aggressive and, in some cases, are willing to bend the rules for the lessee's benefit to win a transaction. For example, some will give a lessee the right to buy the equipment at a predetermined fixed price when the lease ends—a practice that can run the risk of adverse tax consequences. (See Chapter 8—C,6.)

There are two types of independent leasing companies: those that merely buy and lease the equipment to the user ("finance leasing companies"); and those that also offer other services, such as maintenance and repair of the equipment ("service leasing companies").

a.   Finance Leasing Companies

Finance leasing companies—lessors of millions of dollars of equipment each year—operate in much the same manner as banks or other financing companies. They do not maintain an equipment inventory, but rather, after agreeing on a lease with a lessee, buy the specific equipment needed for that lease. The lessee orders and receives the equipment from the vendor. When it arrives, the finance leasing company pays for it, takes title, and leases it to the equipment user.

Finance leasing companies typically write leases—referred to as finance leases—that run from 70 to 80% of the equipment's useful life. The total amounts received under these leases, including the rents payable and the equipment residual value proceeds, are usually sufficient to provide the lessor with a full return of his equipment invesment and a profit. If the equipment purchase is leveraged with third-party debt, the rents will also generally be enough to cover the full repayment of the debt. This type of long-term lease is generally net to the lessee. That is, the lessee must assume substantially all the equipment ownership responsibilities, such as maintenance, taxes, and insurance.

b.   Service Leasing Companies

Service or specialized leasing companies provide nonfinancial services to lessees in addition to the equipment financing. Services may include equipment maintenance and repair or advice on the equipment's operation and design.

Service lessors typically limit their activity to a single type of equipment, such as computers, or to a single type of industry, such as the mining industry. The intense experience gained through the specialization enables them to reduce many leasing risks. For example, because they frequently handle used equipment, they know how to deal efficiently with equipment when it comes off lease, which, in turn, reduces their re-leasing or sale risks. And, because of that reduced risk, they can offer attractive lease termination or equipment exchange privileges.

▶ **Observation:** Many industry participants believe that product specialization is less risky for a lessor than industry specialization. *Reason*: There is a greater likelihood that an industry specialized lessor would suffer more if his industry hit hard times than an equipment specialized lessor would if one of the industries in which his equipment was used hit hard times.

Service lessors typically write leases with much shorter lease terms than finance leases. Nonpayout in nature, those leases do not permit the lessor to recoup his entire equipment investment during the first lease term. Thus, to recover his investment and make a profit, the service lessor must continue to re-lease the equipment. If the equipment becomes obsolete sooner than expected, the lessor may incur a loss. To be compensated for taking that risk, and for providing other services, service lessors will generally charge higher rents than finance lessors.

When should a prospective lessee consider leasing from a service leasing company? Basically, when the lessee needs the specialized services offered by the service lessor or wants a shorter lease term or earlier termination rights. A user may want the shorter term when, for example, there is a high risk of equipment obsolescence or where the user's industry is in a down cycle.

▶ **Recommendation:** A prospective lessee considering leasing equipment that he may want to return early should compare the early termination penalties for finance lessors and service lessors. Frequently, the finance lessors, even though they charge lower rents, will impose stiff penalties for early termination. *Reason*: The financial lessors do not have as strong remarketing capability as the service lessors.

3. Lease Brokers

Also referred to as "lease underwriters" or "syndicators," lease brokers package lease transactions for the account of third parties. Put simply, they match up prospective lessees with prospective lessor-investors. They charge a fee for their service—usually ranging from 0.75 to 8% of the leased equipment's cost—that is typically paid for by the lessor-investors.

To put the lease broker's role into perspective, it is helpful to understand how a broker normally operates. Generally, a lease broker begins by contacting all types of equipment users to determine whether they have any leasing needs. If they do, he will define the rough parameters through discussions with the prospective lessees. At this juncture, the broker may perform a credit check on the prospective lessee to make sure the credit is marketable. If there are not any problems, he will formulate a concise lease structure, including rental rate, and offer it to the equipment user, generally through a formal proposal letter.

If the user finds the proposed arrangement acceptable, the broker then proceeds to find prospective lessor-investors, commonly referred to as equity participants. If the transaction is to be leveraged with third-party debt, a leveraged lease, he may also put out feelers for prospective lenders, commonly referred to as debt participants, although usually the debt side is handled by an investment banker. Having located the equity and debt participants, the broker proceeds to shepherd the transaction through documentation to completion.

Although generally acting exclusively as a broker, a lease underwriter may, on occasion, invest some of his own funds in the equipment along with other third-party lessor-investors and, thereby, become a part owner. By doing so, the lease underwriter can add credibility to the investment and thus be able to sell the lease transaction to potential investors more readily.

One of a lease broker's major assets is his knowledge of the leasing industry. Because he is continually in the market, he will know where to find competitive, cooperative, and realistic equity participants. And he will know how to get those equity participants to agree to what meets the lessee's needs, including, for example, lease rates, overall transaction structure, and documentation.

▶ **Recommendation:**   A prospective lessee considering a finance lease arrangement should invite a cross section of brokers to quote, in addition to regular lessors. Because of their ability to find aggressive equity participants, lease brokers will add a new dimension to the bidding environment.

4.   Captive Leasing Companies

In increasing numbers, equipment vendors are setting up their own leasing companies, generally referred to as captive leasing companies, to service their customers. Although the purpose is usually to offer lease financing on equipment sold by an affiliated company, some captive leasing companies also may be willing to buy and lease equipment sold by an unassociated company.

A captive leasing company marketing its affiliated company's equipment can often offer attractive rates. *Reason:* When it markets its affiliated company's equipment, that company makes a profit, and the captive lessor can then work with a lower financing profit than other types of lessors. Coupled with its knowledge of the equipment's potential residual value, this can result in attractive rents for a lessee.

▶ **Recommendation:**   When considering a certain vendor's equipment, a prospective lessee should also find out whether the vendor has a captive leasing company. If so, the prospective lessee should ask it to submit a lease quotation.

▶ **Observation:**   Although captive leasing companies have a theoretical advantage over other types of lessors because of their connection with the vendor in practice they often do not know how to take advantage of that position effectively. Perhaps this is because the equipment vendors do not have extensive experience in using leasing as a marketing tool and may not support the leasing operation as fully as they should.

5.   Banks

Many banks, particularly national banks, have become actively involved in equipment leasing. They usually are lessors in net finance leases because of regulatory requirements and because those leases provide the least risk and most similarity to their lending activity. (Finance leases are explained later in this chapter at §E,1.)

Banks are not generally inclined to take aggressive equipment residual value positions, thus resulting in a rate increase. Their cost of funds, however, in many cases is lower than that of nonbank lessors, often offsetting their conservative position on residual value assumption.

The terms and prices offered by bank lessors often vary significantly from one transaction to the next. Internal bank policies may contribute to that variation. Banks are not as dependent as most nonbank lessors on their leasing activities for revenues and so can afford to miss out on many deals. Periodically, however, they go on major drives for lease business and, at those times, can be extremely rate aggressive.

▶ **Recommendation:**   Given the unpredictability of bank lessors' responses to potential lease transactions, the prospective lessee is well advised to contact several in hopes of finding one that may offer a particularly attractive deal.

Bank lessors have typically operated with a limited lease marketing staff. As a result, the transactions they saw were fundamentally limited to those coming in through existing customers or lease brokers. Today, however, an increasing number of bank lessors have established strong marketing organizations and, as a group, will undoubtedly become more of a factor in the marketplace in the not too distant future.

It is worth mentioning that banks directly participate in the leasing market in another major way: They frequently act as lenders in leveraged lease transactions.

E. Types of Leases

Significant differences exist among the various types of leases. Unfortunately, the industry jargon used to label the different types is sometimes less than precise. Further compounding the problem is the fact that many hybrid arrangements have surfaced that cross over the lines of the standard descriptive terminology. Once the fundamental characteristics of different leases are identified and understood, however, the confusion can be eliminated.

For explanation purposes, it will be helpful to separate all equipment leases into two main categories: Financial leases and operating leases. The financial, or finance, lease typically represents a long-term lease commitment in which the sum of the rents due will approximate the equipment's purchase cost. Decisions to enter into a financial lease should be part of a company's financial, as opposed to operating, policy considerations. All equipment leases not fitting within the financial lease category can be put into the operating lease category. Because operating leases involve shorter term financial commitments, decisions as to their use typically come within the scope of a company's operating policy.

Within those two broad categories, there are a number of basic variations: Leveraged leases, nonleveraged leases, and service leases. These variations are sometimes incorrectly considered to be separate types of leases rather than what they are, descriptive forms of the basic types. For example, finance leases can be leveraged leases or nonleveraged leases, and service leases can be financial or operating in nature. They will, however, be explained individually to give the reader a working perspective.

Table 1-1 sets out a general overview of some fundamental lease characteristics.

TABLE 1-1

LEASE CHARACTERISTICS

Type of Lease	Lease Term	Typical Type of Transaction	Comments
Finance Lease	Substantial portion of asset's economic life	Underwritten and direct lessor	Payout-type lease
Net Finance Lease	Substantial portion of asset's economic life	Underwritten and direct lessor	Payout-type lease. Lessee has basically all ownership responsibilities.
Leveraged Lease	Usually, substantial portion of asset's economic life	Underwritten	Usually net finance lease
Nonleveraged Lease	Hours to substantial portion of asset's economic life	Direct lessor	Any lease where no third-party debt involved
Operating Lease	Hours to years	Direct lessor	Usually nonpayout

1. The Finance Lease

A common type of equipment lease, finance leases are considered long-term leases because the primary lease terms usually run for most of the equipment's useful life. Typically, the total cash flow over the term—from rents, tax savings, and equipment residual value—will be sufficient to pay back the lessor's investment, take care of his administrative expenses, pay off any equipment-related debt obligations and commissions, and provide a profit. Because they are entered into by lessors as long-term financial commitments, finance lessors usually impose a substantial prepayment penalty for a lessee's early lease termination in an amount that will assure the lessor of a return of his investment and a profit, at least up to the date of termination.

Consistent with its financial nature, a finance lease is usually a net lease. A net lease means that the fundamental ownership responsibilities, such as maintaining and repairing the equipment, paying for the necessary insurance, and taking care of property, use, and sales taxes, are placed on the lessee. A net finance lease can be compared to an equipment loan in that the lessor, like a lender, is involved only in asset funding. The lessor's only basic responsibilities are to pay for the equipment, lease it to the lessee for the agreed-on term, and not interfere with its use.

Because a finance lease's term runs for most of the equipment's useful life, the lessee bears most of the risk of the equipment becoming obsolete. The degree of obsolescence risk that the finance lessor assumes depends on the equipment's anticipated residual value. If, for example, a lessor computes the rent based on a zero equipment residual value at the lease term's end, the lessor has no residual value risk and, thus, no obsolescence risk. This, of course, presumes there is no risk of premature equipment return as a result, for instance, of a lessee default. As a practical matter, however, a lessor must generally use a residual value greater than zero to be price competitive. The risk of obsolescence would then be on the lessor to the extent of the value estimated. If his profit is in part dependent on the anticipated residual value, the greater the risk of obsolescence the greater the chance the transaction will not turn out to be as profitable as anticipated.

One of a financial lessor's principal concerns is the protection of his investment in the event of a lease default or an equipment casualty. Toward this end, finance leases usually include provisions to make the lessor whole if any of these events occur. From a casualty loss standpoint, the lease may include stipulated loss value provisions. Those provisions set out the amount the lessee must pay the lessor if an equipment casualty occurs, depending on when it occurs. The amount of the stipulated loss value is intended to guarantee the lessor a return of his investment, reimburse him for any tax benefit losses, and assure him of at least some of his profit. These stipulated loss values are also sometimes used as a measure of lease default damages, although there are other methods.

Finance leases frequently contain a "hell or high water" rent commitment. Under this type of obligation, a lessee must pay the full rent when due unconditionally and cannot reduce the amount paid even though he has a legitimate claim against the lessor for money owed. This is not as bad as it sounds for a lessee, because he can still bring a lawsuit against the lessor for any claims.

Finance lessors seek hell or high water rent provisions most often in leverage lease transactions involving nonrecourse loans. *Reason*: In a nonrecourse loan, the lender agrees to look only to the lessee's rent payments and the equipment for a return of his investment. With a hell or high water provision, the lender need not be concerned that a dispute between the lessor and lessee will result in the lessee's withholding rent, and so the lender is more willing to offer an attractive loan arrangement.

2. The Operating Lease

Where a lease's primary term is significantly shorter than the equipment's useful life, the lease is referred to as an operating lease. Operating leases typically run anywhere from a few months to a few years, although some are as short as a few hours.

Because the lease terms are relatively short, an operating lessor usually cannot earn much of his equipment investment back through the rents from one lease transaction. Thus, he must either sell or re-lease the equipment on attractive terms to come out ahead. The danger to an operating lessor, of course, is that the equipment's market value will be inadequate to allow him to sell or re-lease it on economically favorable terms. In other words, he has the risk of equipment obsolescence. As a result, such a lessor will attempt to earn his money back faster to lessen his investment exposure by charging higher rent than a finance lessor.

Their short lease terms and easy cancellation provisions make operating leases attractive to users in several situations. One is where the user anticipates using the equipment only for a short time. Another is where the user wants to be able to change equipment if something better comes out. For this reason, users often lease computer equipment under operating leases in view of the constant technological improvements of that equipment.

3. The Leveraged Lease

A leveraged lease is one where a percentage of the funds to buy the equipment, usually 60 to 80%, is loaned by a bank or other lender. Because the lessor has put up only a small percentage of the equipment's cost, his investment is said to be leveraged because his return is based on 100% of the cost. Leveraging generally enables a lessor to provide a lessee with relatively lower rents while at the same time maintaining his return. Frequently, net finance leases are structured as leveraged leases.

The debt used to leverage a lease transaction is usually nonrecourse debt. Where debt is nonrecourse, the lender has no recourse against the lessor for nonpayment of the loan, but rather he can look only to the rental stream, the lessee, and the value of the equipment for its repayment. In such an arrangement, the lessor must assign to the lender its rights under the lease, including the right to the rental payments.

▶ **Observation:**   While a lessor has no repayment obligations to a nonrecourse lender if the lessee defaults, he does bear some risk because his rights against the lessee and the equipment are subordinated to the lender's repayment rights.

4.   The Nonleveraged Lease

Also referred to as an unleveraged or straight lease, a nonleveraged lease is one in which the lessor pays for the equipment from his own funds. Leasing companies often enter into nonleveraged leases.

A distinct advantage in using a nonleveraged lease structure is that there are usually only two principals involved, the lessee and the lessor. Because of the limited number of parties, the mechanics of putting together a transaction are simpler, saving time and documentation costs, such as legal fees. One disadvantage for a lessee, however, is that the rent is usually higher than it would be if the lease were leveraged.

5.   The Service Lease

Leases in which the lessor assumes equipment ownership responsibilities, such as maintenance, repair, insurance, recordkeeping, or payment of property taxes, in addition to providing the asset financing, are usually called service leases. Services leases generally have relatively short least terms.

F.   The Pros and Cons of Leasing

Leasing is not always the best way for every user to acquire equipment. In some circumstances, it is advisable; in others, buying equipment may be preferable. Whether or not to lease certain equipment is not always an easy decision, and in each situation a user must weigh all the advantages and disadvantages. This section will provide the reader with the basic considerations essential to a comprehensive evaluation.

1.   The Advantage of Leasing

a.   Obsolescence Concerns

When a user is concerned that equipment may become obsolete before the end of its useful life, leasing can reduce that concern. High-tech equipment, such as computer equipment, often gives rise to that concern because new, more efficient models are continually being developed that quickly outdate their predecessors.

As a practical matter, as long as the equipment does its job, does it really matter whether there is better equipment available? In some situations it does. For example, a more efficient item of manufacturing equipment can lower production costs by a sufficient amount so that the user would have to acquire a new model before the old model has been written off to insure its price-competitive position in the market. If a user had bought rather than leased the equipment, the overall cost of replacing it could be expensive. And if the old equipment's market value was significantly less than its book value at the time of replacement, the user could be confronted with a potentially undesirable book loss in addition to the replacement cash outlay.

▶ **Observation:**   A lessor also runs the risk of financial loss through equipment obsolescence. Thus, to protect himself he will undoubtedly build a premium into his lease rate to compensate for the risk. A prospective lessee may be willing to pay the premium as a form of insurance against a loss through obsolescence. Of course, if the equipment does not become obsolete the increased rental rate will have reduced the profits he could have made had he owned the equipment.

▶ **Recommendation:**   Because it is impossible to determine absolutely whether equipment will become obsolete, the obsolescence risk issue can cause a real dilemma. Evaluating the past history of the type of equipment under consideration can be helpful in predicting trends. Also, the user can estimate the impact on profits of continuing to use the older, technologically obsolete equipment.

b.   Limited Use Needs

If equipment is needed only for a limited period of time, leasing can be an effective way of acquiring its use. It eliminates the re-marketing risks an owner would have at the end of a short use period, and it also permits a more defined estimate of the effective cost of using the equipment. For example, public utilities building their own power plants often must acquire certain specialized construction equipment to do the job. Once the plant is finished, the equipment may be of no further use to the utility, but it may still have many years of useful life left. If it cannot be sold for a reasonable price, the overall cost of its use can be high. Leasing removes the resale risk and allows the utility to determine in advance the total effective usage cost.

▶ **Observation:** Putting together a lease financing can require less red tape and time than a loan transaction. There are situations in which the documentation time and expense that could be saved can make up for a lower interest cost. This is particularly true when the cost of the equipment involved is relatively small.

c.   Preserving Capital

An advantage of leasing to some users is that it helps preserve their existing funds or bank lines for other uses. The absence of a downpayment—in effect 100% financing—can assist high growth rate companies in maximizing their use of funds. That can be particularly attractive in periods of tight money.

▶ **Observation:** When evaluating whether to lease or to buy equipment, a user must carefully consider the real cost of borrowed funds. For example, a high compensating balance requirement can easily increase the effective cost of a bank loan. As this type of collateral loan cost increases, the attractiveness of leasing usually increases.

d.   Obtaining Technical or Administrative Services

Users lacking the staff or expertise to attend to specialized equipment needs can lease equipment as a way to acquire those necessary technical or administrative services. Through service leases, users can avoid tying up time and manpower in activities that are outside of their normal operations. There is, of course, generally a charge, built into the rent, for the nonfinancial services supplied. Typically, lessors of office equipment, trucks, automobiles, and railcars offer some form of nonfinancial services as a supplement to their financing. For example, railcar lessors frequently offer maintenance services.

e.   Borrowing Problems

Users with credit or borrowing problems may have an easier time getting leasing companies to fund their equipment needs as leasing companies often impose less stringent financial requirements than traditional lenders. *Reason:* They are willing to take greater risks because (1) they actually own the equipment and (2) they can more readily handle used equipment than can banks, if they must take possession from a defaulting lessee.

This is not to say that leasing companies will provide equipment financing to a user regardless of its financial condition. There still must be a reasonable assurance that the user will be able to meet the lease payments.

f.   Inability to Use Tax Benefits

It is common for a user to be in a situation in which it cannot use the tax benefits—currently depreciation deductions—that would result from equipment ownership. It may, for example, have an excess of accumulated tax benefits or insufficient earnings, either due to poor performance or to major acquisitions, that have used up its tax bill, or the user may be subject to the minimum tax and find the tax benefits deferred (explained at Chapter 6, Part III). Such a company can indirectly take advantage of most of the ownership tax benefits through leasing. Because a lessor takes these tax benefits into account when calculating the transaction's economic return, he, in effect, passes these benefits through in the form of a relatively lower rent.

▶ **Observation:**   A lessor will not pass 100% of the equipment ownership tax benefits on to a lessee through a reduced rental charge. He will make a profit on those benefits by adjusting the rent to reflect only a partial recognition. The rent adjustments vary with each lessor and each situation.

g.   Capital Budget Restrictions

Decisions to lease equipment are sometimes made to avoid a user's internal capital budget restrictions. For capital equipment purchases above a certain amount, a manager may be required to obtain prior approval, and that approval may be difficult or impossible to obtain. If the equipment is leased, he may be able to account for the rental payments as an operating expense—even though the lease represents a long-term financing similar to a capital expenditure—to get around the approval problem. In this way, he may also be able to maximize his capital budget.

▶ **Recommendation:**   Top management should prescribe certain rules in this area to avoid budget-end running, particularly with finance leases. Long-term equipment leases can have a significant negative future impact on a company's earnings, particularly when cutbacks are necessary. Thus, management should institute certain reasonable lease commitment restrictions.

h.   Off-balance Sheet Benefits?

In the early days of leasing, many users leased equipment, instead of taking out long-term loans to buy equipment, to avoid burdening their balance sheet with long-term debt liabilities. The lease, regardless of its duration, was basically treated as an operating expense. As a result, a company's profit to fixed asset ratios were improved that, in turn, generally permitted a greater bank borrowing capability. Today, the circumstances have changed. Regardless of whether significant lease obligations have to be recorded on the balance sheet or not, sophisticated lenders factor them into their evaluation of a company's financial condition. Also, and certainly most important, the accounting rules now effectively eliminate the traditional "off balance sheet" benefit in most situations.

2.   Disadvantages of Leasing

a.   Residual Upside Is Lost

When a user leases equipment, he forgoes the possibility of realizing a gain if the equipment appreciates in value during the lease term. Any such gain instead goes to the lessor. This is a common occurrence. For example, through inflation or buyer demand, a 10-year old river barge may be worth more than it originally cost.

Many leases give lessees the option to buy the leased equipment at the lease term's end for its fair market value at that time. If the fair market value turns out to be high, the purchase price, coupled with the rent paid, can result in a very expensive transaction. In such a situation, the lessee would undoubtedly have been better off if he had originally bought the equipment. The problem is that there is no way of telling what the future value is going to be.

There is, however, one way for a prospective lessee to limit his cost exposure if he believes it is likely he will want to buy the equipment at the end of the term and, also, share in any residual upside—a fixed price purchase option. Under this option, a lessee has the right to buy the equipment at the end of the lease at a fixed price, say 25% of original cost, that was agreed on at the time the parties entered into the lease. If the equipment's market value at the lease term's end is high, say 75% of cost, the lessee has the option to taking advantage of the favorable market by buying it for 25% of cost and selling it for 75% of cost. There are, however, two problems with fixed price purchase options. First, not all lessors are willing to grant them and give up their residual upside. Second, fixed price purchase options can jeopardize a lease's true lease status for tax purposes.

▶ **Recommendation:**   If a prospective lessor is willing to grant a fixed price purchase right at 35% of cost, the prospective lessee should request that it be at 35% of cost or at the equipment's fair market value, whichever is less. This way, if the equipment's market value at the time of the option's exercise is lower than the fixed price, the lessee will not have to pay more than the equipment is worth if a purchase is necessary.

Frequently, a prospective lessee's concern over the loss of residual value upside is more emotional than practical. The potential loss must always be kept in the proper economic perspective. This can be done by attempting to put a realistic value on it by, for example, bringing in a qualified appraiser to give an opinion as to what the equipment is likely to be worth in the future and discounting that value to its present worth.

Illustrative Example—*A Residual Perspective:*
   Company Able is considering whether to lease or buy a heavy duty crane. Company Able's financial vice president recommends that it be leased; however, the operational vice president believes that it should be bought because of its potentially favorable market value at the end of the period of use. The facts are as follows:

Crane cost . . . . $3 million
Lease term . . . . 20 years
Depreciated book value at end of 20 years $300,000

If the market value of the crane is estimated to be $500,000 at the end of the lease term, Company Able would lose the chance at a $200,000 upside gain ($500,000—$300,000) if it leased the equipment.

   What if, however, the potential loss is considered in terms of current dollars? The present value of such a loss 20 years out, computed using an annual discount rate of 10%, is approximately $30,000. Compared to the original cost of $3 million and considering the fact that the upside gain may not materialize, the residual concern may be overstated, particularly if any down payment that would have been required in a purchase was put to productive use.

b.   Equipment Control May Be Limited

When a lease ends, so does a lessee's right to use the equipment. This can create a problem for an equipment user if suitable replacement equipment is not readily available and the lessor refuses to re-lease or sell it to the lessee. While purchase or renewal options theoretically eliminate this risk, from a practical standpoint, when a third party owns the equipment, there is no guarantee he will abide by the terms of the options voluntarily. Also, there is always the possibility, although remote, that a lessor will interfere with the lessee's right to use the equipment during the lease term, even though he may have no legal right to do so. Having the legal right of continued use may be of little consequence to a lessee when equipment essential to its continued operations becomes unavailable.

3.   Key Situations: When to Consider Leasing

In summary, there are certain indicators that suggest an equipment user should seriously consider leasing:

- If an equipment user must pay high interest rates for money borrowed, leasing can be an economically attractive equipment funding alternative. Users whose credit dictates high interest rates, however, may also dictate high leasing rates. *Reason*: The lessor must offset the increased credit risks by increased returns. The cost of leasing, however, will probably not increase proportionately as high as the cost of borrowing.
- An equipment user who cannot use a significant part or all of the equipment ownership tax benefits may come out ahead by leasing. This, of course, assumes the tax benefits can be used by the leasing company, and the benefits are passed through in the form of a relatively lower rental rate.
- Leasing is desirable when the equipment involved has unusual service problems that cannot be handled by a company internally, for example, because of the technical nature of the equipment or the company's inadequate staffing.
- If implicit lease interest rates are about the same as debt interest rates and there are significant ancillary costs to borrowing, such as high compensating balances or commitment fees, leasing should be considered.

G.   When-to-Lease Checklist

An equipment user should consider leasing when one or more of the following factors is present:

- There is a high risk that equipment will become obsolete before the end of its useful life.
- The equipment will be needed only for a short period of time.
- It is desirable to use existing lines of bank credit for purposes other than funding certain equipment.
- It is desirable to maximize available capital resources.
- Technical, administrative, or other nonfinancial equipment related services that are not internally available can be easily secured from a leasing company.

- High interest rates must be paid for borrowed money.
- The tax benefits resulting from the equipment ownership cannot be used.
- The equipment will have a poor market value at the end of its term of use.

H.   Checklist for Prospective Lessees Approaching Potential Lessors

As the preliminary step in considering a lease transaction, an equipment user should review the following:

■ What basic type of lease arrangement is to be considered?

- Nonleveraged finance lease

  (1) Net lease

- Leveraged finance lease

  (1) Net lease

- Operating lease

  (1) Long-term

  (2) Short-term

  (3) Nonfinancial services required

■ What potential sources of lease financing will be invited to submit lease quotations?

- Individuals
- Independent nonbank leasing companies

  (1) Finance lessors

  (2) Service lessors

- Banks or other financial institutions
- Captive leasing companies
- Lease brokers

■ If an individual is under consideration:

- Has the individual been involved in lease transactions before?
- Does the individual have experienced lease advisers and management representatives to assist him if issues arise in the future?

■ If an independent nonbank leasing company is under consideration:

- Does it have a good reputation in the financial community?
- Have other existing lessees been contacted to determine how difficult it may be to deal with?
- Is its financial condition sufficient to insure adequate and timely funding?
- Will the equipment be funded entirely from the lessor's own funds?
- If equipment related nonfinancial services will be supplied, does it have an adequate staff and facilities to supply these services on a timely basis?
- How tough is the lessor's lease documentation? (A form of the lessor's lease should be reviewed.)

■ If the prospective lessee's regular bank will be involved, will the lease restrict its future loan availability?

■ If a lease broker is under consideration:

- How many similar transactions has he completed in the last three years?
- What do other companies that have used his service say about his method of operation and his ability to follow through on a proposed transaction?
- Are there any banks or other prospective lessor-investors that should not be approached by the broker?

CHAPTER 2
The Proposal Stage—Where the Leasing Deal Is Made

A. Overview

Chapter 1 describes the array of alternatives open to the prospective lessee in terms of types of lessors and leases. Unfortunately, many prospective lessees deal with that array in an inefficient and disorganized manner, and, as a result may both pay too much and miss out on benefits they could receive.

This chapter gives guidelines to prospective lessees and lessors on how to sort through the array in a reasonable, efficient manner. At the end of this stage, a lessee and lessor will have come together to agree on a proposal letter, a comprehensive outline of the leasing deal they intend to enter. This chapter describes how the prospective lessee and lessor can achieve maximum results during the stage leading up to the accepted proposal letter.

B. Obtaining Bids—The Request-For-Bids Letter

We have an equipment user considering leasing some equipment. How does this prospective lessee get the best lease deal? Put simply, he or she shops the market, that is, finds out what the alternatives are. To do that, the prospective lessee will want to obtain a meaningful number of specific proposals from potential lessors and lease underwriters. While this could be done in a variety of ways, typically the lessee will obtain the best results by preparing and circulating a well thought out and comprehensive written request-for-bids letter, commonly referred to as a bid letter.

While preparing a bid letter may be somewhat time-consuming, it is an investment in time that usually more than pays off. It can save time by cutting down on telephone calls or other inquiries concerning the proposed deal's basic facts. It also ensures that the responses will be on a uniform, and thus comparable basis. Moreover, without a comprehensive bid letter, a lessee may, for example, receive five proposals, each with a different rental payment mode—quarterly, in advance; semi-annually, in arrears; semi-annually, in advance; monthly, in arrears; and monthly, in advance. Because it may be difficult, if not impossible, to make a meaningful comparison, requotes on a specified payment basis will be necessary, thus wasting valuable time.

Another advantage of using a bid letter is that it will cause everyone concerned on the lessee's side to focus on what they need or would like to obtain from the leasing transaction. Generally, if the lessee does not request a particular benefit, it will not be offered.

What issues should be covered in a comprehensive bid letter? Because the bid letter's purpose is to yield proposals, it should address the same subjects as those covered in the proposal letter. At a bare minimum, a prospective lessee should consider the following issues in putting together a bid letter:

- The equipment type and the manufacturer.
- The number of equipment units that will be involved.
- The equipment's aggregate and per unit cost.
- When the equipment delivery is anticipated.
- The lease type desired, that is, net financial lease or service lease.
- The lease term and any renewal periods desired.
- The rental payment mode, that is, monthly, quarterly, semi-annually, or annually—in advance or in arrears.
- The extent of any acceptable tax indemnifications.
- Whether the equipment will be self insured.
- What options are required.
- A request for appropriate casualty and termination values.
- Who will have the responsibility for the transaction's fees and expenses.
- Whether a tax ruling is necessary or desirable.
- Whether it is acceptable for a favorable tax ruling to be a prerequisite to execute the lease documents.
- Whether a favorable tax ruling should relieve any tax indemnification obligations assumed.
- The deadline for the submission of lease quotations.
- When the transaction will be awarded.
- Whether underwriting bids are acceptable.
- If underwriting proposals are permitted, whether the bids may be on a "firm" or "best-efforts" basis.

- Potential equity participants and lenders who may be unacceptable if the transaction is to be underwritten.

These points are explained below in the context of describing the proposal letter.

▶ **Additional Sources:**   The following are included to assist the prospective lessee in drafting the bid letter:
- Section H of this chapter sets out a proposal stage checklist for the lessee;
- The Appendix includes a sample request-for-bids letter.

C.   What Is the Proposal Letter?

After receiving and reviewing the bid letter, interested prospective lessors or underwriters will make their proposal responding to the bid letter's terms. Their response should be written and is referred to as a proposal letter. The proposal letter is significant for several reasons. First, the letter will be the lessee's first opportunity to make preliminary selections from among the respondents to its bid letter. Second, after reviewing the proposal letters received, the lessee may request changes or additions, and the letter forms the focal point for those negotiations. And third, after successful negotiations, the lessee will accept one of the letters, and it becomes the basis for the later deal documentation. It is important that the proposal letter cover the proposed transaction's major business and legal points.

1.   The Proposal Letter's Legal Status

Before reviewing the letter's substance, it is important to realize what the proposal letter does and does not do. After the prospective lessee has signed the letter, do the parties have a contract? Yes and no. While they have a contract—usually the offer, and sometimes the acceptance, are qualified—conditions are imposed that must be satisfied after all parties have signed the lease proposal. Typical conditions, for example, are

- Necessary governmental or regulatory approvals, licenses, or authorizations.
- Favorable opinions of counsel.
- The effective placement of the debt, in the case of a leveraged lease.
- Acceptable financial covenants, such as a minimum debt-to-equity ratio.
- Satisfactory audited financial statements.

- Mutually satisfactory documentation.
- Formal transaction approvals by the prospective equity partici-
  pants and lenders.
- A minimum dollar participation of equity and debt participants.
- A detailed equipment list.
- Favorable equipment appraisals justifying the equipment residual
  value.

The "satisfactory documentation" condition gives the transaction's
participants the most latitude to find justification to back out if they so
desire. *Reason:* Unless the parties can reach agreement on each term
and condition contained in the lease documents, they don't have to go
through with the transaction. This condition leaves room for some wide
open discussions on issues not even anticipated in the proposal stage,
such as whether the lessee should pay for the equipment's return to
any location designated by the lessor.

While the accepted proposal letter is usually not legally enforceable
because of these conditions, it is important, for several reasons, to the
leasing transaction that it be comprehensive, detailed, and in writing.

- While it is not legally enforceable, the parties will almost always
  make significant efforts to complete the deal once the proposal
  letter has been accepted.
- The proposal letter serves as the guideline and reminder for the
  parties and their lawyers when they draft the documents.
- While unlikely, it is possible that if a party unreasonably backs out
  of the deal after the proposal letter has been accepted, there
  could be a legal action. This is so, particularly if financial obligations have been incurred on the other side.

Thus, a comprehensive and formal proposal letter is beneficial to
both parties, and should be used in every transaction.

2. Proposal Stage Negotiating Strategies

Because the major terms are decided and the lessor or underwriter is
selected during the proposal stage, that stage is often determinative of
the transaction. Besides focusing on specific terms and conditions, the
prospective lessee should keep in mind that, during the bidding stage,
he has a considerable amount of negotiating leverage, particularly if
more than one bidder is involved. One bidder's loss will not jeopardize
the transaction, and the bidders know it. Thus, the lessee's time to press
for the tough concessions is before awarding the transaction. Prospective lessors are sometimes willing to concede points just to win the
deal. Once the transaction has been awarded, the winning bidder is in a

stronger negotiating position merely by virtue of the fact that the other bidders are no longer involved.

A prospective lessee's negotiating position will also be improved if he plans adequate lead time between a lease award and the equipment delivery. In this way, if problems develop after the award, there may still be time to go elsewhere for the financing. If this is not possible, and the prospective lessor starts to "get tough," some balance can be put back into the negotiations by letting it be known that because of the problems, the lessee is considering buying rather than leasing.

From the potential lessor's perspective, the negotiating strategy in the bidding stage is the reverse—the faster it can get a prospective lessee to "sign off" on a proposal letter, the less likely that the lessee will make a problem request. Once the lease documentation has begun, particularly if there are near-term deliveries, a prospective lessor's negotiating position is improved. Psychologically, a prospective lessee is more reluctant to start over with new people once the document negotiations have started.

D. What Issues Should The Proposal Letter Address?

Stated simply, the proposal letter should outline the lease "deal." The letter does not have to cover every detail, but it should set the framework for the overall lease arrangement. To do this, however, the parties must know what points should be covered.

▶ **Recommendation:** If an important point comes up after a proposal letter has been accepted by a prospective lessee, but before the lease documentation has begun, the parties should consider amending the letter to include the point. This helps eliminate deal point "misunderstandings" from arising during documentation.

Typically, although an underwritten leveraged lease situation will be more complex than nonunderwritten transactions, they usually contain most of the same basic elements. By understanding the more complex transaction format, the others will fall into place and, thus, the explanation will center on issues that should be addressed in an underwritten leveraged lease proposal.

The Appendix includes several proposal letters. The first is typical of that used by a leasing company acting on its own behalf, a nonunderwritten transaction, and the second is typical of that used by an underwriter acting on behalf of prospective third-party lessors. Both cover the major topics that should be identified and can be used as guidelines when drafting or reviewing a lease proposal. Because there can be many variables in a particular transaction, however, they should be used only for reference purposes. It may be helpful to review them before reading further, to put the following explanation into an overall perspective.

1. What Is the Offer?

While all proposals will offer to provide equipment financing, proposals from different types of bidders have different consequences to the lessee. One type of proposal is a direct offer by a prospective lessor to lease the equipment to the prospective lessee and another is an offer by an underwriter to arrange the lease financing of the equipment for the prospective lessee. In the latter case, the underwriter may or may not have a specific third-party lessor in mind. Even if he does, the name usually will not be disclosed in the proposal to protect his position as a broker.

Illustrative Language—*Lessor Designation:*   An unknown or undisclosed lessor may be described by an underwriter in the following manner: The lessor will be a trustee acting as owner trustee pursuant to an owner's trust for the benefit of one or more corporate investors.

In a nonunderwritten transaction, the prospective lessor will make an offer directly as principal to lease the equipment to the prospective lessee. For example: ABC Leasing Company will purchase and lease to XYZ Company the equipment designated in this proposal under the terms and conditions specified herein.

▶ **Recommendations:**   In an underwriting situation, a prospective lessee is in a better position if he does not make an award to a particular underwriter until the underwriter has disclosed the prospective lessor, and someone with authority to represent the lessor has been contacted by the prospective lessee to confirm their interest. If there is going to be a problem, the time to find out is when the remaining bidders are still in the picture.

An underwriter should make sure his proposal is only an offer to arrange the proposed financing, unless he or she is fully prepared to step in as lessor in the event a third-party investor cannot be found.

There are many types of offer combinations. For example, a direct lessor could offer to purchase and lease equipment using in part its own funds and in part funds from a nonrecourse loan, a simple form of leveraged lease. Or, an underwriter may offer to put together a leveraged lease using one or more lessor-investors and one or more third-party lenders. Another alternative is that the underwriter may propose to bring in a "single source" investor to act as lessor, such as a regional bank, that would pay for the equipment entirely from its own funds.

To the prospective lessee, the choice among the different variations represents a trade off between delivery and price. A prospective lessee seeking a near-term equipment delivery situation may be well advised to limit its consideration to a direct lessor transaction, because dealing with one party directly will lessen the risk that the financing cannot be done within the short time frame. If there is plenty of time, the best approach may be to pursue a syndicated leveraged lease transaction. This type of transaction will certainly be more involved, but it can provide the best rental rate for a prospective lessee.

Because the amount of lead time available before the equipment will be delivered may dictate the type of transaction that can be considered, it is essential that all parties keep this aspect in mind. Table 2-1 on page 208 can be used as a general guide for planning the timing of a proposed lease financing.

TABLE 2-1
RECOMMENDED TRANSACTION LEAD TIME

Type of Transaction	Anticipated Number of Lessor-Investors	Anticipated Number of Lenders	Recommended Lead Time [1] (Months)
Underwritten Leveraged Lease	Two or more	Two or more	Six
Underwritten Leveraged Lease	Two or more	One	Six
Underwritten Leveraged Lease	One	Two or more	Five
Underwritten Leveraged Lease	One	One	Four
Underwritten Single Investor [2]	One	0	Three
Direct Lease [3]	One	One or more	Three
Direct Lease	One	0	Two

[1]*Lead time* is defined as the time between the proposal's due date and the first equipment delivery. The estimates assume an allowable proposal analysis time of one month.

[2]An *underwritten single investor* transaction is defined as one in which the underwriter brings in only one lessor-investor who puts up 100% of the funds required.

[3]A *direct lease* transaction is defined as one in which the prospective lessee will deal directly with the prospective lessor.

2. 'Best Efforts' or Firm Offer

Typically, in his or her proposal, a lease underwriter will state whether the offer is made on a "best efforts" or on a "firm" basis. A best efforts proposal is nothing more than an offer to try to arrange the lease financing on the stated terms and conditions. There are no performance guarantees, and the underwriter is generally not liable to the prospective lessee if he cannot perform.

Illustrative Language— *'Best Efforts' Commitment:*   ABC Leasing Company proposes to use its best efforts to arrange an equipment lease according to the terms and conditions set forth in this proposal.

A firm underwriting bid is simply just that. The underwriter states that he can deliver the financing under the proposed terms and conditions.

Illustrative Language— *Firm Commitment:*   ABC Leasing Company proposes to arrange on a firm commitment basis an equipment lease for XYZ Inc., according to the terms and conditions set forth in this proposal.

From the prospective lessee's viewpoint, whether to go with a best efforts or firm offer is—like the choice among bidders—a trade off between delivery time and price. Underwriters will often offer a better price on a best efforts bid because that way they do not have to market the transaction to potential lessors until it has been awarded to them. Marketing an awarded deal saves the underwriter time, and also may make the potential lessors more willing to offer a better price—they will know the transaction is theirs if they accept the underwriter's bid, and so are more willing to invest time evaluating the transaction than if the transaction has not been awarded.

The best efforts offer, however, has a downside to the lessee—time. If the underwriter cannot, after having been awarded the deal, rapidly find a lessor, valuable documentation time is lost. In fact, if the underwriter takes an extended period to market the deal, the possibility becomes greater that no lessor will accept the deal. *Reason:* Prospective lessor-investors become suspicious when a transaction has been around the market place for a while and may refuse to consider it for that reason alone.

▶ **Recommendation:**   If a prospective lessee has adequate lead time, a best efforts underwriting should be permitted. If the winning underwriter cannot perform quickly, the prospective lessee can move on to the underwriter in second place without creating a timing problem.

As described previously, even an accepted firm offer will not usually be a binding agreement because of the various conditions—such as satisfactory documentation—in the proposal letter. However, as a practical matter, some firm offers may be more likely to go ahead to a completed transaction than others. For example, there are situations when an underwriter will firmly commit to do the transaction, even though he does not have a commitment from any lessor prospects, and is agreeing to buy and lease the equipment himself if he cannot broker it. This type of arrangement can be risky for a prospective lessee because if the underwriter cannot sell the deal, it may not want to go ahead itself, and may seek an excuse to justify a way out. For example, offers conditioned on mutually satisfactory lease documentation can provide an underwriter with an opportunity to create a document "disagreement" and, thereby, a basis to refuse to go forward.

▶ **Recommendation:** A prospective lessee should carefully investigate the financial situation of a lease underwriter offering a firm underwriting bid. If the underwriter does not have the financial resources to stand behind the transaction in the event it cannot deliver a lessor-investor, the fact that the offer is firm may be worth nothing.

If the offer is made directly by a prospective lessor instead of an underwriter, the situation will be different. Because the prospective lessor will use its own money to fund the transaction, the chances of the lessor looking for an excuse to back out are greatly reduced.

Illustrative Language—*Direct Commitment:* ABC Leasing Company, as lessor, offers to purchase and lease to XYZ Inc. the equipment described below under the stated terms and conditions.

3.   Specifying the Exact Cost

The proposal letter should identify total equipment cost. Frequently, a prospective lessor will put a limit on, or "cap," the amount of money he or she is willing to commit to a transaction. For example, he or she may agree to buy and lease an oil tanker at a cost not to exceed $40 million. Without a cap, he runs the risk that unexpected cost escalations will cause him to invest more than he is comfortable with. An unanticipated cost increase thus may give a prospective lessor who no longer finds the transaction desirable an excuse to back out.

▶ **Recommendation:** A prospective lessee entering into a lease agreement covering equipment to be delivered in the future must make sure the lessor's cost commitment is adequate. For example, will it cover any allowable manufacturer price escalations? If there is a problem with determining an exact price, a dollar cushion can be built into the estimate. A word of caution, however, if a fee has been imposed by the prospective lessor for the failure to use all the committed funds (commonly referred to as a non-utilization fee). A prospective lessee should be careful not to build in an excessive cushion because any fee paid on the excess over the amount used will increase the effective cost of the financing.

4. Identify the Real Lessee

While the proposal letter will identify the lessee responsible for the rent, sometimes the *real* lessee is not identified. For example, the proposal letter may name XYZ Inc. as lessee while XYZ Inc. plans to have a subsidiary be the lessee. The lessor will do a credit review and approval based on XYZ Inc.'s statements. If the subsidiary is the lessee, the check on the parent will not be sufficient, and there may not be enough time to make any necessary adjustments. Getting the parent company's guarantee may be enough, but it may be difficult to obtain at the last minute.

5. Rent Payments—Rental Adjustment Clauses

The proposal should specify how often, how much, and for how long rent will be paid. For example, a five-year lease may provide for 20 consecutive level quarterly payments, in arrears, each payment to equal 3.000% of the equipment cost, beginning as of the start of the primary term.

When a leveraged lease is involved, the rent calculation becomes more complicated. The amount of rent a lessor charges is, in part, determined by the debt interest rate. However, the lessor generally will not secure the debt until after the award. *Reason:* It wouldn't be practical to spend the time and money necessary until there is a deal. Thus, to calculate the rent, the lessor will use an assumed interest rate and calculate the rent accordingly. Then, to protect its return in case the actual interest rate varies from the assumed rate, the lessor will often want a rental adjustment clause.

Illustrative Example—*The Need for a Rent Adjustment Clause:* Company B proposes to lease to Company A a $10,000 item of mining equipment. The transaction will be leveraged with 80% debt at an assumed interest rate of 6% per annum. The terms are as follows:

```
Lease term . . . . . . . . . . . . . . . . . . . . . . . . . . . . . . . . . . . . 10 years
Loan term  . . . . . . . . . . . . . . . . . . . . . . . . . . . . . . . . . . . . 10 years
Annual rent  . . . . . . . . . . . . . . . . . . . . . . . . . . . . . . . . . . . $1,200
Annual debt service (level, in arrears)
   ($8,000 @ 6%) . . . . . . . . . . . . . . . . . . . . . . . . . . . . . . . . $1,087
```

The annual rent will cover the annual debt service by $113 ($1,200-$1,087). Assume that when Company B goes into the debt market the best available annual interest rate is 10%. The annual debt service, assuming level payments, will be approximately $1,302. In this case not only will the increased debt service expense erode the lessor's return, but the lessor will have to invest an additional $102 a year ($1,302-$1,200) to make up for the shortfall.

The rental adjustment clause enables the lessor to be protected against an increased interest rate, and this provision should be stated in the proposal letter.

Illustrative Language—*Proposal Rent Adjustment:* Lessee shall make 20 consecutive, level, quarterly payments, in arrears, each equal to 3.000% of equipment cost, commencing on January 1, 19—. The rental percentage factor is based on the assumption that the interest rate on the leveraged debt will be 9.5% per annum. If the interest rate is other than 9.5%, the rental factor will be adjusted, upward or downward, accordingly so that Lessor's economic return shall be maintained.

▶ **Recommendations:**   If a prospective lessor has the right to protect his return by adjustments upward if the actual debt interest rate is higher than assumed, a prospective lessee should require a downward rent adjustment if the debt comes in lower than assumed.

A prospective lessee should determine what criteria the prospective lessor will use to make any rent adjustment so the accuracy of the calculation can be independently confirmed.

Any time a rental adjustment is permitted, the parties should also provide for appropriate adjustments in values that relate to the rent, such as casualty and termination values.

6.   Primary and Interim Lease Terms

The proposal letter must specify the equipment's lease term and, if more than one item of equipment is to be leased, identify each item's lease term.

Also, where numerous items of equipment are involved, using an interim term in addition to the main or primary lease will simplify rental payment mechanics. The interim term covers the period from the time the equipment is accepted for lease to the start of the primary term. The interim term concept is commonly used when many items of equipment are involved and deliveries are scattered over many months. By consolidating the start of the primary lease terms to, for example, calendar quarters, the rent payment and processing mechanics are simplified.

Illustrative Example—*The Interim Technique for Rent Consolidation:*   Company B wants to lease 120 trucks from Company A. The trucks will be delivered over a 12-month period at a rate of 10 trucks a month. Company B wants to pay the lease rent in quarterly, in arrears, payments. Company A proposes this solution:

1. There shall be four primary lease terms starting as follows:
   a. First primary term - April 1, 19—
   b. Second primary term - July 1, 19—
   c. Third primary term - October 1, 19—
   d. Fourth primary term - January 1, 19—
2. All trucks delivered and accepted for lease in the calendar quarter preceding the nearest primary term start date shall be on interim lease until the start date, at which time the primary term shall begin for such trucks.

Without the interim arrangement, Company A could end up with as many as 120 different primary lease term start dates and, thus, 120 different rental payment dates.

7. Credit Support for Lease Obligations

The prospective lessor should evaluate the prospective lessee's financial strength, and if the lessee is not financially strong enough to support a particular leasing financing, the lessor should require, in the proposal letter, some form of credit support. In that event, prospective lessors prefer to get a full and unconditional guarantee of all the lease obligations from a creditworthy entity, such as a parent company, a bank, or possibly, an underwriter. Other acceptable forms of credit support include a manufacturer's deficiency guarantee or a "take or pay" contract assignment. Different forms may be acceptable in different situations. An experienced leasing company or underwriter should be able to offer some viable alternatives to meet the needs of a particular transaction.

▶ **Recommendation:**   If the proposed lessee is a corporate subsidiary and credit support is required, the parent company should pursue a structure that will have the least impact on its future borrowing capabilities. For example, an assignment of a "take or pay" contract between the subsidiary and an outside entity may have little impact on the parent company. However, a full, unconditional guarantee could have a substantial impact.

8. Structure of Owning Entity

In structuring a typical underwritten leveraged lease transaction, an underwriter may propose one of a number of different alternative entities to own the equipment—a trust, partnership, or corporation. The underwriter's choice of entity should be decided in the proposal stage.

Concern for tax issues and limited liability issues will be of greatest concern to a prospective lessor. This is particularly true when two or more are brought together to act as the lessor. On the tax side, the chosen structure should permit a direct flow-through of all the available tax benefits. As to limited liability, the lessors may want protection against direct liability on a specific transaction in the event of a lawsuit.

▶ **Recommendation:** Trust arrangements can be a useful equipment ownership structure for prospective lessor-investors. If set up properly, it is generally agreed that they will be treated, for tax purposes, as a partnership and, for liability purposes, as a corporation.

The ownership vehicle form can also be important to a prospective lessee. For example, if the equipment ownership is not centralized in a multiple lessor-investor situation, the lessee may have to deal individually with each investor throughout the lease. The lessee may then have to issue separate prorated rent checks and, if a lease variance is necessary, obtain separate consents: A substantial inconvenience.

▶ **Recommendation:** In a multiple lessor-investor situation, a prospective lessee should insist that there be a single representative with the authority to handle the day-to-day issues.

9. The Debt Arrangement

If the lessor proposes a leveraged lease, the debt arrangement mechanics and terms should be outlined in the proposal letter. Points to consider concerning the debt:

- Who will find the debt.
- The debt repayment schedule.
- The anticipated per annum interest charge.
- The anticipated principal amount as a percentage of equipment cost.
- The form of lender representative.
- Whether the debt will be recourse or nonrecourse to the lessor.

While the proposal should cover these points, the lessor may need the ability to make changes, if the debt structure eventually obtained is at a variance from the proposal.

Illustrative Language—*Debt Structure:* ABC Leasing Company (ABC), or an investment banker acceptable to the lessee and to ABC, shall arrange for the private placement of a note ("indebtedness") to be issued by the lessor for a principal amount of approximately 80% of the total cost of the equipment to certain institutional investors (Lenders). The Lenders may be represented by an indenture trustee or agent bank.

This proposal assumes that the indebtedness shall be amortized in 20 payments of principal and interest at 9.5% per annum, payable quarterly, in arrears, over five years. The indebtedness shall be secured by a lease assignment and a security interest in the equipment, but otherwise shall be without recourse to the lessor. Any variance from the debt assumptions, other than interest rate which is provided for in the rent adjustment clause, will relieve the offeror from his commitment hereunder, if so elected.

The proposal letter should address which party will handle the debt placement and pay the placement fees. Typically, the underwriter or lessor will pay those costs. If he places the debt himself, he will save the debt placement fee and, thereby, increase his profit. However, where the underwriter or lessor handles the debt himself, and there is a rent adjustment provision, he may have little incentive to make sure he has found a truly rock-bottom rate.

▶ **Recommendations:**   Where the prospective underwriter or lessor is arranging the debt, the lessee should require the right to exclude any potential lender, for several reasons. First, it should be able to protect itself against a lessor obtaining an unreasonably high interest rate and passing it along through the rental adjustment clause. Second, a lessee may not want any of its "line" banks to become involved because of potential future borrowing restrictions. Also, some lenders are difficult to deal with, and they should be brought in only as a last resort.

If a prospective lessor or underwriter must pay the debt placement fee, he or she should have an equal say in the selection of the party that will place the debt. This will prevent him or her from being stuck with an inappropriately high placement fee.

▶ **Documentation Suggestion:**   Many documents used in a leveraged transaction will be subject to lender approval. Some lenders can be difficult to negotiate with and slow in responding. To avoid last-minute problems, the relevant papers should be sent to them as soon as possible and monitored carefully as to their review progress.

10. Tax or Business Reasons May Require a Narrow Equipment Delivery Time Frame

In some instances, the equipment's delivery date may significantly affect the economic benefits to the lessor. Most lessors will be taking depreciation deductions on the equipment, and when the equipment is placed in service determines the first year deduction. Different dates can substantially affect the lessor's deduction. For example, a lessor may want the deduction in a current year because he has substantial income to offset. Or he may want it in his next tax year because he cannot use the benefits in the current year. Or he may want it before or after its last quarter to avoid the mid-quarter convention. (See Chapter 5, Part 1   C,4.)

Business concerns can similarly dictate a narrow delivery time. For example, the lessor may not want to be obligated to provide lease financing at a particular fixed economic return beyond a certain date. Also, the prospective lessor may need to anticipate his cash needs for funding equipment purchases. Late deliveries can particularly be a problem when a long term lease commitment involves many equipment items and the likelihood of delays is increased.

A solution to that problem is to use a commitment period. This limits the lessor's obligation to fund to a designated period, six months for example, after the last expected delivery date. The longer the commitment period, however, the more likely it is that a prospective lessor will impose a fee for holding the funds available. Commonly referred to as a commitment fee, it is usually based upon a percentage of equipment cost. For example, a lessor may charge a fee equal to 0.5% of the total funds committed. Lessors are often willing to hold funds available for up to six months without charging a commitment fee.

▶ **Recommendation:**   A commitment fee should be included in a prospective lessee's cost-to-lease computation. A transaction with a lower rent and a commitment fee may be less attractive than one with a higher rent and no fee. This is not, however, always the case. Therefore, a prospective lessee should not automatically exclude a proposal just because it involves a commitment fee.

11.   Equipment Location

The proposal letter should specify where the lessee intends to use the leased equipment. The lessor may want to make security interest filings to protect its ownership interest against a lessee's creditors. To do so, the lessor will need to know the equipment's location. Also, the lessor's potential tax benefits may depend on the equipment's location. For example, if the equipment is used outside the United States, the lessor will generally have less attractive depreciation deductions.

Another consideration is that the equipment's location may have psychological benefits that affect the marketing effort. Certain lessor-investors or lenders may be more willing to participate in situations involving equipment used in their local area. For example, if the equipment is to be used in Maryland by a division of a California corporation, Maryland regional banks may be interested because of the possibility of doing future business with a company they normally may not be involved with.

12. Purchase or Renewal Options

To have the option to continue to use the equipment, a lessee may want the right to buy the equipment, or renew the lease, under certain conditions, at the primary lease term's end. To do that, the lessee can obtain purchase or renewal options.

Illustrative Language—*Purchase and Renewal Options:*   At the end of the primary lease term, the lessee may (with 180 days written notice prior to the end of such term):

1. Renew the lease with respect to the equipment for an amount equal to its then fair market rental value, or
2. Purchase the equipment for a price equal to its then fair market value.

▶ **Recommendation:** From a lessee's viewpoint, a purchase option should be exercisable not only at the end of the main lease term, but also at the end of each renewal term. Also, the renewal term rights should adequately cover potential periods of extended use.

An alternative is the "right of first refusal" option. Basically, a first refusal option gives the lessee the right to buy or renew the equipment under the same terms as offered by an unrelated third party.

Illustrative Language—*Right of First Refusal:*   At the end of the primary lease term, the lessee will have a right of first refusal as to any sale or re-lease of the equipment.

▶ **Observation:** A right of first refusal can create a potential problem for a lessee. It is conceivable that a competitor would bid for equipment essential to a lessee's operations merely to attempt to interfere with its business.

In some situations prospective lessors want the right to require a lessee to buy the equipment at the lease's end. This type of right is commonly referred to as a "put" and should, as with the other options, be identified in the proposal. However, because of potential tax problems, puts are not generally used.

13. Early Termination Rights

A prospective lessee may want—what is called an early termination option—the right to end the lease prematurely as to any equipment that becomes obsolete or surplus to its needs. Lessors, however, typically do not like to grant termination options because they cut off future earnings. Thus, when granted, the lessee usually must pay a substantial premium to exercise the option, a premium referred to as a termination value payment.

Illustrative Language—*Termination Right:* At the expiration of each year during the primary lease term, the lessee shall have the right, at its option, to terminate the lease. The lessee will be required to give the lessor 90 days prior written notice of its intention to terminate and, during the period from giving notice until the termination date, the lessee shall use its best efforts to obtain bids from unaffiliated third parties for the equipment's purchase. On the termination date, the lessor shall sell the equipment for cash for the highest bid received. The total proceeds of such sale shall be retained by the lessor, and the lessee will pay to the lessor the difference, if any, by which the sales proceeds are less than the appropriate termination value indicated on the attached schedule.

▶ **Recommendation:**   If a prospective lessor is willing to grant a termination right, the prospective lessee should make sure that the termination values along with the right are incorporated into the lease proposal. These values are not standard and can vary significantly depending on the competition and the lessors. Too many times, the values are not seen until after the award, and sometimes only a few days before the anticipated lease document closing. If they turn out to be excessive, it may be too late to go elsewhere for the financing.

14.   Equipment Damage or Loss

The proposal letter should identify the lessee's basic financial responsibilities in the event of a casualty loss. Typically, to protect its equipment investment, the lessor requires the lessee to pay a defined casualty value. How the casualty value amount will be determined should be set out in the proposal letter.

▶ **Recommendation:**   Lessees required to insure equipment against casualty losses for the lessor's benefit should make sure any insurance proceeds received by the lessor will be credited against any casualty value due.

15.   Tax Assumptions and Indemnification

A prospective lessor generally anticipates receiving certain tax benefits, such as depreciation, as a result of owning the leased equipment, and incorporates the assumed tax benefits into the rental computation. Those benefits, thus, become critical to the lessor's transaction economic return. A prospective lessor should spell out in the lease proposal exactly what tax benefits are expected. Without doing so, there is a greater likelihood that factors that could have an adverse impact on the anticipated ownership tax benefits may not be identified in a timely manner during lease documentation. Worse yet, they may not be identified at all!

Because of the adverse impact the loss of anticipated tax benefits can have for tax-orientated lessors, they frequently want lessees to indemnify them against any loss of expected tax benefits. Lessees, for their part, will usually agree to some indemnification, but will want to limit the circumstances triggering the indemnity as much as possible. While the precise terms of the indemnification will be negotiated during the documentation, the basic terms should be determined at the proposal stage.

16.   Tax Law Changes

Where a lessor is anticipating tax benefits, a change in tax laws can affect the lessor's economic return. For example, changes in the tax laws affecting the equipment's depreciation life, the equipment depreciation method, or the federal tax rate on corporate income can have a substantial positive or negative impact.

▶ **Observation:**   Because of the intense ongoing governmental focus on the federal tax laws in the equipment and the corporate tax rate area, lessors and lessees should pay particular attention to the implications of anticipated changes.

One way to handle this risk is to quote the rent subject to an appropriate adjustment to reflect any tax law change affecting the lessor's expected economic return. The parties may agree, for example, that the rent will be adjusted to maintain the lessor's net return.

▶ **Recommendation:**   The particular parameter that is to serve as a guide for the rent adjustment should be defined precisely to prevent a calculation disagreement. "Net return," for example, can mean different things to different people. If a lessee does not know how to check an adjustment, it may pay more than necessary if the lessor tries to squeeze a little higher return. By the same token, a lessee may incorrectly object to a legitimate adjustment.

17.   Tax Rulings

In response to a taxpayer's request, the IRS will rule on a transaction's tax consequences, and—provided the taxpayer's request is complete and accurate—the IRS letter (called a private letter ruling) will be dispositive of the tax consequences. (See Chapter 8, § A,1.) Where a leasing transaction is particularly complex, or involves uncertain tax law issues, a lessor may require a private letter ruling on the tax consequences before entering the transaction. If a favorable ruling is received, the lessor may be willing to release a lessee from certain indemnification obligations on the tax treatment of issues addressed in the ruling. If such a ruling will be sought, the proposal letter should include that an IRS private letter ruling is required.

Illustrative Language—*The Use of a Private Letter Ruling:* The lessor plans to obtain a private IRS ruling with respect to the assumptions stated in this proposal letter. The lessee shall agree to indemnify the lessor for the tax assumptions that are the subject of the ruling request. Such indemnity shall remain in effect until a favorable ruling has been obtained on each of these points.

18. Transaction Expenses

The proposal letter should address which parties will pay transaction expenses, particularly in deals involving an underwritten leveraged lease. Where the lease is not an underwritten leveraged lease, the primary expense is legal fees, and the party incurring the expense usually pays for it. The matter is less simple in an underwritten transaction. Because this type of transaction can involve many parties—equity participants, lenders, trustees, and the underwriter—a variety of substantial expenses may be incurred. For example:

- Fees and disbursements of special counsel for the lenders and their representative.
- Acceptance and annual fees of the lenders' representative—usually found in a trust arrangement.
- Special counsel fees and disbursements for the equity participants and their representative.
- Acceptance and annual fees of the equity participants' representative—usually found in a trust arrangement.
- Fees and disbursements related to the filing for a private letter ruling.
- Documentation expenses, such as reproduction and printing expenses.
- Fees related to the placement of the debt.

In practice, the expense allocation is not as great a problem as it may appear. *Reason:* Very often, the underwriter agrees to pay substantially all the expenses. An underwriter can, however, cap these expenses by agreeing to pay only up to a specified percentage, usually around 0.75 to 1.25% of the equipment cost, and the lessee must, then, pay the excess. Because an underwriter makes his money by charging the lessor-investors a set fee for bringing them the transaction, the more he can limit his expense responsibility, the less he has to worry about fees and expenses eroding his profit. In a competitive market, however, many underwriters are willing, particularly if pushed a little, to assume the entire expense responsibility.

Illustrative Example—*The Underwriter Expense Problem:* Company A, an underwriter, arranged for Company C and Company D to participate as the equity investors in the leveraged lease financing of one ocean-going tugboat to be leased to Company B. Companies C and D agreed to pay Company A a brokerage fee equal to 2% of the equipment's cost for bringing in the transaction. As a condition of the transaction award, Company A had to commit to Company B that Company B would not have to pay any expenses, except its own counsel fees. At the closing, the following costs were incurred:

Tugboat cost . . . . $6 million
Fees for the lender's counsel 20,000
Counsel fees for Companies C & D 50,000
Counsel fees for Company A 2,000
Counsel fees for Company B 35,000
Printing expenses 21,000

What does Company A's profit picture look like?

Company A's "gross" fee from the transaction is $120,000 (2% × $6 million). All fees and expenses, excluding Company B's counsel fees, total $93,000 ($20,000 + $50,000 + $2,000 + $21,000). Therefore, Company A "nets" $27,000 ($120,000 − $93,000). If Company A had a 1% "cap," its expense responsibility would have been limited to $60,000 (1% × $6 million) and it would have made $60,000 ($120,000 − $60,000) instead of $27,000.

The difficult expense question is who must pay what expenses if a proposed underwritten transaction collapses. The lenders and the prospective lessor-investors will refuse to have any responsibility if the transaction does not go through, so that leaves the underwriter and the prospective lessee. Some underwriters attempt to put the responsibility for all expenses incurred in such a situation on the prospective lessee by inserting an appropriate clause in the proposal letter. Typically, the clause provides that the prospective lessee may pay all expenses if the transaction is not consummated for any reason whatsoever. This can be a dangerous position for a prospective lessee, particularly when the underwriter's poor performance may be the reason the transaction failed.

▶ **Recommendation:**   In a major underwritten lease financing, the expenses can be substantial. For example, it is not unheard of for the legal fees and other expenses in a complicated $10 million leveraged lease financing to run anywhere from $200,000 to $400,000. Thus, underwriters and prospective lessees should each carefully evaluate their potential expense exposure and clearly define the responsibilities in all events.

19.   The Lease Type

As described in Chapter 1, there are a variety of different lease types, each having different responsibilities for the lessor and lessee. Without fully understanding what the equipment related expense obligations will be, for example, the overall costs cannot be properly assessed. Many equipment lease transactions involve net finance lease arrangements. Under this type, the lessee must pay all fixed expenses relating to the equipment during the lease term, such as maintenance, insurance, and certain taxes. It can be an expensive surprise for a lessee to discover after the equipment is on lease that he must pay a substantial sales tax.

E.   Agreement to the Proposal Letter

Following any negotiations concerning the proposal letter, the lessee accepts the proposal by acknowledging his willingness to proceed on the basis of the terms presented. If the proposal is written, it can be accepted by an appropriate officer signing his acceptance directly on the letter or in a separate writing properly referencing the proposal letter. Any acceptance condition should be clearly a part of the acceptance and identified as such. For example, if the acceptance is made by signing in a designated space on a proposal letter, the condition should precede the signature.

▶ **Recommendation:**   If a proposal letter is used, a prospective lessee should "accept" directly on the proposal letter, not in a separate writing, particularly if the acceptance is conditioned. Separate papers can easily be lost or misplaced.

F.   The Prospective Lessee's Obligations After a Proposal Is Accepted

Because a proposal letter is generally not a contract, it may have no more than a psychological hold on the transaction because of various stated conditions, such as mutually satisfactory documentation, which are usually imposed. Thus, except for any obligation to pick up a collapsed transaction's expenses, the prospective lessee's obligations may be minimal or nonexistent at the time of the proposal acceptance. As a result, prospective lessors may be unable to require a prospective lessee to go through with a transaction or recover damages for his failure to proceed.

▶ **Recommendation:**   Inasmuch as a prospective lessee's obligations to go forward may be nonexistent after the acceptance of the offer, prospective lessors and underwriters must make sure transactions are quickly and efficiently completed.

G. The Prospective Lessor's Obligations After a Proposal Is Accepted

Because the lease proposal is conditioned, the offeror's obligations after the prospective lessee accepts the proposal will probably be limited. For example, if the offer is conditioned on acceptable documentation, a prospective lessor may have no trouble finding "unacceptable" points and walking away from the transaction. Of course, there may be an ethical obligation to go forward, but this will be of little value to a prospective lessee when left standing at the last minute without the essential financing.

▶ **Recommendation:** If a proposal is conditioned on certain lessor committee approvals, a prospective lessee should request written verification once the approvals have been given. Psychologically, this will bring the prospective lessor further into the transaction.

H. A Proposal Stage Checklist for the Lessee

The following lists the issues that a prospective lessee must address during the proposal stage. The lessee will want to review the list in preparing its bid letter and again to make sure the issues are addressed in the proposal letter.

■ Equipment Description
  ● What type will be involved?
  ● Who is the manufacturer?
  ● What is the model?
  ● How many units will be involved?
■ Equipment Cost
  ● What is the total cost involved?
  ● What is the cost per item?
  ● Is the cost per item fixed?
    (1) If not, what is the probable cost escalation?
■ Equipment Payment
  ● When must the equipment be paid for?
  ● Must the entire purchase price be paid at once?
■ Equipment Delivery
  ● What is the anticipated delivery date?
  ● How long should the lease commitment run past the last anticipated delivery date?

■ Equipment Location

- Where will the equipment be located?

  (1) At the lease inception

  (2) During the lease term

■ Equipment Lease

- What type of lease is desired?

  (1) Net finance lease

  (2) Service lease

  (3) Other

■ Lease Period

- How long must the lease run?

- Will an interim lease period be acceptable?

  (1) If so, what is the latest date on which the primary term can begin?

- How long a renewal period is desired?

- How will the renewal right be structured? For example, five one-year periods, one five-year period, etc.

■ Rent Program

- When should the rent be payable?

  (1) Annually

  (2) Semi-annually

  (3) Quarterly

  (4) Monthly

  (5) Other

- Should the payments be "in advance" or "in arrears"

- If there is an interim period, how should the interim rent be structured?

  (1) Based on the primary rent (for example, the daily equivalent of the primary rent)

  (2) Based on the long-term debt interest rate

  (3) Other

- If there will be a renewal period, how should the renewal rent be structured?

  (1) Fixed

  (2) Fair rental value

- Options
  - What type of options are desired?
    (1) Fair market value purchase right
    (2) Fixed price purchase right
    (3) Fair market rental value renewal right
    (4) Fixed price renewal right
    (5) Right of first refusal
    (6) Termination right
    (7) Other
  - Is a right of first refusal specifically unacceptable?
- Casualty and Termination Values
  - If a termination right is required, will the termination values be a primary factor in the lease decision?
  - Must the termination and casualty values be submitted at the time of the proposal?
- Maintenance and Repair
  - Who will have the equipment maintenance and repair obligations?
- Tax Indemnifications
  - What tax indemnifications will be acceptable, if any?
- Insurance
  - Is the right of self-insurance desired?
- Taxes
  - What taxes will be assumed?
    (1) Sales
    (2) Rental
    (3) Other

■ Transaction Expenses

- What expenses other than lessee's legal fees, if any, will be assumed if the transaction is completed?*
    (1) Counsel fees for any lenders and their representative
    (2) Acceptance and annual fees of any lender's representative (trust arrangement)
    (3) Counsel fees for the lessor-investors and any representative
    (4) Acceptance and annual fees of any lessor-investor's representative (trust arrangement)
    (5) IRS private ruling letter fees
    (6) Documentation expenses
    (7) Debt placement fee
    (8) Other
- What expenses, if any, will be assumed if the transaction collapses?

■ Tax Ruling

- Is an IRS private letter ruling necessary or desirable?
- Can a favorable letter ruling be a prerequisite to any of lessor's obligations?
- Should a private letter ruling relieve any tax indemnification obligations?

■ Submission Date

- What is the latest date on which the proposal can be submitted?

■ Award Date

- On what date will the transaction be awarded?

■ Type of Proposals

- Is an underwritten transaction acceptable? If so:
    (1) Will "best efforts" or "firm" proposals be accepted?
    (2) Is a leveraged or single source transaction preferred?
- If "best efforts" proposals are acceptable, how long after the award will the underwriter have to firm up the prospective lessor-investors and any lenders?

■ Prospective Lessors—Underwritten Transaction

- Are any prospective lessor-investors not to be approached?

I.   A Proposal Stage Checklist for the Lessor

The following checklist will serve as a guide to the prospective lessor in identifying issues, and in preparing and negotiating a proposal letter.

---

*Usually only a concern in underwritten transactions.

■ The Offer
- Will an underwritten or direct lessor proposal be involved?
- If an underwritten offer is involved:
  (1) Will it be on a "best efforts" or "firm" basis?
  (2) Must there be more than one equity participant?
  (3) If it can be on a "best efforts" basis, is there any deadline when the equity participants must give their formal commitment?
  (4) Will the transaction be leveraged with third-party debt?

■ The Lessee
- Has the lessee been accurately identified?
- Has the lessee's financial condition been reviewed?

■ Credit Support
- Can the lessee's financial condition support the entire lease obligation?
- If the lessee's "credit" is not sufficient, are there additional credit support alternatives available?
  (1) Parent company guarantee
  (2) Affiliated company guarantee
  (3) Unrelated third-party guarantee
  (4) Deficiency guarantee
  (5) Bank support
  (6) Other
- If credit support is necessary, has the financial condition of the entity giving the support been reviewed?

■ The Equipment Description
- What type will be involved?
- Who is the manufacturer?
- What is the model?
- How many units will be involved?

■ The Equipment Cost
- What is the total cost involved?
- What is the cost per item?
- Is the cost per item fixed?
  (1) If not, what is the probable cost escalation?

■ The Equipment Delivery
- What is the anticipated delivery date?
- Must the lease commitment run past the anticipated delivery date? If so, for how long?
  (1) Will a fee be charged for the commitment to lease future delivered equipment?

- ■ The Equipment Location
  - ● Where will the equipment be located?
    - (1) At the lease inception?
    - (2) During the lease term?
- ■ The Rent Program
  - ● What is the primary rent payment program structure?
    - (1) Will the rent be payable "in advance" or "in arrears"?
    - (2) Will the rent be payable annually, semi-annually, quarterly, monthly, or other?
  - ● Will interim rent be involved? If so,
    - (1) Will it be based upon the primary rent, the long-term debt interest rate (if leveraged), or other?
    - (2) When will the payments be due?
- ■ The Term of the Lease
  - ● How long will the lease run?
    - (1) Primary lease term
    - (2) Renewal period
  - ● Will an interim lease term be involved? If so,
    - (1) When will the interim term lease term start?
    - (2) When will the primary lease term start?
- ■ The Lessor
  - ● How will the equipment be owned?
    - (1) Directly
    - (2) Indirectly through a partnership, trust, or corporation
  - ● Will the ownership structure satisfy any tax and liability criteria?
    - (1) Flow-through of tax benefits
    - (2) Corporate-like liability protection
    - (3) Other

■ The Debt—if the Transaction Is Leveraged
  ● What is the loan repayment program?
    (1) "In advance" or "in arrears"
    (2) Debt service to be payable annually, semi-annually, quarterly, monthly, or other
  ● Who will be responsible for arranging for the placement of the debt?
  ● Will the rent be quoted on the basis of an assumed debt principal amount, per annum interest charge, etc.?
    (1) If so, will the rent quoted be subject to adjustment if other than assumed?
  ● If the rent is subject to a debt assumption adjustment, what adjustment criteria will be used?
    (1) After-tax yield
    (2) Cash flow
    (3) Net return
    (4) Other
  ● Who will be responsible for fees related to the debt?
    (1) Placement fee
    (2) Lender's commitment fee
    (3) Other
■ Options
  ● What special rights will the lessee have?
    (1) Fixed price purchase right
    (2) Fair market value purchase right
    (3) Fixed price renewal right
    (4) Fair market rental value renewal right
    (5) Termination right
    (6) Other
  ● What special rights will the lessor have?
    (1) Fixed price sale right
    (2) Fixed price renewal right
    (3) Termination right
    (4) Other
■ Casualty Loss
  ● What financial responsibilities will the lessee have in the event of a casualty loss?
■ Casualty and Termination Values
  ● What amounts are to be used?

■ Tax Aspects

- What are the relevant tax assumptions?
- What tax assumptions, if any, will the lessee have to indemnify the lessor for in the event of loss or inability to claim?
- If there are lessee tax indemnifications, what events that result in tax benefit unavailability will trigger an indemnification payment?
  (1) Any reason
  (2) Acts or omissions of lessee
  (3) Acts or omissions of lessor
  (4) Change in law
  (5) Other

■ Tax Ruling

- Will a tax ruling be involved?
- If so, will a *favorable* ruling:
  (1) Relieve the lessee from any tax indemnifications?
  (2) Be a prerequisite to the lessor's obligation to lease the equipment ?

■ Transaction Expenses

- Who must pay for the expenses if:
  (1) The transaction goes through without problems?
  (2) The transaction collapses before the lease documents are executed?
  (3) The transaction collapses after the lease documents are executed but before the equipment is delivered?

■ Type of Lease

- What type of lease will be involved?
  (1) Net finance lease
  (2) Service lease
  (3) Other

■ Conditions

- What conditions must be satisfied before the lessor is committed?
  (1) Governmental or regulatory approvals
  (2) Licenses or authorizations
  (3) Favorable opinions of counsel
  (4) Maintenance or achievement of certain financial tests
  (5) Satisfactory audited financial statements
  (6) Acceptable documentation
  (7) Approvals by prospective lessor or equity participants
  (8) Minimum dollar participation by equity and debt participants
  (9) Favorable equipment appraisals justifying equipment residual value
  (10) Other

■ Form of Proposal
  ● Will a written proposal be used? If so,
    (1) How should acceptance be acknowledged?
■ Submission and Award Dates
  ● When is the latest date on which the proposal can be submitted?
  ● What is the anticipated transaction award date?
    (1) Is there adequate time to do the deal?
■ Offer Termination Date
  ● How long will the prospective lessee have to accept the offer?

CHAPTER 3
Negotiating the Lease Document

A. What Is the Lease's Central Purpose?

Although a lease agreement can involve many complex, highly technical, and sometimes overwhelming concepts, its central purpose is very simple—it's a contract in which a property owner—the lessor—transfers the right to use the property to another—the lessee—for a period of time. The lessor retains title.

A lease differs from a conditional sale, an outright sale, or a mortgage type of transaction. Under a conditional sale, the property owner sells the property, not merely its use, to the buyer. At the time the agreement is reached, the seller transfers the property to the buyer, but retains title until the buyer performs certain conditions, usually the payment of the purchase price in installments. Following satisfaction of the conditions, the seller transfers title to the buyer.

In an outright sale, the property owner unconditionally transfers the property, including title, to the buyer and, at the same time, the buyer pays the seller the full purchase price. In a mortgage situation, a buyer of property borrows from a third-party lender some or all of the money necessary to buy the property. The lender, or mortgagee, as security for the repayment of its loan, requires the borrower, or mortgagor, to give it a security interest in the property. The borrower has possession of, and title to, the property subject to the lender's right to foreclose on the property in the event of a loan default.

B. The Common Lease Forms

Generally, leases fall into one of three common forms—the standard lease, the master lease, and the custom lease. These types, however, follow the same fundamental structure and reflect the same concepts. The differences, and the choice among the different approaches, is mostly determined by the practicalities of the situation, particularly the size and cost of the transaction.

1.   The Standard Lease

Lessors, particularly in small transactions and "vendor" programs, frequently use a "standard" preprinted lease. The form has fill-in blanks for those aspects, such as rent, that typically vary with each transaction. Although this type of lease format can be tailored to meet certain required variations, it is difficult to incorporate too many into the form and still come out with a readable document. The standard lease— particularly attractive in small dollar lease transactions—cuts down on drafting and negotiation, and thus helps keep documentation costs, such as legal fees, to a minimum. That can help both parties because the greater the expenses, the less the profit to a lessor, and the greater overall cost to the lessee.

▶ **Recommendation:**   The parties should always consider the estimated costs involved in documenting a lease in determining the transaction's economic attractiveness. Documentation expenses can be the same regard-less of the dollar amount of equipment involved. A $10,000 legal fee may be reasonable for a $500,000 transaction but it will not be for a $20,000 transaction.

2.   The Master Lease

A lease that is set up to permit future delivered equipment to be easily added is commonly referred to as a master lease. It may be either in a preprinted form or specifically prepared for a particular transaction (a custom lease approach).

A master lease has two parts: The main, or "boiler plate," portion contains the provisions that will remain the same from transaction to transaction (such as basic representations, warranties, tax obligations, and maintenance responsibilities); and the second part, sometimes called the "schedule," contains the items that will vary among the transactions (such as equipment type, rent, and options). Typically, the schedule will be short—often only one or two pages—while the main portion may be 40 to 50 typed pages. The advantage to using a master lease format is that the parties can document future transactions with a minimum amount of time and expense by merely adding a schedule containing the information pertaining to the specific transaction.

▶ **Observation:**   A lessor with a master lease in place with a particular company has a competitive advantage over other prospective lessors in any new bidding situation. Because documenting new equipment additions is simpler than negotiating an entire new lease agreement, companies with master leases frequently go out of their way to let an existing lessor win, such as giving him the chance to match a lower proposal.

3.   The Custom Lease

Frequently, an equipment lease will involve a great number of unique elements. In these cases, it is usually not practical, or even possible, to consider using a preprinted form, and a lease must be specifically drafted from scratch. Leases of this nature are often referred to as custom leases and are frequently found in major equipment lease transactions.

C.   Subjects to Address in Negotiating the Lease

Before starting and during the lease negotiations, the parties must understand the legal, financial, and practical aspects of a lease. Without that understanding, a party may inadvertently give up on an issue that is important, be too adamant about a point of little consequence, or miss an issue altogether. The following explanation identifies and describes issues that can arise in a major equipment lease, and suggests ways that the parties may resolve them. In preparing for the negotiations, the parties must weigh the relative values to them of different alternative approaches so that they will be able effectively to make necessary tradeoffs.

▶ **Reminder:**   Besides the transaction's participants, another party must be considered in negotiating a tax-oriented lease—the IRS. While the parties may find that a particular approach is in their business interests, the approach may jeopardize the lease's status as a true tax lease. The tax lease rules are explained in Chapter 8, and particular issues that may give rise to tax problems are noted below.

The following explanation uses a net finance lease as an example because it is generally the most comprehensive and complex form. Generally, understanding the issues arising in a net finance lease will enable an individual to deal with virtually any kind of equipment lease.

▶ **Note:**   The Appendix includes a sample net finance lease. The reader is urged to read it in conjunction with the following explanation.

▶ **Recommendation:**   In drafting a lengthy lease document, the parties should compile an index containing all the topic headings and page numbers to help the participants to the negotiation process be able to locate relevant provisions.

1.   Identify the Parties to the Lease

The lease should begin by clearly stating each party's full legal name, the jurisdiction in which each is organized, and the mailing address of their principal places of business. This will prevent disputes as to who is intended to be bound by the contract.

Illustrative Language—*The Proper Name Designations:*   This lease made as of the 25th day of February, 19XX, by and between ARROW CORPORATION, a Delaware corporation, having its principal place of business at 200 Curtis Street, New York, New York (hereinafter called "Lessor") and THE HARRIS CORPORATION, a Missouri corporation, having its principal place of business at 100 Barkley Street, St. Louis, Missouri (hereinafter called "Lessee").

▶ **Recommendation:**   Sometimes a corporation leases equipment to be used exclusively by one of its divisions. When such a division has been organized as a "profit center," the corporation frequently wants it to be the named "Lessee." However, if the division is not a separate legal entity, it cannot be bound by a contract. If the "division" is a corporate subsidiary, however, this problem will not be present because it will have a separate legal existence. A prospective lessor should, therefore, make sure that the lessee entity has been properly identified and is capable of being legally bound in the capacity indicated in the lease.

2.   The Factual Summary

At the outset, a lease document should summarize the basic facts surrounding the transaction. Writing the summary may help the parties focus on the overall transaction. Also, it may be helpful for future reference by individuals who were not involved at the time the lease was negotiated. For example, a summary can describe an equipment purchase contract that the lessee had entered into before the lease transaction and that was assigned to the lessor as part of the transaction. The factual summary is often incorporated into what are referred to as "whereas" clauses.

While not necessary, it helps if the factual summary describes the consideration for the lease, generally stated as the mutual obligations of the lessor and the lessee under the agreement. This is usually done in a "Now, Therefore" clause following the "Whereas" section.

Illustrative Language—*A Factual Summary:*   Whereas, pursuant to a purchase agreement (the "Purchase Agreement") dated January 2, 19XX between White Aircraft Corporation (the "Manufacturer"), a

Delaware corporation, and the Lessee identified above, the Manufacturer has agreed to manufacture and sell to the Lessee, and the Lessee has agreed to purchase from the Manufacturer, one White Model A-14 aircraft, that is to be financed pursuant to this Lease; and

Whereas, the Lessee and the Lessor will enter into an assignment of the Purchase Agreement simultaneously with the execution of this Lease whereby the Lessee assigns to the Lessor all the Lessee's rights and interests under the Purchase Agreement, except to the extent reserved therein;

Now, therefore, in consideration of the mutual agreements contained in this Lease, the parties hereto agree as follows:

3.   Definitions of the Key Terms

The lease should define the fundamental terms used repeatedly in the lease agreement that have special meaning in one section, preferably at the document's beginning. For example, terms such as "fair market purchase value," "fair market rental value," "manufacturer," "purchase contract," "stipulated loss value," and "termination value" will usually have certain meanings in a particular transaction, and the parties must agree on their meaning to prevent future ambiguities. Using such a definition section makes the text clearer, permits the parties to locate definitions more readily, and lessens the risk that an important term will accidentally be left undefined.

4.   Dealing With Future Delivered Equipment

Often the parties will want to enter into the lease well before the equipment's delivery date. Coming to terms on the lease in advance of the equipment's delivery can often benefit both parties: the prospective lessee can then be sure that no insurmountable problems will arise before it is too late to find another lessor; and an equally anxious prospective lessor may want to make sure that the lessee does not change its mind.

a.   Putting the Equipment Under the Lease

When a lease transaction is documented before the equipment's delivery, the parties must prescribe a method for putting the equipment under lease when it arrives. Usually the arrangement is for the lessee to notify the lessor in writing of the equipment's delivery and its acceptability for lease. The notification is usually in what is referred to as an "acceptance supplement," a written statement that lists the equipment delivered and states that the lessee has accepted it for lease as of a specified date. If the equipment conforms to the agreement, the lessor automatically puts it on lease.

When the lease relates to equipment to be delivered in the future, the lessee's obligation to lease the equipment must be clearly spelled out. For example, the lessee may want the option to accept or reject the equipment when delivered. And the lessor should clearly be aware of the lessee's obligation. An ambiguous phrase such as "the lessee *may* accept the equipment when delivered by executing the appropriate acceptance supplement," can cause problems—the lessor may anticipate that the lessee is bound to accept the equipment, while the lessee may not believe it is bound.

b. Nonutilization and Commitment Fees

Where the lessee wants the right to reject equipment to be delivered in the future, there are two ways a lessor can have some protection: A nonutilization fee and a commitment fee.

A nonutilization fee compensates a lessor for funds committed to future delivered equipment that remain unused at the end of the commitment period. Usually, the fee is expressed as a percentage of originally estimated equipment cost and is payable in a lump sum at the end of the commitment period. If all or an agreed-on portion of the funds are used, the lessee owes nothing.

Illustrative Example—*The Nonutilization Fee:* Company Able, a leasing company, has agreed to give Company Baker a lease line of credit for 10 river barges. The barges' total cost will be $1 million, and they will be delivered over a 12-month period. Company Able, however, has a limited amount of funds available and wants to be sure it will be protected from an opportunity loss if the barges are not delivered or Company Baker decides not to lease them. Therefore, it imposes a 1% nonutilization fee. If only $400,000 worth of barges are delivered during the commitment period, how much of a fee is due?

Company Baker would owe Company Able $6,000: 1% of the funds remaining unused, $600,000. If none of the equipment was put on lease, Company Baker would owe $10,000 (1% $\times$ $1 million). If $1 million worth of equipment was leased, Company Baker would not owe anything.

A nonutilization fee arrangement has its risks for a lessee. An unexpectedly high equipment purchase cost (whether from a mistaken estimate or a price escalation) or a delivery delay may give the lessor the right to exclude equipment from the lease. If this happens, a lessee can end up paying a nonutilization fee based on the unused funds remaining at the end of the commitment period. It is not, however, generally considered unreasonable, in cases other than where a lessor could arbitrarily choose not to lease certain agreed-on equipment when it arrives, for the lessee to bear this type of risk.

▶ **Recommendation:** Confronted with a nonutilization fee arrangement, a prospective lessee can lessen the payment impact resulting from equipment exclusions by negotiating a commitment percentage leeway. For example, the lease can provide for the fee to be payable only to the extent that greater than 10% of the committed funds are not used.

The other approach, a commitment fee, is more commonly used. Under this arrangement, a lessee can pay a flat fee at the time the lease is entered based on the total equipment cost involved for the lease funding commitment. Generally, the fee is expressed as a percentage of total cost, commonly ranging from 0.375 to 1%. Because the commitment fee pays a lessor for holding funds available, the lessee can freely elect not to put equipment on lease.

▶ **Observation:** In a competitive lease market, lessors may find it difficult to make a lessee accept nonutilization and commitment fees because many other lessors may be willing to hold funds available without a fee to win business.

c. Minimum Grouping Requirements

When a lease involves many less expensive equipment items to be delivered over a long period of time, a lessor can require a minimum equipment acceptance grouping to reduce its administrative handling expenses. For example, a lessee may not be able to accept equipment for lease in aggregate cost groups of less than $100,000.

An equipment grouping requirement can cause serious problems for a lessee. For example, if the dollar minimum was set high, the lessee may have to manipulate deliveries to avoid having to pay for equipment for which it does not yet have lease funding until the specified amount is accumulated.

▶ **Recommendation:** When confronted with a minimum dollar amount equipment grouping requirement, the prospective lessee should seek a "best efforts" qualification. Under this provision, if, after using its best efforts to assemble the required minimum, it becomes impractical to do so, the lessee will be permitted to have a smaller amount accepted.

5.   The Lease Terms

The parties must clearly negotiate the lease terms. Generally, the lease terms are of two types: (1) a main lease term, referred to as the "base lease term," the "primary lease term," or the "initial lease term"; and (2) a renewal term. Some transactions also call for an "interim lease term," beginning when the equipment becomes subject to lease until the start of a predetermined base term. The interim term concept is frequently used when many equipment items will go on lease at various times. For example, the base term may start on January 1, 19XX for all equipment delivered during the prior three-month period. By consolidating the primary lease term's start, there will be less administrative work.

In setting up the renewal term options, from the lessee's viewpoint, the more the alternatives the better. For example, one four-year renewal term is less preferable than four one-year terms because the lessee can compare market prices at more intervals. For the lessor, a longer renewal period will generally be preferable because it will want to have a longer period where its rents are predictable and it does not have to undertake to remarket the equipment.

6.   The Rent Payment Structure

Because when the rent payments are due and how much the lessee must pay are key elements of every lease transaction, the lease must precisely set out in detail those terms. For example, a 10-year lease may call for rent to be payable in 20 consecutive, level, semiannual in arrears payments, each payment to be equal to 2% of the total cost of the equipment.

a.   Payment Mechanism

To avoid problems, the lease should specify: (1) where the rent is payable, such as at the lessor's place of business; (2) the form of payment, such as in immediately available funds; and (3) when it is to be deemed received by the lessor, such as when deposited in a U.S. mailbox. Unless the lease specifies those terms, a lessee runs the risk of a lessor claiming a technical default based on what the lessor deems to be an incorrect or late payment, and a lessor runs the risk of losing interest it could have earned had the rent been paid in a manner that would have permitted an earlier use of the money. For example, a lessor will lose interest if payment is made by regular check that would take time to clear, as opposed to immediately available funds.

▶ **Recommendation:**   Lessees should establish appropriate internal rent payment procedures to avoid technical defaults through, for example, accidental late payments. If the rent must be sent to a special P.O. box number, all individuals responsible for handling the payments should be separately advised so that the rent does not instead get sent to the lessor's regular business address.

b.   Fixing the Rental Amount

Besides using fixed dollar amounts, the lease may express the rent in different ways. One way is as a percentage of equipment cost. The parties frequently use this method when equipment is to be delivered after the lease is signed because then the rent does not have to be recalculated if the purchase price varies from that anticipated. For example, if the annual rent is expressed as 2% of equipment cost, changes in cost will not require a lease adjustment. If, on the other hand, the lease sets rent at $2,000 a year based on a $100,000 item of equipment and the price later turns out to be $105,000, a lease amendment is needed to incorporate the proper rent.

When the rent is based on a percentage of equipment cost, the lease should define what expenses may be included, or "capitalized," in the "cost" term. If a prospective lessor has ample funds available, he may be eager to include more expenses into the rent computation cost base. For example, he may readily pay for sales taxes, freight charges, and installation costs and thereby increase the rent. If, however, his money supply is limited, he will probably want to exclude the extras. Also, when "soft" costs, such as installation costs, are substantial in relation to the raw equipment purchase price, a prospective lessor may not be willing to exceed a certain dollar amount on such costs because to do so would lessen his collateral value protection. For example, if a lessor financed the installation costs, and they ran 25% of the raw equipment cost, the lessor's collateral position would be diluted. In other words, 25% of the total amount financed would relate to installation charges that would have no re-marketing value.

▶ **Recommendation:**   The equipment related cost items that a prospective lessor is willing to finance can vary with each transaction. A prospective lessee should, therefore, define the ground rules in the proposal letter stage to eliminate potential misunderstandings or misconceptions.

c.   Tax Law Rental Adjustment

When a prospective lessor's economic return depends in part on anticipated equipment ownership tax benefits, he may want to be able to make rent adjustments if unexpected tax law changes occur that adversely affect his return. For example, the lease can incorporate a provision that would allow the lessor to adjust the rent to maintain his "yield and after-tax cash flow." Instead of a yield and after-tax cash flow, leases sometimes use a maintenance of earnings or net return standard.

▶ **Recommendations:**

■ A prospective lessor with the right to make rent adjustments in the event of adverse tax law changes should also have the ability to make appropriate adjustments to values that are based on the rent, such as termination or stipulated loss values. Without being able to adjust these rent-related values, the financial integrity of the transaction may not be maintained in the event, for example, of an early termination or a casualty loss.

■ A prospective lessee should always make sure that the lease clearly defines any lessor rent adjustment criterion. Terms such as yield or earnings, for example, do not have standard meanings and can be subject to many interpretations. The lease must set out the exact formula to be used in making any adjustment to enable an independent verification of any of the lessor's computations.

■ If a lessor has the right to adjust the rent up in the event of an adverse change in the tax laws to compensate for any loss, a lessee should request the right to have the rent adjusted downward if there is a tax law change that is economically favorable to the lessor.

Where It appears that the tax law may change, the parties can determine in advance what the rents and rent related values will be should the change occur and put them in the lease agreement. In this way, everyone knows how they would stand, and the parties can work out any problem before a final commitment is made.

d.   Conditions on Payment

In many equipment leases, particularly finance leases, the lessee's rent obligation is absolute and unconditional. That is, the lessee must pay the rent in full and on time regardless of any claim the lessee may have against the lessor. Commonly referred to as a "hell or high water" obligation, the provision at first sight shocks many new prospective lessees. The provision, however, is not as troublesome as it seems initially because it does not prevent a lessee from independently bringing a lawsuit against the lessor on any claim.

▶ **Recommendation:**   Although not technically necessary, a prospective lessee may want to insert a statement in a hell or high water provision to the effect that any rights of action it may have for damages caused by the lessor will exist regardless of the hell or high water rent commitment.

Typically, a lessor will want a hell or high water provision when he is leveraging his investment through using a nonrecourse loan. With this provision, a lender is more likely to lend on a nonrecourse-to-lessor basis because potential claims against the lessor would not affect the rental stream that is being relied on for the loan repayment.

▶ Observations:

■ Using nonrecourse debt as opposed to recourse debt is the most desirable way for a lessor to leverage a lease transaction. For financial reporting purposes, the nonrecourse nature permits a lessor to disregard the loan obligation on its books because the lender may look only to the lessee and the collateral for repayment, not to the lessor's general funds.

■ Sometimes a lessor's general lending bank requires a lessor to include hell or high water lease provisions in all leases. If so, the obligation is included in the lending agreement and is usually coupled with a right to require an assignment of all the lessor's rights under each lease, including the right to the rent payments, as an additional form of security for their loans.

7.   The Lessor's Right to Receive Reports

The lessor, to be able to monitor the transaction, may want the right to receive certain reports from the lessee. The utility of the various possible lessee reports depends on each transaction. It is usually advisable, however, for a prospective lessor to at least require financial reports, accident reports, lease conformity reports, equipment location reports, and third-party claim reports. These will enable him to stay on top of a transaction.

a.   Financial Reports

One of the best methods for a lessor to monitor a lessee's financial condition during the lease term is to require the lessee periodically to submit financial reports, such as current balance sheets and profit and loss statements. With these, a lessor will be in a good position to spot potential financial problems and take whatever early action may be necessary to protect his investment.

▶ Recommendations:

■ A prospective lessor should require quarterly, as well as annual, balance sheets and profit and loss statements. And each should be certified by an independent public accounting firm.

■ A prospective lessee should insure that the time between that period when the information is gathered and when a financial report is due is adequate for its preparation and submission to avoid a potential default situation.

b.   Accident Reports

A lessor should receive immediate notification of every significant or potentially significant accident involving the leased equipment, whether the damage is to the equipment or to persons or other property. Because it is not uncommon for a lessor to be sued solely on the basis of his ownership interest, lessee accident reports are a must. The reports should be in writing and contain a summary of the incident, including the time, place, and nature of the accident, and the persons and property involved. Reviewing all incidents may be a tedious job, particularly when many items of equipment are on lease, but it can prevent some costly surprises.

▶ **Recommendations:**
■ When an accident could involve major dollar liability, the lease should require the lessee to notify the lessor by telephone immediately in addition to submitting a written report. A lessor's early arrival on the scene can produce facts that would otherwise be lost.
■ A prospective lessee should limit accident notification responsibility only to incidents involving serious accidents. Minor accidents can create an unnecessary volume of paperwork. One approach is to set an estimated damage dollar amount below which notification is not required. If there is such a cutoff, the lessor should make the lessee responsible for inaccurate estimates because the lessor may not hear about a major claim until it has received notice of litigation.

c.   Lease Conformity Reports

Lessors sometimes require lessees to submit annually an officer's certificate stating whether any events of default under the lease have occurred during the reporting year, and whether there were any existing conditions that could eventually result in an event of default. If there are any, an appropriate factual summary must accompany the certificate. From a lessor's viewpoint, this type of report can be a good early warning technique. Although the reports are somewhat of a burden from a lessee's viewpoint, they are useful in avoiding inadvertent lease default situations.

d.   Equipment Location Reports

Requiring a lessee to prepare and submit equipment location reports is frequently advisable and sometimes necessary. Where practical, a lessor should periodically inspect the leased equipment, particularly when the lessee has an obligation to maintain it. If the location is known, it is easy for the lessor to "drop in" to check up on its condition. Location reports may be essential if a lessor intends to keep any security interest or other collateral protection filings up to date, as a location change sometimes necessitates a new filing.

▶ **Recommendation:**   When the lessor has filed or intends to file security interests, the lease should require the lessee to notify the lessor at least 45 days before a change of equipment location to give the lessor enough time to make any additional filings or amendments to existing filings.

e.   Third-Party Claim Reports

Generally, a lessor has a measure of security because he can take his equipment back if the lessee defaults. However, tax liens or other third-party claims imposed on the equipment, viable or not, can seriously jeopardize this protected position. Thus, the lease should require that the lessee notify the lessor of any events that result, or could result, in such an imposition so that he will have the opportunity to protect his position and equipment.

f.   Other Reports

The lessor should request the right to have the lessee submit reports that may be determined to be necessary in the future because unforeseeable events may require that the lessor receive certain additional information concerning the equipment. However, the lessee should seek to qualify any general reporting obligation so that only reasonable information relevant to the lease transaction can be requested.

8.   Equipment Maintenance and Alterations

a.   Equipment Maintenance

The lease must specify which party has the obligation for maintenance and what will be acceptable maintenance. Many types of leases, such as net finance leases, put the normal maintenance responsibilities on the lessee. Regardless of the arrangement, however, the maintenance issue should be specifically addressed in the lease.

Usually, the lease will describe the maintenance requirements in terms of the condition in which the equipment will have to be maintained. A common provision requires the lessee to keep the equipment in "good working order, ordinary wear and tear excepted." Unfortunately, such a general requirement may be difficult to apply because it is somewhat vague, and more specific guidelines are difficult to come up with. Two ways to minimize the difficulties:

- If the lessee will use the equipment in a manner that may cause extra wear and tear, the maintenance provision can exclude ordinary wear and tear resulting from the lessee's intended use.
- If the equipment's manufacturer provides maintenance instructions, the lessee should follow them exactly.

Some types of equipment must be specially maintained. A leased aircraft, for example, must be maintained under standards put out by the Federal Aviation Administration. Failing to meet those standards may mean that the aircraft cannot be flown, or, even worse, could result in lawsuits.

▶ **Recommendation:**   The parties should seek expert advice in specialized maintenance situations. Parties negotiating lease agreements frequently do not fully appreciate the cost effect of a proposed maintenance arrangement and, as a result, fail to protect themselves adequately.

A lessee responsible for maintenance should also be required to keep maintenance records and make them available to the lessor. Keeping records helps both parties: the lessor can determine whether the equipment is being properly serviced, and the lessee has greater protection should the lessor raise a claim of inadequate maintenance.

▶ **Recommendation:**   If the lease permits the lessor access to the lessee's maintenance records, the lessee should limit access to normal business hours.

b.   Equipment Alterations

A lessor should have the right to prohibit the lessee from making equipment alterations not related to normal maintenance. A lessee making alterations can affect the true lease status of the lease for tax purposes, thereby jeopardizing the lessor's tax benefits. These are explained in Chapter 8. In addition to the tax considerations, an alteration could affect the equipment's market value and impair its value to the lessor following the lease term. Generally, this is handled by a lease provision requiring the lessee to get the lessor's prior written consent to a proposed change.

9.   The Lessor's Ownership Should Be Specifically Protected

There are certain basic possession, use, and operational conditions that may be necessary for a lessor to impose to protect its ownership interest in the leased equipment. This section will be devoted to a description of the most essential considerations.

a.   Filings Must Be Made

In many cases, it will be necessary that filings be made to protect the lessor's ownership status. The lessor may want to file security interests under the UCC to ensure priority over other creditors. Certain types of equipment require special filings. An aircraft lessor, for example, must make certain filings with the Federal Aviation Administration to protect its ownership interest.

Who should be responsible to make the required filings? If the lessee has that obligation, the lessor must require the lessee to confirm promptly that the designated action was taken. The lease should also obligate a lessee to pay for any out-of-pocket losses incurred as a result of an improper filing.

b.   An Equipment Marking Requirement

The lease should require the lessee to mark the leased equipment with the lessor's name and its principal place of business. Marking the equipment has two basic benefits for a lessor: A marking will help fend off a creditor of the lessee trying to claim the equipment for the lessee's unpaid debts; and it will enable a lessor to identify his equipment more readily during an inspection trip or if a reclaiming action is necessary.

Illustrative Language—*Ownership Marking:*   White Leasing Corporation, Owner-Lessor, San Francisco, California.

c.   Certain Broad Use Prohibitions

The lease should prohibit the lessee from "using, operating, maintaining, or storing the leased equipment carelessly, improperly, in violation of law, or in a manner other than contemplated by the manufacturer." If, for example, improper handling or storing damages the leased equipment, and the lessor becomes responsible to a third party for damages caused through any of these actions, the lessor may have a basis for making a claim against the lessee.

▶ **Recommendations:**

■ Because of the scope of some general usage prohibitions, a lessee can easily find itself in technical default for relatively minor violations. A prospective lessee should, therefore, attempt to define the parameters more specifically, such as pinpointing the exact laws with which it must comply.

■ Lessees prohibited from using equipment other than in conformity with the manner contemplated by the manufacturer can unknowingly run into trouble. Frequently, equipment is acquired for a use different from that it was originally built to meet because, for example, nothing else is available. In such a case, a prospective lessee should attempt to get a use exception, a specific authorization to use the equipment as necessary.

10. The Lessor Should Require Certain Key Assurances

The lease should require the lessee to make certain key representations on matters related to a lease transaction. The representations should be given as true on the date of the lease document's execution and, where relevant, should also be ongoing during the lease period. The lease should provide that the remedy for the lessee's failure to maintain the representations is that the lessor may declare an event of default and get out of its commitments.

a.   That the Lessee Is Legally in Existence

The prospective lessor must assure itself through an appropriate lessee representation that the prospective lessee is a legal entity authorized to do business where the equipment will be used. A corporate lessee should, for example, be required to represent that it is properly organized, validly existing, and in good standing under the laws of its state of incorporation and that it is duly authorized to do business in those states where the equipment will be used. If the lessee is not, the lessor may have a difficult time suing the lessee, should it become necessary to do so. Also, any lack of proper legal standing can result in a seizure of the equipment by state authorities. The lessor's secured position could be jeopardized.

b.   That the Lessee Has the Transactional Authority to Enter Into the Lease

A lessor must have the lessee represent that it is authorized to enter into the lease transaction and that the persons executing the lease, by name or official title, are fully authorized to sign on the lessee's behalf. For example, if the lessee is a corporation and it had not been properly empowered by its board of directors to make the lease commitment, a lessor may be unable to enforce the agreement against the corporation.

The lessor's only recourse may be against the individual executing the lease "on behalf of the corporation." Because it is unlikely that the signing party, in his individual capacity, would have enough personal wealth to satisfy any substantive claim, the lessor would be in a precarious position.

▶ **Observation:** Merely because a lessee represents a particular point does not mean it is necessarily true as stated. If, however, a falsehood is deemed an event of default, the lessor would have the ability to reclaim the equipment.

c. That There Are no Conflicting Agreements

Existing agreements may restrict a prospective lessee's ability to enter into a lease transaction. A bank credit agreement, for example, could prevent the borrower from taking out additional loans without the lender's consent. If "loans" are defined to include lease obligations, the failure to secure the lender's consent would most likely be treated as a loan default. Typically, if there is a loan default, the lender would have the right to demand an immediate repayment of the outstanding money, which, in turn, could adversely affect a lessee's financial condition. Any lessening of the lessee's financial strength can jeopardize its ability to meet its lease obligations. The lease should include a provision that by entering into the lease agreement the lessee is not violating any existing credit or other agreements.

d. All Necessary Regulatory Approvals Have Been Obtained

In some situations, a prospective lessee may be required to secure regulatory approval for certain aspects of a lease transaction. For example, a public utility may be required to clear certain lease commitments with the appropriate utility regulatory authority. If they are not cleared, the lease commitments may be unenforceable. It is essential, therefore, that a lessor get a representation from the lessee that all necessary regulatory approvals have been obtained or, if none are needed, a representation to that effect.

▶ **Recommendations:**
■ Because of the regulatory complexities existing in certain industries, such as public utilities, it may be wise for a prospective lessor to verify independently that the lessee has complied with all necessary regulatory aspects, rather than relying on the lessee's representation or its counsel's opinion. Failure to comply can result in a major problem. Although the lessor can reclaim the equipment if a misrepresentation is deemed an event

of default, the expense and time involved in getting the equipment back, combined with the problem of having to dispose of, for example, 100 heavy duty used trucks at a reasonable price, can present serious practical problems. Securing a favorable opinion from independent counsel expert in the area is advisable, but it is not an "ironclad" solution. The safest course of action, if possible, is to get the appropriate regulatory authority to issue a favorable written opinion on the relevant issues.

■ Regulatory approval processes frequently take time. To avoid major delays, a prospective lessee should start the process as soon as possible so that, if necessary, it will be in a position to deliver the necessary assurances at the lease closing, such as supplying certified copies of any approvals obtained.

e. That There Are no Adverse Proceedings

A lessor must require the lessee to represent that there are no pending or threatened legal or administrative proceedings that could adversely affect the lessee's operations or financial condition. If there are such proceedings, the lessee should indicate what they are, and the lease (or another document) should expressly describe them. For example, it is not inconceivable for an impending lawsuit to be potentially serious enough to bankrupt a company. If it comes to a lessor's attention after the lease is signed, a no adverse proceeding representation would allow a lessor to terminate the transaction.

▶ **Recommendations:**
■ It is sometimes impossible for a prospective lessee to be aware of all threatened lawsuits or similar proceedings, particularly those involving minor incidents. Thus, the proceeding representation should be qualified to the effect that there are no proceedings that would have a material adverse impact on the lessee's operations or financial condition of which it is aware.

■ A no adverse proceeding representation, from a lessor's viewpoint, should be broad enough to cover not only the lessee, but also its subsidiaries and affiliated companies, because a proceeding against a related company could jeopardize the lessee's financial condition.

f. That the Lessee's Financial Statements Are Accurate

Because the lessee's financial condition is a critical consideration in a lessor's credit analysis, the lessee should represent that all financial statements delivered to the lessor, including those prepared by the lessee's outside accountants, accurately represent its financial condition. Such a representation should be requested whether or not the statements have been certified by the lessee's independent accountants. If, for example, a mistake were made, the lessor could reassess its willingness to continue with the transaction when it is discovered.

11.   The Lessee Should Require Certain Key Assurances

The lessee should also require that the *lessor* make certain representations—a point often overlooked by prospective lessees.

a.   That the Lessor Has the Transactional Authority to Lease the Equipment

Even though a prospective lessor presents itself to the public as being in the leasing business, there may be restrictions, such as in a credit agreement, prohibiting the lessor from entering into particular types of transactions. Also, a prospective lessor may have to go through prescribed internal procedures before a lease is in fact an authorized transaction. Violating any restrictions or procedures could jeopardize the lessee's right to continue using the equipment. Of course, an appropriate representation from a lessor will not guarantee there will be no use interference, but it will provide the lessee with another ground on which to base a claim in the event of a problem.

In underwritten transactions, the lessor-investors, "equity participants," are frequently not in the leasing business per se. Many corporations, for example, invest in leases on an irregular basis as equity participants, and if the lessor corporation has not obtained all the appropriate internal approvals for the transaction, a lessee may have some enforceability problems. In such a case, if a lessor backs out, a lessee may try to sue for performance on the basis that the lessor should be held to the contract based on its apparent authority to enter into the lease. If a lessor-investor is involved who is not regularly in the leasing market, this possible ground may be unavailable. Thus, it is important in underwritten transactions for a lessee to secure a representation that the transaction has been duly authorized by the lessor-investor.

b.   That the Equipment Will Be Paid for

The lease must include a statement by the lessor, particularly when the lease is executed in advance of equipment deliveries, that the lessor will pay for and lease the equipment to the lessee. While a firm commitment will not guarantee that funds will be available, it will assist in a legal action for damages in the event the lessor does not follow through. The lessor, in turn, will want the commitment to be subject to the lessee fulfilling certain obligations, such as equipment inspection and acceptance. As long as those conditions are within the lessee's capability, they should not be of concern.

▶ **Recommendations:**

■ A lessor payment commitment representation is particularly important when a prospective lessee is dealing with smaller, less well financed leasing companies. It cannot, however, be relied on exclusively if the dollar amount of the equipment involved is significant, or last minute funding problems could cause a budgeting disruption. Thus, the reputation and financial background of a prospective lessor should be investigated to insure that funding risk is at a minimum. A cheaper rental rate from a lesser known leasing company, or equity participant in the case of an underwritten transaction, will quickly lose its appeal if the funds are not available when needed.

■ The lessor should represent that the equipment will be, and will remain, free of all liens and encumbrances, except those of which the lessee is aware, such as the debt in a leveraged lease. That representation will help assure that there will not be any interference with the lessee's equipment use from the lessor's third-party creditors.

c.   That There Will Be no Interference With the Equipment's Use

A lessee's right to the quiet enjoyment and peaceful possession of the equipment during the lease period is fundamental, provided, of course, the lessee is not in default under the lease. A prospective lessee should require a representation to that effect.

▶ **Recommendation:**   A prospective lessor should limit its representation of quiet enjoyment to its own actions, as opposed to guaranteeing that the lessee will be entitled to quiet enjoyment in all events. If the representative is not so qualified, a lessor can be liable for damages if an unrelated third party, not claiming directly or indirectly through the lessor, interferes with the lessee's use of the equipment.

12.   The Lessor Should Disclaim Certain Product Responsibility

If the lessor is not the equipment vendor, he will not typically be responsible to the lessee for anything that goes wrong with the equipment. However, to be on the safe side, a lessor should make an appropriate product warranty disclaimer to prevent any possible exposure to a lessee for defects in the equipment's design, suitability, operation, fitness for use, or merchantability. The lessee should be able to accept such a disclaimer because it can rely on the usual manufacturer's, subcontractor's, or supplier's product warranties.

13.   It Is Advisable for the Lessee to Get an Assignment of Product Warranties

Where equipment is supplied by a manufacturer, subcontractor, or supplier, the lessee may be responsible for defects during or at the end of the lease term even though they were caused by the manufacturer, subcontractor, or supplier. To prevent that, a prospective lessee should obtain an assignment of any rights that the prospective lessor would have as equipment owner against any manufacturer, subcontractor, or supplier during the lease term. If these rights are not assignable because, for example, of a warranty restriction, a lessee should have the power to obligate the lessor to sue on its behalf if it deems it necessary.

▶ **Recommendations:**

■ If a prospective lessee finds it necessary to have the right to require the prospective lessor to sue in the name of the lessor because, for example, the product warranty rights cannot be assigned, that right should be coupled with the right to control the action, including the selection of counsel and the grounds of the lawsuit.

■ If a prospective lessor agrees to allow the prospective lessee to be able to require it to sue on its behalf, it should also specify the extent of the lessee's obligation to pay the legal expenses. Generally, these will be the lessee's responsibility.

14.   The Party With the Risk of Loss Should Be Specified

Generally, the lessee will bear the risk of equipment loss, whether due to damage, theft, requisition, or confiscation, because the lessee possesses the equipment. Net finance leases, for example, frequently require the lessee to guarantee that the lessor will receive a minimum amount of money, usually referred to as the "stipulated loss value" or "casualty value," if there is an equipment loss. The stipulated loss value, which decreases as the lease term runs, is calculated so that the lessor will not have to report a loss on its books. That obligation basically puts the lessee in the position of being the equipment's ultimate insurer.

▶ **Recommendations:**

■ Where the lease imposes a stipulated loss obligation, a prospective lessee should:

- Request an offset for any insurance proceeds or other awards resulting from the loss and
- Make sure its obligations, including rent, under the lease as to the affected equipment, terminate as of the loss date.

■ When a stipulated loss provision is incorporated, a prospective lessee should insist on a clear definition of the term "loss", because it can be susceptible of various interpretations. Generally, unless a defined loss has occurred, the rent must continue with the possible result that the lessee would be paying on unusable equipment. Typically, "loss" means destruction to the extent the equipment is no longer usable to the lessee. It is also worth noting that loss for the use intended may be somewhat less than actual total destruction. Thus, a prospective lessee should be careful in agreeing to the ground rules.

If a prospective lessee must repair equipment damaged by a third party at its own expense, it should insist on the right to claim any money received, at least up to the costs incurred, from the party causing the damage.

15. Responsibility for Certain General Taxes

In a typical net financial lease, the lessee is responsible for paying taxes—such as sales, property, and rental taxes—imposed by any local, state, or federal taxing authority. A prospective lessee should take into account any tax payment obligations when determining its effective leasing cost. Note: Some taxes can be significant.

▶ Recommendations:

Frequently, lease agreements require a lessee to pay equipment related taxes that, by law, the lessor must pay. If a lessor is improperly assessed by a taxing authority and refuses to institute a proceeding to correct the problem, the lessee may have to pay an incorrect assessment. Thus, a prospective lessee should require a right to be able to have any tax assessment contested or reviewed.

Where the lessee wants to contest a tax imposed on the lessor, the lessor should require that the lessee deliver an opinion from its counsel setting out that there is a legitimate basis for the action and should require the lessee to put up a reasonable amount of money in advance to cover the expenses.

The lease should require each party to notify the other party timely of potential or actual imposition of any taxes or similar assessments on the equipment. This will allow the interested party to participate at the earliest possible time.

16. Protecting the Lessor's Tax Benefits

Generally, the parties to a lease will want the transaction to be classified as a "true" lease for federal income tax purposes (see Chapter 8). It is absolutely essential, therefore, that the parties draft the lease to insure that the desired tax treatment will not be endangered.

If a "lease" does not qualify as a true tax lease, the lessor would undoubtedly lose ownership tax benefits, such as depreciation. Because such a loss can turn a favorable transaction into a highly unfavorable one, sophisticated tax lessors try to build protections into the lease documentation in two basic ways—prohibiting inconsistent actions and filings and requiring tax indemnifications.

a.   Inconsistent Actions and Filings Should Be Prohibited

The lease should prohibit the lessee from taking any action or filing any documents, including income tax returns, that would be inconsistent with the true lease intent. Normally, this does not present a problem for lessees because by doing so they could lose their right to deduct the rent charges as an expense—often the reason the transaction was structured as a lease.

b.   Tax Indemnifications—A Way to Protect a Lessor's Economics

The second way that lessors can attempt to protect themselves against tax benefit losses is through tax indemnification provisions. Typically, these provisions require the lessee to pay the lessor an amount of money that, after taxes, will put him in the same economic position as before the loss.

Tax indemnification provisions can be extremely complex and, to assess properly their effect and workability, one must understand how the ownership tax benefits can be lost. Basically, there are three ways: through acts or omissions of the lessor; through acts or omissions of the lessee; or through a change in law. For obvious reasons, lessors would like to put the economic burden of a loss or inability to claim all of the expected tax benefits on the lessees, regardless of the cause. Lessees, however, object to assuming the entire burden, and, as a result, a compromise is usually reached.

It is fairly standard in true leases to include a tax indemnity based on the *lessee's* acts or omissions. An indemnity based on the *lessor's* acts or omissions is rare, and a lessee should agree to such an indemnity only if the transaction provides significant other benefits. The third situation giving rise to potential tax problems, a change in law, can go either way, usually depending on the overall bargaining position of the parties.

c. Tax Law Changes

How significant is assuming the risk of tax benefit losses resulting from changes in tax law? To begin with, it should be recognized that the "risk" breaks down into a retroactive risk and a prospective risk. That is, changes that affect equipment already delivered and those that affect equipment to be delivered in the future.

▶ **Observation:**   A prospective lessee sometimes successfully shifts the burden of a retroactive change in tax laws to a prospective lessor by arguing that it is a "normal" leasing business risk that a lessor should assume. There is some logic to this position.

What about prospective changes in tax law, those affecting equipment that a lessor has made a commitment to lease, but that has not yet been delivered? In this case, the risk does not really have to be assumed by either party. For example, the lessor could be given the right to adjust the rent upward an appropriate amount if there is adverse change in the tax benefits before the equipment arrives or have the right to exclude affected equipment. The lessee, in turn, could exclude the equipment if the adjusted rent is too high. Alert prospective lessees usually make sure when a rent adjustment right is given that the lessor will have to make a downward adjustment if there is an increase in the available tax benefits.

▶ **Recommendations:**
■ Before a prospective lessor agrees to adjust the rents downward, if there is an increase in tax benefits affecting future delivered equipment, it should carefully determine whether it can use the increased tax benefits. If not, a downward rent adjustment will merely erode his economic return.
■ As explained in the above section, if the parties agree to provide for a rent adjustment and couple it with a mutual exclusionary right if the adjustment is unfavorable, certain disadvantages must be considered. A lessor can lose alternate investment opportunities if a lessee excludes equipment at the last minute, and a lessee may not have enough time to find substitute lease financing if the lessor exercises its rights.
■ If a prospective lessor excludes equipment based on a tax law change, it is possible that a nonutilization fee may be triggered. Thus, a prospective lessee should ensure that any nonutilization fee excludes the cost of equipment not leased as a result of a lessor's change-in-law exclusion right. If this is not provided for, a lessee will have to pay a fee on funds that remain unused as a result of the lessor's exclusion election.

d. Tax Loss Payment Formula

When the lease includes a tax indemnification provision, the provision must set out a precise formula for determining the amount the lessee must pay. Because the indemnity formula's purpose is to make the indemnified party "whole," the formulas are typically broad in scope and provide for a payment that, after deduction of all fees, taxes, and other changes payable as a result of the indemnification payment, will put the indemnified party in the same economic position as before the loss.

Frequently, this will be expressed as paying the lessor enough money to maintain the lessor's "net return." Unfortunately, that term can have many meanings, for example, total earnings, discounted rate of return, or after-tax cash flow. Thus, the lease should define such terms and provide a precise formula for determining the amount of the loss.

The formulas can become complicated, particularly if the lessor or equity participant is a large multinational corporation, because the payment may affect other aspects of the corporation's tax picture. As a result, where there are significant sums involved, it is usually necessary to retain experienced tax lawyers to work out the formulas.

In terms of the payment timing, there are two basic alternatives: A lump sum or a rent readjustment. Lessors often prefer the lump-sum payment so they can recoup their entire loss as quickly as possible.

e.   The Tax Loss Date

The lease must identify the time when the lessee becomes obligated to pay the indemnity. For example, would the lessee become responsible to pay for a tax benefit loss when the lessor discovers the problem or when a court rules on it? In many situations the "loss date" is defined as the time when the tax benefit loss has been established by the final judgment of a court or administrative agency having jurisdiction over the matter.

▶ **Recommendations:**

■ A prospective lessee should not agree to any provision that obligates it to make any tax indemnification payment until the lessor has actually incurred, or is about to incur, an out-of-pocket expense.

■ A lessor should have the right under a tax indemnification clause to make justifiable tax adjustments without prompting from the IRS and call on the lessee to pay if it realizes that it may not properly claim a tax benefit. However, it may not always be clear what is a justifiable adjustment, and without some means of making that interpretation, the lessee could be required to pay an indemnity solely at the lessor's discretion. To avoid that problem, the indemnity provision should provide that the lessor will claim a benefit only after receiving the opinion of a jointly chosen lawyer, or under some other similar arrangement where each party will have some control.

■ The lessee should have the right to require a lessor to contest any tax claim that will trigger an indemnification payment. Without it, a lessor could decide not to defend against a claim because he will not ultimately have to pay it.

f. Reimbursement for Erroneous Tax Loss Payments

The right to be reimbursed for any money incorrectly paid under a tax indemnification provision is an important concept to include within this arrangement. If the tax loss is determined not to exist, the indemnified party should be required to return any money paid promptly.

▶ **Recommendation:**   When a lessee has the right to force a lessor to contest a tax claim, he should also have a right to the return of any amount that he has had to pay before a final resolution, if the lessor later, without justification or consent, settles or discontinues the action. The purpose, of course, is to make sure the claim will be fully contested.

17. Equipment Return

The condition in which and the place where the leased equipment must be returned to the lessor are important considerations. Overlooking either can result in a costly omission for the lessor or the lessee.

When the equipment is returned, a dispute can arise concerning whether the equipment's condition meets the standards required in the lease. If a lessor determines that the lessee did not properly maintain the equipment, it can insist that the lessee pay for any repairs necessary to restore the equipment. And even if the lessor's claim for repairs is legitimate, a lessee may believe that the maintenance standards in the lease were met and dispute payment. Thus, the lease should provide a means to determine whether the lessee has met the standard of care criteria defined in the lease.

The best approach is to set an objective, easy-to-measure "outside" standard, for example, agreeing that an aircraft under lease will be returned with no less than 50% of remaining engine operation time before the next major overhaul. Where an easily measurable objective criterion is not available, the parties might agree to use an independent equipment appraiser to assess the equipment's condition. The lease can either identify the equipment appraiser or set out a method to select appraisers if their services become necessary. A selection method can call for each party to pick an appraiser at the appropriate time, and, if the two selected appraisers cannot reach an agreement, the parties will then jointly select a third independent appraiser whose opinion will be final and binding.

The lease should specify where the equipment is to be returned and who will bear the delivery expense. If, at the lease's end, a lessor, for example, unexpectedly had to pay for the transportation of 200 trucks from 10 of a lessee's plants scattered up and down the East Coast to a central sale point in the Midwest, his profit margin could be noticeably affected. Although who pays for shipping expenses varies with each transaction, it is not unusual for a lessee to pay only for shipping charges to a general transportation shipping point near where the equipment is used.

▶ **Recommendations:**
■ Prospective lessors without access to inexpensive equipment storage facilities should consider negotiating the right to store equipment on the prospective lessee's premises at the end of a lease until a buyer or new lessee can be found.
■ Prospective lessees must carefully consider the potential expense exposure in agreeing to return equipment to a particular return point, particularly when many items are involved. For example, a trucking pickup location may be much closer and, therefore less expensive, than the nearest railhead. Having the right to choose between alternative return locations may also be advisable. Circumstances can change, and it may turn out to be more practical to transport the equipment to, for example, the nearest railhead instead of the nearest truck pickup point.

18.   Events of Default

If a problem arises that would jeopardize a lessor's rights or interest in the lease or the equipment, the lessor should be in a position to end the lease, and take other action as may be appropriate, such as reclaiming the equipment. The various "problem" situations that could give rise to this type of lessor right should be clearly specified in every lease agreement. Those situations are generally referred to as "events of default."

a.   Where There Is a Nonpayment of Rent

The lessee's failure to pay the rent, when and in the amount due, should always be an event of default. Rent payment is a fundamental obligation, and a lessor should expect the fullest attention to it, perhaps allowing for a reasonable overdue payment grace period for unavoidable delays.

▶ **Recommendations:**

■ Prospective lessees should seek both a reasonable overdue rent payment grace period, and a lessor notice requirement. For example, the lease could provide that the failure to pay rent will not result in an event of default until a period of time, say five days, after the lessee has received written notice from the lessor of the nonpayment.

■ If a lessor agrees to an overdue rent notice provision as described in the above Recommendation, he should make sure the proper controls are instituted to monitor the timeliness of the rent payments.

b.   When There Is an Unauthorized Transfer

The lease should provide that if the lessee assigns or transfers the lease agreement or the equipment without the lessor's consent, there will be an event of default. *Reason:* The lessor enters into a lease transaction to a great extent relying on the quality and reputation of the lessee, so if assignments or transfers were freely permitted, the equipment could end up in the hands of an unacceptable third party. A sublease, for example, to someone who intended to use the equipment in a high wear operation could seriously jeopardize the equipment's anticipated residual value. By controlling transfers and assignments, a lessor can protect its investment position.

c.   When There Is a Failure to Perform an Obligation

It is in the lessor's interest to have an expansive definition of event of default, so it may seek to be able to declare a lease default if the lessee fails to observe or perform any condition or agreement in the lease. Whether or not a court would allow a lessor to actually terminate a lease agreement, no matter how minor the failure, may be open to discussion; however, the potential threat may keep a lessee in full compliance. Lawsuits are expensive even for the winner.

▶ **Recommendations:**

■ Many conditions and agreements in a lease may not be fundamental to the essence of the lease transaction, such as the correct marking of the equipment. Therefore, a prospective lessee should attempt to minimize the default risk by requiring that the breach be "material" before it gives rise to a default event.

■ A good way for a lessee to avoid inadvertent lease defaults is to have the lessor obligated to give at least 30 days' prior written notice before a default can be declared. Lengthy notice requirements, however, could hinder a lessor's ability to move quickly to protect its equipment and should be carefully considered before being given.

d. When the Lessee Has Made a Material Misrepresentation

As explained above, a lessor will often require the lessee to represent certain facts that a lessor deems critical to its decision to enter into the lease. Any misrepresentation of a material nature could subject a lessor to a risk that it would not otherwise have assumed had it known the actual facts. In many cases a lessor will rely on the lessee's representation that there have been no adverse changes in the lessee's financial condition between the date of the latest financial statements and the transaction's closing date. If a lessor discovers the representation was not true after the lease is signed, it should be entitled to declare a default even if the misrepresentation was inadvertent.

e. When the Lessee Is Going Bankrupt

The following should also constitute events of default: a court order or decree declaring the lessee bankrupt or insolvent; the appointment of a receiver, liquidator, or trustee in bankruptcy for a lessee under any state or federal law; any similar action that would expose the leased equipment to a third-party claim or otherwise endanger the lessor's position; or any voluntary act by the lessee that would lead to any of these events.

19. Lessor's Remedies Following an Event of Default

The lease should set out what remedies a lessor can pursue if a lessee defaults under a lease. Although doing so will not necessarily guarantee a lessor that a particular action will be permitted if the parties end up in court, it will put a lessee on notice, and thus may weigh against any lessee objection.

Lease agreements incorporate many types of default remedies, usually representing nothing more than a common sense approach to dealing with the default issue. The various remedies listed in a lease sometimes overlap, but from a lessor's viewpoint it is better to be somewhat redundant than to risk a claim that a certain course of action was waived by implication because it was omitted.

a. Court Action

The most obvious default remedy that should be included is a right to bring a court action to require the lessee to perform any breached obligation or to get money damages for the failure to do so. This is the standard type of remedy available in a basic contract action.

b.   Termination of the Lease

The lessor's right to terminate a lessee's rights under the lease, including its right to use the equipment, is a basic default remedy. As a part of this right, a lessor usually has the ability to enter the lessee's premises immediately and take possession of the equipment. The reclaiming right is particularly useful when a lessee's creditors are trying to attach assets as security for their claims.

c.   Redelivery of the Equipment

Lessors commonly have the right to require a lessee to redeliver the equipment in an event of default. It usually imposes a greater burden than if the lease normally ran its course. For example, the lessee may have to redeliver the equipment at its own expense and risk to any location that the lessor designates rather than to the nearest general transportation pickup point. In an adversary proceeding, the expanded right may not have much more meaning than helping to measure damages because a great deal of cooperation cannot be expected from the lessee.

d.   Storage of the Equipment

In a default situation, the lessor may not have a place to store the equipment readily. Thus, the lessor may want to obligate the lessee to store the equipment on its premises, free of charge, until the lessor can dispose of it following a default. Whether or not it is actually advisable to let a lessee retain control over the equipment is a separate issue that would have to be considered by the lessor when a default occurs. For example, a lessor may run the risk that other creditors would seize the equipment. Even though the creditors did not have a valid claim, the possible renting time lost and equipment deterioration could endanger the lessor's investment.

▶ **Recommendations:**
■ To avoid a prolonged storage obligation, a prospective lessee should place a time limit on any lessor storage right. If a time cannot be negotiated, the lessor at least should be committed to proceed to sell, lease, or otherwise dispose of the property diligently.
■ Any lessor right to have the lessee store the equipment should be accompanied by a right to enter the storage area for any reasonable purpose, including inspection by a prospective buyer or new lessee.

Although there are no industry standard formulas used to measure the damages that a lessor would suffer because of a lessee's default, two types frequently are used. One provides for the lessee to pay an amount equal to the present worth of the aggregate remaining rentals that the lessor would have received, but for the default, reduced by the equipment's fair market sales value or the present worth of the equipment's fair market rental value over the original remaining lease term. The other calls for the payment of an amount equal to the equipment's stipulated loss value as of the date of default, reduced by the equipment's fair market sales value or the present worth of the equipment's fair market rental value over the original remaining lease term. A prescribed per annum discount rate, such as the prime commercial lending rate in effect at the time of termination, is incorporated into the liquidated damage "formula" for present worth computation purposes.

▶ **Observation:** The discount rate agreed on to compute the present worth of the remaining rental stream can significantly affect what will be owed. Too often parties agree to arbitrary rates without considering the consequences. The higher the rate, the less the offsetting credit and the greater the damage amount payable.

Illustrative Example—*Liquidated Damage Formula Computation:* Company Able leased a $1 million aircraft to Company Baker for a 10-year term. As part of the agreement, the parties incorporated a liquidated damage formula that they considered to be a fair measure of the damages Company Able would suffer if Company Baker defaulted. The formula provided that Company Able would be entitled to an amount equal to the present worth of any remaining rents that would otherwise have been due but for the default, offset by the present worth of the aircraft's fair market rental value over the original remaining lease term. The per annum discount rate to be used to compute the present worth was specified as 10%, the current prime lending rate at Company Able's bank. At the end of the fifth year Company Baker defaulted. For simplicity we will assume that the rents are payable annually, in advance. The facts are:

Unexpired lease term	5 years
Annual rent	$120,000
Annual fair market rental value	$100,000

The present worth of the remaining rents under the lease, calculated using a 10% discount rate is $500,384. The present worth of the aggregate fair market rental value over a five-year period is $416,986. The amount that the lessee owes is $83,398, the difference between the present worth of the unpaid rents and the fair market value rents.

If the parties had agreed on a discount rate of 8% instead of 10%, the lessee would owe $86,242, instead of $83,392. On the other hand, if the discount rate were 12% instead of 10%, the lessee

$80,747. As the reader can see, the discount rate should not be treated lightly.

▶ **Recommendation:** Because the future fair market rental value is an estimate, the actual rentals may be higher or lower, resulting in either an underpayment or overpayment by the lessee. To solve this situation, both parties might consider the possibility of allowing for a future adjustment if the actual amounts vary from the appraisal.

20. A Lessor May Want Certain Lease Assignment Rights

Prospective lessors frequently ask for the right to assign their interest in a lease and the equipment at any time during the term. While a general assignment right sometimes makes prospective lessees uneasy, this should not cause concern if it is properly negotiated. To help protect its rights, a prospective lessee could insist that any assignment not adversely affect his lease rights.

a.   Assignment to a Lender

In many cases, a lessor's lenders will require as part of their credit arrangement that the lessor incorporate in all leases a provision giving the lenders a right to an assignment of the rights, including title to the equipment, if certain loan restrictions are violated. Generally, the purpose of the assignment provisions is to enable a lender to take over the leases as security if there is a loan default. If an assignment requirement exists in a lessor's loan agreement, it must be in each lease agreement, and it is not a negotiable point between the lessor and lessee. In certain situations, a lessor may want to have the ability to borrow a portion of the equipment purchase cost from a lender on a nonrecourse basis. To do that, the lessor usually must assign to the lender all the lessor's lease contract rights, such as the right to receive uninterrupted rentals.

▶ **Recommendation:** Any time a prospective lessee must agree to allow a lessor to be able to assign any or all of its interest in a lease to its lenders, the lessee should require that any such transfer be subject, and subordinate, to the terms of the lease. Thus, if there is an assignment, the lessee's rights, including the right to use the equipment, will not in any way be jeopardized by the lessor's assignment of its rights to the bank. The lease should provide that any transfer will not relieve the lessor from any of its obligations under the lease. This will give a prospective lessee the assurance that it will always have what it originally bargained for.

b. Assignment to an Investor

A lessor will sometimes want the right to "sell" the lease, including title to the equipment, to a third party. Under this arrangement, the third-party buyer would become the equipment owner, would take subject to the terms and conditions of the lease agreement, and would, therefore, become the "lessor." The original lessor would no longer have any rights or *duties* under the lease.

A broad assignment right can expose a lessee to certain risks. A lease sold to a financially unstable lessor, for example, may endanger the lessee's right to the continued use of the equipment because of potential creditor actions against the new lessor. Also, an assignment to a lessor who is difficult to deal with can create problems, for example, where the lease must be modified.

▶ **Recommendations:**

■ A prospective lessor seeking a lease assignment right should also seek the right to require the lessee to execute any documents necessary to effect the assignment. Without that right, a lessee could, intentionally or unintentionally, block the assignment.

■ A lessee may want some control over a lease assignment. For example, if the lessor assigned the lease to any of the lessee's banks or lending institutions that assignment could restrict the lessee's borrowing capability. To prevent that, the lessee could request the right to pass on any potential transferees or, if a prospective lessor is unwilling to grant such a right, it could specifically define the limits of who would be acceptable.

21. A Lessee May Want Certain Equipment Sublease Rights

A lessee with the right to sublease equipment is in the best position to lessen or eliminate the impact of having to pay rent on assets that become unproductive because of changes in use needs during the lease term. If there are no restrictions, such as those that would limit transfers to affiliated companies only, a lessee will have the maximum flexibility.

▶ **Recommendations:**

■ Prospective lessors consenting to a subleasing right should insist that the lessee remain primarily liable under the lease agreement during the sublet period.

■ Prospective lessees desiring subleasing rights should try to avoid agreeing to any exercise conditions, such as having to obtain the lessor's prior written consent. Time wasted waiting for a consent could result in lost revenue.

■ From the lessor's perspective, however, it may not be advisable to give a prospective lessee an unrestricted right to sublease the equipment to any party, even though the original lessee will remain primarily liable under the lease. Having the right to pass judgment on any proposed sublessee will prevent knowing transfers to parties who may misuse the equipment or who are financially unstable. Regardless of the original lessee's primary responsibility, misuse can diminish the equipment's value, and a sublessee's bankruptcy could interfere with the equipment's return.

22.   Lessor's Options to Renew, Sell, or Terminate

There are a few situations when a prospective lessor will want certain rights that are not usually requested, such as a right to terminate the lease in a non-default situation, a right to force a sale of the equipment to the lessee, a right to force the lessee to renew a lease, or a right to abandon the equipment. These rights can create substantial tax problems or be otherwise undesirable from a lessee's viewpoint. Thus, if proposed, their possible effect should be carefully reviewed.

a.   The Right to Terminate the Lease

It is conceivable, although extremely unlikely, that a prospective lessor would want to be able to terminate a lease *for any reason it chooses* during its term without the lessee's consent. For example, if a prospective lessor believes the rental market will rise before the end of the negotiated lease term, it may want to have the ability to go after a better rate.

▶ **Recommendation:**   For obvious reasons, a prospective lessee should not put itself in a position where a lessor could prematurely terminate the lease without the lessee's prior consent and without reason.

b.   The Right to Force a Sale of the Equipment to the Lessee

In certain situations a prospective lessor will insist on having the right (commonly referred to as a "put") to force a lessee to buy the equipment under lease at the end of the term. Generally, this right is expressed as a fixed percentage of the original equipment's cost rather than a defined dollar amount. For example, a lessor may have the right to sell the equipment to the lessee for an amount equal to 10% of cost. In effect, a put eliminates any risk that a lessor will not realize his assumed residual value that, in turn, protects his anticipated profit. Transactions involving certain types of store fixtures or equipment that will be difficult or uneconomical to move, such as certain heavy storage tanks, sometimes incorporate a forced sale right.

▶ **Recommendations:**
■ The use of a put may impair the tax status of a lease transaction. (See Chapter 8.) They should be incorporated only with the advice of tax counsel.
■ If a prospective lessor insists on having a put, the prospective lessee should make sure it will not be required to indemnify the lessor for any loss of tax benefits a lessor can suffer if the put causes the lease not to qualify as a true tax lease.

c.   The Right to Abandon the Equipment

In the past, equipment abandonment rights had been used in leases of equipment that would be difficult and costly, if not totally impractical, to reclaim if the lessee decided not to buy it at the end of the term. A good example of the type of leases that involved abandonment rights were those relating to certain kinds of commercial storage tanks that were so large that the only way to move them was to cut them into pieces and then reweld them at the new site. In these situations, the expenses involved could be so great that the lessor could not reasonably recoup them through a releasing or a sale.

Lessors sometimes attempt to solve an equipment removal expense problem by requiring the equipment to be delivered to them at the end of the term at the lessee's expense. If the lessee refuses to do so, however, the lessor's only recourse, without a right of abandonment, would be to bring a lawsuit to force the lessee to live up to its agreement or, possibly, pay for any resulting damages. If the lessee is in financial trouble, a lawsuit may be of little use. Having an abandonment right allows the lessor to drop the property in the lessee's lap and rid itself of any lingering responsibility or expense exposure.

▶ **Recommendation:**   The lessor's right to abandon the equipment is prohibited under the IRS Guidelines and can create serious tax lease treatment problems (See Chapter 8 §C,7.) It should be used only on the advice of tax counsel.

d.   The Right to Require a Lease Renewal

In situations where an abandonment right or a put might be considered, a lessor may instead use a forced lease renewal right. Under this right, a lessor could make the lessee re-lease the equipment at a predetermined rental.

▶ **Recommendation:**   The right of a lessor to require a lessee to renew a lease could also run afoul of the IRS Guidelines and can create serious tax lease treatment problems. It should be used only on the advice of tax counsel.

23. Lessee Options to Buy, Renew, or Terminate the Lease

Invariably, a prospective lessee will ask for certain rights, referred to as "options," that will enable him to maintain some form of control over the equipment's use, such as an equipment purchase right, a lease renewal right, or a lease termination right. Generally, these types of options are willingly granted by prospective lessors.

a.   The Right to Buy the Equipment at Fair Market Value

A prospective lessee typically wants to be able to buy the leased equipment at the lease's end. In many situations, this is done through a fair market value purchase option. Basically, the option gives the lessee the right to buy the equipment for whatever its fair market value is *at the time it is exercised.*

Although the term "fair market value" appears self-explanatory, the parties should agree on a method for its determination. Generally, the "fair market value" of a piece of equipment is the amount that a willing buyer under no compulsion to purchase would pay a willing seller under no compulsion to sell in the open market. As a practical matter, however, how is the value actually determined between a lessor and a lessee? Typically, it is done through an equipment appraisal. The parties can designate in the lease an independent appraiser who will evaluate the equipment at the appropriate time. Alternatively, the parties can each select an independent appraiser to come in and make an assessment when necessary. If the two appraisers cannot agree on a satisfactory value, then they must jointly select a third appraiser, whose opinion will be binding.

▶ **Recommendation:**   A fair market value purchase option can be an expensive way for a lessee to acquire equipment with a typically strong resale value. A purchase price "cap" is sometimes negotiated to limit how much the lessee would have to pay. For example, the lessee would have the right to buy the equipment at fair market value or 30% of the equipment's original cost, whichever is less. However, a cap can present tax problems. (See Chapter 8§C,6.)

b.   The Right to Buy the Equipment at a Fixed Price

When equipment has traditionally maintained a favorable re-sale value, many companies refuse to lease because a fair market purchase option coupled with the lease rents could result in an economically unfavorable way of acquiring it. As a result, a fixed price purchase option is sometimes given to induce them to lease. Under a fixed price purchase option, commonly referred to as a "call," the lessee can buy the equipment at the end of the lease for a predetermined price. The price is usually expressed as a percentage of the equipment's original cost. For example, the lessee may have the right to buy designated equipment for 35% of cost. In this way, the lessee knows the maximum amount of money he will have to spend if he wants to buy the equipment when the lease is over.

▶ **Observation:** A lessee fixed price purchase option can cause a lease to fail to be characterized as a lease for federal income tax purposes. If the exercise price is so low that the lessee may, in effect, have a bargain purchase right, the IRS may be able to challenge successfully its status as a true tax lease. Fixed price purchase options, therefore, should be granted with care, and only with the advice of tax counsel, if it is important that a lease qualify as a true tax lease.

c. The Right to Renew the Lease at Fair Rental Value

Providing a lessee with the right to renew a lease at the equipment's fair market rental value at the time of renewal is acceptable, both from the standpoint of the IRS and, generally, a lessor. The parties can determine the fair rental in a manner similar to that for the determination of the fair market purchase value, through independent appraisal at the time of the intended renewal.

▶ **Recommendation:** When equipment is vital to a prospective lessee's operations, it should make sure the lease renewal terms are adequate to cover any anticipated needs. For example, if a four-year renewal is desirable, an option that would allow a selection of two two-year periods, four one-year periods, one one-year period followed by a three-year period, or a four-year period would provide a great deal of flexibility as to term and as to rental rate. A structure such as this would give the lessee the ability to limit its renewal costs in a high rental market or to "lock in" for a longer period of time in a low rental market. From a lessor's viewpoint, of course, too much latitude on the lessee's side can lessen its chances of maximizing its renewal profits and, therefore, any such arrangement should be carefully thought out as to the possible future effects.

d.   The Right to Renew the Lease at a
Fixed Price

Prospective lessees sometimes request a fixed price renewal option. By knowing in advance the exact dollar amount of the renewal rents, they know where they would stand if they wanted to continue to use the equipment beyond the main lease term. This would, of course, not be possible with fair market renewal option.

▶ **Observation:**   A fixed price renewal right may result in adverse tax consequences. (See Chapter 8§C,1 and 2.) Thus, the amount of fixed renewal option must be carefully considered.

e.   The Right to Terminate the Lease

It is not uncommon for a prospective lessee to have the ability to terminate a lease early, particularly when it believes the equipment could become technically obsolete or surplus to its needs before the lease would normally end. When this right is granted, the lessee frequently will be required to pay the lessor a predetermined amount of money, commonly referred to as the "termination value," on exercise. Because most lessors do not like to grant termination rights, the termination amount is usually high.

f.   The Right of First Refusal

A purchase "right of first refusal" is sometimes used as an alternative to a fair market value purchase option. Under this option, a lessee is given the right to buy the leased equipment at the end of the lease term under the same terms and conditions as offered by an unaffiliated third party. The disadvantage to using it is that a lessee may run the risk that a competitor may bid for the equipment either to push the price up or to acquire it for its own operations.

Illustrative Language—*Right of First Refusal:*   Unless an Event of Default shall have occurred and be continuing at the end of the term of this lease, or any event or condition which, upon lapse of time or giving of notice, or both, would constitute such an Event of Default shall have occurred and be continuing at such time, the lessor shall not, at or following the end of the term of this lease, sell any item of equipment (including any sale prior to the end of such term for delivery of such equipment at or following the end of such term) unless:

(1) the lessor shall have received from a responsible purchaser a bona fide offer in writing to purchase such equipment;

(2) the lessor shall have given the lessee notice (a) setting forth in detail the identity of such purchaser, the proposed purchase price, the proposed date of purchase, and all other material terms and conditions of such purchase, and (b) offering to sell such equipment to the lessee upon the same terms and conditions as those set forth in such notice; and

(3) The lessee shall not have notified the lessor, within 20 days following receipt of such notice, of its election to purchase such equipment upon such terms and conditions.

If the lessee shall not have so elected to purchase such equipment, the lessor may at any time sell such equipment to any party at a price and upon other terms and conditions no less favorable to the lessor than those specified in such notice.

24. A Defaulting Party Should Lose Certain Options

Generally, the lease should provide that the party holding an option forfeits its exercise right, if it is in default under the lease. For example, a lessee should lose its right to buy the equipment under a purchase option if the lease is terminated because of a default on its part.

25. Designate the Law Governing the Lease

It is always advisable for the parties to specify what jurisdiction's law will apply to their rights and obligations under a lease agreement. For example, the parties can agree that all actions on lease issues will be decided under the laws of New York State, regardless of whether the proceedings are instituted in a New York court. By doing this, the attorneys are able to draft the documents under the law they believe will give the fairest known outcome.

26. Severability Clause

The lease should include a severability clause, providing that any lease provision determined to be legally unenforceable will be severed. Under this clause, the severed provision is treated as though it never existed. This may prevent the entire lease agreement from being held invalid if only certain provisions are unenforceable.

27.   The Interest Penalty for Late Payments

A lease agreement should prescribe the interest rate that will be charged on any overdue payments, such as delinquent rent payments. This will eliminate disputes over late charges, and will assist in assessing damages if a lawsuit arises.

▶ **Recommendations:**

■ When the lease specifies an overdue payment interest penalty, the prospective lessor should also incorporate a qualification that the rate will in no event be higher than the maximum enforceable legal rate to avoid any potential enforceability problems if the legal limit is inadvertently exceeded.

■ Prospective lessors will want interest on overdue obligations to run from the date the money is due to the payment date. Prospective lessees, on the other hand, should attempt to get it to run from the date the lessee receives written notice of the overdue obligation from the lessor.

28.   The Lease Should Identify Where and How to Send any Required Notifications and Payments

While leases usually provide that all required notifications and payments, such as loss notifications and rent payments, must be promptly made, they sometimes fail to identify exactly *where* they should be sent. As a result, payments or notifications could be misdirected and money or valuable time lost. The lease should, therefore, expressly state the appropriate mailing addresses.

In addition to specifying where payments and notifications must be sent, the lease should specify the notification and payment manner. For example, it may be agreed that a notice will be deemed given when it is deposited in a U.S. mail box, sent by prepaid telegraph, or sent by certified mail.

29.   The Lease Should Be Correctly Signed

All parties to a lease should make sure it is signed in the proper capacities. Leases to be signed by an individual representing himself generally do not present any problems. Leases to be signed by an individual representing a firm, such as a partnership, corporation, or trust, sometimes do. If, in the latter case, the signature is not made in the correct representative capacity, the represented firm may not be bound. For example, if a vice president intends to sign on behalf of his corporation, the signature block should be set up as follows:

XYZ Corporation

by _____

R. Smith, Vice President

If the signature form is not correct, the signing individual may run the risk that he is *personally* liable on the contract—certainly, a less-than-desirable outcome for all parties concerned.

D.   A Checklist for Drafting and Negotiating a Lease Agreement

In preparing a well-drafted lease agreement, the parties should cover all the important issues involved in a transaction. The following checklist pinpoints the issues frequently encountered.

■ What form of lease is appropriate?
- A standard lease
- A custom lease

■ Should a master lease be used?

■ Does the lease agreement cover the following issues?
- Has a page index of all topic headings been included?
- Have the parties been properly identified?
    (1) Lessor
    (2) Lesser
- Is the lessee a valid legal entity?
- Has a factual summary of the circumstances giving rise to the transaction been included?
- Has the consideration for the transaction been stated?
- Have the key terms been defined in a definition section? For example:
    (1) Affiliate
    (2) Business day
    (3) Buyer-furnished equipment
    (4) Equipment delivery date
    (5) Equipment manufacturer
    (6) Event of default
    (7) Event of loss
    (8) Fair market value
    (9) Indenture
    (10) Interim rent
    (11) Lease

(12) Lease period

(13) Lease supplement

(14) Lessor's cost

(15) Lien

(16) Loan certificates

(17) Loan participant

(18) Overdue interest rate

(19) Primary rent

(20) Casualty loss value

- If equipment will be delivered after the lease is signed, has a procedure for adding it been established?
  - (1) Can the lessee decide not to lease future delivered equipment when it arrives? If so, will the lessee be obligated to pay:

    (a) A non-utilization fee?

    (b) A commitment fee?

  - (2) Can future delivered equipment be accepted for lease as it arrives or must the lessee aggregate a minimum dollar amount?

- The lease period should be defined
  - (1) Will there be an interim lease term? If so, when will it begin and end?
  - (2) When will the primary term begin?
  - (3) How long will the primary term run?
  - (4) Will the lessee be permitted to renew the lease? If so, what is the renewal period arrangement?

- The rent structure must be defined
  - (1) Will a percentage rent factor be used? If so, what may be included in the equipment cost base?

    (a) Sales tax

    (b) Transportation charges

    (c) Installation charges

    (d) Other

  - (2) How much rent must be paid?
  - (3) When will the rent be due?
  - (4) How must the rent be paid?

    (a) Check

    (b) Wire transfer

    (c) Other

  - (5) Where must the rent be paid?

    (a) Has a post office box or other address been specified?

(6) Can or must the lessor adjust the rent charge if there is a tax law change affecting, favorably or unfavorably, the lessor's economic return?

    (a) If a rent adjustment is provided for, has the exact criterion for making it been clearly specified?

    (b) If the tax law change applies to future delivered equipment and a rent adjustment is not acceptable, can the party adversely affected elect to exclude the equipment?

(7) Will the rent obligation be a hell or high water obligation?

- What is the lessor's total dollar equipment cost commitment?

    (1) Will a percentage variance be permitted?

- Will the lessee be required to submit reports? For example:

    (1) Financial reports

        (a) Profit and loss statements

        (b) Balance sheets

        (c) Other

    (2) Accident reports

        (a) Has a minimum estimated accident dollar amount been agreed upon below which a report is not required?

        (b) Will the lessee be obligated to immediately telephone if a serious accident occurs?

    (3) Lease conformity reports

    (4) Equipment location reports

    (5) Third-party claim reports

- Has a time been established for when lessee reports are due?
- Has a general lessee reporting requirement been imposed as to reports that may be deemed necessary by the lessor in the future?
- Equipment maintenance

    (1) Who has the responsibility for insuring proper maintenance?

        (a) Lessor

        (b) Lessee

        (c) A third party

    (2) Who must bear the cost of the maintenance?

        (a) Lessor

        (b) Lessee

    (3) Will maintenance records be required?

        (a) Will the lessor be permitted access to the maintenance records? If so, at what times:

           1. Normal business hours

           2. Any time requested

- Will equipment alterations be permitted? If so,
    - (1) Will the lessor's consent be required before:
        - (a) An addition that may impair the equipment's originally intended function or that cannot be removed without so impairing such function
        - (b) Any change
    - (2) Who will have title to any addition or other alteration?
        - (a) If it can be easily removed without equipment damage?
        - (b) If it cannot be removed without function impairment?
        - (c) What rights will the lessor have to buy the alteration?
- Will certain lessor ownership protection filings be advisable or necessary?
    - (1) Federal regulatory agencies, such as the Federal Aviation Administration
    - (2) Uniform Commercial Code
    - (3) Other
- If lessor ownership protection filings will be made, who has the responsibility for making them and who must bear the expense?
    - (1) Lessor
    - (2) Lessee
- If the lessee must make required filings for the lessor, will the lessee have to confirm they have been made?
- Will the equipment be marked with the lessor's name and address? If so, who will have the marking responsibility and expense?
    - (1) Lessor
    - (2) Lessee
- Has the lessee been specifically prohibited from using, operating, storing, or maintaining the equipment carelessly, improperly, in violating the law, or in a manner not contemplated by the manufacturer?
    - (1) If the lessee must use the equipment for a purpose other than intended, an exception should be negotiated
- The lessee must be required to provide certain key representations
    - (1) That the lessee is properly organized, validly existing, and in good standing
    - (2) That it has proper authorization to do business in the state where the equipment will be located
    - (3) That the lessee has the transactional authority to enter into the lease
        - (a) That necessary board of director approvals have been obtained covering the transaction *and* the person signing the lease on behalf of the lessee
        - (b) That any other required approvals have been obtained

(4) That there are no conflicting agreements

    (a) Bank credit agreements

    (b) Other loan agreements

    (c) Mortgages

    (d) Other leases

(5) That all necessary regulatory approvals have been obtained

(6) That there are no pending or threatened adverse legal or administrative proceedings that would affect the lessee's operations or financial condition

(7) That there have been no adverse changes as of the lease closing in the lessee's financial condition since the latest available financial statements

- The lessor must be required to provide certain key representations

  (1) That the lessor has the transactional authority to lease the equipment

      (a) That any necessary board of director approval has been obtained

      (b) That any other approvals have been obtained or, if none are required, a statement that none are required

  (2) That the lessor will pay for the equipment in full

  (3) That the lessor will not interfere with the lessee's use of the equipment

      (a) Has an exception when the lessee is in default been negotiated by the lessor?

- The lessee should require product warranties to be assigned if the lessor has no equipment defect responsibility

  (1) If the warranties are not assignable, the lessor should be required to act on the lessee's behalf

- Who has the responsibility for equipment casualty losses?

  (1) Lessor

  (2) Lessee

- Do the casualty loss values give adequate financial protection to the lessor?

- Are the casualty loss values competitive from the lessee's viewpoint?

- As of what time will a casualty loss be deemed to have occurred—has a "loss date" been defined?

  (1) What obligations change or come into effect on the loss date?

- When is the casualty loss value payable and when does interest on the amount payable begin to run?

- What taxes must be paid?

  (1) Sales tax

  (2) Property taxes

(3) Rental taxes

(4) Withholding taxes

(5) Income taxes

(6) Other

- Who must pay the taxes?
  (1) The lessor
  (2) The lessee
- For any taxes that a lessee must reimburse a lessor for payment, does the lessee have the right to have the taxes contested?
  (1) What happens if the lessor does not fully pursue its contest remedies?
- Is each party required to immediately notify the other of any tax imposition for which they will be responsible?
- Do the parties intend a true tax lease? If so,
  (1) Inconsistent actions and filings should be prohibited
  (2) Will tax loss indemnifications be required?
  (3) Will any tax indemnity cover all lessor tax losses or only those resulting from the lessee's acts or omissions?
- Who has the economic risk of a change in tax law?
  (1) For past delivered equipment
  (2) For future delivered equipment
     (a) Can either party elect not to lease if the economics are no longer favorable?
- Has a formula been agreed on for measuring the amount of any tax benefit loss and the amount of any required reimbursement?
  (1) Does the formula make the indemnified party whole?
  (2) Is the formula absolutely clear?
- Has the tax loss date been determined?
- Who has the expense responsibility for the equipment return and where must it be returned to:
  (1) If the lease ends normally?
  (2) If the lease ends prematurely?
- May either party designate an alternate return location? If so, what is the expense responsibility?
- The lessor should be able to terminate the lease early or take other protective action in certain situations
  (1) When the rent is not paid
  (2) When the lessee makes an unauthorized transfer of the equipment or any of its rights under the lease
  (3) When there is a general failure to perform the obligations under the lease

- (4) When the lessor discovers the lessee has made a material misrepresentation
- (5) When there is a bankruptcy or similar event that would jeopardize the lessor's position
- The actions that the lessor may take in the event of default must be specified
  - (1) Court action
  - (2) Terminate the lease
  - (3) Cause a redelivery of the equipment
  - (4) Cause the lessee to store the equipment
  - (5) Sell the equipment under its own terms
  - (6) Be able to hold or re-lease the equipment
  - (7) Be entitled to a predetermined amount of money as damages for a lease default
- Certain lessor assignment rights may be desirable or required
  - (1) To a lender as security
  - (2) To an investor
- Will the lessee be able to sublease the equipment? If so,
  - (1) Will the lessee remain primarily liable under the lease during the sublease period?
  - (2) Will the lessor have any control over who the sublessee will be?
- Have all the lessor's options been included? For example:
  - (1) Right to terminate the lease
  - (2) Right to force a sale to the lessee
  - (3) Right to abandon the equipment
  - (4) Right to force a lease renewal
- Have all the lessee's options been included? For example:
  - (1) A purchase right
    - (a) Fair market purchase value
    - (b) Fixed purchase price
  - (2) A renewal right
    - (a) Fair market rental value
    - (b) Fixed price rental
  - (3) A termination right
  - (4) A right of first refusal
- Will a defaulting party retain any of its option rights under the lease?
- Has the law of a jurisdiction been specified to control any issues that arise under the lease?
- Is there a severability clause?
- Is there any interest penalty for overdue payments?

- Has each side specified how and where any required notifications and payments will be made?

  (1) The address where notifications and payments must be sent

  (2) The manner in which the notifications and payments must be made

      (a) U.S. mail

      (b) Other

- Has the signature section been set up properly for:

  (1) An individual

  (2) A corporation

  (3) A partnership

  (4) A trust

  (5) Other

- Has the signature been made in the proper capacity?

CHAPTER 4
Supplemental Lease Documents

A. Overview of Supplemental Lease Documents

While the lease is the core document in any equipment lease transaction, depending on their size and complexity, most transactions will involve additional documents. These collateral documents range from those that essentially provide the parties with comfort on specified issues, such as opinions of counsel, to those that define critical supportive arrangements, such as guarantee agreements.

While drafting the supplemental papers will be the transaction's lawyers' responsibility, the other participants should also understand the fundamental concepts involved, so they can review the documents to ensure they accurately reflect the parties' agreements. Also, understanding the purpose of the supplemental documents will enable the participants to more readily negotiate compromises when the lawyers reach impasses.

Many major equipment lease financings are structured as leveraged leases, arrangements in which the lessor borrows a portion of the equipment's purchase cost from a third-party lender. Leveraged lease transactions do not radically differ from standard lease transactions, although additional documents are usually involved, such as a security and loan agreement, to accommodate various business or legal aspects. (The latter part of this chapter explains the basic additional documents that may be called for in a leveraged lease.)

While this chapter provides a general working knowledge of the typical collateral lease documents, remember that most transactions have their own unique aspects that must also be taken into account.

■ When the lessee stores the equipment, there is the issue as to the responsibility for damage to the equipment. A prospective lessee, therefore, should specify that the risk of damage through third party acts during any forced storage period is on the lessor.

e.   Sale of the Equipment

A prospective lessor should insist that, after a lessee defaults, it can sell or otherwise dispose of the leased equipment, free and clear of any of the lessee's rights. However, the lessee should seek the right to have an offset of any proceeds received against any damages it otherwise owes.

▶ **Recommendations:**
■ The more a lessor receives from an equipment disposition, the less default damages a lessee may owe if it has a right to an offset. To insure that the lessor undertakes the maximum disposal effort, a lessee should insist on an accounting of the disposition proceeds.
■ If a prospective lessor agrees to credit any sale or re-leasing proceeds received from third parties against any amounts that a defaulting lessee would owe, it should limit the credit obligation to the "net" proceeds actually received. The expenses that the lessor incurs, for example, to lease the equipment should be deducted from the amount that the lessee would be entitled to receive as a credit. Also, until the money is in fact in the lessor's hands, it should not have to recognize any credit.

f.   Right to Hold or Re-Lease the Equipment

Besides being able to dispose of the equipment, a prospective lessor would want the right to "hold, use, operate, lease to others, or keep idle" any equipment that it has re-acquired as a result of a lease default. Ideally, then, a lessor could take what action it deems to be in its best interest. Of course, if a court finds that the lessor did not act in a manner to minimize the damages suffered, it may limit any recovery that a lessor may be able to get.

g.   Liquidated Damages

A "liquidated damage" provision should always be included as an alternate default remedy. Under this provision, the parties agree on a method for determining what damages the lessor is entitled to if a default occurs. Generally, courts will uphold a liquidated damage arrangement if it fairly anticipates the losses that may result from the lessee's nonperformance, and is not a penalty.

B.   Legal Opinions

1.   The Function of Legal Opinions

Before considering which, if any, legal opinions a participant to a leasing transaction may want, the threshold question is what is the practical value of a legal opinion? While that question cannot be precisely answered, it is important to realize what a legal opinion does not do. It is not a guarantee that the conclusions expressed in the opinion are correct. Regardless of the quality of the lawyer's work in preparing the opinion, a court or administrative agency may interpret the law or facts differently, and, of course, their decision, not the legal opinion, will be controlling. However, receiving a legal opinion does have value:

- It provides the participants with a significant, if not complete, degree of comfort, because the lawyer's opinion usually will be correct.
- Because in drafting the opinion, the lawyer will need access to relevant information, writing the opinion may help bring to light troublespots in the transaction that can be corrected.
- And, if the unlikely result occurs that a court or agency disagrees with the opinion, having the opinion may help show that the parties exercised due care in entering the transaction and may prevent the imposition of any penalties.

Lawyers frequently will qualify their opinions by setting out the facts on which they relied. Thus, to the extent that the participants do not convey the relevant facts to their lawyer, his opinion will have less value.

▶ **Recommendations:**

■ Although legal opinions can make a party feel secure as to the issues addressed, there are times when even more certainty is required. For example, if a prospective lessor is concerned about whether a certain type of lease structure will qualify as a lease for federal income tax purposes, it may be worthwhile applying to the IRS for a ruling on the issue (see Chapter 8).

■ The "expertness" of the lawyer giving an opinion is an important consideration when complex legal issues are involved. Choose a lawyer who has experience in leasing arrangements.

2.   Opinion From Lessee's Lawyer

The lessor should ask the lessee to submit a legal opinion. The opinion's goal is to provide the lessor with assurance that there are no legal issues that will undermine the lease transaction. Thus, a lessor will typically want the lessee's lawyer to opine on the following:

- Whether the lessee has been properly organized, is validly in existence, and is in good standing under the laws of its state of incorporation.
- Whether the lessee has the authority to enter into the lease documents.
- Whether the lessee has the ability to perform all its obligations under the transaction's documents.
- Whether all the lessee's lease commitments are legally binding.
- Whether any consents, such as those of the shareholders or lenders, are necessary and, if so, whether they have been obtained.
- Whether any regulatory approvals, such as a state public utility commission, are necessary. If so, whether all the proper action has been taken.
- Whether there are any adverse pending or threatened court or administrative proceedings against the lessee, and, if so, their probable outcome.
- Whether, by entering into the lease arrangement or complying with any of its terms, the lessee would violate any law, rule, or provision of any of its existing agreements.

3. Opinions From Lessor's Lawyer

a. To the Lessee

The lessee should obtain an opinion from the lessor's lawyer concerning the legal consequences of the lessor's ability to enter into and perform its obligations. That opinion should include that:

- The corporate lessor is properly incorporated at the time the lease is signed.
- The lessor is properly qualified to do business in the state where the equipment will be used. (There may be a risk that the equipment could be attached by the state authorities for the nonpayment of any taxes that the lessor may owe.)

b. To the Lender

A prospective lender should seek a written opinion from the lessor's lawyer on key issues relating to its loan arrangement with the lessor. The opinion will generally cover the same issues as those covered in the opinion given to the lessee. For example,

- Whether the lessor is duly organized, validly existing, and in good standing in its state of incorporation.
- Whether all the necessary authorizations have been secured.
- Whether the lessor's obligations under the loan documents are fully enforceable.

Also, when the loan will be nonrecourse and so the lender can look only to the lease payments and equipment for repayment, the lender will want an opinion that:

- The lessor has good and marketable title to the equipment covered by the lease.
- The equipment is free and clear of any liens or encumbrances other than those of which the lender is aware.
- The lessor has not made any other lease assignments.
- It has a free and unencumbered right to receive all payments, such as rent under the lease agreement.

▶ **Recommendation:**   A prospective lessor should consider requiring an opinion from the prospective lender's lawyer confirming that all the necessary action in connection with the loan's authorization has been taken. Many prospective lessors are so grateful to get the loan they sometimes neglect to determine whether it was properly authorized. But, a loan without proper authorization may be withdrawn.

4.   Opinion From the Guarantor's Lawyer

In many situations, a third party will guarantee the lessee's lease obligations. For example, the parent company of a prospective financially weak corporate lessee may have to provide a guarantee to induce the prospective lessor to enter into the transaction. The strength and viability of the guarantor's commitment will be important to a prospective lessor (and a prospective nonrecourse lender if the transaction is leveraged), and to help confirm the guarantee's worth, a lessor should request a favorable opinion from the prospective guarantor's lawyer on the relevant aspects.

Such an opinion should address issues that relate to the legal aspects bearing on the guarantor's ability to fulfill the guarantee. The subjects to cover include whether:

- The guarantor is duly organized, validly existing, and in good standing.
- There is anything that could adversely affect the guarantee's quality, such as material litigation.
- The guarantee has been fully and properly authorized.
- It is a legally enforceable obligation.

5.   Opinion From the Vendor's Lawyer

Usually the leased equipment's vendor is not asked to provide any legal opinion because he has only to deliver clear title to the equipment. An adequate bill of sale containing proper seller representations and warranties typically gives the necessary comfort. In certain situations, particularly if a substantial dollar amount of equipment is involved, a prospective lessor will ask the vendor for its lawyer's opinion corroborating, for example, the delivery of clear title and the due authorization of the sale.

C.   Financial Reports

The financial weakness of any party to a lease transaction could jeopardize the transaction. Therefore, it is important to obtain reliable information concerning the parties' financial strength. The degree of information necessary depends on the transaction's size—a lease of several office typewriters may not warrant the degree of investigation that would be called for in a lease involving expensive equipment.

1.   Why Financial Information Is Necessary

a.   Of the Lessor

All too often prospective lessees fail to check the prospective lessor's financial condition (apparently operating under the assumption that a lessor will always have the money for a committed purchase, and that once the purchase is made there is nothing to worry about). This is not necessarily true. A financially weak lessor may not have the necessary funds to buy the equipment when it's ready for lease. Also, once the equipment has been bought and is on lease there is always a risk that one of the lessor's creditors could seize the leased equipment as security for unpaid obligations.

Whether adequate funds are available for equipment purchases is of particular concern when the transaction involves a lease line of credit—that is, when a lessor has agreed to buy and lease equipment that will be delivered over a long period. If the lessee needs equipment for immediate use, the lack of financing could be a serious problem for a would-be lessee.

b.   Of the Lessee

Similarly, a prospective lessee's financial condition is a critical element in a prospective lessor's decision whether to enter into a particular lease financing, particularly when a major long-term lease is involved, and the prospective lessor wants to be sure there is little risk the lease will end prematurely.

c.   Of a Controlling Corporation

If a prospective lessee is owned by another corporation, many prospective lessors, regardless of how financially strong the potential lessee is, also review the parent corporation's financial statements. Such a review is useful—even when the parent does not guarantee the lease obligations—because the weaker its financial condition, the greater the likelihood that it will drain a lessee's cash to solve its own problems.

▶ **Recommendation:**   When there is a risk that a controlling corporation could drain a prospective lessee's cash, a lessor must take precautions. One such precaution is to impose a restriction on the amount of dividends that the lessee can declare and distribute to the controlling corporation.

d.   Of the Guarantor

If the lessee's financial condition is inadequate, a lessor can require the transaction to be guaranteed by a financially stronger entity. In that case, the guarantor's financial strength is an important consideration.

2.   Type of Financial Information Needed

Usually, a company's financial condition can be adequately assessed by reviewing its past and present financial statements, including profit and loss statements and balance sheets. Also, to bring the participant's financial picture up to the transaction's closing date, a financial officer of each participant can deliver a certificate at the closing presenting relevant financial information since the last published statement. For example, if the most current financial statements reflect a company's condition as of May 15, 19XX and the transaction does not close until June 2, 19XX, the certificate should provide that as of the closing date, June 2, 19XX, there have been no materially adverse financial changes since the date of the latest financial statements, May 15, 19XX. Of course, it would be more comforting to get the company's independent accountants to issue the certificate, but this is generally not practical.

▶ **Recommendation:** Financial certificates should be sought not only from the prospective lessee. They should be requested from any party whose financial condition may affect the transaction's viability, such as a prospective guarantor.

D. Corporate Authorization Documents

When a corporation participates in a lease transaction, the other parties should require a copy of the corporation's board of directors' resolutions authorizing the transaction. The resolutions should be certified by the corporate secretary or assistant secretary and delivered at the closing. A resolution from a prospective lessee's board of directors should, for example, provide that the prospective lessee has been duly authorized to enter into the transaction for the specified dollar amount and that a certain person has been authorized to execute the documents on behalf of the corporation.

▶ **Recommendations:**
■ Prospective lessors and lenders usually require prospective lessees to deliver appropriate board of directors' resolutions at a lease closing. While lessees frequently do not request authorizing resolutions from the other parties, they should do so, particularly from prospective corporate lessors and lenders not regularly engaged in leasing or lending.
■ If, after the parties have entered the lease, it is discovered that any other party has failed to get necessary board of directors' approval, that party should be requested to deliver appropriate resolutions approving, ratifying, and confirming all actions that have been taken.
■ While board of directors' resolutions should be reasonably broad in scope, corporate directors must be careful not to grant more than is necessary. For example, if a lease transaction is to involve a vessel, its cost should be specified with leeway for reasonable changes. Without designating the cost, an individual representing the corporation may be able to bind it to a lease even if there were unexpected and significant cost increases.

E. Guarantees

When a prospective lessee wants to lease more equipment than its credit capability justifies, a financially strong third party may have to be brought in to guarantee the lessee's obligations. These guarantees can vary anywhere from a full guarantee of all the lease obligations to something significantly less.

In a typical full lessee guarantee, the guarantor would unconditionally obligate himself to insure the lessee's full and prompt performance of all the lease obligations, covenants, and conditions. For example, if the lessee does not pay the rent, the lessor would have the right to go directly to the guarantor for payment. Generally, the guarantor would have the right to go against the lessee for reimbursement of any amounts paid.

Under a partial guarantee, the guarantor may, for example, guarantee the repayment of only 10% of the total lease payments. Partial guarantees frequently come about when the proposed transaction is very attractive to the prospective lessor, and he or she is willing to make compromises.

F.   Proof of Insurance Documents

Frequently, the lease will require the lessee to take out personal injury and property damage insurance as to the leased equipment. In these cases, the prospective lessor must make sure the insurance will be in effect when it accepts the equipment for lease. One of the best ways to do this is to have the agreed-on insurance company deliver a certificate of insurance at the closing stating that the necessary insurance has been bought.

▶ **Recommendations:**

■ A certificate of insurance must be carefully reviewed to verify that the coverage is proper and that it will be in effect when necessary. Any coverage limitations, such as restricted equipment usage, should be carefully considered.

■ A prospective lessor must make sure the required insurance coverage cannot be cancelled without prior written notice to him, followed by an adequate grace period. In this way, if the lessee does not keep the insurance in force, the lessor has the opportunity of taking over the insurance payments to prevent the insurance from lapsing.

G.   Equipment Purchase Agreements

Unless the lessee constructed or already owned the equipment, the lessor must buy it from a vendor to be able to lease it. If the equipment is available from the vendor at the time the lease agreement is entered into and the lessee wants it then, the lessor can buy the equipment at that time.

What should the lessor do if the parties enter the lease agreement before the equipment is ready to be leased? Should the lessor enter into a purchase agreement directly with the supplier for the equipment to be leased? No, because if the lessee, with or without justification, refuses to accept the equipment for lease, the lessor can still be legally obligated to buy the equipment. Thus, if a purchase agreement must be executed early, the prospective lessor should insist that the prospective lessee be the signing party.

When the equipment becomes available to be leased—particularly when new equipment is involved—it is advisable for the lessor to have direct contract rights with the supplier to obtain equipment warranty and other purchase rights. Thus, the lessor should contract directly to receive such rights but should not be obligated to purchase the equipment until it is ready to be leased. The lessor can achieve those two goals by using a purchase agreement assignment together with the purchase agreement.

Under this arrangement, the prospective lessee and the equipment supplier enter into the necessary purchase agreement, and then the prospective lessor and lessee enter into an assignment of this agreement. Under the assignment, the prospective lessor typically acquires the prospective lessee's contract purchase rights, but not its obligations. The rights generally transferred include not only the right to buy the designated equipment, but also the rights to any service, training, or information that the prospective lessee would be entitled to as buyer and any buyer warranties or indemnities.

▶ **Recommendations:**
■ If a prospective lessor enters into a purchase agreement assignment, he must be careful not to assume any of the buyer's duties or obligations under the purchase agreement. The assignment should specify that the prospective lessee will remain liable on the purchase contract as if the assignment had not been made.
■ When a prospective lessor enters into an equipment purchase agreement assignment, it should, at the same time, get the supplier's written consent to the assignment. The consent should acknowledge the assignment and provide that any rights assigned (such as, supplier warranties), will accrue to the lessor's benefit, just as though it had been originally named as the buyer. Also, the supplier should be asked to acknowledge that the prospective lessor will not be liable for any of the purchase contract duties or obligations.

H.   An Equipment Bill of Sale

A prospective lessor generally requires the seller to deliver a bill of sale when it pays for the equipment. Frequently, the bill of sale is a warranty bill in which the seller not only transfers title to the subject equipment, but also warrants that he has full legal and beneficial title to it, free and clear of any encumbrances, mortgages, or security interests. Also, the seller generally represents that he has the lawful right and the appropriate authority to sell the equipment.

▶ **Recommendation:**   A prospective lessor should require the seller to represent in an equipment bill of sale that he will defend the prospective lessor's title to the equipment against any person or entity claiming an interest in the equipment.

I. Waivers From Land Owners or Mortgagees

Frequently, the leased equipment will be located on real property that is leased from a third party or is subject to a mortgage. In this case, statutory lien rights may exist that, for example, would permit a landlord to attach any equipment on his land, including leased equipment, if his rent was not paid. Similarly, the holder of a mortgage on a lessee's building may, under a general mortgage claim right, be able to go after leased equipment located in the building. When this situation exists, the prospective lessor should get a waiver from the landlord or mortgagee of any claim to the leased equipment.

J. Security Interest Filings

Where the leased equipment is expensive, the lessor should file appropriate Uniform Commercial Code (UCC) financing statements to insure priority over other parties who may claim an interest in the equipment, particularly the lessee's creditors. If the UCC statement is not correctly filed, the lessor's claim to the equipment will not be perfected as to third parties (such as, the lessee's general creditors), and may not give the necessary protection. Simple in form, the statement basically requires nothing more than a description of the parties and the equipment. The filing procedures are routine, and the expenses are nominal.

▶ **Observation:**   Although, theoretically, a lessee's creditors could not prevail against a lessor in a claim against the leased equipment under applicable state law even if a UCC financing statement had not been filed, the possibility always exists that a claim can succeed.

K. Participation Agreement

Frequently used in underwritten lease transactions, particularly leveraged transactions, a participation agreement sets out the lease financing's general parameters. Typically, the parties to the agreement are the lessee, the equity participants, the debt participants, and any trusts established for the debt or equity participants. The participation agreement prescribes the terms under which the debt participants must make their loans and the equity participants must make their equity investments. It also usually provides for a method for substituting any defaulting participants, and also may set out any prescribed tax indemnification provisions.

L.   The Owner's Trust Agreement

Often, a trust is established for equity participants in a leveraged lease transaction, typically when more than one equity participant is involved. The trust arrangement provides the equity participants with corporate-like liability protection and partnership-like income tax treatment and thus can be a desirable ownership vehicle for equity participants.

To set up a trust, the equity participants enter into a trust agreement with an entity, such as a bank, that will act as the trustee, referred to as the "owner trustee." The trust agreement spells out in detail how, and to what extent, the trustee will act on behalf of the equity participants.

Typically, the trustee will execute all relevant documents, including the lease, any participation agreement, the indenture, and any purchase agreement assignment, on behalf of each equity participant. The right, title, and interest in the equipment, the lease, any purchase agreement, and any purchase agreement assignment is collectively referred to as the trust estate, and legal title to it is held in the owner trustee's name. The owner trustee is, however, only a figurehead owner, the beneficial interest in the trust estate resting with the equity participants. The equity participant's interests are represented by certificates, referred to as owner certificates, issued by the owner trustee.

M.   A Lender's Trust Agreement

In leveraged lease transactions, the debt participants frequently act through a trust arrangement to receive favorable tax treatment and liability protection. The arrangement is typically set up through a trust indenture and mortgage agreement entered into between the equity side and debt side. A trust indenture and mortgage agreement defines the basic debt financing parameters and provides for issuing loan certificates that set out the debt repayment obligations. The agreement also grants a security interest to the lenders in the equipment and the lease while the loan is outstanding.

The debt participants are represented by a trustee, referred to as the "loan trustee." The loan trustee stands in the same position to the debt participants as does the owner trustee to the equity participants. As the "watchdog" for the debt participants, the trustee can take any prescribed action that may be necessary to protect the loan participants' interests, such as foreclosing on the lease in case of default.

N. Using a Partnership Instead of Trusts

If multiple equity or debt participants find it undesirable or impractical to act through a trust arrangement, they can use a partnership structure instead. Here, the "lessor" or "lender," as the case may be, is the partnership with the equity or debt participants partners in the partnership. Although not always absolutely necessary, it is advisable for a formal partnership agreement to be entered into that defines each partner's rights and obligations.

O. The Underwriter's Fee Arrangement

The lease underwriter's job is to bring together the equity participants, the lessee, and, if the transaction is leveraged, the debt participants. Performed for a fee that varies with each transaction and each broker, the underwriter's services are typically payable by the equity participants. To protect itself and prevent later misunderstandings as to the payment terms, the underwriter should require the equity participants to enter into a formal fee agreement clearly defining the fee arrangement.

P. A Supplemental Lease Document Checklist

Although the type of supplemental documents used in a lease transaction vary with each situation, the following checklist can be used as general guidelines.

■ Concerning the required legal opinions:

- Is the lawyer rendering the legal opinion thoroughly experienced in the area to be covered by the opinion? For example, if an opinion is required on complex tax issues, is he or she fully knowledgeable on all the relevant aspects?

- How much has the legal opinion been conditioned? In other words, has the lawyer left himself so many outs as to his position that he really has provided little comfort?

- To the extent that the legal opinion is based on facts supplied to the lawyer, are the facts accurate and complete?

■ Does the opinion of the lessee's lawyer, to be delivered to the lessor, address the following issues:

- Proper organization, valid existence, and good standing of the lessee.

- The lessee's full authority to enter into the lease.

- The lessee's complete and unrestricted ability to perform all obligations.

- Whether all the lessee's lease commitments are legally binding.

- Whether all necessary consents have been obtained.

- Whether all necessary regulatory approvals have been obtained.

- Whether there are any pending or threatened adverse court or administrative proceedings. If so, what the potential impact may be.

- Whether any law, rule, or collateral agreement will be violated by the lessee entering the lease transaction.

■ Does the opinion of the lessor's lawyer, to be delivered to the lessee, address the following issues:

- Whether the lessor is properly organized, validly existing, and in good standing.

- Whether the lessor is properly authorized to do business in the jurisdiction where the equipment will be located.

- Whether the transaction has been fully authorized by the lessor. For example, have all necessary committee and board of director approvals been secured?

- Whether all the lessor's commitments are binding.

- Whether the lessor's ability to perform its obligations is unrestricted.

- Whether any shareholder, lender, etc., consents are necessary. If so, have they been obtained?

- Whether the transaction will violate any law, rule, or collateral agreement as to the lessor.

■ Does the opinion of the lessor's lawyer, to be delivered to a third-party lender, address the following issues:

- Whether the lessor is properly organized, validly existing, and in good standing.

- Whether all necessary authorizations, both as to the lease financing and the loan financing, have been obtained.

- Whether the loan obligations are fully enforceable against the lessor.

- Whether the lessor has good and marketable title to the leased equipment.

- Whether the equipment has any liens or encumbrances on it.

- Whether the lessor's rights under the lease are unencumbered, including its right to receive the rent payments.

- Does the opinion of the guarantor's lawyer, to be delivered to the lessor, address the following issues:
  - Whether the guarantor is properly organized, validly existing, and in good standing.
  - Whether all necessary authorizations as to the lease financing have been obtained?
  - Whether the lease obligations are fully enforceable against the guarantor.
- Does the opinion of the vendor's lawyer, to be delivered to the lessor, address the following issues:
  - Whether the title to the equipment will be delivered free and clear to the lessor.
  - Whether all necessary internal authorizations have been obtained.
- Has the lessor obtained adequate lessee, lessee controlling corporation, and guarantor financial statements?
  - Profit and loss statements.
  - Balance sheets.
  - Officer's certificate updating to the closing.
- Has the lessee obtained adequate lessor financial statements?
  - Profit and loss statements.
  - Balance sheets.
  - Officer's certificate updating to the closing.
- Have all the critical financial statements been certified by an independent certified public accounting firm?
- Has a certified copy of any relevant corporate board of director resolutions been delivered?
- If the lease obligations will be guaranteed by a third party, will it be a full and unconditional guarantee? If not, is the limited extent of the guarantee understood?
- If personal injury and property damage insurance is required, does the insurance company's certificate of insurance properly represent the required insurance?

- If the lessor must enter into an equipment purchase agreement directly with the vendor, is it prepared to buy the equipment if the lessee backs away? If not, can a purchase agreement assignment be used?
  - Does any equipment purchase agreement assignment specifically provide that only the rights, not the obligations, will be transferred to the lessor?
  - Under an equipment purchase agreement assignment, will the lessor be entitled to all vendor supplied services, training, information, warranties, and indemnities?
  - Has the vendor's consent been obtained as to the purchase agreement assignment? If so, does it
    (1) Acknowledge the assignment?
    (2) Acknowledge that the lessor will not have to buy the equipment if the lessee backs out before the lease is executed?
- Has an equipment bill of sale been included? If so,
  - Is it a warranty bill of sale?
  - Does it contain a representation that the seller has the lawful right and authority to sell the equipment?
- If the equipment will be located on leased or mortgaged property, has the landowner or mortgagee supplied a written waiver of any present or future claim to the leased equipment?
- Have appropriate UCC financing statements (UCC-1's) been prepared for filing?
- If the transaction is underwritten:
  - Has a participation agreement been prepared?
  - Will the lenders and the equity participants each act through:
    (1) A trust arrangement?
    (2) A partnership arrangement?
- Has a fee agreement been prepared to formalize the underwriter's fee arrangement?

CHAPTER 5
Depreciation Advantages in Lease Transactions

Introduction

A lessor's ability to write off, or depreciate, the cost of the leased equipment is crucial to the lease transaction's economic viability. The '86 TRA magnified depreciation's importance by doing away with the investment tax credit and, correspondingly, enhancing depreciation deductions for most equipment. A prospective lessor, therefore, must have a thorough understanding of the depreciation rules to evaluate a leasing transaction. These rules are also important to a prospective lessee, for two reasons:

- Unless the benefits available are fully understood and evaluated, an intelligent lease versus purchase analysis cannot be made.
- If a prospective lessor requires depreciation indemnities, the lessee cannot properly assess the potential risks without a clear appreciation of the technical intricacies.

This chapter proceeds in three parts. First, it describes the Modified Accelerated Cost Recovery System (MACRS), the system that, because it determines the available depreciation deductions for most property placed in service after 1986, will apply to most future leasing deals. The second part describes the Accelerated Cost Recovery System (ACRS), the system that applied to most property placed in service between 1981 and 1987 and that will apply to certain future transactions not covered by MACRS. The third part describes the depreciation methods in effect before 1981. This chapter explains the rules concerning personal property only, and does not cover real property depreciation.

▶ **Caution:** The depreciation rules explained in this chapter may be altered if the alternative minimum tax applies, so Chapter 6 must be read in conjunction with this chapter.

PART I: DEPRECIATION AFTER 1986

A. An Overview

Among the wide-reaching changes introduced by the '86 TRA was the Section 168's Modified Accelerated Cost Recovery System (MACRS)—a revised depreciation system. Replacing the Accelerated Cost Recovery System (ACRS), the MACRS rules generally apply to property placed in service by a taxpayer on or after January 1, 1987, with certain exceptions.

Although MACRS incorporates some of the ACRS concepts, there are substantial and fundamental differences. MACRS, for example, retains the concept of property classes, but reclassifies certain assets into different property classes (also called recovery classes), and adds more classes. There were also changes in depreciation methods and in depreciation conventions.

Under MACRS, three depreciation methods, six recovery periods, and two averaging conventions apply to equipment, depending on a variety of factors.

B. Property Eligible for MACRS

Besides meeting the MACRS requirements, to be depreciable, equipment must pass muster under Section 167(a). Section 167 establishes the basic rule authorizing an equipment owner to a deduction, in computing federal income tax liability, for the exhaustion, wear, and tear of property used in a trade or business or held for the production of income. All depreciation deductions under MACRS and previous systems must fulfill those threshold requirements: the property must be depreciable (for example, land is considered not to wear out and so is not depreciable) and must be used in a business or income producing activity.

Generally, property qualifying under Section 167(a) may be depreciated under MACRS. The following types of property however, are excluded:

- Intangible property (for example, copyrights, licenses etc.). This property also does not qualify for ACRS and is amoritized under other rules.
- Property that is classified as public utility property (unless the taxpayer uses a normalization method of accounting).

- Certain property that a lessor has elected to apply a depreciation method not expressed in terms of years (such as the unit of production method).
- Motion picture films, video tapes, sound recordings (such as music tapes).
- Property covered by MACRS antichurning or transition rules.

Where property is transferred in a nonrecognition transaction under Sections 332, 351, 361, 371(a), 374(a), 721, or 731, MACRS may be used for only a portion of the equipment's basis.

Also, certain property must be depreciated under an alternative MACRS method.

C.   MACRS Deduction Computations

Four steps determine the annual MACRS depreciation deduction amount for any leased equipment. First, determine the total amount to be depreciated; next, determine the applicable MACRS recovery class from among the six classes; third, apply the appropriate depreciation method; and fourth incorporate the applicable convention.

1.   Total Amount to Be Depreciated

The total amount a lessor can write off for acquired equipment, and thus the annual deduction amount, depends on the lessor's basis in the equipment. For MACRS purposes, basis is determined under general Internal Revenue Code rules for determining the gain or loss on the sale or other disposition of an asset, and includes not only what the lessor paid for the equipment, but also the costs incurred in acquiring the equipment.

However, a lessor must reduce the basis so calculated by any amount expensed under Section 179 and, if the investment tax credit (ITC) is available, because of a grandfathering provision, to account for that ITC. There is, however, no reduction for salvage value.

2.   MACRS Recovery Classes

MACRS continues, with modifications, the recovery class concept instituted by ACRS. The recovery class concept represents the current solution to the longstanding tax question—over how long a period should depreciation deductions be spread. Before 1971, the lessor took depreciation deductions over an estimate of the equipment's useful life—determined based on the facts and circumstances. While having the virtue of potential accuracy, the facts and circumstances method was cumbersome and difficult for both taxpayers and the IRS to administer.

In 1971, the IRS simplified matters by promulgating the Class Life Asset Depreciation Range System (ADR). ADR set out a list of prescribed asset classes. Generally, an asset's useful life was determined by referring to the list. (For an explanation of pre-ACRS property, see Part III of this chapter.)

In 1981, the Economic Recovery Tax Act (ERTA) introduced ACRS. ACRS grouped assets based on their ADR class lives into recovery classes. For example, property with an ADR class life of more than 4 years, but less than 10, was put into the 5-year class. Under ACRS, all personal property fell into one of four personal property recovery classes. ERTA also replaced the various optional depreciation methods with statutory write-off periods.

MACRS continues the recovery class concept, grouping equipment into one of six recovery classes. Like ACRS, the MACRS recovery class grouping is based on the equipment's class life, assigned by the ADR tables. The ADR class lives for MACRS purposes from Revenue Procedure 87-57 [IRB 1987-42.] are reproduced in the Appendix.

MACRS also assigns certain equipment to particular recovery classes notwithstanding their ADR classification. Property neither assigned to an ADR class life, nor specifically assigned by MACRS, falls within the 7-year class. The Treasury has the authority to shift the property assigned by MACRS from one class to another, but such change generally can't affect property placed in service before January 1, 1992.

The following are the six recovery classes applicable to equipment:

- **3-Year Property.** The 3-year MACRS class generally includes property with an ADR class life of four years or less (for example, special tools and devices for the manufacture of rubber products and special handling devices for the manufacture of food and beverages). Automobiles and light general purpose trucks that have ADR lives of less than four years have been expressly assigned to the 5-year class.
- **5-Year Property.** The 5-year property class generally includes equipment with an ADR class life of greater than 4 years and less than 10 years. Heavy general purpose trucks, computer equipment, trailers and trailer-mounted containers, duplicating equipment and typewriters are examples of types of equipment that come within the 5-year classification. Certain equipment is assigned to the 5-year class notwithstanding its ADR classification: automobiles; light general purpose trucks; computer-based tele-

phone central office switching equipment; semi-conductor manufacturing equipment; qualified technological equipment; equipment used in connection with research and experimentation;
certain specified biomass properties that qualify as small power
production facilities under the Federal Power Act; and ocean
thermal, geothermal, wind, and solar energy properties.

- **7-Year Property.** The 7-year MACRS class generally includes
  property with an ADR class life of 10 years or greater but less than
  16 years, for example, office furniture, fixtures, and equipment,
  and equipment used in the manufacture of tobacco and food
  products (other than those listed in the 10-year class). Railroad
  track and single purpose agricultural and horticultural structures
  are specifically assigned by MACRS to the 7-year class.

- **10-Year Property.** The 10-year MACRS property class generally
  includes property with an ADR class life equal to 16 years or
  greater but less than 20 years. This class includes equipment used
  in the manufacture of grain and grain mill products, sugar and
  sugar mill products, and vegetable oils and vegetable oil products,
  and equipment used in petroleum refining.

- **15-Year Property.** The 15-year MACRS property class includes
  property with an ADR class life of 20 years or greater but less than
  25 years. This class includes municipal sewage treatment plants,
  telephone distribution plants, and comparable equipment that is
  used for two-way exchange of voice and data communications.
  Cable television equipment that is used primarily for one-way
  communication isn't "comparable equipment" for the purposes
  of this asset classification.

- **20-Year Property.** The 20-year MACRS property class includes
  property with an ADR class life of 25 years and greater. Specifically included in this class by statute are municipal sewers.

3.   Depreciation Methods

Under MACRS, the lessor recovers the equipment's cost over the
number of years in the recovery class plus one, for example, three-year
property yields deductions over a four-year period. For equipment in
the 3-, 5-, 7-, or 10-year class, the lessor uses the 200% declining
balance method of depreciation, with a switch to straight-line depreciation at the time that maximizes the deduction. For property in the 15-
and 20-year classes, the lessor uses the 150% declining balance
method with a switch to the straight-line method at a time that maximizes the deduction.

Under the declining balance method, the equipment owner calculates the depreciation deduction for any year by multiplying the asset's

basis—reduced by any prior years' depreciation deductions—by the declining balance rate, and then multiplying by the percent available each year. Thus, for example, an asset with a $100 basis and a five-year recovery period, the first year's depreciation is $40 (ignoring the averaging conventions):

$100 basis $\times 2 \times 20\% = \$40$

For the second year, the MACRS deduction would be $24:

$100 basis $-$ $40 first-year deduction $= \$60$

$60 $\times 2 \times 20\% = \$24$

And so on, for three more years.

At the point when the declining balance method yields smaller deductions than straight-line, the method switches to straight-line. (Depreciation methods are explained in more detail below at Part III, §C.) The 200% balance method resulted in more accelerated deductions than had been available under ACRS. The IRS has calculated and published, in Revenue Procedure 87-57 [IRB 1987-42], the appropriate annual deductions applying the 200% and 150% methods for each MACRS recovery class (set out in the appendix).

A lessor can elect to use the straight-line depreciation method instead of the prescribed MACRS accelerated method established for MACRS property classes. If the election is made, it's irrevocable and applies to all the MACRS eligible property within the same asset class that is placed in service during the relevant tax year. The assets within the class for which a straight-line method is elected are to be written-off over the recovery period prescribed under the applicable regular recovery period.

4.   MACRS Averaging Conventions

In determining how to handle depreciation deductions under any system, there is an issue of how to handle placements in, and retirements from, service that occur during the year.

Generally, under MACRS a lessor recovers equipment costs using the half-year convention. Under that convention, equipment is deemed to have been placed in service at the mid-point of the year in which it was placed in service, regardless of when during the year it was placed in service. Similarly, an asset is deemed to have been disposed of or retired from service at the mid-point of the year during which it was disposed of or retired, regardless of when in fact it was disposed of during the year. Thus, a lessor is entitled to one-half a full year's permitted depreciation in the year he places an eligible asset in service, and one-half a full year's depreciation in the year he disposes of or retires the asset from service. When there is a short tax year (a year less than 12 months), an asset is deemed to have been placed in service for a period of time equal to one-half the number of months in the short tax year.

To prevent taxpayers from abusing the half-year convention by bunching purchases at year's end, MACRS includes a mid-quarter convention. That convention kicks in if a taxpayer places in service, in the tax year's last quarter, over 40% of the aggregate bases of property placed in service during the tax year. Under the mid-quarter convention, all property placed in service (or disposed of) during a tax-year quarter is treated as though placed in service (or disposed of) in the middle of such quarter.

5.   Applying MACRS

To summarize: Find the appropriate recovery class and check the averaging convention. Then refer to Revenue Procedure 87-57 to find the MACRS deduction annual percentage. Set out in the Appendix are some tables from that Revenue Procedure. (Note: 3-, 5-, 7-, and 10-year classes are based on 200% declining method; 15- and 20-year classes use 150% method.)

D.   The Alternative MACRS Depreciation Approach

The '86 TRA established an alternative depreciation system (ADS) that the lessor must use in certain select cases and can elect in other situations. Under ADS, a taxpayer generally is to compute its permitted depreciation allowance by applying the straight-line method, without making a basis reduction for salvage value, over a recovery period typically longer than that specified under the other MACRS approaches. The applicable averaging conventions—the half-year or mid-quarter convention—apply in the same situations as under the regular MACRS.

1.   When Must ADS Be Used?

A taxpayer must use ADS to depreciate the following:

- **Equipment used predominantly outside the United States.** This is equipment located for more than 50% of the time during a tax year outside the United States. To determine U.S. use, the rules relating to the ITC have been deemed to apply. Under the '86

TRA rules, there is an additional special exception to the predominant use outside of the United States classification for property that qualifies as a satellite or other spacecraft or interest therein held by a U.S. person and that is launched within the United States.

- **Tax-exempt bond financed property.** This is equipment that has been financed out of the proceeds of tax-exempt bonds that were issued after March 1, 1986. It includes any property to the extent that it's financed directly or indirectly by an obligation if the interest from that obligation is tax exempt.

- **Tax-exempt use property.** This includes equipment that's leased to a tax-exempt entity under certain types of leases that don't fit specified Code requirements (known as "disqualified" leases). A lease is considered to be a disqualified lease if, for example, its lease term exceeds 20 years.

- **Imported property.** This is equipment produced or manufactured in a foreign country and is the subject of an Executive Order issued by the U.S. President. It is considered made outside the United States if it's completed outside the United States or 50% or more of its basis is attributable to value added outside of the United States. The President has the authority to issue an Executive Order for property brought in from a foreign country that either maintains burdensome trade restrictions that aren't consistent with trade agreements or engages in discriminatory or other acts that unjustifiably restrict U.S. commerce.

- For alternative minimum tax depreciation preference computation purposes. [Section 56(g)(4).]

- To figure the earnings and profits of a domestic corporation or a controlled foreign corporation. [Section 312(k)(3).]

- For "listed property," if the property's business use doesn't exceed 50% for the year.

2.   When Can ADS Be Elected?

A lessor can elect to use ADS as to any MACRS property for any MACRS eligible tax year. The election, once made, is irrevocable and applies to all property in the class that the taxpayer has placed in service during the election year.

3.   ADS Recovery Periods

Under ADS, the lessor will generally depreciate the equipment over the ADR class life period. The following are assigned specific recovery periods notwithstanding their ADR class lives:

- **5 years.** Automobiles, light general purpose trucks, semiconductor manufacturing equipment, computer or peripheral equipment, any high technology telephone station equipment installed on the customer's premises, and any high technology medical equipment.
- **9.5 years.** Any computer-based telephone central office switching equipment.
- **10 years.** Any railroad track.
- **12 years.** Personal property with no class life.
- **15 years.** Single-purpose agricultural or horticultural structures.
- **24 years.** Any municipal waste water treatment plant and any telephone plant and comparable equipment used for two-way exchange of voice and data communications.

4.   Applying ADS

Revenue Procedure 87-57 sets out tables to find annual deduction percentage amount for equipment depreciated under ADS with a recovery period of 2.5 to 50 years. Table 8 prescribes the percentages for the half-year convention; Tables 9 through 12 set out the percentages for equipment subject to the mid-quarter convention. These tables are included in the Appendix.

E.   Antiabuse Rules Under MACRS

Because MACRS generally permits more rapid deductions than prior systems, Congress was concerned that certain taxpayers might try to use MACRS on equipment previously placed in service through transfers not resulting in substantive ownership changes. To address this concern, MACRS incorporates antichurning provisions that precluded specified property from qualifying under MACRS rules. As a result, the '86 TRA incorporated into the law special provisions to prevent the improper "churning" so as to obtain enhanced benefits under the MACRS method. If one of the antichurning provisions apply, the taxpayer can't use MACRS. Thus, MACRS can't be used if the equipment was any of the following:

- Owned or used at any time during 1986 by the taxpayer or a related person.

- Acquired from a person who owned the property at any time during 1986 and, as part of the transaction, the property user remained the same.
- Leased by the taxpayer to a person, or any person related to such person, who owned or used the property at any time during 1986.
- Acquired in a transaction where the property user didn't change, and it wasn't MACRS eligible property in the transferor's hands.

CAVEAT: These antichurning rules don't apply if, by using them, a taxpayer would receive a more generous writeoff for the year the property was placed in service than under the MACRS method. These rules also don't apply to property, used for personal use before 1987, that first was used for business purposes after 1986, so that the property is deemed to have been placed in service when it is first used for business.

F. Special Depreciation Rules for Automobiles and Listed Property

Section 280F specially limits MACRS deductions available for automobiles and certain other equipment. MACRS deductions available for automobiles are limited to $2,560 for the first tax year, $4,100 for the second tax year, $2,450 for the third tax year, and $1,475 for each succeeding tax year. Also, a lessor must use ADS, rather than regular MACRS for automobiles and other listed property costs, if the business use of the property fails to exceed 50% of its use. Listed property includes:

- Any property used as a means of transportation.
- Any property of a type generally used for purposes of entertainment, recreation, or amusement.
- Any computer or peripheral equipment (unless used exclusively at a regular business establishment and owned or leased by the person operating that establishment).

If the business use exceeds 50% of annual usage, and then, in a later year, drops below 50%, the lessor must recapture the excess of accelerated depreciation over the straight-line amount claimed in earlier years.

G. Recapture

Generally, on disposition of MACRS equipment, the equipment owner must recapture, as ordinary income, the MACRS deduction—

including any Section 179 deduction—up to the amount realized on the equipment disposition.

H. Expensing

Under Section 179, an equipment owner can elect to deduct currently up to $10,000 of MACRS property used in the active conduct of his business. (The $10,000 limit is the total per taxpayer, not for each equipment item.) However, if a taxpayer places in service over $200,000 of Section 179 property in a year, the amount that can be expensed is reduced dollar-for-dollar by the excess over $200,000. Expensing is available to noncorporate lessors only if they meet the requirements of Section 46(e)(3) (describing when a non-corporate lessor may be eligible for ITC).

I. MACRS Effective Dates

The '86 TRA depreciation rules are generally effective for property placed in service on or after January 1, 1987 for tax years that end on or after that date. A lessor can elect to use the MACRS rules for property placed in service after July 31, 1986, and before January 1, 1987, if the property isn't transition property. That election can be on an asset-by-asset basis and is irrevocable.

1. Transition Rules

The general effective dates don't apply to property subject to transitional rules. Under the general transitional rules, MACRS doesn't apply to property placed in service after December 31, 1986, and pre-MACRS rules apply if the property:

- was constructed or acquired by the taxpayer under a written contract binding on March 1, 1986;
- was an equipped building (including equipment and machinery to be used in or incidental to the building), or a plant facility not housed in a building, on which construction began no later than March 1, 1986 under a specific written plan and greater than 50% of the cost was either incurred or committed no later than March 1, 1986; or
- was self-constructed property (constructed or reconstructed by the taxpayer) where that the construction or reconstruction started by, and at least the lesser of 5% of the property's cost or $1 million was incurred or committed by, March 1, 1986.

Transition property with an ADR class life of at least 7 years but less than 20 years must be placed in service before January 1, 1989. Transition property with a class life of 20 years or greater must be placed in service before January 1, 1991.

Special transition property rules apply to certain specified property. These include property that is an integral part of a qualified urban renewal project, certain projects that qualify under the 1978 Public Utility Regulatory Policies Act, property that is integral to carrying out certain supply or service contracts, and certain solid waste disposal facilities. The lessor writes off property that comes within the special transitional rules under pre-1987 depreciation rules.

2. The Sale-Leaseback Rule

Property that qualifies as transition property in a lessee's hands, or that was originally placed in service by the lessee before January 1, 1987, may come within the pre-1987 depreciation rules if it meets certain sale-leaseback date requirements. The lessee must (1) have placed the property in service by January 1, 1987 or the property must be covered by one of the transition rules described above and (2) the property must be sold and leased back by the lessee not later than the earlier of the applicable transition date or three months after it was placed in service.

PART II: ACRS DEDUCTIONS

A. Overview

Generally, for property placed in service between January 1, 1981 and December 31, 1986, an equipment owner depreciated property using ACRS. Part of ERTA, ACRS both substantially simplified the previous depreciation methods and, by accelerating depreciation deductions, was designed to provide incentives to stimulate capital investment in an economic climate where inflation was eroding the value of existing depreciation allowances.

MACRS has replaced ACRS for most equipment placed in service after 1986. The ACRS rules, however, continue to apply to the numerous leasing deals entered into between 1981 and 1987. Also, ACRS will apply to future leasing transactions where property is covered by a MACRS antichurning or transition rule.

B. Property Eligible for ACRS

Generally, ACRS applied to the same property as does MACRS. The following are specific exclusions:

- Certain public utility property.
- Property covered by antichurning rules.
- Property depreciated using a method not based on a term of years.
- Certain property amortized under the tax rules, such as rehabilitated low-income housing.
- Property that a taxpayer acquired in specified types of transactions where gain or loss wasn't recognized for tax purposes.

C. Computing ACRS Deductions

Calculating an ACRS deduction was similar to the method described above for MACRS deductions. The same steps are involved: calculate the basis and then determine the recovery class. The equipment owner then simply multiplies the applicable recovery property class percentage for the appropriate tax year times the equipment basis. In statutory tables, ACRS prescribed the applicable percentage deduction for each class, incorporating the following:

- The method used was the 150% declining balance method switching to straight-line at the time that maximizes the deduction. (Depreciation methods are explained below in Part III, §C.)
- The averaging convention, like MACRS, was the half-year convention under which the equipment owner received a half-year deduction for all property placed in service during the year. Unlike MACRS, there was no deduction in the year the property was retired from service, and the deductions were spread out over the number of years in the recovery class (without the additional year as under MACRS).

ACRS recovery classes, based on ADR class lives—set out for ACRS purposes in Revenue Procedure 83-35, [1983-1 C.B. 745]— grouped personal property into the four classes—3-year, 5-year, 10-year, and 15-year classes:

- **3-Year Recovery Property.** The three-year recovery property class includes, generally, all Section 1245 property (essentially depreciable personal property) having an ADR class life of not greater than four years. Thus, three-year property includes cars, light trucks (trucks with an unloaded weight of less than 13,000 pounds), over-the-road tractors, and certain specified manufacturing activity tools and handling devices. Also, the statute specifically includes equipment and machinery used in connection with research and experimentation.

The recovery property percentages applicable to three-year property were:

YEAR	PERCENTAGE
1	25%
2	38
3	37

- **5-Year Recovery Property.** The 5-year recovery property class included, in general, Section 1245 property that did not qualify as 3-year property, 10-year property, or 15-year public utility property. As a practical matter, most equipment was 5-year property.

The recovery percentages applicable to five-year recovery property were:

YEAR	PERCENTAGE
1	15%
2	22
3	21
4	21
5	21

- **10-Year Recovery Property.** The 10-year recovery property class included public utility personal property that had an ADR class life of greater than 18 years but not more than 25 years. Railroad tank cars and certain coal utilization property were also part of this ACRS property class.

The recovery percentages applicable to 10-year recovery property were:

YEAR	PERCENTAGE
1	8%
2	14
3	12
4	10
5	10
6	10
7	9
8	9
9	9
10	9

- **15-Year Public Utility Recovery Property.** The 15-year public utility recovery property class included public utility personal property with an ADR class life of greater than 25 years. Public utility personal property used in connection with research and experimentation was deemed to be three-year recovery property even though it might have qualified in another recovery property class.

The recovery percentages applicable to 15-year public utility recovery property were:

YEAR	PERCENTAGE
1	5%
2	10
3	9
4	8
5	7
6	7
7	6
8	6
9	6
10	6
11	6
12	6
13	6
14	6
15	6

D. Straight-Line Election

Like MACRS, under ACRS, an equipment owner could elect to depreciate ACRS property more slowly, by using the straight-line method and a longer depreciation period. For each recovery class, two longer periods, in addition to the normal recovery period, may be used; for 3-year property, the alternative periods are 5 or 12 years; for 5-year property, 12 or 25 years; for 10-year property, 25 or 35 years, and for 15-year public utility property, 35 or 45 years. *Note:* If an equipment owner makes a straight-line election, the same election has to be made for all property in the same recovery class put into service in the election year.

E. Equipment Used Outside the U.S.

The ACRS recovery classes did not apply to equipment used predominantly outside the United States. Generally, a taxpayer had to recover the equipment's cost over the property's ADR class life. Where the equipment did not have a class life, a 12-year period was used.

Under proposed regs, property is deemed used outside the United States, if it is physically located outside the United States during more than 50% of the tax year. If property is placed in service after the start of the tax year, then the 50% test is applied from the time the property is placed in service until the end of the tax year.

F. ITC Adjustment

The 1982 Tax Equity and Fiscal Responsibility Act (TEFRA) amended ACRS to require an equipment owner intending to claim ITC on ACRS property placed in service after 1982 to either (1) reduce the asset's basis by 50% of the ITC claimed or (2) reduce the ITC amount claimed by 2%. For example, a taxpayer allowed to claim a 10% ITC on an item of computer equipment that cost $1 million could have claimed an $80,000 ITC [8% × $1 million = $80,000] and depreciated the computer in an amount equal to $1 million. As an alternative, the taxpayer could have claimed a $100,000 ITC [10% × $1 million = $100,000] and depreciated the computer in an amount equal to $950,000 [$1 million – $50,000 (5% × $1 million) = $950,000)].

▶ **Observation:** Generally speaking, equipment lessors who could use the ITC found it more advantageous to claim the full available ITC and take ACRS reductions, rather than take the reduced ITC.

G. Antichurning Rules

Like MACRS, ACRS incorporated antichurning provisions into the law that precluded specified property from qualifying under the ACRS rules. The antichurning provisions disqualified personal property from ACRS treatment that:

- The taxpayer or a related person, owned or used at any time during 1980.
- Was acquired from a person who owned the property at any time during 1980 and, as a part of the transaction, the property user remained the same.
- Was leased by the taxpayer to a person, or a person related to that person, who owned or used the property at any time during 1980.
- Was acquired in a transaction where the property user did not change, and the property was not considered recovery property in the transferor's hands because it came within the scope of the second or third rule above.

Of particular importance to lessors were the antichurning rules requiring the user to change because those rules precluded equipment lessors from exchanging equipment to fit within the ACRS recovery rules.

The term "related person" for these antichurning rule purposes casts a wide net. The related persons rule of Sections 267(b) [limiting losses between related parties] and 707(b)(1) [disallowing losses among certain partnerships] apply with 10% substituted for 50%. Also, persons engaged in trades or businesses under common control are related persons.

H. The Short Tax Year Rule

If the taxpayer's tax year was less than 12 months long, the taxpayer had to reduce the full year's ACRS deduction by a fraction, the numerator of which was the number of months in the short tax year and the denominator of which was 12; the ACRS deductions for later years were also affected.

PART III: PRE-1981 DEPRECIATION

As explained, ACRS made sweeping changes to the depreciation rules, generally effective for property placed in service after December 31, 1980. The pre-ACRS depreciation rules, however, continue to govern leasing transactions entered into before that date, many of which are ongoing. Also, those rules cover certain other limited transactions, such as those excluded from both ACRS and MACRS by antichurning rules. Thus, the pre-ACRS rules have some continuing importance and are explained below.

Governed by Section 167, calculating depreciation deductions before ACRS was more complex, but followed the same pattern:

- Over how long a period was that amount spread?
- What is the total amount that could be depreciated?
- What depreciation methods could be used?
- How were placements and retirements during the year treated?

This portion of the chapter first addresses these questions for pre-1981 depreciation, generally. Then, the Classified Asset Depreciation Range System (ADR), instituted in 1971, which provided additional depreciation options, is explained.

A. Useful Life

Under pre-ACRS rules, an equipment owner depreciated an asset over its "useful life." And an asset's useful life was determined under the facts and circumstances method.

Under that method, an equipment owner determined an asset's useful life based on its experience with similar property. To do that, it had to take into account any current or anticipated future conditions that could affect its conclusion. For example, the equipment owner had to consider (1) wear and tear and decay or decline from natural causes; (2) normal progress of the state of the art; (3) economic changes, inventions, and current developments inside that taxpayer's industry and trade or business; (4) climatic and other relevant local conditions that could affect the taxpayer's trade or business; and (5) the taxpayer's repair, renewal, and replacement program. If it lacked enough experience with a particular asset to make a judgment, it could base its estimate on the general experience in its industry. Once the useful life determination had been made, it could not be varied unless the anticipated conditions forming the basis for its determination changed. If these conditions did change, the useful life had to be revised.

B. The Total Amount to Be
Depreciated—Salvage Value

Generally, in determining the total amount to be depreciated, an equipment owner started with the asset's basis, calculated under the general Code principles. Next, an equipment owner had to determine the asset's salvage value.

What is an asset's salvage value? It is that amount that a taxpayer estimates, at the time the asset is acquired, that it will bring when the taxpayer retires it from service, whether through sale or other disposition. This value is sometimes referred to as the asset's "gross salvage value." In computing the depreciation allowance, the asset's "net salvage value" could be used instead of its gross value, provided the taxpayer's choice was consistent with its prior practice. The net value is nothing more than the gross value reduced by removal, disposition, or other similar costs.

Depending on the method chosen to depreciate an asset, that is, declining-balance, sum-of-the-years-digits, or straight-line, the salvage value would either be deducted from the amount that is to be depreciated or act as a depreciation cut-off:

- Using the straight-line or sum-of-the-years-digits method, salvage value had to be deducted from the asset's basis.
- Using the declining-balance method, the asset's basis did not have to be reduced by its salvage value before computing the annual deductions; however, the taxpayer no longer could depreciate the asset when it had been written down to its salvage value.

If the ADR was elected, the salvage value did not have to be deducted from an asset's basis before determining the depreciation allowance regardless of the way it was depreciated, that is, whether the declining-balance, sum-of-the-years-digits, or straight-line method was used. The asset could not, however, be depreciated below its salvage value.

In computing the depreciation allowance for personal property having a useful life of at least three years, a taxpayer could, generally, have elected to reduce the property's expected salvage value by an additional amount up to 10% of its basis. This, in effect, increased the amount that could be written off.

C. Depreciation Methods

When depreciating equipment, an equipment owner could use the straight-line, the sum-of-the-years-digits, or the declining-balance method. However, an equipment owner could basically use any consistent method it wanted to use to compute its annual equipment depreciation allowance, provided the sum of the annual allowance and all its prior allowances did not exceed the total amount that would have been permitted during the first two-thirds of the asset's useful life had the declining-balance method been used. The consistent method requirement was met if the treatment was consistent for a particular asset or group of assets. The requirement did not prevent other depreciation methods from being chosen for other assets or groups of assets, or the same asset or group of assets acquired in a later year.

Although there appeared to be reasonable leeway in the choice of depreciation rate methods, lessors typically selected one of three methods, or a combination thereof, specifically prescribed in Section 167(b). They were, as already mentioned, the straight-line method, the sum-of-the-years-digits method, and the declining-balance method.

1.   The Straight-Line Method

To use the straight-line method, the equipment owner simply divides the asset's basis, after subtracting its salvage value by its useful life. This method produces the smallest write-off in the early years of an asset's use. The straight-line method could be elected whether the asset was new or used.

2.   The Declining-Balance Method

Under the declining-balance method, the equipment owner multiplied the asset's basis (reduced by any prior years' depreciation deductions) by the declining-balance rate. This method could be used only if the asset had a useful life of at least three years. This method could produce, for new assets, an initial deduction far greater than either of the other two methods.

For new equipment, the user could use the 200% or double-declining method; for used equipment, the lessor was limited to the 150% method. When the declining-balance method was used, the asset's salvage value did not have to be deducted from its basis before calculating the annual depreciation allowance. The asset could not, however, be depreciated below its salvage value.

3.   The Sum-of-the-Years-Digits Method

Under the sum-of-the-years-digits method, the deduction for any year was determined by multiplying the basis of the asset (reduced by its salvage value) by a prescribed fraction that would vary for each year. The numerator of the fraction was the number of years remaining in its useful life as of the beginning of the computation year, and the denominator was an amount equal to the sum of the number of years of the asset's useful life. This method could be used only for new assets with a useful life of at least three years.

▶ **Illustrative Example**—*Depreciation Methods:* In 1980 Able Company bought a new truck for $10,000. Able estimated the truck's useful life to be 10 years, and its salvage value at the end of the 10-year period to be $1,000. Under the various depreciation methods, how much could Able have written off each year?

Straight-Line: The annual straight-line deduction (($10,000—$1,000) × 10%) would have been $900 for each of the 10 years.

Declining Balance: The 200% declining-balance rate is two times the straight-line rate, here 10%. Thus, the following deductions were available:

$$1\text{st year–}\$2,000 \ (2 \times 10\% \times \$10,000)$$
$$2\text{nd year–}\$1,600 \ (2 \times 10\% \times \$ 8,000)$$
$$3\text{rd year–}\$1,280 \ (2 \times 10\% \times \$ 6,400)$$
$$4\text{th year–}\$1,024 \ (2 \times 10\% \times \$ 5,120)$$
$$5\text{th year–}\$ \ 819 \ (2 \times 10\% \times \$ 4,096)$$
$$6\text{th year–}\$ \ 655 \ (2 \times 10\% \times \$ 3,277)$$
$$7\text{th year–}\$ \ 524 \ (2 \times 10\% \times \$ 2,621)$$
$$8\text{th year–}\$ \ 419 \ (2 \times 10\% \times \$ 2,097)$$
$$9\text{th year–}\$ \ 336 \ (2 \times 10\% \times \$ 1,678)$$
$$10\text{th year–}\$ \ 268 \ (2 \times 10\% \times \$ 1,342)$$

▶ **Sum-of-the-Years:** The denominator of the multiplying fraction is the sum of $10 + 9 + 8 + 7 + 6 + 5 + 4 + 3 + 2 + 1 = 55$. Therefore, for each of the 10 years the depreciation deductions are calculated as follows:

1st year–$1,636 $\left[\frac{10}{55} \times (\$10,000 - \$1,000 = \$9,000) \right]$

2nd year–$1,473 $\left(\frac{9}{55} \times \$9,000 \right)$

3rd year–$1,309 $\left(\frac{8}{55} \times \$9,000 \right)$

4th year–$1,145 $\left(\frac{7}{55} \times \$9,000 \right)$

5th year–$ 982 $\left(\frac{6}{55} \times \$9,000 \right)$

6th year–$ 818 $\left(\frac{5}{55} \times \$9,000 \right)$

7th year–$ 655 $\left(\frac{4}{55} \times \$9,000 \right)$

8th year–$ 491 $\left(\frac{3}{55} \times \$9,000 \right)$

9th year–$ 327 $\left(\frac{2}{55} \times \$9,000 \right)$

$$10\text{th year} - \$ \ 164 \left(\frac{1}{55} \times \$9,000 \right)$$

Comparing the three methods reveals that the 200% declining balance method yielded the largest early year deductions, the sum-of-the-years-digits the next largest, and the straight-line the smallest. For later years, of course, the result was the opposite. Thus, to maximize the available depreciation deductions, lessors initially using the declining-balance method sometimes switched to the straight-line method when it would produce a greater annual allowance. At the time the change was made, the original depreciable amount, reduced by the sum of the previous deductions, was to be straight-lined over the remaining useful life. If, in the preceding example, the switch to the straight-line method were made *after* the fifth year, the annual allowance would be computed on the remaining basis of $3,277($10,000–$6,723). If an election had been made to reduce the salvage value by the permitted 10% of original basis and if the remaining basis were multiplied by the straight-line rate, 20% over the remaining five years, the depreciation deduction for the sixth year would be equal to $655(20%×$3,277). Because for the seventh through tenth year the amount would also be equal to $655, it is easy to see what the increase in benefit would be by switching to the straight-line method.

D.   How to Account for Depreciation

An equipment owner could record equipment subject to depreciation in one of two ways—on an *item by item* basis or on a *group* basis. Under the group approach, the taxpayer would put two or more assets into a single depreciation account, referred to a *multiple asset accounting.*

The grouping into one account may be done in a number of ways. One method was to group those used in a particular business into one account. These accounts were referred to as composite accounts because no weight was given to the type or useful life of the asset. Another way—called group accounts—was to group them on the basis of similarity in kind and useful lives. Under a third way—called classified accounts—assets could be grouped on the basis of similar use. And, finally, if the ADR method was elected, all ADR eligible assets had to be put into vintage accounts. A vintage account was essentially a grouping of assets based on the year the assets were first placed in service.

E.   Mid-year Placements in Service and Retirements

The general rule is that an asset's depreciation begins when placed in service and ends when retired. Generally, if an asset was placed in service during the year, only a percentage of a year's depreciation could be taken for the first year. Similarly, only a portion was available for a year in which the asset was retired from use before the end of the taxpayer's full reporting year. In these situations, the depreciation percentage available was the percentage of the year the asset was held.

For multiple asset accounts, however, the treatment was different. The beginning and ending annual depreciation amounts were determined on the basis of certain averaging conventions that, in effect, created artificial beginning and ending depreciation dates. For example, under a certain convention, all equipment additions and retirements in the first half of a tax year were treated as having taken place on the first day of that year, and all those in the second half were treated as having taken place on the first day of the following year. In this case, for the year the assets were placed in service, a full year's depreciation was permitted on first half assets and none was permitted on the second half assets. Correspondingly, no depreciation could be claimed on assets retired in the first half of the year, and assets retired during the second half of the year were entitled to a full year's depreciation deduction.

How was the depreciation calculation handled for assets that were not placed in service on the first day of a month or retired on the last day of a month? There were a number of methods commonly used. One provided that an asset placed in service after the first day of a month, but on or before the 15th of that month, would be entitled to a full initial month's depreciation. If the asset was placed in service after the 15th day of the initial month, the taxpayer had to exclude the initial month in computing the available depreciation. For example, an asset placed in service on June 14th would have been entitled to a full seven months depreciation for a calendar-year taxpayer. If the asset were placed in service on June 19th, only six months could be claimed. Under this method, asset retirements had to be treated in a consistent manner. Another method often employed was for the initial month to be consistently excluded, and the retirement month consistently included. The specific acquisition or retirement date was ignored. A third alternative was for a taxpayer to claim the exact number of days an asset was held, and, thereby, not lose or gain any depreciation for the acquiring or retiring year. Generally speaking, however, this technique may not have been practical to use when many assets were involved.

F.   The ADR System

In 1971, to reduce potential factual disagreements concerning useful life, salvage value, and treatment of repairs, the IRS instituted the Class Life Asset Depreciation Range System (ADR). ADR grouped assets into classes, including either a range of years (asset depreciation range) or a specified year life (class life) from which an equipment owner would choose a useful life. Called the asset depreciation period, the ADR life provided an alternative to the facts and circumstances approach and, in many instances, resulted in shorter depreciation, and thus quicker writeoffs.

Generally, ADR followed the facts and circumstances method for computing depreciation. However, ADR also entailed other requirements, highlighted below.

1.   Eligible Property

To qualify for ADR treatment, equipment had to be

- depreciable;
- tangible;
- first placed in service by the taxpayer after 1970;
- subject to a taxpayer's ADR election;
- property for which a class and class life were in effect;
- property qualifying under Section 1245 (basically, depreciable personal property or certain other tangible property that is not a building or a buildings structural component); and
- not subject to certain special depreciation or amortization deductions.

2.   Election Required

To use the ADR method for a particular tax year, an equipment owner had to elect ADR when it filed its federal income tax return. Generally, once the election was made, all ADR eligible property first placed in service during the electing year had to be included within the election. Any related ADR elections, such as the choice of the preferred first year convention, also had to be made at that time.

A taxpayer generally couldn't revoke or modify an ADR election after the last day that was prescribed for filing for the election. Also, other modifications, such as changes in the vintage accounts, depreciation periods, or first-year conventions, generally could not be made after this time unless required by the rules. An example of a required change would be when an incorrect asset guideline class had been selected.

3.   Selecting the ADR Depreciation Period

To determine the appropriate ADR asset depreciation period, certain terms—asset guideline class, asset guideline period, and asset depreciation range—which form the conceptual basis of the system, had to be understood.

Asset guideline class meant essentially a specified asset category for which a separate asset guideline period was provided. An asset guideline period was defined as the average class life that had been prescribed for a particular assets' class. Generally, the average class life, or mid-range ADR depreciation life, was referred to simply as the class life of an asset. Typically, a particular class of assets had a range of years above and below their class life. This range was referred to as the asset depreciation range of the assets' class. The range lower limit was set at 80% of the *asset guideline period*, and the upper limit was set at 120% of the asset guideline period. If an *asset depreciation range* existed for a particular asset, a taxpayer could generally choose any number of years, plus a half year, within the established asset depreciation range. The period selected was the period over which the asset was depreciated and was referred to as the *asset depreciation period*. If an asset depreciation range was not in effect for an asset class, the asset depreciation period would be the prescribed asset guideline period. Assets used predominantly outside the United States, for example, did not have an asset depreciation range.

ADR included both *type* categories—such as trucks—and *activity* categories— such as mining. To make the asset guideline selection, an equipment owner would use an asset's type category, unless none existed, in which case he referred to the activity category. The asset's primary use during the election year determined the asset's appropriate activity class. The fact that a taxpayer used the asset in a different activity in a later year would not affect the initial choice.

For the most part, the asset depreciation period was treated as the asset's useful life for all federal income tax purposes, including the ITC computation. It was not used, however, for the purpose of determining salvage value, whether a true tax lease existed, or whether an expenditure added to an asset's useful life.

The ADR asset guideline periods, as well as asset guideline classes and asset depreciation ranges, for classified assets were embodied in Revenue Procedure 77-10 [1977-1 CB 548]. Generally, the periods, classes, and ranges in effect on the last day of an ADR election year were to be referred to for all vintage accounts established during an election year. A taxpayer could not make changes in its selection to incorporate modifications effective following the last day of the election year.

4. The ADR Vintage Account

To elect ADR treatment for a particular year, the equipment owner had to establish a "vintage account" for each eligible asset, or group of assets, covered by a single asset guideline class. An asset vintage account was a closed-end depreciation account that contained ADR eligible assets, or groups of assets, which had first been placed in service during the election year. The tax year during which the asset, or group of assets, was placed in service established the account's vintage. Each account could only contain ADR eligible property that came within a single asset guideline class and could have only one ADR depreciation period. The number of vintage accounts that could be established, however, was unlimited, and different assets within the same asset guideline class could be placed in separate vintage accounts.

A taxpayer had to set aside a certain amount of money as a "depreciation reserve" for each vintage account, and the reserve had to be included on each federal income tax return. Essentially, an account's depreciation reserve was the total accumulated depreciation on the assets in the account, adjusted for certain required increases and decreases.

5. ADR Depreciation Methods

An equipment owner using ADR generally faced the same options— the straight-line, declining-balance, and sum-of-the-years methods— as one using the facts and circumstances approach. Other ADR points included:

- An equipment owner had to select a depreciation method for each vintage account and depreciate all account assets under that method.
- The annual ADR depreciation allowance was computed without regard to salvage value. The assets, however, could not be depreciated below salvage value. *Note:* Salvage value for these purposes is based on the asset's value at the end of its non-ADR useful life.
- When applying a depreciation method to vintage account assets, the account's *unadjusted* basis was used. An asset's unadjusted basis is, generally, its undepreciated, or unamortized cost. The

excess of an unadjusted basis over the allowable depreciation is called the adjusted basis of an asset.

- An equipment owner could, without IRS approval, switch (1) from the declining-balance depreciation method to the sum-of-the-methods or (2) from the declining-balance or the sum-of-the-years method to the straight-line method. Most other changes required IRS approval.

6. First Year Conventions

An equipment owner could select either of the two specified conventions available under ADR—the *modified half-year* convention or the *half-year* convention. While an equipment owner had to apply the same convention to all vintage accounts established during an ADR electing year, it could, however, change its vintage account conventions in any other year.

a. The Modified Half-Year Convention

Under the modified half-year convention, an equipment owner calculated the amount of first-year depreciation for a vintage account by considering all the account's assets placed in service during the first half of the tax year as having been placed in service on the year's first day. All assets placed in service during the year's second half were treated as having been placed in service on the first day of the following tax year. A taxpayer had to follow certain specific rules for assets subject to the modified half-year convention that were extraordinarily retired.

b. The Half-Year Convention

Under the half-year convention, an equipment owner computed the depreciation allowance for the first tax year by treating assets placed in service anytime during the tax year as placed in service on the first day of the second half of the tax year. For example, for a calendar year taxpayer, an asset placed in service in January and an asset placed in service in November of the same year would each be entitled to one-half year's depreciation. Extraordinary retirements under this convention were treated as all having taken place on the first day of the second half of the retirement year.

7. Leased ADR Equipment

A lessor using the ADR approach determined the ADR asset depreciation range, and the asset depreciation period for leased equipment, without regard to the lease term. The asset guideline class that generally had to be used was the class the lessee would use if it had been the equipment owner, unless there was a class in effect for lessors covering the particular equipment.

CHAPTER 6

The Minimum Tax's Role in Leasing

Introduction

The '86 TRA enacted a tax applicable to corporations, an *alternative* minimum tax (AMT), replacing the previous add-on minimum tax. The '86 TRA also expanded the coverage of the AMT applicable to noncorporate taxpayers.

The key to understanding the AMT is to understand that it is an "alternative" tax system. Essentially, it sets up a separate system of taxation that runs parallel with the regular tax system, with its own rules for deductions, credits, and income inclusion.

In the leasing community, the revised AMT has given rise to questions for both the prospective lessee and lessor:

- For equipment users, the key question is whether the AMT has made leasing equipment more attractive than buying it.
- For prospective lessors, the question is how to take account of the AMT in making their rent pricing decisions.

To answer these questions, it is necessary to understand the overall AMT. This chapter describes the AMT in three parts. The first part explains the corporate AMT, in general. The second part summarizes the individual AMT. And the final part shows how the AMT affects leasing transactions.

PART I: THE CORPORATE AMT

A. Overview

Before the '86 TRA, corporations had been subject to an add-on minimum tax—simply a tax corporations had to pay in addition to their regular tax under certain conditions. A corporation became subject to that additional tax—computed at a 15% rate—if it reduced its tax liability through the use of certain tax preference items. For example, the amount by which accelerated depreciation claimed on real property the corporation owned exceeded straight-line depreciation could give rise to add-on tax liability.

The current AMT will alter the tax picture for many more corporations than had the prior add-on tax. Congress's intent in enacting the AMT was to stop profitable corporations from excessively reducing their tax liability through deductions, credits, and exclusions, in effect ensuring that corporations pay their "fair" share of federal income taxes.

This chapter will provide the reader with a general understanding of the AMT rules so that the leasing implications can be addressed.

B. The AMT's General Approach

The conceptual approach under the corporate income tax rules is straightforward. The corporation first computes its income tax liability under the regular method prescribed by the Internal Revenue Code. It then calculates its AMT "tentative" tax under the AMT rules (referred to as the tentative minimum tax or, simply, the TMT). If the TMT exceeds the "regular" income tax liability, the taxpayer must pay the TMT excess in addition to its regular tax liability. If there is no excess, only the regular tax is paid.

Illustrative Example: White Corporation determines that its federal income tax liability computed under the prevailing "regular" rules is $120,000. Under the AMT tax system, White Corporation calculates that its TMT is $150,000. What is White Corporation's federal tax liability?

Because the TMT is greater than the tax liability computed under the regular rules, White Corporation must pay its regular tax liability of $120,000 and, in addition, must pay another $30,000; the excess of the TMT ($150,000) over the regular tax liability ($120,000). If its TMT were $110,000, White Corporation would pay only $120,000, its tax liability computed under the regular tax rules.

To determine its AMT, a corporation first calculates its regular taxable income. To the taxable income, the corporation adds preferences, adds or subtracts adjustments, and subtracts the AMT NOL, resulting in its alternative minimum taxable income (AMTI). From that amount, the corporation subtracts an exemption, if available, up to $40,000.

The corporation then multiplies the result by the AMT tax rate (currently 20%) and subtracts any allowed foreign tax credits (FTCs) and investment tax credits (ITCs). This total is the corporation's TMT. The excess over the regular tax liability is the corporation's AMT.

▶ **Observation:**   At first glance it may seem that the TMT would always be lower than the regular corporate tax liability because the AMT tax rate is 20% and the regular corporate income tax rate is 34%. Frequently, that will not be the case because the AMT's income base, the AMTI, may be significantly greater than the regular corporate tax base.

The following sets out the steps involved in computing the AMT, explained further in the following pages.

AMT Road Map

Regular Taxable Income
+ AMT Tax Preferences
± AMT Adjustments <u>(Other Than Book Income Adjustment)</u>
= Tentative AMTI
+ AMT Book Income Adjustment
<u>− AMT NOL</u>
= AMTI
− AMT Exemption
× 20% AMT Rate
<u>− AMT FTCs and AMT ITCs</u>
= TMT
<u>− Regular tax liability (after allowable tax credits)</u>
= AMT

1.   The AMT Tax Preferences

In determining whether it has any AMT liability, a corporation's first step is to calculate the amount of its AMT tax preferences. The tax preferences that must be added to taxable income include:

a.   Tax Exempt Interest

Tax exempt interest on certain "private activity bonds" issued after August 7, 1986 is an item of AMT tax preference. A "private activity bond" is essentially one issued by a state or local authority in which (1) more than 10% of the proceeds are to be used for private business use and (2) either (a) more than 10% of the bond proceeds are secured with private business activity property or (b) more than 10% of the principal or interest on the bond is to be repaid from private business activity revenue.

There are certain exceptions to the tax-exempt interest inclusion rule. For example, tax-exempt interest on certain bonds issued to benefit specified charitable organizations is not a preference.

b.   Charitable Contributions

For contributions of appreciated capital gain property, there is an AMT preference in the amount that the donated property's fair market value exceeds the property's adjusted basis. The preference applies for tax years after 1986, but does not apply to carryovers arising from charitable contributions made before August 16, 1986.

c.   Percentage Depletion

Under the percentage depletion method of determining deductions for certain natural resource reserves, corporations can take percentage depletion deductions exceeding the property's basis. When a corporation does that, it gives rise to a preference in the amount by which percentage depletion deductions exceed the property's adjusted basis. This was also a tax preference item under the prior tax law.

d.   Intangible Drilling Costs (IDCs)

IDCs were an item of tax preference for individuals under the prior tax law, and they are an AMT tax preference for corporations under the '86 TRA. The portion treated as a preference item is the amount by which the excess of (1) deductions determined by expensing IDCs over (2) deductions that would result from 10-year straight-line amortization of such costs is greater than 65% of the net income from oil, gas, and geothermal properties for such year.

e.   Bad Debt Reserves for Financial Institutions

The amount by which the bad debt reserve deductions exceeds the deductions that would be computed based on the prior year's actual bad debt loss of certain financial institutions is deemed to be an item of AMT tax preference. The bad debt reserve preference was an item of preference under the prior tax law.

f.   Pre-1987 Real Property Depreciation

The amount by which the accelerated depreciation deductions on real property placed in service before 1987 exceeds the straight-line depreciation deductions on such property is an item of AMT tax preference. For personal holding companies, the same rule applies to leased personal property.

g.   Pre-1987 Pollution Control Facilities

The excess of the allowable amortization deductions (generally over 5 years), on certified pollution control facilities that were placed in service before 1987 over otherwise permitted depreciation deductions (usually 15 years) must be included as an item of tax preference.

2.   AMT Adjustments

In determining a corporation's AMT liability, certain specified adjustments must be made to its regular taxable income in computing its AMTI. The concept of adjustments evolved to address items that are really deferral preferences—items where the timing of the deduction or income, as opposed to its amount, is the basis for its being treated as a tax preference. For an equipment item that a taxpayer depreciates on an accelerated basis, for example, the adjustment will be positive (added to regular taxable income in computing AMTI) in early years and negative (subtracted from regular taxable income in computing AMTI) in later years. The aggregate of the adjustments made over the item of equipment's depreciable life will net to zero.

▶ **Further Explanation:** Before the '86 TRA, the AMT (applicable only to individuals) did not fully address a tax preference resulting from a timing difference. For example, for a deferral preference resulting from the excess of accelerated over straight-line depreciation, the later years AMT liability calculations did not take into account the fact that the regular tax deductions would be less than they would have been if the equipment had been depreciated on a straight-line basis over the equipment's depreciable life.

The corporate AMT includes numerous tax adjustments. The following briefly describes the most important ones, and lists adjustments of more limited application.

a.   Depreciation on Personal Property Placed in Service After 1986

A corporation must make an AMT adjustment for personal property placed in service after 1986, in the amount of the difference between the regular accelerated depreciation deduction and the AMT depreciation deduction. The AMT alternative depreciation deduction uses the 150% declining balance method (switching to a straight-line at the time to maximize the allowance) over a specified AMT recovery period. The AMT recovery period for personal property is the period used for the Alternative Depreciation System: With certain exceptions, it is the ADR class life. (See Chapter 5—D,3.) The regular tax depreciation averaging conventions apply to AMT depreciation deductions. (See Chapter 5—C,4.)

The AMT depreciation deductions result in slower writeoffs than the regular MACRS deduction. *Result:* There will be a positive adjustment in the earlier years of an item of equipment's depreciation, and a negative adjustment in the later years.

▶ **Note:**   To determine gain or loss on an asset's disposition for AMT purposes, the asset's basis is adjusted using the AMT depreciation rules. As a result, the AMT basis may often be higher than the regular tax basis, causing any gain for regular tax purposes to be larger than the gain for AMT purposes.

b.   Post-1986 Real Property Depreciation

For real property placed in service after 1986, the Alternative Depreciation System deduction, generally computed by using the straight-line method of depreciation over a 40-year period, must be used instead of the more regular accelerated depreciation deduction.

c.   Post-1986 Pollution Control Facility Depreciation

For certified pollution control facilities that are placed in service after 1986, a corporation must substitute, in calculating its AMTI, the straight-line method of depreciation over the facilities' Alternative

Depreciation System life for the 60-month amortization period permitted under the regular tax rules.

d. Mining Exploration and Development Costs

Mining exploration and development costs, that otherwise may be currently deducted, must be amortized over a 10-year period. Only costs that have been incurred or paid after 1986 come within this rule.

e. Long-Term Contracts

Long-term contracts that have been entered into by a corporation on or after March 1, 1986 can give rise to an AMT adjustment. A corporation must use the specified "percentage of completion" method of accounting for these contracts in computing its AMTI, if a completed contract method of accounting had been used.

f. Dealer Installment Sales

Generally, a corporation that sells property in the regular course of business must report for AMT purposes all gains on property sales in the year in that the property is actually sold. In other words, a dealer is not permitted to recognize profits on the sale of dealer property for AMT purposes on the installment method. Property that is disposed of on or after March 1, 1986 is subject to this rule.

g. Other Adjustments

Other adjustments pertaining in more limited circumstances are:

- Merchant marine capital construction fund deposits and earnings;
- Blue Cross/Blue Shield special deductions;
- Passive activity losses (applicable to closely held corporations and personal service corporations only);
- Farm losses (applicable to personal service corporations only);
- Circulation expenses (applicable to personal holding companies only).

3.   The Book Income Adjustment

Probably the most significant—or at least time-consuming—AMT adjustment for corporations in general, and for those considering leasing transactions in particular, is the book income adjustment. Basically, this adjustment requires an addition to tentative AMTI of 50% of the difference between a corporation's book profits or loss and its tentative AMTI. This adjustment applies to tax years beginning in 1987, 1988, and 1989.

The book income adjustment works as follows: All other preferences and adjustments are computed and added or subtracted from taxable income to arrive at tentative AMTI. The tentative AMTI is compared to the corporation's "adjusted net book income," and if that book income is greater, then 50% of the excess is added to the tentative AMTI. (There is no adjustment if the book income is less than the tentative AMTI.)

The "adjusted net book income" is the corporation's income or loss reported on its "applicable financial statement", subject to adjustments. The first step, then, in determining the adjusted book net income, is identifying the corporation's applicable financial statement from which the book income is taken. As different corporations will have different types of statements, the IRS has issued temporary regulations [Temporary Reg. §1.56-1T(c)] that provide priority rules. Statements filed with the Securities and Exchange Commission are given the highest priority. The regulations must be consulted for additional guidelines on the relative priorities of other statements.

Once the corporation has selected its applicable financial statement it must make the required adjustments [see Temporary Reg. §1.56-1T(d)]. The adjustments can be complex, and the regulations must be consulted in many instances. In summary, adjustments are required:

- For certain taxes;
- To prevent omission or duplication;
- For footnote disclosure or other supplementary information; and
- To take account of related corporations.

There are also special rules where the corporation's tax and financial years differ [see Temporary Reg. §1.56-1T(b)(4)].

The book income adjustment applies to all regular corporations. S corporations, regulated investment companies (RICs), real estate investment trusts (REITs), or real estate mortgage investment companies (REMICs) are excluded.

The book income adjustment presents corporations with numerous planning possibilities and raises other issues not directly affecting leasing. [A detailed explanation of those is outside this book's scope.]

For tax years starting in 1990, the book income adjustment is scheduled to be replaced by an adjustment based on the corporation's earnings and profits (E&P). The adjustment will be an amount equal to 75% of the difference between the corporation's "adjusted current earnings" and its tentative AMTI. If the adjusted current earnings exceeds the tentative AMTI amount, the corporation must add 75% of the excess to its tentative AMTI. If the tentative AMTI exceeds the adjusted current earnings, 75% of that excess is subtracted, with certain exceptions.

Determining adjusted E&P will involve complexities for many corporations. Generally, E&P is a concept used to determine the tax status of corporate distributions to shareholders. While its starting point is taxable income, there are numerous modifications to E&P. (See for example, IRC, Section 312.) After making those modifications, the result is then adjusted further under IRC, Section 56(g)(4). Regulations will presumably be issued in the future to give more guidelines on how to calculate the adjustments.

▶ **Observation:** The AMT book income adjustment cannot reduce tentative AMTI; if the adjusted net book income is lower than the tentative AMTI, there is simply no change. By contrast, the E&P adjustment can either add to tentative AMTI or reduce it.

4.   AMT Net Operating Losses (NOLs)

After taking into account its preferences and adjustments, the next step in computing the AMT is to subtract any AMT NOL. A corporation computes its AMT NOL in the same way it computes its regular tax NOL, with one exception. To compute its AMT NOL, the corporation must add back its loss year tax preferences and adjustments to its regular tax NOL.

When carried over, the AMT NOL may offset only 90% of AMTI (before taking into account the loss deduction). AMT NOLs can be carried back 3 years and carried forward 15 years. The amount of AMT NOL that cannot be used because of the 90% limitation may also be carried over.

▶ **Observation:** The AMT NOL rules will keep corporation's tax departments busy because a corporation must keep track of its AMT NOLs separately from its regular tax NOLs.

A special transition rule permits corporations to carry forward for AMT purposes all pre-1987 law regular tax NOLs as AMT NOLs. While those NOLs must be applied to the corporation's first tax year to which the AMT applies, they then can be carried forward until they are used up. If, however, the corporation had a pre-1987 deferral of add-on minimum tax liability, a reduction is required to be made to the loss amount that is carried forward to the first tax year beginning after 1986 for any preferences that gave rise to the deferred AMT liability.

5.   Corporate AMT Exemption

After a corporation subtracts its AMT/NOL, the next step is to subtract the exemption amount, if any. A corporation is permitted a $40,000 exemption, if its AMTI is less than $150,000. The exemption is phased out beginning at AMTI over $150,000, and, if the corporation's AMTI exceeds $310,000, no exemption is permitted.

6.   Applying AMT Rate

After subtracting any exemption from the AMTI, the corporation multiplies the result by the AMT tax rate (currently 20%).

7.   Foreign Tax Credits (FTCs) and Investment Tax Credits (ITCs)

A corporation then substracts any AMT FTCs. Basically the AMT FTC is computed by making AMT substitutions to the regular tax FTC calculation. The reader should consult the new FTC rules in making the determination.

ITCs may also be used to reduce the AMT liability. The use of ITCs after 1986 is generally limited (see Chapter 7, Part III, D), and those limitations apply to AMT. Additional limitations include

- If the corporation has AMT NOL and FTC carryovers, these are used before ITCs.
- The ITCs cannot offset more than 25% of the TMT liability.
- The combined total of the NOLs, FTCs, and ITCs cannot reduce the TMT below 10% of its amount before those reductions.

8.   TMT

After the credits are subtracted, the result is the corporation's TMT. The corporation must pay the amount that the TMT exceeds its regular tax liability.

9.   AMT Credit

A corporation having to pay the AMT may be able to obtain a credit, called the AMT credit, for use in future years. Designed to prevent double taxation, the AMT credit is the amount of the TMT that exceeds the regular tax liability and is attributable to deferral-type adjustments. Those include all adjustments except tax-exempt private activity bond interest, percentage depletion, and appreciated property contributed to charity.

The AMT credit can only be used to reduce a corporation's regular, not AMT, tax liability. It can be carried forward indefinitely, but cannot be carried back to earlier tax years.

PART II: THE INDIVIDUAL AMT

A.   Overview

The '86 TRA expanded the prior version of the individual AMT. Because its format is the same as the corporate AMT, this section will only summarize its provisions.

B.   Computing the Individual AMT

The individual AMT is calculated as follows: The taxpayer starts with taxable income. To that, preferences are added, adjustments added or subtracted, and the AMT NOL is subtracted, resulting in AMTI. The AMT exemption, if available, is then subtracted, and the result is multiplied by the AMT tax rate. AMT foreign tax credits are subtracted. The result is compared with the taxpayer's regular tax liability, and the taxpayer must add any AMT excess to its tax liability.

1.   AMT Preferences

Many of the individual AMT preferences are the same as those for corporate AMT. Those include:

- Charitable contributions of appreciated capital gain property.
- Intangible drilling costs.
- Interest on private-activity bonds.
- Percentage depletion.

There are two additional preferences:

- Certain gains on incentive stock options.
- Pre-1987 accelerated depreciation and amortization. Basically, this preference covers leased personal property and real property placed in service before 1987. The amount of the preference is the excess of the accelerated depreciation deduction over the

deduction that would have been allowable if the deduction had been calculated using the straight-line method over an extended recovery period.

2.   AMT Adjustments

Many of the individual AMT adjustments are the same as those for the corporate AMT. They are:

- Excess depreciation on personal property placed in service after 1986.
- Excess depreciation on real property placed in service after 1986.
- Long-term contracts.
- Installment sales.
- Mining exploration and development costs.
- Passive activity losses.
- Farm losses.
- Circulation expenses.

Additionally, there are individual AMT adjustments not applicable to corporations:

- Research and experimentation expenses. For AMT purposes these expenses are amortized over 10 years.
- Certain itemized deductions. An individual must add back the standard deduction, consumer interest, and certain state, local, and foreign taxes. The deductions for medical expenses, investment interest, and qualified residence interest are subject to certain adjustments.

▶ **Note:**   There is no book income adjustment for non-corporate taxpayers, even if they are doing business as partnerships or in other forms.

After the taking into account the preferences and adjustments, the AMT NOL is subtracted. The result is the taxpayer's AMTI.

3.   AMT Exemption

The next step is to apply the AMT exemption. The exempt amounts are

- For married couples filing joint returns, the exemption is $40,000. It begins to be phased out when AMTI exceeds $150,000 and is completely phased out at $310,000.
- For singles or heads of households, the exemption is $30,000, phased out at AMTI between $112,500 and $232,500.

- For married taxpayers filing separately, the exemption is $20,000, phased out at AMTI between $75,000 and $155,000.

After subtracting the applicable exemption, the result is multiplied by 21%, the AMT rate for tax years after 1986.

4.   AMT Foreign Tax Credit

The taxpayer then can subtract its AMT foreign tax credit. This is the only credit available for individual taxpayers. The result is the TMT liability. This is compared with the taxpayer's regular tax liability, and the taxpayer must pay the amount by which the TMT exceeds the regular tax liability, in addition to its regular tax liability.

5.   AMT Credit

Taxpayers who have AMT liability may be able to use the AMT credit in later years. Basically, the AMT credit is the amount by which AMT exceeds regular tax for that year attributable to timing differences—all adjustments and preferences except percentage depletion, charitable contributions of appreciated property, itemized deductions disallowed for AMT purposes, and certain private activity tax-exempt bond interest. The AMT credit can offset regular tax liability in later years, but cannot reduce the AMT liability in later years.

PART III: THE AMT CONSIDERATIONS FOR LEASING

A.   The Public Reaction to the AMT

It is apparent that the AMT rules are complex. Corporate and non-corporate taxpayers must consider their entire tax and financial situation to assess their AMT liability and its implications. As with any extensive tax law change, it takes time before all the ramifications are understood. There are always concerns, some unfounded, in the early stages. Companies and their advisers struggle frantically to get a handle on what the new law changes mean, how they actually work, and how to deal with any vagueness or ambiguity. Of great interest is whether there are any legitimate tax incentives that could be of use. The arrival of the corporate AMT and the expanded non-corporate AMT and their perceived effects on leasing transactions are no exception.

B. Overview

It is apparent from the above that the revised corporate and individual AMT will have an effect on equipment leasing for both lessors and lessees. From the prospective lessee's standpoint, the issue is whether the AMT makes leasing equipment more desirable than buying it. To the potential lessor, the question is how the AMT will alter the tax benefits that the lessor may receive by owning the leased equipment, and thus what lease rate it can profitably charge a lessee.

A taxpayer's first step in answering both those questions is to review the AMT steps described above, as applied to its overall tax position. If the taxpayer determines that he may be subject to the AMT, he must analyze the leasing deal taking that possibility into account.

The following explanation shows how the AMT impacts leasing transactions. The explanation will center around two key adjustments: The personal property depreciation adjustment and the book income adjustment (and its replacement, the E&P adjustment). As the book income adjustment applies only to corporations, noncorporate taxpayers can ignore that part of the explanation.

C. The Deferral Effect

Before explaining the AMT in the context of leasing transactions, it is important to remember that, with adjustments, the AMT defers, rather than eliminates, the deductions. The deferral effect is achieved by means of the AMT credit. As described above, a credit in the amount of the AMT paid—to the extent it is based on deferral adjustments—may be used to offset regular tax liability in later years. The two adjustments that impact leasing transactions—the depreciation of personal property and the book value adjustment—are deferral adjustments. Thus, the amount lost through the AMT, as described below, may be recouped through the use of the AMT credit.

While it may be recouped, there are two caveats. First, the AMT credit can be used only to offset regular tax liability. Thus, a taxpayer subject to the AMT in many or most years may not receive the AMT credit benefit for many years, or not at all. Secondly, depending on how long it is before the taxpayer can use the credit, the taxpayer is losing the time value of money. The funds that the taxpayer does not have as a result of the deferral could be earning other money; if nothing else, interest could have been earned if the unavailable funds were invested in attractive investment instruments.

▶ **IMPORTANT:** Thus, in summary, in the following explanation, it is important to remember that when the AMT reduces a deduction by reason of either adjustment described above, it is usually merely deferring it. Thus, the taxpayer's loss is, for the most part, the loss of the time value of money.

D.   The AMT and the Lessee

1.   AMT's Impact on a Lessee

When a lessee leases equipment and pays rentals, those payments are not preferences or adjustments under the AMT. Thus—assuming the lease is a true lease and the lessee is not the equipment owner—the lessee may deduct its lease payments without increasing its AMTI.

However, for corporations there may be some AMT consequences. Under the accounting principles applicable to lease payments, a lessee may account for its lease payments in specific ways on its financial statements. As explained in Chapter 11—B, how the lessee accounts for its lease generally depends on whether it is classified as a capital or operating lease.

Rents under both capital and operating leases are treated somewhat differently from the manner in which the payments are deducted for tax purposes. Thus, there may be some small book income adjustment. That amount, however, is not likely to be significant.

After 1989, there will probably be no adjusted E&P adjustment as a result of a lessee's rents because—under current law—rent deductions are not adjusted for E&P purposes.

2.   Purchasing Equipment

If the lessee instead bought the equipment, there would be greater AMT consequences. For AMT computation purposes, a taxpayer must depreciate equipment he owns and places in service after 1986 by using the prescribed 150% declining-balance method over a longer recovery period. As compared with the regular MACRS depreciation, generally, the AMT writeoff period is longer, and the rate of depreciation is slower. *Reason:* The regular MACRS depreciation method is the 200% declining-balance method. Thus, if for AMT calculation purposes (1) the depreciation rate is less than for regular tax purposes (150% rather than 200% declining-balance method) and (2) the required writeoff period is longer than for regular tax purposes, the ownership of the equipment under consideration will result in a relative increase in a corporation's potential AMT as a result of the AMT depreciation preference adjustment.

Illustrative Example: In 1988, John Jones buys and places in service a $10,000 printing press for use in his company. For regular

MACRS purposes, the press is seven-year property. He is, however, subject to the AMT in 1988. The press has an 11-year ADR class life. Assuming the mid-quarter convention did not apply, the depreciation deductions under the regular MACRS and AMT are as follows:

Year	Regular MACRS	AMT
1	$1,429	$ 662
2	2,449	1,271
3	1,749	1,097
4	1,249	948
5	893	818
6	892	798
7	893	797
8	446	798
9		797
10		798
11		797
12		399

Also, if a corporation buys equipment, it may be subject to the book income adjustment, assuming that the corporation's overall reporting method makes it subject to the book income adjustment. Because the book income adjustment is calculated after the depreciation adjustment is taken into account, there will be an adjustment if the corporation's depreciation method for reporting purposes is slower than the AMT method. Because typically corporations will use the straight-line method over a useful life that is longer than the applicable AMT recovery period, there will be a book income adjustment if the corporation buys equipment.

After 1989, when the adjusted E&P adjustment goes into effect, there may also be an adjustment for purchased equipment, again assuming that the corporation is subject to the E&P adjustment. For property placed in service after 1989, the depreciation deduction to be used is the smaller of the deduction allowed under the alternative depreciation system (ADS) or the method used for book purposes. As explained in Chapter 5—D, the ADS system requires that the straight-line method be used over the property's applicable ADS recovery period. As this is slower than the AMT method, there will usually be a further AMT adjustment. (Different rules apply for property placed in service before 1989; see IRC Section, 56(g)(4)(A).)

E.   The Lessor and the AMT

The lessor's decision in considering the AMT is how it will impact the lessor's lease economic return. As the lease rate will be determined in large part by the transaction's tax benefits, the lessor must decide whether the tax benefits will be sufficient, if the AMT applies, so that it can make an attractive offer to a prospective lessee.

Both corporate and noncorporate lessors will be affected by the adjustment on depreciation of personal property. As described above, this means the lessor must use the slower AMT depreciation method. It will thus have lower writeoffs in earlier years and larger writeoffs in later years, for AMT computation purposes.

For corporate taxpayers, the book income adjustment complicates matters. As explained in Chapter 11—D and E, a lessor's accounting requirements are complex. The way a lease is accounted for depends on whether it is classified as a sales-type, direct financing, leveraged, or operating lease. Assuming the corporation is otherwise subject to the book income adjustment, the lease classification could further affect the book value adjustment if the resulting reporting method is slower that the AMT depreciation rate.

When the adjusted E&P adjustment goes into effect, that adjustment will also probably affect lessors. As described above, for property placed in service after 1989, the depreciation for adjusted earnings is the slower of the ADS method or the book income method. Presumably, the book income method will be similar to the financial reporting methods for leases described above. Because both the ADS method and the book value method will be slower than the AMT depreciation, there will be an adjustment in the amount of 75% of the difference, if the corporation becomes subject to the E&P adjustment.

CHAPTER 7
Investment Tax Credit

Introduction

Before 1986, the investment tax credit (ITC) offered a taxpayer a big reward for buying new equipment—a 10% credit. Like other credits, the ITC did not merely reduce taxable income, but rather offset, dollar-for-dollar, the equipment owner's federal income tax liability. The '86 TRA dramatically changed the ITC picture. Except for certain transition property—generally property in the works before 1986—the ITC's gone.

Gone perhaps, but not forgotten. Where the ITC was claimed on leased property before 1986, its rules may still come into play—for example, the equipment may be disposed of or damaged, or the IRS may contest the ITC claimed. Additionally, there is little doubt in the author's and most tax practitioners' minds that the ITC will again reappear.

▶ **Observation:** Before the actual general ITC repeal, equipment lessors were extremely concerned over the adverse impact a general repeal would have on their business. As it turned out, the innovative equipment lessors made the appropriate adjustments and have gone forward with few, if any, problems. In fact, many lessors have come out ahead because their transactions do not have to be as tax sensitive as they did before the ITC repeal.

The ITC's purpose was to encourage investment in new equipment to stimulate economic growth. The taxwriters also used it to encourage the growth, development, and stabilization of a business area that the federal government sought to promote.

The ITC rules implemented that purpose by permitting an equipment owner to claim a tax credit in an amount equal to a specified percentage of the cost of equipment bought in a particular tax year against its potential tax liability for that same year. Generally, for equipment placed in service before January 1, 1986, a taxpayer could claim a maximum investment tax credit equal to 10% of the cost of equipment acquired during a tax year. Thus, for example, a taxpayer buying an equipment item in a particular tax year that cost $1 million could reduce its federal income tax liability by an amount equal to $100,000 (10% × $1 million = $100,000) for that year. If a taxpayer would have owed $250,000 in federal income taxes for the purchase year apart from the ITC, he would actually have to pay only $150,000 ($250,000 – $100,000 = $150,000) after claiming the ITC.

Given that tax reduction, the ITC played a major role in equipment leasing. If the lease qualified as a true lease (explained in Chapter 8), the lessor was treated as owner, and could claim the ITC. The ITC has numerous requirements, and the prospective lessor had to understand the ITC rules before entering a leasing transaction.

It was also important for prospective lessees, and their representatives, to have a solid appreciation of the ITC for two reasons:

- Prospective lessees could not evaluate whether to buy or lease equipment unless they knew how to work with those rules.
- Lessors frequently require lessees to indemnify them against an ITC loss that may arise in certain circumstances. Thus, the prospective lessee would not be able to understand the indemnity risks unless he was fully aware of what he was asked to provide.

This chapter proceeds in three parts. Part I explains generally how the ITC worked before 1986. Part II covers how events in an on-going leasing transaction could result in a retroactive loss of a previously claimed ITC. This part may be particularly useful to parties who had entered leasing transactions before 1986. Part III explains what remains of the ITC for equipment placed in service after 1986.

PART I: ITC BEFORE 1986

A.   Computing the ITC

The amount of ITC that a taxpayer could claim for a tax year was calculated by multiplying the appropriate investment credit rate times its "qualified investment" in eligible property. Calculating a taxpayer's qualified investment took a little work.

The basic determining rule provided that a taxpayer's qualified investment for any tax year was equal to the sum of

- The applicable percentage of the basis of each item of *new* Section 38 property that the taxpayer placed in service during that tax year plus
- The applicable percentage of the cost of each item of *used* Section 38 property that the taxpayer placed in service during that tax year.

The resulting ITC amount was then subject to annual limitations. The steps to be taken to arrive at that amount were:

- Determining what property was Section 38 property.
- Calculating the basis of the new Section 38 property.
- Calculating the cost of the used Section 38 property.
- Determining the applicable percentage for the property.
- Determining when the property was placed in service.
- Deciding whether the property was new or used.
- Applying the annual limitations on the amount that could be claimed.

1. Section 38 Property

ITC was available only on Section 38 property. To be Section 38 property, the property must be depreciable—that is, subject to wear and tear and used in the taxpayer's trade or business or held for the production of income—and had to be either tangible personal property or other tangible property. The other tangible property, property that generally would have been considered real property, must meet one of the following tests. It had to be

- Used as an integral part of a manufacturing, production, or extraction activity, or be an integral part of the furnishing of transportation, communication, electrical energy, gas, water, or sewage disposal services;
- A research facility used in connection with any of the activities specified above; or
- A facility used in connection with any of the activities specified above for the bulk storage of fungible commodities, including commodities in a liquid or gaseous state.

Generally, most office equipment and machinery qualified under the tangible personal property test. Even equipment affixed to the ground generally qualified.

To satisfy the integral part test, the other tangible property had to be used directly in, and essential to the completeness of, the qualifying activity. For example, docks, railroad tracks, or bridges, may be considered to be an integral part of a manufacturing activity. (See Reg. Sec. 1.48-1(d) for additional examples.)

Generally, a building and its structural components do not qualify as Section 38 property. (These are defined in Reg. Sec. 1.48-1(e).)

2.   Basis for ITC Purposes

Before 1983, basis for ITC purposes was determined under general Code principles. For example, if a taxpayer bought new Section 38 property, its basis in the property was its cost. In making the computation, the taxpayer could include such items as freight, sales, and installation charges.

The 1982 Tax Equity and Fiscal Responsibility Act (TEFRA) introduced an ITC adjustment rule. For ITC eligible property placed in service after December 31, 1982, a taxpayer had to reduce his or her basis in that property for depreciation and disposition purposes by 50% of the ITC claimed. Alternatively, a taxpayer could elect to reduce the amount of available ITC by 2%, in which case the property's basis did not have to be reduced.

3.   Applicable Percentage

As explained in Chapter 5, the 1981 Economic Recovery Act (ERTA) introduced the Accelerated Cost Recovery System (ACRS). ACRS greatly simplified depreciation, including introducing recovery classes to determine the period over which an asset's cost was recovered. ERTA made corresponding changes to the way a taxpayer determined the applicable percentage for ITC purposes. For property placed in service after 1980, the applicable percentages were:

- For property in the 5-, 10-, or 15-year public utility recovery class, 100% of the basis could be used to compute ITC.
- For property in the 3-year class, 60% of the property's basis was eligible for ITC. Certain property, assigned to the three-year recovery class for ACRS purposes, (for example, commuter highway vehicles) was assigned a 100% applicable percentage.

Determining the applicable percentage for property placed in service before 1981 was more complex. The percentages depended on the property's useful life:

- For property with a useful life of at least three years, but less than five years, the applicable percentage was equal to 33 1/3%.
- For property with a useful life of at least five years, but less than seven, it was 66 2/3%.
- For property which had a useful life of at least seven years, the applicable percentage was 100%.

- Property with a useful life of less than three years was not eligible for the ITC.

Determining property's useful life was done under the facts and circumstances approach or using the Class Life Asset Depreciation Range System. These are explained in Chapter 5.

▶ **Observation:**   A taxpayer's choice of useful life for depreciation purposes would "lock in" the useful life for ITC computation purposes. Thus, if a taxpayer depreciated an asset over a five-year period useful life, the applicable percentage would be 66 2/3% for qualified investment determination purposes.

4.   Placed in Service

Except for qualified progress expenditures, a taxpayer could claim ITC generally only for the year the equipment was placed in service, regardless of when during the year it is so placed. For ITC purposes, property was deemed placed in service in the *earlier* of the following years:

- The year in which, under the taxpayer's depreciation practice, the taxpayer began to depreciate the property or
- The year in which the property was placed in a condition or state of readiness and availability for a specifically assigned function, whether in a trade or business, in the production of income, in a tax-exempt activity, or in a personal activity.

The second test was designed to prevent taxpayers from postponing the ITC by delaying the start of the property's depreciation. Determining whether property was in a condition or state of readiness could be a difficult judgment; the regs [Reg. Sec. 1.46-3(d)(2)] provide guidelines by examples.

▶ **Leasing Pitfall:**   The condition or state of readiness for use test could wreak havoc on a leasing deal where the parties were not careful. If the lessee constructed and completed the equipment, or it was delivered to the lessee, before the deal was completed, the equipment could have been deemed placed in service at that point by the lessee, not the lessor. Then, when the lessor bought the equipment and leased it back to the lessee, the lessor could not claim the ITC. The best way to minimize this risk was for the lessee to pay close attention to construction or delivery schedules, and for the parties and their lawyers to complete the transaction before the equipment was constructed or delivered. Also, many lessors wanted to protect themselves against the risk that the property could inadvertently have been deemed placed in service before they bought it by using tax indemnification provisions, under which the lessee would indemnify the lessor for its lost tax benefits.

5.   New and Used Property

ITC was generally available on both new and used Section 38 property. However, only $125,000 of used Section 38 property could qualify for the credit in any one year. Also, ITC on used property could not be passed through to the lessee.

Equipment was considered new when its original use began with the taxpayer. "Original use" is considered to be the first use to which the property is put, regardless of whether the use corresponds to the taxpayer's use. Under this rule, the original use could not begin with a taxpayer, if the property had been reconditioned or rebuilt before it was acquired. The fact that property had used parts, however, did not automatically disqualify it as new property unless there were so many used parts that it would fall within the rebuilt or reconditioned category.

Property initially qualifying as new Section 38 property would not lose its status if the owner sold the property and simultaneously leased it back. The rationale was that the property continued to be used by the person who used it before its sale. However, the lessor could then not claim the ITC. If a lessee leased equipment that was new Section 38 property in the lessor's hands at the time the lessee leased it, it would remain new to the lessor. *Reason:* By being used by the lessee, it is deemed used by the lessor. Also, if certain corporate, partner, or related taxpayer relationships existed between a seller and a buyer, new Section 38 property in the hands of the seller did not, on transfer, become used Section 38 property.

6.   Annual Limitations on ITC Claimed

While a taxpayer could earn an unlimited amount of ITC in any given year, the amount he or she could claim in a year was limited. In calculating the limitation, the taxpayer combined its available ITC, energy credits, targeted jobs credit, alcohol fuels credit, and ESOP credit into a single, general business credit. If the taxpayer's federal tax liability for a year, apart from the credits, was $25,000 or less, he or she could use $25,000 of credits. If the taxpayer's tax liability exceeded $25,000, then the limit was $25,000, plus 85% (for years before 1986) of its tax liability apart from the credits. Unused business credits were first carried back 3 years, and then any remaining unused credits could be carried forward 10 years. The annual limitation applied to carryback and carryover amounts.

B.   ITC Pass through to Lessee

Generally, a lessor of new Section 38 property could, under Section 48(d), elect to treat the lessee as the equipment's buyer for ITC purposes. In other words, the lessor could "pass through" the credit to the lessee so that the lessee could claim it directly.

The lessee's qualified investment in property on which a Section 48(d) election had been made was generally the property's fair market value on the transfer date. In the case of a lease between certain related corporations, however, the lessee's qualified investment was instead equal to the equipment's basis in the lessor's hands on the transfer date.

The determination of the property's "original use" as to a lessee was made within the same guidelines as if the lessee were the owner. In this regard, if the lessor or any third party had used the property before the lessee, or if it had been reconstructed, rebuilt, or reconditioned property, the lessee would not be able to claim any investment credit. *Reason*: The property's original use would not have begun with the lessee. The lessor's mere testing or storing of property was not considered prior use.

▶ **Observation:**   A lessee could elect to "pass through" to a sublessee the ITC that had been passed through to the lessee. The lessee's ITC "pass-through" was treated as if the original lessor had leased the property directly to the sublessee for the sublease term.

The "pass-through" election could be made either (1) on an item-by-item basis or (2) on a general basis as to all property that was leased by the electing lessor to the lessee. In either case, the lessor made the election by filing an appropriate statement with the lessee, on or before the lessee's federal income tax return was due for the tax year during which possession was transferred to the lessee. The election was irrevocable as of the time the statement was filed with the lessee.

C.   Limits on Noncorporate Lessors

Noncorporate lessors could claim ITC on property they leased to third parties only in two situations:

- The noncorporate lessor either manufactured or produced the leased property in the ordinary course of business or
- The lease term (including any renewal options) was less than 50% of the property's estimated useful life, and the lessor's total allowable Section 162 deductions during the initial 12-month period beginning on the date the property was transferred to the lessee exceeded 15% of the lease rental income.

▶ **Observation:** The noncorporate lessor rule did not apply to corporate lessor-partners. Thus, each corporate partner could claim ITC on its proportionate investment in Section 38 property held by the partnership.

D.   Use Outside the United States

An equipment owner could not claim ITC on property used predominantly outside of the United States during a tax year. Property would be considered "predominantly" used outside the United States if it was physically located for more than 50% of the tax year outside the United States. In the event the property was placed in service during a tax year, the 50% test would be applied against the portion of the year beginning when it was so placed in service. If a lessor elected to "pass through" the ITC to the lessee under Section 48(d), the predominant use test would be based on the property's predominant use during the lessee's tax year.

Property that was used predominantly outside the United States during the tax year it was placed in service would not qualify as Section 38 property even though, in a later year, it was permanently returned to the United States. If the predominant use test was satisfied when the property was placed in service, but in a later year it was not satisfied, the property would cease to be Section 38 property regardless of who, in fact, used the property outside the United States during that year.

There are several exceptions to the predominant use test, including certain aircraft and vessels. (See Reg. Sec. 1.48-1(g)(2).)

E.   Qualified Progress Expenditures

Where Section 38 property had a construction period of over two years, it was possible to claim a portion of the ITC before the property was placed in service. Called qualified progress expenditures, these are costs incurred in constructing the property. To take qualified progress expenditures, it had to be reasonable to expect that the equipment would qualify for ITC when placed in service, and the equipment must have had a normal construction period of at least two years.

PART II: LOSING ITC

A.   ITC Recapture

While the ITC on an item of equipment was all earned in the year the taxpayer placed the property in service, some or all of it could be lost if the property ceased to qualify as Section 38 property or was disposed in later years. This later ITC loss is referred to as ITC recapture.

For property placed in service after 1980, and subject to ACRS rules, the recapture rules are straightforward. For each year the property continued to be Section 38 property, 2% of the ITC vests. Put another way, for each year short of the end of the recapture period in which the recapture event occurs, 2% must be recaptured. The 2% rule applies whether the ITC claimed was 10% or 6%. The following chart illustrates the recapture amounts.

If Disposed Of:		Recapture
	3-year property	15-year, 10-year, and 5-year property
Within one Year	6%	10%
After one Year	4	8
After 2 Years	2	6
After 3 Years	–0–	4
After 4 Years	–0–	2
After 5 Years	–0–	–0–

Illustrative Example: In 1983, Company Able bought a $10,000 drill press and claimed the $1,000 ITC. In 1987, it sold the drill press. As the press was in its fourth year of use, Company Able would have recapture of $2,000 (2% of the $10,000 investment). The $2,000 is added directly to Company Able's otherwise computed tax liability. It also cannot be offset by ITC or other business credits earned on other property in that year.

For ITC earned before 1981, where the ITC was determined under pre-ACRS rules, the recapture amount was based on a redetermination of the property's useful life. The amount that had to be recaptured was equal to the difference between the total credit originally claimed and an ITC computed on the basis of a useful life, computed from the time the property was placed in service by the taxpayer to the date of the disqualifying event. Thus, if a taxpayer disposed of property four years after he bought it (on which he had initially claimed an ITC based on a useful life of nine years), his federal income tax liability for the year of disposition would have been increased by an amount equal to two-thirds of the credit initially claimed because the qualified investment applicable percentage for a four-year useful life is 33 1/3%, as opposed to 100%, for a nine-year useful life.

For the purpose of ITC recapture calculations, the determining useful life was the shortest life within the useful life category used to establish the appropriate qualified investment applicable percentage. That is, if the taxpayer claimed a credit when the property was placed in service based on a four-year useful life, but the property was disposed of or ceased to be Section 38 property in the third year, the property would not have been deemed to have been disposed of before the end of its useful life.

B.   Events Triggering Recapture

Generally, a recapture event occurs when the taxpayer either disposes of the property or it ceases to be Section 38 property in the taxpayer's hands. There are certain exceptions, some of which are explained below. (See Reg. Sec. 1.47-2—1.47-6 for further explanation.)

1.   Special Rules Concerning Leased Equipment

- Where a taxpayer has placed Section 38 property in service, and later enters into a sale-leaseback of that property, there is no disposition for ITC purposes. This was true even though the taxpayer had to recognize a gain or loss on the property and could no longer depreciate it.
- If the lessor was entitled to claim ITC on property, but later the lessee stopped using it for a qualified use, the lessor was subject to ITC recapture.
- Where the lessor had elected to pass through the ITC to the lessee, normally the lessor could dispose of the property without causing a disposition. However, if the new lessor was not eligible to make the pass-through election, the lessee was subject to ITC recapture.

2.   Changes of Ownership Form

Generally, if a taxpayer changed the form of the trade or business in which Section 38 property was used, a "disposition" or "cessation" for ITC purposes was not deemed to have occurred. For example, if the taxpayer were initially a partnership when it acquired ITC eligible equipment, a change to a corporate form would not result in ITC recapture. The rule, however, was subject to the following conditions:

- The property must have been retained as Section 38 property in the same trade or business.

- The transferor of the property must have retained a substantial interest in the trade or business.
- Substantially all the assets of the trade or business necessary for its operation must have been transferred to the transferee of the Section 38 property.
- The basis of the Section 38 property must have been carried over in part or in whole.

Whether a transferor had retained a "substantial interest" in a trade or business was sometimes a difficult issue. The criterion was satisfied if, after the change in form, its interest was substantial in relation to the remaining interests or was at least equal to its prior interest. For example, a taxpayer who formerly held a 5% interest in a partnership that was converted into a corporation and who, after the conversion, had a 5% interest in the corporation, retained a "substantial interest" in the trade or business.

3.   S Corporations and Partnerships

Where an S corporation or a partnership acquired Section 38 property, the shareholder or partner took the ITC individually. If the S corporation or partnership disposes of the property, the shareholder or partner must take any recapture. Also, if a shareholder of an S corporation having ITC that has not completely vested sells his stock, he has made a disposition and may be subject to recapture. Similarly, If a partner's proportionate interest in the general partnership's profits is reduced, there may be recapture.

C.   Whether Section 38 Property Had Lost Its Status Had to Be Regularly Reviewed

During the ITC vesting period, a taxpayer had to, at the end of each tax year following the year the ITC was claimed, determine whether any Section 38 property had ceased to be Section 38 property. If any of that property would no longer qualify as Section 38 property, the taxpayer had to recompute the amount of credit to which he was entitled and make the appropriate adjustment to his federal income tax liability.

▶ **Observation:** If property otherwise qualified as Section 38 property, the fact that it could no longer be depreciated under the taxpayer's depreciation practice would not cause it to lose Section 38 status if the taxpayer continued to use the property in its trade or business or in the production of income.

PART III: ITC AFTER 1985

A.   ITC Repeal

The '86 TRA essentially wiped out the regular ITC for equipment placed in service after 1985, except for ITC transition property and qualified progress expenditures. The '86 TRA also curtailed the use of many ITCs still available to taxpayers and increased the required basis adjustment for property on which ITC could still be claimed after 1985.

B.   ITC Transition Property

To assuage some of the harshness of the ITC repeal, the '86 TRA allowed ITC to be claimed on transition property—basically, property as to which the taxpayers had committed sufficient resources before 1986.

Specifically, ITC transition property is property placed in service after 1985 that

- is self-constructed property (that the taxpayer constructed or reconstructed) on which the construction or reconstruction started by December 31, 1985, and at least the lesser of (1) 5% of the property's cost or (2) $1 million was incurred or committed by December 31, 1985;
- is constructed, reconstructed, or acquired under a written contract binding on December 31, 1985;
- is an equipped building (equipment and machinery to be used in or incidental to the building come within this rule), or a plant facility that is not housed in a building, on which construction began no later than December 31, 1985, under a specific written plan, and greater than 50% of the cost was either incurred or committed no later than December 31, 1985;
- is readily identifiable as belonging to and necessary to be used in connection with performing a written supply or service contract, or lease agreement, that was binding as of December 31, 1985.

A special sale-leaseback provision permits lessors to claim ITCs after 1985 under certain conditions. First, the property must have been placed in service by the lessee before 1986 or be ITC transitional property in the lessee's hands. Second, the property must be leased back by the lessor to the lessee by the earlier of (1) the placed in service date for the applicable property class (set out below) or (2) three months following the date when it was originally placed in service.

The '86 TRA does set cutoff dates by which the transition property must have been placed in service. Those dates, set out below, are based on the property's ADR class life (explained in Chapter 5).

- Transitional property with an ADR midpoint of less than five years must have been placed in service before July 1, 1986;
- Property with an ADR midpoint of at least five years, but less than seven years (and computer-based telephone switching equipment) must have been placed in service before January 1, 1987;
- Property with an ADR midpoint of at least 7 years, but less than 20 years, must be placed in service before January 1, 1989;
- Property with no ADR midpoint must be placed in service before January 1, 1989; and
- Property with an ADR midpoint of 20 years or more must be placed in service before January 1, 1991.

In addition to the above rules, ITC transition property must comply with detailed guidelines. Parties considering a lease of transition property must consult those guidelines (see Revenue Ruling 87-113, IRB 1987-45, p.4).

C.   Qualified Progress Expenditures

Before the '86 IRA, taxpayers could claim a portion of the property's ITC in advance when the property's construction lasted over two years. Taxpayers can still claim those credits after 1986, but only as to property that it is reasonable to expect will be ITC transition property when placed in service. If the property is not transition property when placed in service—for example, it is not placed in service by its extended deadline—the credits must be adjusted.

D.   ITC Reductions

Not only did the '86 TRA virtually eliminate the ITC, it cut down on the value of those ITCs that remained. Generally, a taxpayer claiming ITC after 1985 under an ITC transitional rule or an ITC carryforward provision from a tax year ending before July 1, 1987, must reduce the ITC amount by 35%. The reduction is effective for tax years beginning after June 30, 1987. For tax years that begin before and end after July 1, 1987, the 35% ITC amount reduction is prorated under a ratio based on the post-June 30, 1987 tax year months over the total tax year months. The ITC amount not available because of the 35% reduction cannot be taken in a prior or succeeding year.

E.   Basis Reductions

Before the '86 TRA, taxpayers had to reduce their equipment's basis—for depreciation or disposition purposes—by 50% of the ITC claimed. After 1986, the equipment's basis is reduced by the full amount of the ITC claimed. Thus, if in 1988 a taxpayer were to claim $100,000 ITC on $1 million of equipment his or her basis would be $900,000. If the 35% ITC reduction applies, the basis reduction is limited to that reduced amount.

CHAPTER 8
How to Cope Successfully With The Tax Lease Rules

A. The True Lease

When the parties sign a document entitled a "lease," and the document is a lease under state and local law, is it a lease for federal income tax purposes? Not necessarily. The lease must pass muster as what is called a "true" lease—a lease for federal income tax purposes. Failure to do so will cause the lessor to lose tax benefits (and even possibly be subjected to penalties) and the lessee to forfeit rent deductions. *Result*: The leasing transaction sinks into a pool of red ink.

What, then, characterizes a "true" lease? The term is not defined in the Code or regulations. The bottom line—as summarized by the Supreme Court—is whether the lessor, rather than the lessee, is the equipment's tax owner, having "significant and genuine attributes of the traditional lessor status . . . What those attributes are in any particular case will necessarily depend upon its facts" [*Frank Lyon Co. v. U.S.*, 435 U.S. 561, 41 AFTR 2d 78-1142 (1978) (sale-leaseback of building upheld)].

While the ultimate "true" lease test is based on the transaction's facts and circumstances, the IRS has provided guidelines which, if followed, will help assure that a leasing transaction stays afloat. In the form of four published Revenue Procedures, called the *Guidelines*, the IRS sets out what the parties must do to obtain a private ruling on a leveraged lease. While nominally limited to ruling requests, the *Guidelines* provide helpful advice on achieving true lease status, even where the parties to the transaction do not request an IRS private ruling. Revenue Ruling 55-540 [1955-2 CB 39] also provides general guidelines.

177

B.   Procedural Alternatives

How do the parties maximize their chances of obtaining true lease status? The best two alternatives—obtain an IRS private ruling letter or proceed without one while following the *Guidelines* and Revenue Ruling 55-540.

1.   A Private Letter Ruling

As a general matter, if a taxpayer submits a ruling request to the IRS concerning a transaction, the IRS, after reviewing the request, will rule on some or all of the transaction's tax consequences. Then, provided the information submitted was accurate and complete, the issues on which the IRS has ruled will be dispositive. In leveraged leasing transactions, taxpayers must follow the specific instructions set out in the *Guidelines* when submitting their request. If the parties to a leasing transaction receive a favorable ruling from the IRS, they can rest assured that the transaction's anticipated tax results will survive.

While the safest route is to obtain a ruling, it is not always the optimum alternative for several reasons. First, it is costly: Preparing and submitting the request involves a significant amount of legal work, resulting in higher legal fees, and a several-hundred-dollar fee must be paid to the IRS. Second, submitting a request takes time—both to prepare the request and for the IRS to rule. Third, if the IRS's ruling is unfavorable and the transaction has been closed, there is a risk that this will draw attention to an issue that may otherwise have gone unnoticed. Weighing those downside factors against the increased certainty, a request should be considered when:

- Most important, where the lessor will not go ahead without a ruling.
- For certain reasons, there is considerable doubt as to the lease's true lease status or other tax issues.
- The deal's overall costs are substantial enough to sustain the added costs.
- The lessee has time to wait for the ruling to be issued before closing the deal.

2.   Proceeding Without a Ruling

Where, for one or more reasons above, a ruling is not practical, the next safest approach is to comply with the IRS's *Guidelines*. Those *Guidelines* tell taxpayers what they must submit to obtain an advance ruling on a leasing deal and do not specifically address situations where there is no ruling. And while the IRS does not promise that compliance with the *Guidelines* will guarantee favorable treatment on audit, as a practical matter, the *Guidelines* creep into the audit process. Thus, compliance with the *Guidelines* can let the parties to a lease transaction feel comfortable that the arrangement will in fact qualify as a true lease.

And, as the *Guidelines* do not guarantee lease treatment, failure to comply precisely with each *Guideline* provision does not necessarily doom a lease. *Reasons*: (1) The IRS's *Guidelines* are its position only on advance rulings. They do not necessarily reflect the IRS's view of the law so a slight variation may not raise a problem on audit. (2) If the transaction goes to court, the *Guidelines* will carry less weight; under *Frank Lyon* the court will look at all the facts and circumstances, and may well find, on balance, that a true lease exists.

An advisable course of action, particularly where there is some variation from the *Guidelines*, is to obtain a written opinion from experienced lease tax counsel that the arrangement will have the desired lease treatment. While this increases costs, it may provide some assurance either on audit, or, if necessary, in litigation.

C.   The Guidelines

The following comprise the *Guidelines*:

- Revenue Procedure 75-21 [1975-1 CB 715] generally sets out conditions that must be met for there to be an advance ruling on a leveraged lease.
- Revenue Procedure 75-28 [1975-1 CB 752] sets out information and representations required to be furnished by taxpayers in a leveraged leasing transaction ruling request.
- Revenue Procedure 76-30 [1976-2 CB 647] supplements Revenue Procedure 75-21 on issue of limited use property.
- Revenue Procedure 79-18 [1979-2 CB 529] supplements Revenue Procedure 75-21 on improvements to leased property.

As explained above, the *Guidelines* are expressly designed to tell taxpayers what they must do to obtain an advance ruling. However, following the rules, even where no ruling is sought, is advisable to help assure true lease treatment. Also, while the *Guidelines* apply only to leveraged leases, parties to a nonleveraged transaction should review the portions of the *Guidelines* not applicable to the debt aspect of leasing transactions.

In addition to the *Guidelines*, prospective lessors and lessees will want to comply with Revenue Ruling 55-540 [1955-2 CB 39], explained below, which gives some general guidelines on leasing transactions.

▶ Observations:

■ Syndicators must be careful when deviating from the *Guidelines* in structuring a lease financing, even though each party initially states a private ruling will not be required. Invariably, once the parties, particularly the equity investors, hear all about the theoretical risks from their lawyers, they get nervous and frequently ask for a favorable opinion from tax counsel as to the true lease nature. In many situations, when there is a *Guideline* variance, counsel is reluctant to give an opinion, because of the uncertainty as to the variance's effect. Coming at the last minute, this can lead to a serious roadblock to completing the deal.

■ When a private ruling will not be involved, the *Guideline* rules are sometimes stretched to keep all the parties satisfied. For example, a company may not be willing to lease equipment unless there is a low fixed-price purchase option. Although prohibited under the rules, a prospective lessor may grant such a right just to win the transaction.

At first glance, the *Guideline* rules do not appear complex. This is not the case. In structuring a particular transaction, take care not to violate them inadvertently—not a simple task. The best protection against that is a thorough understanding of the principal *Guideline* concepts. We will now examine the various aspects of the *Guidelines*.

1. The Lessor Must Maintain a Minimum Investment

Under the *Guidelines*, the lessor must initially make an unconditional equity investment in the equipment equal to at least 20% of its cost. This can be done in a number of ways: with cash, with other consideration, or by personally assuming the obligation to buy the equipment. Typically, the lessor makes a cash payment from its own funds. The 20% equity investment is referred to as the "minimum investment."

The IRS requires the unconditional nature of the initial investment to prevent the lessor from arranging to receive, either from the lessee or certain lessee-related parties, all or any part of his equity back once the equipment is put into service. This is so because the IRS believes that if a lessor wants to be treated as an equipment owner for tax purposes, and thus be entitled to claim the tax benefits, there must be an ownership risk.

If the personal liability assumption alternative is used to meet the minimum equity test, the lessor's net worth must be sufficient to make the assumption in fact meaningful.

The lessor must also maintain this 20% "minimum investment" in the equipment during the lease term. The test for determining whether the minimum investment rule has been met during the term is complicated; follow it carefully. The test will be met if the excess of (1) the cumulative payments that the lessee is obligated to pay over (2) the cumulative disbursements that the lessor is obligated to pay as a result of the equipment ownership is never greater than the *sum* of (a) any excess of the initial equity investment over 20% of the equipment cost and (b) the cumulative pro rata portion of the transaction's projected profit, not considering tax benefits. Simply, this means that the excess of the amounts coming in to the lessor over the amounts going out must never be more than the sum of any equity investment amount greater than 20% of equipment cost and the pro rata portion of the anticipated profit. The tax benefits accruing from ownership cannot be considered as profit in the computation.

▶ **Recommended Computation:** In Revenue Procedure 75-28, the IRS provides a mechanical formula to establish the 20% investment during the lease term. It may be useful to run the following test on a computer and retain it for audit purposes.

Verify that throughout the lease term the items designated as (1), (2), (3), and (4) below comply with the formula "(1) − (2) never exceeds (3) + (4)."

1. The projected cumulative payments required to be paid by the lessee to or for the lessor.

2. The projected cumulative disbursements required to be paid by or for the lessor in connection with the ownership of the property, excluding the lessor's initial equity investment, but including any direct costs to finance the equity investment.

3. The excess of lessor's initial equity investment over 20% of the cost of the property.

4. A cumulative pro rata portion of the projected profits from the transaction (exclusive of tax benefits). Profit for this purpose is the excess of the sum of (a) the amounts required to be paid by the lessee to or for the lessor over the lease term plus (b) the value of the residual investment referred to in section 4(1)(C) of Revenue Procedure 75 21, over the aggregate disbursements required to be paid by or for the lessor in connection with the ownership of the property, including the lessor's initial equity investment and any direct costs to finance the equity investment.

Also, the minimum investment test must be met at the end of the lease term. It consists of two basic parts:

- The lessor must show that the leased equipment's estimated fair market residual value is equal to at least 20% of its original cost.
- The lessor must show that a reasonable estimate of the equipment's useful life at the end of the lease term is the longer of one year or 20% of the equipment's originally estimated useful life.

Illustrative Example—*At-Risk Residual Test:*   Company A wants to lease a $10,000 steel shipping container from Company B for an 11-year lease term. The container has an estimated useful life of 12 years and an estimated fair market value at the end of 11 years of $2,300. Will the end-of-the-lease-term "at risk" investment test be met?

The estimated fair market residual value test has been met. That is, the $2,300 residual meets the first test (20% of $10,000 = $2,000, the minimum).

The useful life test has not been met. Twenty percent of 12 years is 2.4 years. When the lease term is over there will only be 1 year of useful life left, and the second test says the remaining useful life must be the longer of 1 year or, in our example, 2.4 years.

In making the fair market residual value determination, no weight can be given to any inflationary increases or deflationary decreases during the lease term—the determination must be made as to future value base on current dollars. Also, the estimated residual amount must be reduced by any anticipated costs that may be incurred in removing and delivering the property to the lessor at the end of the lease term.

The calculations cannot be made without first figuring out what the "lease term" will be for a particular transaction. The lease term is not merely the "primary term" designated by the lease document. By definition, the "term" must include all renewal and extension periods other than those that are at fair market rental value and are at the lessee's option. For example, the lessor would have to include any period for which it could require the lessee to continue to lease the equipment even though it would be at fair market rental value. This rule prevents a lessor from avoiding its "residual risk" through a forced renewal of the lease, which would in effect run until the lessor had no residual value risk. This again reinforces the *Guideline* intent that if an equipment owner wants to be a "lessor" he must incur real ownership risks.

2.   The Transaction Must Produce a Profit

The *Guidelines* provide that the lessor must make a profit on the transaction. At first this statement seems ridiculous. What businessperson would be involved in a situation in which he or she didn't make a profit? None, so what is the IRS getting at? Simply, that the lessor must make money on the deal aside from the return generated by the tax benefits. In other words, the lessor must be able to show that the lease transaction makes economic sense without considering the tax benefits. The IRS wants to make sure that lease deals are not merely tax avoidance devices.

How does a lessor know whether the profit requirement has been met? By meeting the following *Guideline* test: The total rent and other amounts that the lessee is obligated to pay over the lease term, when added to the equipment's estimated residual value, has to be greater than the amount of money that the lessor is obligated to pay out for the equipment, such as debt service and equity investment, including any related direct equity financing costs. Simply, the lessor must anticipate having money left over, when adding in the estimated residual value, at the end of the lease term after repaying any transaction debt, the money it took out of its own pocket to acquire the equipment, and any other direct equity investment financing costs.

Illustrative Example—*the Profit Test:*   Company B has leased a new $100,000 barge to Company A under the following facts:

Lease term	10 years
Barge residual value	$20,000
Equity investment	$20,000
Debt principal	$80,000
Debt interest rate	10%
Loan term	10 years
Total aggregate rentals	$125,000
Legal fees	$5,000
Miscellaneous fees	$1,000

For simplicity, assume that the debt repayments are based on an average outstanding principal of $40,000 over the 10-year period. Based on the above, the deal evolves as follows:

Total debt interest due	$40,000
Total principal payment	$80,000
Total fees ($5,000 + $1,000)	$6,000

Does the lessor pass the IRS profit test? The formula is:
Aggregate rentals + residual value must exceed cash out.

Aggregate rentals + residual —
$125,000 + $20,000 = $145,000

Equity investment + debt service + fees = cash out =
$20,000 + $80,000 + $40,000 + $6,000 = $146,000

The lessor fails the test.

The net result: The rents must be increased to pass the test.

▶ **Recommended Computation:**   Run the following test from Revenue Procedure 75-28:
Demonstrate that the items identified as (1), (2), and (3) below will solve the formula "(1) + (2) exceed (3)."

1. The projected aggregate payments required to be paid by the lessee to or for the lessor over the lease term.

2. The value of the residual investment described in Section 4(1)(C) of Revenue Procedure 75-21.

3. The projected sum of the aggregate disbursements required to be paid by or for the lessor in connection with the ownership of the property, including the lessor's initial equity investment, and any direct costs to finance the equity investment.

Not only must a lessor anticipate a profit, he must also demonstrate that the transaction will produce a positive cash flow that is "reasonable" in amount. That is, the aggregate rents and other required lessee payments must comfortably exceed the aggregate outflows, basically the debt service and the direct equity financing costs.

▶ **Recommended Computation:**   Run the following test from Revenue Procedure 75-28:

Demonstrate that the lessor will have a projected positive cash flow from the lease transaction. This analysis must contain the following information to demonstrate that the items identified as (1) and (2) will solve the formula "(1) exceeds (2) by a reasonable minimum amount."

1. The projected aggregate payments required to be paid by the lessee to or for the lessor over the lease term.

2. The projected aggregate disbursements required to be paid by or for the lessor in connection with the ownership of the property, excluding the lessor's initial equity investment, but including any direct costs to finance the equity investment.

3.   No Lessee Investment

Generally, the lessee cannot invest in the equipment by providing funds necessary to buy, add to, modify, or improve the equipment. There are several exceptions. The lessee may make "severable improvements," additions or improvements that can easily be removed without causing material damage, so long as they are not necessary for the equipment's intended use, and the lessor does not have the right to buy them at below market price.

The lessee generally cannot make nonseverable improvements, those that cannot readily be removed by the lessee without causing material damage. However, the lessee can make nonseverable improvements if they (1) are not required to complete the property for the lessee's intended use, (2) do not constitute a lessee or lessee-related party equity investment (as, for example, if the lessor is required to buy the improvement), and (3) do not cause the property to become limited use property (property of use only to the lessee). Also, the nonseverable improvements must meet one of the following tests: (1) be furnished to comply with governmental standards; (2) not modify the leased property for a materially different use; or (3) not substantially increase the original property's productivity or capacity. The rules governing severable and nonseverable improvements are extensive, and an in-depth explanation is beyond the scope of this chapter. The reader can refer to Revenue Procedure 79-48 for a full explanation.

Also, ordinary maintenance and repairs that the lessee must make at its expense are not deemed "additions or improvements" and are thus excluded from the rule. The problem with this exception is that the *Guidelines* do not set up any parameters for determining what is considered "ordinary maintenance and repairs." If the IRS successfully challenges any expenses as not "ordinary," there may be a risk that the true lease nature will be lost.

Under the same basic concept, the lessee cannot pay for any equipment cost overruns. Usually this may be a problem only when equipment with a long construction period is involved. In many of these situations, the purchase contracts have price escalation clauses. Some prospective lessors committing to lease such equipment before completion limit their cost exposure by specifying they will not pay for any excess over a certain amount. If a lessor had this type of "cap," he could refuse to pay for any excess, with the possible result that the prospective lessee would run the risk of having to negotiate a new lease deal at the last minute or buy the equipment.

4.   The Lessee Cannot Be a Lender

Before the IRS issued Revenue Procedure 75-21, some lessees and parties related to them loaned money to the lessor to be used toward buying the equipment. For example, a prospective lessee may want to lease equipment manufactured by its parent company. The parent company would offer to sell the equipment to the lessor on a favorable installment basis. The payment delay would "pump up" a lessor's time value yield over a non-delayed payment, and at least part of the benefit would be reflected in a more attractive rental rate.

Under the *Guidelines*, the lessee and members of the lessee group are specifically prohibited from lending funds to the lessor to assist in the equipment financing. Thus, direct loans and other credit-extending techniques similar to that described in the previous paragraph will transgress the *Guidelines* and prevent the issuance of a favorable private ruling on the transaction.

5.   Certain Guarantees Cannot Be Used

The lessee and certain lessee-associated parties, such as its parent company or sister subsidiary, cannot guarantee any equipment debt. For example, a lessee's parent company cannot guarantee the repayment of a leveraged lease third-party loan. In most cases this will not be a great loss; however, it was a handy technique for lessors to use when, for example, third-party, nonrecourse lenders wanted added security.

The *Guidelines* permit lessee-related parties to guarantee certain conventional obligations found in a net lease, such as rent, maintenance, or insurance premium obligations. This takes some of the sting out of the debt guarantee prohibition.

6.   Lessee Purchase Options Must Be at Fair Market Value

To insure that the lessee is not the equipment owner, the *Guidelines* prohibit any arrangement granting a lessee or lessee-related party the option to buy the leased equipment at a price below its fair market value. The lessee may have a purchase option only if the price is no less than the equipment's fair market value at the time of purchase under the option.

That rule eliminates below-market fixed-price purchase rights, including so-called nominal purchase options. A typical nominal purchase right is one in which the lessee can buy the equipment at the end of the lease term for $1.00. In the past, some lessors had used this option to induce a prospective lessee to take their deal by claiming that lessees could have the best of both worlds: A rental deduction during the lease term and, in effect, an equipment purchase credit for the rent paid.

Low fixed-price purchase options are also in trouble. These types of options are particularly attractive to companies that are aware certain equipment will have a "high residual" at the end of the term. With a fair market value purchase option, they run the risk that their cost to buy will be substantial in relation to the original price. This would, in turn, relatively increase their effective leasing cost. Therefore, the lower the option's exercise price, the less the overall cost.

Illustrative Example—*The Purchase Cost Is Critical:*   Company A wants to lease a barge from Company B. The facts are as follows:

Original barge cost $100,000
Estimated residual value $20,000

If the lessee, Company A, had an option to buy the barge at the lease term's end for $20,000, its cost for leasing could be easily determined in advance. The rents and the purchase price are known. Assume instead that the lessee was granted only a fair market value purchase option under the *Guidelines*. If, at the end of the lease term, the barge was actually worth $50,000 because of the current demand, the lessee would have to pay out an additional $30,000—thus increasing the overall cost.

The above example is not unrealistic. There are many cases where items, such as barges, have a market value after years of use equal to or greater than the original cost. Leasing that equipment, therefore, can be expensive if the lessee wants to buy it at the end of the term and must pay the fair market value.

7. Lessor Cannot Have Right to Require Sale

A lessor is specifically prohibited from having any initial right to require "any party" to buy the leased equipment for any reason, except when there are nonconformities with written supply, construction, or manufacture specifications. The lessor's investment in the equipment would, therefore, be said to be subject to the "risks of the market."

Thus, a lessor cannot have the right—called a "put"—to force an equipment sale at a predetermined price at the lease term's end to, for example, the lessee, a manufacturer, or a dealer. What does this mean for a lessor concerned about whether certain equipment will have any residual value? Simply, that a zero residual value may have to be assumed in calculating the rent to insure that the return will be maintained. Were "puts" permitted, a lessor could base his investment return analysis on an anticipated residual value equal to the "put." As a result, a lessee could then be charged a relatively lower rent amount during the lease term on potentially poor residual value equipment. If the equipment could be sold at the end of the lease for an amount equal to, or greater than, the "put" amount, the lessee would have had a rent savings because the lessor would not need to force the lessee to buy the equipment to get his required economic return.

The right of a lessor to abandon the property is considered to be a right to require a purchase and, therefore, is also prohibited.

The rule provides some leeway. The *Guidelines* provide that after the equipment goes on lease the IRS may, depending on the particular facts and circumstances, permit an arrangement in which the lessor could require someone to buy the equipment.

▶ **A Word of Caution:**   Parties can be tempted to try to get around this rule by entering into a side agreement before the lease is closed, giving the lessor a sale right. After the equipment is placed in service, the side agreement is to be submitted to the IRS for approval as a proposed arrangement, without mention that it had been agreed to during the prohibited period. This is dangerous and clearly not recommended. Private ruling letters are granted strictly on the basis of the facts submitted in the ruling request, and if the facts actually vary from those as presented, the IRS may not adhere to the tax treatment stated.

8.   Uneven Rent Programs Must Meet Certain Tests

"Step rentals," such as "low-high" or "high-low" rent structures, had been a valuable lessor marketing tool. Particularly attractive to lessees were rents that started low and increased during the lease's term, for a variety of reasons, including showing higher profits in early years, anticipating inflation, or increasing cash flow.

The *Guidelines* ask a taxpayer submitting a ruling request to submit certain information on any rent payment variations during the lease term.

Uneven rent payments, however, under the *Guidelines*, will not impact the IRS's ruling on whether the lease is a true lease. Rather, under the *Guidelines*, uneven rents can result in a portion of the uneven rent being treated as prepaid or deferred rent.

The *Guidelines* set out two safe harbor tests, so that if the rent payments satisfy either test there will be no issue as to prepaid or deferred rent. If the lease fails to meet either test, then the ruling request must also contain a request for a determination of whether any portion of the uneven rent payments will be deemed by the IRS as prepaid or deferred rent.

a.   Ten Percent Variation Test

Under the first test, rent payments come within the safe harbor if the rent for each year does not vary more than 10% above or below the average annual rent payable over the lease term. The average annual rent is computed by dividing the aggregate rent payable over the entire lease term by the number of years in the term. As a practical matter, this does not permit a lessor to offer anything significant, when compared to some of the pre-guideline uneven rent programs.

Illustrative Example—*Uneven Rent Test:* Company A wants to lease a fuel truck for 10 years for a start-up operation, but anticipates that its cash flow will allow only a $1,000 annual rent expense for the first 3 years. Company B, the prospective lessor, proposes the following rent program:

Lease term:	10 years
Annual rent for years	
1-3	$1,000
Annual rent for years	
4-10	$2,000

Company A finds the rent to be within its cash flow projections. Is there a deferred rent issue?

Let's examine the numbers. The rule says the rent for each year cannot be above or below 10% of the average annual rent. The average annual rent is computed by dividing the total of the 10-year rents $(3 \times \$1,000 + 7 \times \$2,000 = \$17,000)$ by the number of years in the lease.

Annual average rent = $17,000/10 = $1,700

Because 10% of $1,700 is $170, the rent per year cannot be above $1,870 ($1,700 + $170) or below $1,530 ($1,700 − $170). Therefore, this rent program does not meet the test, and the issue of deferred rent must be addressed.

b. Initial Period Test

The second safe harbor is designed to permit, to some degree, rental payments that fluctuate during the lease term. Lease payments satisfy that test if, during at least the initial two-thirds of the lease term, the yearly rent is not more than 10% higher or lower than the average annual rent for such selected initial portion, and the remaining individual yearly rent is not greater than the highest annual rent payable during the initial portion and not less than one-half of the initial term average yearly rent. There is somewhat more flexibility in using this alternative, but it is still limited.

Illustrative Example—*Initial Period Test:* Assume the following rent program:

Lease term	9 years
Annual rent for years	
1-3	$1,000
Annual rent for years	
4-6	$1,200
Annual rent for years	
7-9	$600

Will this rent structure pass the IRS alternative test?

First the average rent must be computed for the initial two-thirds of the lease term as follows:

$$\text{Average rent} = \frac{(3 \times \$1,000 + 3 \times \$1,200)}{6 \text{ years}} = \$1,100$$

The yearly rent cannot be greater than $1,210 ($1,100 + 10% × $1,100) or less than $990 ($1,100 – 10% × $1,100). The test is met for the initial two-thirds of the lease.

What about years seven through nine? The annual rent ($600) cannot be greater than the highest rent payable during the initial two-thirds of the lease term ($1,200) and less than one-half of the initial term average annual rent (1/2 × $1,100 = $550). This program just meets the test, so the IRS under the *Guidelines* would not object to the steps as presented.

▶ **Tax Law Observation:**   Section 467, added by the 1984 Deficit Reduction Act, may require certain lessors and lessees to accrue uneven lease rental income and deductions in a level manner. Section 467 applies to an equipment lease totaling over $250,000 in rental payments under which either (1) at least one amount is allocable to the use of property during a calendar year or (2) there are increases in the amount of rent to be paid over the lease term. Accrual will not be required where the lease payments satisfy a presumptive tax-avoidance test. Parties to a leasing transaction should review Section 467 when considering an uneven rent structure.

9.   Limited Use Property

Limited use property is property not expected to be useful to or usable by the lessor except for purposes of continued leasing or transfer to the lessee or a member of the lessee group. The IRS says this means that, at the lease term's end, there will probably be no potential lessees or buyers other than the lessee or members of the lessee group. As a result, the lessor will probably sell or rent the property to the lessee or a member of the lessee group, so that, in effect, the lessee will receive the equipment's ownership benefits for substantially its entire useful life. To obtain a favorable ruling, it is necessary to establish that it is commercially feasible for a party, not the lessee or a member of the lessee group, to lease or buy the property from the lessor—demonstrating that it is not limited use property.

D.   Ruling Request Submission Requirements

In submitting a ruling request, the taxpayer must present the information the *Guidelines* require in the manner prescribed by Revenue Procedure 75-28, as modified by Revenue Procedure 79-48.

Generally, all the parties to the transaction, including the lessor and the lessee, must join in the ruling request. The request must contain a summary of the surrounding facts. The request must be accompanied by certain relevant documents, such as the lease, or, in the case of a brokered transaction, any economic analysis, prospectus, or other document used to induce the lessor to invest.

The request must include detailed information covering, for example:

- The type and quality of the leased equipment.
- Whether the equipment is new, reconstructed, used, or rebuilt.
- When, how, and where the equipment will be, or was, first placed in service or use.
- Whether the equipment will be permanently or temporarily attached to land, buildings, or other property.
- The flow of funds among the parties.

The request must disclose the lease term, and any renewals or extensions, and any purchase and sale options. This includes any right the lessor has to force a purchase or to abandon the equipment, and any intention to give this right in the future.

If the lessee, or any related party, must pay for any cost overruns or will invest in the equipment, by, for example, contributing to its cost or paying for an improvement, modification, or addition, this must be disclosed. The request must also identify any unrelated parties who will provide funds.

Information covering any lessee related guarantees, whether the profit and positive cash flow tests have been satisfied, and any uneven rent structure must be presented. An economic analysis showing that the minimum "at risk" investment rules will be satisfied has to be submitted. A detailed description of the debt and the repayment terms; any lease provisions relating to indemnities, termination, obsolescence, casualty, or insurance; and the party who is to claim any investment credit must be set out. The request must include representations that the property is not limited use property. The parties must submit an expert's opinion on the equipment's residual value, setting out the manner in which the conclusion was determined, any removal or delivery costs at the end of the lease term, and the useful life of the equipment remaining at the end of the term.

E.   The Foundation Tax Rules

Two decades before issuing the *Guidelines*, the IRS issued Revenue Ruling 55-540 [1955-12 CB 39] setting out the factors that it considers in deciding whether a leasing transaction is really a conditional sale for tax purposes. Unlike the *Guidelines*, Revenue Ruling 55-540 sets out the IRS audit position rather than dealing with what is required to obtain a ruling. The ruling is, however, much less useful than the *Guidelines* because it is less precise. But, by checking its tests you will help assure a leasing transaction's viability.

In that ruling, the IRS stated generally that whether:

an agreement, which in form is a lease, is in substance a conditional sales contract depends upon the intent of the parties as evidenced by the provisions of the agreement, read in the light of the facts and circumstances existing at the time the agreement was executed.

In addition, it provided that in "ascertaining such intent no single test, or any special combination of tests, is absolutely determinative," no "general rule, applicable to all cases can be laid down," and that each "case must be decided in the light of its particular facts." The IRS then went on to state that an intent that would cause an arrangement to be treated as a sale instead of a lease for tax purposes is found if one or more of the following factors exist:

- Portions of the periodic payments are specifically made applicable to an equity interest to be acquired by the lessee.
- The lessee will acquire title to the property under lease on the payment of a stated amount of "rentals" that the lessee under the contract must make.
- The total amount that the lessee must pay for a relatively short period of use constitutes an inordinately large proportion of the total sum required to acquire title.
- The agreed "rental" payments materially exceed the current fair rental value.
- The property may be acquired by the lessee under a purchase option at a price that is nominal in relation to the property's value at the time the option may be exercised (determined at the time the agreement was entered into) or which is relatively small when compared to the total payments that the lessee must make.
- Some portion of the periodic payments is specifically designated as interest or is otherwise readily recognizable as the equivalent of interest.

▶ **Observation:** Revenue Ruling 55-540 provides guidelines for determining whether a conditional sale contract exists. The assumption is that, if a conditional sales contract does not exist and the parties structured the transaction as a tax lease, everyone is on safe ground. If the transaction is structurally complex, experienced tax leasing counsel may be necessary to get adequate assurances.

F.   Potential Penalties

Not only do the parties risk losing their tax benefits if a transaction fails to qualify as a true lease, they also run a risk of incurring penalties. The 5% negligence penalty is possible if the parties fail to exercise reasonable care. In addition, in several Tax Court cases, the Section 6659 overvaluation penalty has been imposed on lessors where the court found that there was no reasonable expectation that the lessor could make an economic profit—apart from tax benefits—from the leasing transaction. The Section 6659 penalty is 30% of the amount of the understatement attributable to the overvaluation (here, the equipment's basis). Applying only to individuals (including partnerships) and closely held or personal service corporations, Section 6659 is not applicable to all lessors, but is a potential risk in certain leasing transactions.

G.   A Quick 'True' Lease Checklist

The following checklist can be used as a guide to determine whether a lease transaction's basic features comply with the *Guidelines'* requirements. If any answer is "No," there may be a problem.

	YES	NO
1. Has the lessor made an initial equity investment equal to at least 20% of equipment cost?	☐	☐
2. Is the initial equity investment unconditional in nature?	☐	☐
3. Will the lessor's minimum investment remain equal at least to 20% of equipment cost during the lease term?	☐	☐
4. Is the estimated residual value of the equipment at least equal to 20% of equipment's original cost?	☐	☐
5. Will the useful life of the equipment remaining at the end of the lease term be equal to the longer of one year or 20% of the originally estimated useful life?	☐	☐
6. If there is a lessee purchase option, is it at fair market value as of the time of exercise?	☐	☐
7. Is the lessor without any rights to force a sale of the equipment to any party?	☐	☐

8. Is the lessor without any specific right to abandon the equipment?   **YES**   **NO** □ □

9. Has the lessor furnished all the equipment cost other than any third-party debt? □ □

10. Will the lessor have to bear the cost of any permanent equipment improvement, modification, or addition? □ □

11. If the lessee pays for a severable improvement, could the equipment be used for its intended use without it? □ □

12. If the lessee pays for a severable improvement, can the lessor buy it only at a price at least equal to its fair market value? □ □

13. If the lessee pays for a nonseverable improvement, could the equipment be used for its intended use without the improvement? □ □

14. If the lessee pays for a nonseverable improvement, will someone other than the lessee be able to use the equipment? □ □

15. Does every nonseverable improvement that is paid for by the lessee, not constitute a lessee investment? □ □

16. Will the lessor pay for any equipment cost overruns? □ □

17. Are all the equipment loans from lenders unrelated to the lessee? □ □

18. Is the transaction devoid of any indebtedness guarantees by the lessee or related parties? □ □

19. Will the lessor make a profit on the lease without considering the tax benefits? □ □

20. Will the transaction generate a positive cash flow for the lessor? □ □

21. Will the equipment have a use at the end of the lease term to someone other than to the lessee? □ □

22. Have the required backup information and material been submitted with the request for ruling? □ □

CHAPTER 9

Advantages and Risks of Leveraged Leasing Decisions

A. What Is the Concept of Leveraged Leasing?

The leveraged lease can be one of the most complex and sophisticated vehicles for financing capital equipment in today's financial marketplace. The individuals and firms in the leveraged leasing industry are aggressive and creative. As a result, the environment is one of innovation and intense competition.

Is the concept of a leveraged lease complex? Not really. It is simply a lease transaction in which the lessor puts in only a portion, usually 20% to 40%, of the funds necessary to buy the equipment and a third-party lender supplies the remainder. Because the benefits available to the lessor are generally based on the entire equipment cost, the lessor's investment is said to be "leveraged" with third-party debt.

Generally, the third-party loan is on a nonrecourse-to-the-lessor basis and ranges from 60% to 80% of the equipment's cost. The nonrecourse nature means the lender can only look to the lessee, the stream of rental payments that have been assigned to it, and the equipment for repayment. The lessor has no repayment responsibility even if the lessee defaults and the loan becomes uncollectible.

The fact that a nonrecourse lender cannot look to the lessor for the loan repayment if there is a problem is not as bad as it seems for two reasons:

- The lender will not make a nonrecourse loan unless the lessee is considered creditworthy, and,
- The lender's rights to any proceeds coming from a sale or re-release of the equipment comes ahead of any of the lessor's rights in the equipment and lease.

The lessor's equity investment is subordinated to the loan repayment obligation. If a lender only contributed, for example, 70% of the funds necessary, the subordination arrangement would put him in an over-collateralized loan position that, in turn, would decrease his lending risk.

Although the third-party loan is usually made on a nonrecourse basis, this is not always so. If the lessee's financial condition is weak, a lender may only be willing to make a recourse loan. Under this type of loan the lender can look to, or has recourse against, the lessor for repayment if it cannot be satisfied through the lessee or the equipment. The lessor still, however, has the economic advantage of a leveraged investment.

Although the concept of leveraging a lease investment is simple, the mechanics of putting the concept together is often complex. Leveraged lease transactions, particularly ones involving major dollar commitments, frequently involve many parties brought together through intricate arrangements. The "lessor" is typically a group of investors joined together by a partnership or trust structure. The partnership or trust is the legal owner, or "titleholder," of the equipment. The "lender" is often a group of lenders usually acting through a trust arrangement. This is further complicated by the fact that each participant will be represented by counsel with varying views. As a result, the job of organizing, drafting, and negotiating the necessary documents is generally very difficult.

▶ **Observation:** Because the expenses involved in documenting a leveraged lease can be substantial, transactions involving less than $2 million worth of equipment can be economically difficult to structure as a leveraged lease. If, however, documentation fees (such as counsel fees) can be kept within reason, smaller equipment amounts can be financed in this manner. In many cases a prospective lessor or underwriter has an in-house legal staff with the ability to originate and negotiate the required documents. If so, this will help keep costs down.

Generally, leveraged lease financings are arranged for prospective lessees by companies or individuals who specialize in structuring and negotiating these types of leases. These individuals and firms are referred to as lease underwriters. Essentially, their function is to structure the lease economics, find the lessor-investors, and provide the necessary expertise to ensure that the transaction will get done. In a limited number of situations, they also find the debt participants. They do not generally participate as an investor in the equipment. Because the vast majority of leveraged leases are brought about with the assistance of lease underwriters, lease underwriting has become synonymous with leveraged leasing.

The premise on which lease underwriting services are provided by an underwriter (that is, on a "best efforts" or "firm" basis) varies significantly. It is, therefore, worthwhile at this stage to explore the two types of underwriter offers: "best efforts" and "firm commitment" underwriting arrangements.

1. A 'Best Efforts' Underwriting Arrangement Can Be Risky

Lease underwriting transactions are frequently bid on a "best efforts" basis. This type of bid is an offer by the underwriter to do the best he can to put a transaction together under the terms set out in his or her proposal letter. There are no guarantees of performance. As a result, a prospective lessee accepting the offer may not know for some time whether he or she has the financing.

In practice, a best efforts underwriting is not as risky as it appears. Most reputable underwriters have a good feel for the market when bidding on this basis and usually can deliver what they propose. Thus, there is a good chance they will be able to get "firm commitments" from one or more prospective lessor-investors to participate on the basis offered.

▶ **Recommendations:**
■ A prospective lessee must always keep in mind that a best efforts underwriting proposal gives no guarantee the transaction can be completed under the terms proposed. Thus, he or she must give careful consideration to the experience and reputation of an underwriter proposing on this basis before awarding a transaction to him or her. An inability to perform as presented can result in the loss of valuable time.
■ When there is adequate equipment delivery lead time, a prospective lessee may be inclined to award a transaction to an unknown underwriter who has submitted an unusually low bid. There is, however, a risk that must be considered. If the transaction is so underpriced that it cannot be sold in the "equity" market, it may meet resistance when it is reoffered on more attractive investor terms. This can happen merely because it has been seen, or "shopped," too much. It is an unfortunate fact that when an investor is presented with a transaction that he knows has been shopped, even if the terms are favorable, he may refuse to consider it. This can happen merely because it has been around for a long time. A prospective lessee, thus, should not be too eager to accept a "low ball" best efforts bid unless he has taken a hard look at the underwriter's ability to perform.
■ Best efforts underwriters sometimes submit proposals that are substantially below the market. At times this happens by mistake. For example, transactions may have been priced in good faith based on acceptable investor market yields, but by the time the award is made the market has moved upward. At other times, an underwriter may intentionally underprice a

transaction to make sure he wins it. If it cannot be placed as proposed, he will go back and attempt to get the prospective lessee to agree to a higher rental rate. With his competitors no longer involved, he may be in a good position to do this. A prospective lessee with near-term deliveries must be particularly careful in recognizing this possibility. Otherwise, he or she may have little choice but to be pushed into a less favorable deal.

■ A prospective lessee can control the risk of nonperformance under a best efforts proposal by putting a time limit on the award, for example, by requiring the underwriter to come up with, or "circle," interested parties within one week following the award and securing formal commitments by the second week.

■ It is not unheard of for a prospective lessee to make a time limit award to an unusually low bidding, or unknown, underwriter without telling the remaining bidders. The purpose is to try to keep them around just in case the underwriter cannot perform. This can be unfair to an underwriter who, in good faith, is continuing to spend time and money on the transaction in the hope of winning it. Doing this can also hurt a prospective lessee in the long run. *Reason*: It is likely that the other underwriters will find out that this happened. Once the word gets around that a company does business in this manner, reputable underwriters may refuse to participate in future biddings. Even if they do participate, they may quote rates that have not been as finely tuned as possible. *Reason*: They will not spend the time or money necessary in situations in which they may not be treated fairly. Thus, this tactic is not recommended because a prospective lessee may, as a result, not see the best possible market rates.

2. A 'Firm Commitment' Underwriting Arrangement Is Often the Best

From a prospective lessee's viewpoint, a "firm commitment" underwriting proposal is generally the preferred type of offer. When an underwriter has "come in firm" he is guaranteeing to put the proposed lease financing together. Typically, before an underwriter submits this type of proposal, he or she has solid commitments from lessor-investors to enter into the transaction on the terms presented. This, however, is not always the case. His or her firm bid may only represent his or her willingness to be the lessor if he or she cannot find a third-party lessor.

▶ **Recommendations:**
■ If an underwriter proposing on a firm basis does not have "committed equity" at the time his proposal is submitted, a prospective lessee may be subject to certain risks. Unless the underwriter is in a strong financial position, his commitment may be worthless if a third-party lessor cannot be found. Thus, a prospective lessee must always investigate whether an underwriter has lined up one or more lessor-investors. If not, the underwriter's

financial condition must be reviewed to determine, before making the award, whether he has the financial ability to stand behind it.

■ Underwriters sometimes state they have firm "equity" even though they have nothing more than a verbal indication from a prospective lessor-investor's contact that he will recommend the transaction to his approving committee. Thus, a prospective lessee must ask to be put in touch with each lessor-investor to confirm his position. Doing this will also ensure that there are no misunderstandings as to the transaction terms.

B. Leveraged Lease Participants Have Unique Characteristics

Generally, a leveraged lease transaction will involve more parties than a nonleveraged one. At a minimum, the participants will include an equity participant (lessor-investor), a debt participant, a lessee, and an equipment supplier. In the event the equity or debt participant acts through a trust arrangement, a trustee will also be a party. Often, these participants have certain unique characteristics.

1. The Equity Participants

An investor in a leveraged lease is referred to as an "equity participant." Generally, more than one investor is involved on the "equity side" of a leveraged lease. These equity participants, or owners, often act together through a trust arrangement. A trust provides partnership-like tax treatment, while at the same time giving corporate-like liability protection. The equity participants are deemed the beneficial owners of the equipment. Legal title is held by the representative (the trustee) of the trust.

It is possible when more than one lessor-investor is involved for them to act through a partnership arrangement, rather than a trust. Here, the partnership is the lessor. Legal title to the equipment is held in the partnership name.

▶ **Recommendation:** The actual form of equipment owning entity, (that is, trust or partnership), will depend on the particular needs of each transaction and the participants. Counsel must be used to select the best form for a particular situation.

The typical leveraged lease equity participant is an "institutional investor." Banks, for example, come within this category. Because, however, a leveraged lease can be an attractive investment, many "regular" corporations and, in a limited number of situations, wealthy individuals are also potential lessor-investor candidates.

Some prospective leveraged lease investors have their own leasing companies actively looking for lease investment opportunities. But many do not. Those that do not, often referred to as "passive" investors, usually rely exclusively on the lease underwriting community to locate leveraged lease investments for them. Typically, the passive type investor also depends heavily on underwriters for advice on the structure and documentation of these investments.

2.   The Lessee

A leveraged lease transaction, as with any lease transaction, does not begin to come into existence until an equipment user, the prospective lessee, decides to consider leasing as a way to finance the acquisition of equipment it needs. Thus, the lessee is the key participant in any lease financing.

Because documenting a leveraged lease transaction tends to be expensive, this type of lease usually makes economic sense only for financings involving a significant dollar amount of equipment. As a result, the type of potential lessee is usually a large equipment user who has the financial strength to support the obligations involved.

3.   The Debt Participants

A lender in a leveraged lease transaction is generally referred to as a "debt participant." It is common for there to be more than one debt participant involved in a particular lease. When this is the case, they frequently form a trust through which they will act. The document setting out the trust's terms is referred to as the trust indenture. The amount of money each debt participant intends to loan is transferred to the trust, which in turn lends it to the lessor. The loan made to the lessor is generally nonrecourse in nature. The loan is represented by a note or series of notes payable over the lease term from the rent proceeds the lessor receives.

If properly organized, the lender's trust will receive partnership-like income tax treatment and corporate-like liability protection. Each participant, as a beneficial owner of the trust estate, is treated for income tax purposes as though he made his loan directly to the lessor and will not have a direct exposure to any third-party claim.

Leveraged lease third-party debt is often supplied by banks or insurance companies. However, because a leveraged lease loan is no different from any other loan secured by personal property, generally any lender able and willing to make a secured loan is a potential loan source. There is, however, one limiting factor—the prospective lender's ability to offer competitive market interest rates. The debt interest rate is a critical factor in the rent computation. A leveraged lease rent quotation is usually premised on an assumed debt interest rate. Thus, the lower the interest rate the more profit a lessor makes and vice versa. This is so, unless the prospective lessee gets the benefit or bears the risk of interest rate variations. In the latter case the underwriter's proposal will provide that if the debt interest rate comes in other than assumed, the rent will be adjusted upward or downward to appropriately reflect the variance. As a result only the most rate aggressive lenders (such as, banks and insurance companies) are usually able to compete, particularly in the better credit transactions.

4. The Underwriter

The lease underwriting business has a relatively low capital entrance requirement. Because of this there is an overabundance of "packagers" offering lease underwriting services. These packagers run the gamut from individuals operating out of telephone booths to investment bankers to specialized lease underwriting firms. Some are well versed in leveraged leasing economics and documentation and others know little more than the basics. The choice of an underwriter is critical to the success of a transaction. Those who have a solid understanding of the business and who are continually active in the underwriting market are more likely to be able to better structure and ensure leveraged lease financing success.

▶ **Recommendation:**   Prospective lessees entert...ning leveraged lease proposals must make sure before awarding a transaction that the intended underwriter has the qualifications to do the job necessary, both from an experience and a technical standpoint.

5. The Equipment Manufacturer

The equipment manufacturer or distributor involved in a leveraged lease transaction usually does nothing more than sell the agreed on equipment to the lessor at the negotiated price. Once the full price has been paid, his only obligation is to stand behind his product for any warranty period.

In some situations, the vendor's role is not limited to merely selling the equipment to the lessor. He sometimes provides various inducements to a lessor to assist in selling his equipment. For example, he may be willing to guarantee some of the lessee's lease obligations in situations when the lessee's financial condition is weak.

6.   The Investor's Representative—The Owner's Trustee

In the event equity participants act through a trust, a trustee will be appointed to be the trust's representative. The trustee is sometimes referred to as the owner's trustee and is usually a commercial bank or trust company.

The owner's trustee is considered the mechanical arm of the trust. *Reason*: The trust arrangement specifically defines the trustee's responsibilities. For example, one of his prescribed duties will be to divide up and disburse the lease funds among the various equity participants under a predetermined formula. As the equity participants' representative, he makes sure their investment is protected by monitoring their rights under the lease.

7.   The Lender's Representative—The Indenture Trustee

When a trust arrangement is established for the debt participants, a trustee, referred to as the indenture trustee, is employed to represent the trust. The trust agreement clearly defines the indenture trustee's duties. For example, the indenture trustee collects the money to be loaned from the debt participants and then turns it over to the lessor. As a part of the loan transaction, the indenture trustee takes an assignment of the lease and a security interest in the equipment as security for the loan repayment. Typically, a commercial bank or trust company is selected to act as the indenture trustee.

C.   How Different Is the Leveraged Lease Document?

The format of a typical leveraged lease document is essentially the same as that of any other finance lease. However, the terms and provisions are usually more detailed. *Reason*: The major dollar commitments involved usually dictate that greater attention be paid to each aspect.

What about the supplemental documents? There are typically a greater number involved in a leveraged lease transaction than in a "straight" lease transaction. For example, in addition to those found in nonleveraged lease situations, such as the lease, opinions of counsel, and board of director resolutions, the leveraged transaction documentation will at a minimum usually include trust agreements, a participation agreement, promissory notes, and a security and loan agreement.

D.   Three Advantages to the Lessee in a Leveraged Lease

In certain situations, a leveraged lease transaction offers many benefits for a prospective lessee. It may in some cases be the only economically viable approach to take.

1.   The Rent Can Be More Attractive

As a rule of thumb a competitively bid leveraged lease transaction will provide a lower cost to a lessee than a comparable term nonleveraged lease. Logically, if a company can borrow at a more favorable interest rate than a lessor, it stands to reason that if the lessor pays part of the equipment's cost with a loan based on the lessee's credit he can charge lower rents without sacrificing his economic return. There are, of course, exceptions to this rule, and each situation must be examined on its own. For example, if the dollar amount of equipment financed is small, the documentation expenses involved can offset the economic benefits gained through leveraging.

2.   There Is a Better Market for Large Transactions

Major dollar equipment lease financings can generally be arranged more readily by using a leveraged lease structure. This is because a lessor-investor only has to come up with a portion of the required equipment, the remainder being provided by a third party lender.

Because many investors and lenders are unwilling to make a major dollar investment in one transaction, a number of lessor-investors and lenders must frequently be brought together. By forming investor and lender syndicates, they can keep the dollar exposure for each within desired limits.

Bringing together more than one investor and lender can be beneficial for a lessee. When the investment risk is spread among a greater number of participants, there is a better likelihood that a large dollar lease financing can be done at more reasonable rates. No one party has such a great exposure that he believes he must charge a premium for the risk. The disadvantage is the added paperwork. However, a competent and experienced underwriter will be able to successfully usher everyone through the documentation tangle—a reason why the choice of the underwriter is a critical factor.

▶ **Observation:**   There are a small number of prospective lessor-investors willing to act as the sole equity participant in major equipment lease financings. The advantage to using such an investor is that the necessary approvals and potential complications will be kept to a minimum. Generally, however, this type of investor realizes not many others are willing to take an entire major transaction and their rent charge will usually be high. Whether the extra rate is worth the reduced risks of a simpler transaction is a matter of judgment. An experienced underwriter should be of great assistance in evaluating the tradeoff.

3.   The Lessors Can Be More Competitive

The type of lessor interested in pursuing a leveraged lease investment is often most concerned over the available equipment ownership tax benefits. As a result, such a lessor may be more willing to be more aggressive on those aspects of a lease transaction not impacting the lease's tax consequences.

E.   Investment Pitfalls and Recommendations for Prospective Lessors

A prospective lessor must consider many factors before deciding whether to enter into a particular lease transaction, leveraged or not. These considerations, however, are particularly crucial for leveraged lease investors. *Reason*: The transactions are typically very competitive and the investment economics finely tuned. A slight mistake or change in the investment assumptions, thus, can have a major adverse impact.

For a prospective lessor-investor to evaluate the risks involved, he must know what they are. The following explanation will alert the reader to the fundamental points that must be considered by every lease investor.

1.   Equipment Delivery Delays Can Destroy Profits

The date when the equipment is delivered determines when the ownership tax benefits will be available to a lessor. When these benefits are available is a critical factor in a prospective lessor's analysis of his anticipated economic return. An unexpected delivery delay can have a serious negative impact. Consider, for example, a transaction entered into by a calendar year taxpayer-investor based on the assumption that the equipment will be delivered no later than the end of the current year. A following year delivery could jeopardize his contemplated return. *Reason*: The equipment ownership tax benefits would not be available until the next year. If the transaction had been priced in a competitive market, that slippage could easily make the transaction's economics completely unacceptable to the investor.

▶ **Recommendations:**

■ A prospective lessor-investor can protect himself against a potential yield deterioration because of equipment delivery delays in two ways. The first is by establishing a commitment cutoff date. That is, setting a point in time after which he will no longer be obligated to buy and lease delivering equipment. A second way is to provide for a rent adjustment that preserves the transaction's economics if a certain delivery date is passed.

■ From a lessee's viewpoint, either of the lessor delivery delay solutions explained in the above Recommendation can create problems. The first solution, however, is generally considered the more dangerous. When a delivery cutoff date is imposed, a prospective lessee could end up without a lease financing source for the late equipment. When a rental adjustment is permitted, a lessee may be confronted with an undesirably high rent. In the latter situation, however, he at least knows that lease financing will be available regardless of the delay.

■ A prospective lessor should be careful when establishing the rental adjustment criterion to apply to equipment delivered late. For example, if the rental analysis is based on certain yield and after-tax cash flow standards, he should make sure the adjustment provision will permit him to maintain both criteria because they will not run parallel. In other words, maintaining yield will not necessarily maintain after-tax cash flows and vice versa.

2. The Lessee's Financial Condition Is Crucial

The financial strength of a prospective lessee is an important lessor consideration in any lease transaction. It should be of prime concern to a passive type lessor-investor with limited equipment knowledge and remarketing capability. A lease default could easily endanger his invested capital and anticipated economic return. It is of utmost importance, therefore, for the prospective lessee's financial standing to be thoroughly reviewed.

3. Changes in Tax Law Can Eliminate Profits

If the tax benefits anticipated by investing in an equipment lease are eliminated or reduced because of a change in tax law, a lessor-investor could be confronted with an extremely unfavorable investment. The possibility of a tax law change is difficult, if not impossible, to predict. It is not, however, generally considered an unreasonable risk to assume in certain situations.

In major leveraged leases, lessees are sometimes "forced" to indem-nify the lessor against any adverse change in the tax law that causes loss of a tax benefit. The tax indemnification provisions are usually incorpo-rated directly in the lease agreement.

▶ Observations:

■ Prospective lessees have become increasingly successful in placing the tax benefit loss risks from changes in law on the lessor. It usually depends on who has the most negotiating strength. A favorite lessee argument is that the burden properly belongs on the lessor. *Reason*: He is better able to assess them through his experience. The argument has some validity as to "regu-lar" leasing companies. It may not be true, however, as far as the typical leveraged lease investor is concerned. In his passive role he may not have the type of exposure necessary to make the appropriate evaluation.

■ A prospective lessor-investor can hedge against the change-in-tax-law risk by having the right to appropriately adjust the rental rate or to exclude equipment that will be affected and that has not yet been delivered. The danger to a prospective lessee with these lessor solutions is that he may have to pay too high a lease rate or may be without financing at the last minute.

4. Income Variations Can Be Dangerous

A typical leveraged lease transaction may not be economically via-ble for a lessor-investor unless he can use all of the available equipment ownership tax benefits in a timely manner. If the investor had, for example, an unexpected net loss for the year the equipment was placed in service, he would have no taxable income against which to apply the tax benefits. The inability to use the tax benefits when anticipated would reduce the transaction's expected time value return. The time value concept says $1 received today is worth more than $1 received a year from today because of its earning capability. Thus, a lease investment must be looked at by a prospective lessor-investor in light of a careful and realistic appraisal of his present and future earning situation.

5. Tax Rate Variations—Consider the Possibility

How valuable the tax benefits that are available from owning equip-ment are to a lessor-investor depends to a large extent on his overall effective income tax rate. The greater his effective tax rate the more tax savings he will realize from the tax benefits. Any decrease in his tax rate will reduce the favorable impact of the available write-offs. Thus, a prospective lessor-investor must consider any potential income tax rate change in light of the future tax benefits coming from a lease investment.

▶ **Observation:**   A prospective lessor-investor can protect himself against an adverse tax rate change by getting the prospective lessee to agree to indemnify him in the event it occurs. In today's market, however, it is unlikely that any prospective lessee would agree to provide this type of indemnity.

6. Incorrect Residual Value Assessment—
An Easy Trap

Generally, the value of the equipment at the end of a lease, referred to as its "residual value," can have a dramatic impact on the profitability of the transaction. If a prospective lessor's residual value estimate is too high when he analyzes a lease investment, his return will be adversely affected. For example, if a prospective investor makes his investment analysis assuming a certain return based on selling the equipment at the end of the lease for 20% of its original cost, the transaction's profitability is reduced if the equipment sells for only 5% of its original cost. The overall effect of the diminished value depends on its importance in the investor's analysis. Very often it is a significant factor.

▶ **Recommendation:**   It is advisable for a prospective lessor-investor to consult an equipment appraiser for assistance in making a reasonable residual value estimate. Remember, however, that an appraiser's opinion as to future value is nothing more than a professional guess. It does not assure the investor of the equipment's future worth. It does, of course, provide a degree of comfort that would otherwise not exist.

7. An Early Lease Termination Must
Be Considered

A prospective lessor-investor must make sure that a permitted early lease termination will have little, if any, impact on his lease investment economics. Consider, for example, a 20-year full payout lease that is terminated at the end of 2 years. To begin with, the investor's future lease profits will be cut off. Depending on how the rents have been reported for income purposes, an early termination can cause a "book" loss. For example, if the rent income was reported faster than actually received the early termination might make it necessary to report as a loss the difference between what was reported on the income statement and what has actually been taken in.

If the equipment cannot be favorably re-leased in a timely manner, the lessor may be forced to sell the equipment immediately. An unplanned sale situation can make it difficult for a lessor to realize the best price. This is particularly so if large amounts of equipment scattered all over the country are involved. Having adequate and inexpensive storage space can ease the problem. *Reason*: The lessor may be better able to afford to wait the market out. Lessors sometimes negotiate the right to store it on the lessee's premises free of charge. However, this may not be a good solution if the parties are in an adversary situation.

Having to sell equipment early may also create another problem—a recapture of tax benefits claimed. If the tax benefits are an important part of the lessor's yield, a recapture can further destroy the already faltering lease economics.

Incorporating a "termination value" concept into the lease can solve the early termination economic risk. Essentially a termination value is an amount a lessee would be obligated to pay to the lessor to help protect his investment and anticipated return.

8.   Casualty Loss—Are There Protections?

The types of problems confronting a lessor if there is an equipment casualty loss are similar to those that must be addressed if a lease termination occurs, that is, future profits will be unavailable, tax benefit recapture may result, and a "book" loss may have to be reported. There is, however, an important difference—the equipment will have little, if any, value. When a casualty loss occurs, therefore, the lessor is left without its collateral protection and must look to the lessee and any insurance proceeds for loss repayment. This is a good reason why prospective lessor-investors must make sure that the lessee is a creditworthy entity and, also, that adequate insurance is secured and maintained.

▶ **Recommendation:**   If a prospective lessee will be obligated to insure the leased equipment, the prospective lessor should require evidence at the time of the lease closing that the appropriate insurance coverage has been secured. Also, arrangements should be made for the insurance company to notify the lessor if the lessee does anything, such as neglecting to pay the premiums, that could cause the policy to lapse. In this way, the lessor will have the opportunity of taking over any lapsed obligations to assure continued coverage.

Even though the lessee must maintain casualty loss insurance, prospective lessors should also incorporate a "casualty loss value" concept. Casualty values, sometimes referred to as "stipulated loss values," are calculated in much the same manner as termination values. Their purpose is to protect the lessor's investment position in the event of a casualty loss. Under this concept, the lessee in effect guarantees that the lessor will receive a certain amount of money if there is an equipment casualty. The amount decreases after each rent payment is made, to reflect an appropriate recognition of the lessor's decreased financial exposure. It typically will be sufficient to repay the lessor's outstanding investment and any remaining equipment loan obligations. Also, it will provide the lessor with his profit, at least to the date of the loss. Typically, the lessee is given a credit for any insurance money received as a result of the loss against the amount owed. In effect, the lessee becomes an insurer of the lessor's investment and profit.

9.   The Economic Analysis—A Critical Aspect

When a lease underwriter presents a lease investment to a prospective lessor-investor, he generally submits an economic analysis showing the return the investor can expect. If the method of analysis is incorrect, or unrealistic, a prospective investor can end up with a disastrous investment. It is not uncommon, for example, for an underwriter to incorporate a sinking fund arrangement in his analysis calculations. The sinking fund simply improves the investor's economics by assuming that cash available over the lease term will earn a certain amount of interest. If for some reason the interest rate assumption is too high, the return analysis will be misleading. Thus, a prospective investor must always verify any economic presentation on which it intends to base its investment decision.

▶ **Recommendation:**   If a prospective lessor-investor cannot independently analyze the resulting economics of investing in a lease submitted by an underwriter, he should bring in an independent expert to review the presentation.

10.   A Long Term Commitment Can Present a Problem

Frequently, an equipment lease agreement is entered into well before the equipment actually delivers. This is done for a number of reasons. From a lessor's viewpoint, the faster he gets the lease "signed up," the less risk there will be that the prospective lessee will change his mind. Prospective lessees on the other hand, are often interested in proceeding as quickly as possible to avoid last minute documentation problems. If the transaction calls for the lessor to hold a substantial amount of money available over a long delivery period, an unexpected decision by the lessee not to lease the equipment when it arrives will result in an alternate investment opportunity loss for the lessor during the commitment period. To avoid this type of problem, lessors frequently require lessees to agree to pay commitment fees or nonutilization fees. In effect, these fees guarantee that they will be compensated for holding their funds available.

11.   Documentation Expenses Can Ruin a Lease Investment

Expenses, such as legal fees, involved in documenting a lease transaction can be substantial. Depending on the transaction's complexity, it is not unheard of for the expenses to run into the hundreds of thousands of dollars. A $30,000 expense for a $3 million lease investment may be acceptable, a $500,000 expense will probably not be. If an investor must pay these expenses, a substantial bill could ruin his investment economics. Thus, it is essential for a prospective lease investor to know who is responsible for the various charges and what the estimated amounts will be. Of particular concern will be who is responsible for the expenses if the transaction falls apart before the lease is signed.

▶ **Recommendations:**

■ In an underwritten leveraged lease transaction, the responsibility for the various documentation expenses is frequently outlined in the underwriter's proposal letter. In many cases, the underwriter will offer to pay most of the expenses. It is, however, an area of negotiation between the parties. A prospective investor must make sure he has not inadvertently assumed any expense responsibility that has not been considered. The more the expense burden can be shifted to someone else, the less the risk the economic integrity of the investment will be endangered.

■ Frequently, a lease underwriter will place the burden for expenses incurred in a collapsed lease transaction on the prospective lessee. It is recommended, however, that a prospective lessee at least require a sharing of the expenses with any other party contributing to the failure.

F.   A Checklist for the Leveraged Lease Investor

Before making a commitment to invest in a leveraged lease, a prospective lessor-investor must consider the following points:

■ If the equipment will not be put on lease at the time the lease commitment is signed, does it matter when the equipment actually delivers? If so:

- Does the lease agreement provide for a cutoff date beyond which the lessor will not be obligated to buy and lease the equipment?

- If there is not an equipment delivery cutoff date, does the lease permit the lessor to appropriately adjust the rents if his economics are affected?

- Can the lessee substitute equipment if specific equipment delivers late or never arrives? If so, are there controls on the type that will be acceptable?

■ Has the prospective lessee's financial condition been thoroughly reviewed?

■ If any credit support for the lessee's lease obligations will be provided, has the financial condition of the supporting party been carefully reviewed?

■ Has tax counsel been consulted as to any near-term possibility of the tax laws changing so as to affect the anticipated equipment ownership tax benefits?

■ In the event there is a tax law change affecting the equipment ownership tax benefits, will the lessee have to indemnify the lessor for any resulting adverse effect?

■ Can the entire future tax benefits generated by a lease investment be used? That is, will the lessor's taxable income be sufficient to cover the available writeoffs?

■ Has tax counsel been consulted as to any future federal income tax rate changes? If there is a change adversely affecting the leased equipment, who must bear the burden?

■ Is the residual value of the equipment an important factor in the lessor's economic analysis? If so:

  ● Has it been properly assessed?

  ● Has a qualified equipment appraiser been consulted?

■ Will the lessor's economics be protected if there is an early lease termination?

  ● If it results from a lease default?

  ● If it results from a permitted termination?

■ If a termination value concept has been incorporated to protect a lessor's investment position, have the values been verified?

■ Will the lessor's investment position be protected if there is an equipment casualty loss?

■ If a stipulated loss value (also referred to as casualty loss value) concept has been incorporated in the lease, has each value been verified?

■ Will an underwriter's economic analysis of a proposed lease investment be relied on? If so:

  ● Has it been independently checked?

  ● Are all the investment criteria assumptions, such as sinking fund interest rate, realistic from the prospective lessor's standpoint?

■ Must the prospective lessor make a long-term commitment to buy and lease equipment? If so will the lessee be able to decide at the last minute not to lease the equipment without a penalty? If not, has a proper commitment fee or nonutilization fee been incorporated?

■ Have the expenses for documenting the lease and the responsibility for payment been clearly defined

  ● If the transaction actually goes through?

  ● If the transaction collapses before the lease documents are signed?

CHAPTER 10
Financial Analysis Of Leases

A. Overview

While, as described in Chapter 1, there are a variety of factors to be considered when a prospective lessee or lessor decides whether to enter into an equipment lease, the lease's financial consequences are always important, and often decisive.

A prospective lessee, thus, should not choose to lease before making a financial comparision with the other available methods of financing the equipment's acquisition. The extent of the analysis will, of course, depend on how significant the commitment will be. Similarly, a prospective lessor should not commit to a lease until he has reviewed it for investment soundness.

This chapter explains the financial concepts involved in the analysis of a finance lease, both from a prospective lessee's and a prospective lessor's viewpoint. While not exploring every possible method of financial lease analysis, the explanation provides the reader with a concise foundation in lessee and lessor financial lease analysis.

B. The Importance of Cash Flow and Timing for a Lessee

In making a financial assessment of whether to lease or buy equipment, a prospective lessee must take the varying cash flows, and their timing, into account for each alternative. Stated simply, how much are the cash inflows and outflows, and when do they occur? The timing of the cash inflows and outflows is critical because of the principle— referred to as the time value of money—that money received earlier is worth more than money later received.

The following example illustrates how taking cash flow and its timing into account alters the result of an analysis.

Illustrative Example—*Cash Flow and Time Value*:   An equipment user is considering two options: Leasing equipment over a seven-year period with an annual rent of $990 payable at the beginning of each year; and buying the equipment using a seven-year loan with $1,000 annual payments due at each year's end. By choosing to lease, the company would have to pay the $990 out one year earlier than the $1,000 loan payment. If, for example, the company could earn 6% a year after taxes on its available funds, giving up the $990 in advance would result in a "loss" of $59.40 (6% × $990=$59.40) the first year. In this case, the advance payment could be said to cost $1,049.40 ($990 + $59.40=$1,049.40). Putting other considerations aside, the $1,000 loan payment would have been less expensive.

If the company were able to earn only 1% a year after taxes, paying the $990 yearly in advance rather than in arrears would result in only a $9.90 "loss" (1% × $990=$9.90). That is, the effective cost of payment in advance would have been $990.90, instead of $1,049.40.

C.   The Prospective Lessee's Analysis

Once a company has decided it needs certain equipment, it must determine how to finance its acquisition. The following will address three alternatives:

- The user leases the equipment (the Leasing Alternative).
- The user draws on his general funds to buy the equipment (the Purchase Alternative).
- The user takes out a specific loan to buy the equipment (the Financing Alternative).

This section will compare those three financial alternatives by using a common method for taking cash flows and their timing into account, sometimes referred to as the discounted cash flow—or present value—analysis method. The first step will be to compute the periodic costs and tax savings for each alternative. The next step will be to factor in the timing of those cash flows so there is a basis for comparison by calculating the present value of each alternative's cash flows. To compute the present value of a series of future cash flows, an interest rate—referred to as the discount rate—must be selected to discount the flows back to their present worth. The result will be the present value cost of the alternatives.

Because getting to these results involves numerous computations, the analysis will be set out using a hypothetical lease situation.

▶ **Note:**   The financial analysis computations from which the examples in this chapter were developed were done on SuperTrump™ a lease analysis computer software program, by Ivory Consulting Corp., Berkeley, California. The information from the computer analysis results was at times summarized by the author to aid in the explanation of the concepts described in the text material.

1.   A Typical User's Alternatives

White Industries wants to acquire a new computer and can use all available tax benefits. White is considering three financing alternatives—the Lease Alternative, the Purchase Alternative, and the Financing Alternative. Additional facts include (assumed for ease of illustration without regard to whether any applicable tax or other rules will be satisfied):

General Data
Computer Cost . . . .$1 million
Depreciable period . . . . .5 years
Residual value $0
ITC 0%
White Industries income tax rate 34%
White Industries tax year . . . . .Calendar year
Delivery date . . . . .January 1, 1987
Depreciation method . . . . .MACRS
Proposed Financial Lease
Lease term . . . . .7 years
Rental payments . . . .$206,303, payable in 7 annual payments in arrears.
Lease simple interest rate 10.1325%
Commencement date . . . . .January 1, 1987
Proposed Bank Loan
Loan amount . . . .$1 million, repayable in 7 equal annual payments of $222,603 in arrears.
Long term . . . . .7 years
Long term interest rate 12.5%
Commencement date . . . . .January 1, 1987

2.   The Cost of the Leasing Alternative

The first step is to compute the after-tax cost of the various alternatives. Table 10-1 sets out those costs, for the Leasing Alternative.

TABLE 10-1

Year	Rental Payments	Tax Savings From Rent Deductions	After-tax Cost	Cumulative After-tax Cost
1987	$ 0	$ 0	$ 0	$ 0
1988	206,303	70,143	136,160	136,160
1989	206,303	70,143	136,160	272,319
1990	206,303	70,143	136,160	408,479
1991	206,303	70,143	136,160	544,639
1992	206,303	70,143	136,160	680,799
1993	206,303	70,143	136,160	816,958
1994	206,303	70,143	136,160	953,118
Total	$1,444,118	$491,000	$953,118	n/a

Table 10-1 is computed as follows:

- The Rental Payments are the annual payments the lessee must make. These begin in 1988 because the rent is payable in arrears.
- The Tax Savings From Rent Deductions represents the federal income tax savings White Industries would realize from the rent deductions, computed at White Industries' assumed 34% bracket.
- The After-tax Cost is derived by subtracting the Tax Savings from the Rent Deductions from the Rental Payments.
- The Cumulative After-tax Cost represents the transaction's total after-tax cost as of each year end.

The result is a total after-tax cost of $953,118, if White Industries leases the computer.

3.   The Cost of the Purchase Alternative

The next step is to compute the after-tax cost of an outright purchase, shown in Table 10-2. The Annual Depreciation Expense is the amount White Industries would be entitled to deduct under MACRS as the computer owner over a five-year period. The other columns are computed as in the leasing example (Table 10-1):

TABLE 10-2

Year	Equity	Annual Depreciation Expense	Tax Savings	After-tax Cost	Cumulative After-tax Cost
1987	$1,000,000	$200,000	$ 68,000	$932,000	$932,000
1988		320,000	108,800	(108,000)	823,200
1989		192,000	65,280	(65,280)	757,920
1990		115,200	39,168	(39,168)	718,752
1991		115,200	39,168	(39,168)	679,584
1992		57,600	19,584	(19,584)	660,000
TOTAL	$1,000,000	$1,000,000	$340,000	$660,000	n/a

4. Comparing Cash Flows

Thus, at this point in the analysis, the Purchase Alternative seems substantially less expensive than the Lease Alternatives as its total after-tax cost is only $660,000 compared with $953,118 for leasing. However, this ignores the leasing cash flow advantage because, as shown in Table 10-3, the total cost of the lease is less until the sixth year.

TABLE 10-3

CASH FLOW COMPARISON

Year	Lease Cumulative After-tax Cost	Purchase Cumulative After-tax Cost	Lease Cash Advantage
1987	$ 0	$932,000	$932,000
1988	136,160	823,200	687,040
1989	272,319	757,920	485,601
1990	408,479	718,752	310,273
1991	544,639	679,584	134,945
1992	680,799	660,000	(20,799)
1993	816,958	660,000	(156,958)
1994	953,118	660,000	(293,118)

Plainly, leasing does conserve money in the early years, and those available funds could be put to use elsewhere. The resulting earnings on those funds would offset the disparity in total cost between the two alternatives. Thus, it cannot be concluded that leasing is more expensive until the present value of the two alternative's cash flows is compared.

To calculate the present value of the leasing and buying cash flows, White Industries must discount both alternatives' cash flows to their present worth. Choosing a 10% annual discount rate and assuming White Industries pays its taxes on December 15 of each year, the after-tax cash flows for the Leasing and Purchase Alternatives are as follows:

TABLE 10-4

PRESENT VALUE COMPARISON

| | --------LEASE------- | | --------PURCHASE------- | |
Year	After-tax Cost	Present Value	After-tax Cost	Present Value
Jan 1, 1987	$ 0	$ 0	$1,000,000	$1,000,000
Dec 15, 1987	0	0	(68,000)	(62,069)
	0	0	932,000	937,931
Jan 1, 1988	206,303	187,548	0	0
Dec 15, 1988	(70,143)	(58,204)	(108,800)	(90,282)
	136,160	129,343	(108,800)	(90,282)
Jan 1, 1989	206,303	170,432	0	0
Dec 15, 1989	(70,143)	(52,893)	(65,280)	(49,245)
	136,160	117,539	(65,280)	(49,245)
Jan 1, 1990	206,303	154,879	0	0
Dec 15, 1990	(70,143)	(48,066)	(39,168)	(26,861)
	136,160	106,813	(39,168)	(26,861)
Jan 1, 1991	206,303	140,744	0	0
Dec 15, 1991	(70,143)	(43,679)	(39,168)	(24,419)
	136,160	97,065	(39,168)	(24,419)
Jan 1, 1992	206,303	127,900	0	0
Dec 15, 1992	(70,143)	(39,693)	(19,584)	(11,100)
	136,160	88,207	(19,584)	(11,100)
Jan 1, 1993	206,303	116,228	0	0
Dec 15, 1993	(70,143)	(36,071)	0	0
	136,160	80,157	0	0
Jan 1, 1994	206,303	105,621	0	0
Dec 15, 1994	(70,143)	(32,779)	0	0
	136,160	72,842	0	0
Total	$ 953,118	$ 691,967	$ 660,000	$ 736,025

The discounted cash flow analysis clearly reverses the outcome. The Leasing Alternative's present worth is $691,967, while the Purchase Alternative's is $736,025. Based on this analysis, leasing the computer would be less expensive than buying with internal funds.

5.   The Financing Alternative

The next step is to calculate the Financing Alternative's cash flow in the same manner. The computation is the same as the Purchase Alternative (Table 10-2) with the additional factors being the payment of the 12.5% interest and the tax savings on deducting the interest. The after-tax cost calculations are as follows:

TABLE 10-5

Year	Debt Payments	Year-end Principal Balance Outstanding	12.5%Interest On Principal	Tax Savings On Interest	Tax Savings (Depreciation & Interest)	Net After-tax Cost
1987	$ 0	$1,000,000	$ 0	$ 0	$ 68,000	$(68,000)
1988	222,603	902,396	125,000	42,500	151,300	71,303
1989	222,603	792,593	112,800	38,352	103,632	118,971
1990	222,603	669,064	99,074	33,685	72,853	149,750
1991	222,603	530,095	83,633	28,435	67,603	155,000
1992	222,603	373,753	66,262	22,529	42,113	180,490
1993	222,603	197,869	46,719	15,885	15,885	206,719
1994	222,603	0	24,734	8,409	8,409	214,194
Total	$1,558,221		$558,222	$189,796	$529,795	$1,028,426

The present worth calculation, again using a 10% discount rate, results in the following:

TABLE 10-6

| | -------LEASE-------- | | -------FINANCING------- | |
Year	After-tax Cost	Present Value	After-tax Cost	Present Value
Jan 1, 1987	$0	$0	$0	$0
Dec 15, 1987	0	0	(68,000)	(62,069)
	0	0	(68,000)	(62,069)
Jan 1,1988	206,303	187,548	222,603	202,288
Dec 15, 1988	(70,143)	(58,204)	(151,300)	(125,500)
	136,160	129,343	71,303	76,788
Jan 1, 1989	206,303	170,432	222,603	183,828
Dec 15, 1989	(70,143)	(52,893)	(103,632)	(78,116)
	136,160	117,539	118,971	105,712
Jan 1, 1990	206,303	154,879	222,603	167,051
Dec 15, 1990	(70,143)	(48,066)	(72,853)	(49,904)
	136,160	106,813	149,750	117,148
Jan 1, 1991	206,303	140,744	222,603	151,806
Dec 15, 1991	(70,143)	(43,679)	(67,603)	(42,082)
	136,160	97,065	155,000	109,725
Jan 1, 1992	206,303	127,900	222,603	137,952
Dec 15, 1992	(70,143)	(39,693)	(42,113)	(23,822)
	136,160	88,207	180,490	114,130
Jan 1, 1993	206,303	116,228	222,603	125,363
Dec 15, 1993	(70,143)	(36,071)	(15,885)	(8,165)
	136,160	80,157	206,719	117,198
Jan 1, 1994	206,303	105,621	222,603	113,922
Dec 15, 1994	(70,143)	(32,779)	(8,409)	(3,928)
	136,160	72,842	214,194	109,994
Total	$953,118	$691,967	$1,028,426	$688,625

6. Cash Flows Comparisons

As Table 10-6 shows, the Financial Alternative results in a present value cost of $688,625, the least expensive of the three alternatives. This result is not intended to mean that financing with borrowed funds is always the best alternative because the specific result was based on the assumed facts. Rather it is intended to show how dramatically the present value cash flow analysis alters the result. The Financing Alternative, with the highest cumulative cost, results in the lowest present worth cost, and Purchase Alternative, with the lowest cumulative cost, results in the highest present worth cost.

D. The Lessor's Lease Investment Analysis

The prospective lessor, in making its financial analysis, wants to know how much its return will be on the leased equipment. The concepts of cash flow and present value also play an important part in the lessor's analysis.

This section will analyze two types of leases, the nonleveraged lease—where the lessor uses its own funds entirely to buy the equipment—and the leveraged lease—where the lessor borrows to pay for a portion of the equipment cost.

1. Nonleveraged Lease

As explained earlier, in a nonleveraged lease, the lessor supplies all the money necessary to buy the equipment from his own funds. Whether this type of investment will make economic sense depends on how profitable the transaction will be to the lessor. Thus determining the profit—commonly referred to as the rate of return (usually computed on an after-tax basis)—is a threshold issue in any financial lease investment evaluation.

Traditionally, an after-tax lessor's rate of return has been defined as the interest rate—sometimes referred to as the discount rate—that will discount a lease's after-tax cash flows back to a value equal to his initial cash outlay. Or, looking at it another way, it is the rate that, when applied to the original cash investment, will produce the future cash flow amounts generated by the lease.

To explain the investor rate of return analysis approach, we will work through a hypothetical nonleveraged lease example, assuming the following facts:

Equipment Data

Cost	$1 million
Depreciable life	5 years
Residual value	$0
Delivery date	January 1, 1988
Lease commencement date	January 1, 1988
Description	Computer

Lease Investment Data

Lease term	7 years
Rental payments	7 annual payments in arrears, each equal to $206,303
ITC	0%
Investor income tax rate	34%
Depreciation method	MACRS

Based on those facts, Table 10-7 sets out the lessor's cash flow.

TABLE 10-7

Year	Rent Income	Annual Depreciation	Federal Taxable Income	Total Taxes Paid	Equity	Pre-tax Cash Flow	After-tax Cash Flow
1988	$ 0	$ 200,000	$ (200,000)	$ (68,000)	$(1,000,000)	$ (1,000,000)	$ (932,000)
1989	206,303	320,000	(113,679)	(38,657)	0	206,303	244,960
1990	206,303	192,000	14,303	4,863	0	206,303	201,440
1991	206,303	115,200	91,103	30,975	0	206,303	175,328
1992	206,303	115,200	91,103	30,975	0	206,303	175,328
1993	206,303	57,600	148,703	50,559	0	206,303	155,744
1994	206,303	0	206,202	70,143	0	206,303	136,160
1995	206,303	0	206,303	70,143	0	206,303	136,160
TOTAL	$1,444,118	$1,000,000	$ 444,118	$151,000	$1,000,000	$ 444,118	$ 293,118

The columns in Table 10-7 are computed as follows:

- Annual Depreciation represents the amount of the annual MACRS deduction available to the lessor on the computer as five-year recovery property and applying the half-year convention.
- The Federal Taxable Income is the result of subtracting the annual depreciation deduction from the rent income.
- The Total Taxes Paid represents the dollar savings or cost on the income or loss in the Federal Taxable Income column based on a 34% income tax rate. Where the figure is negative, the lessor reduces his overall tax liability by that amount.
- The After-tax Cash Flow results from adjusting the Pre-tax Cash Flow by the amount of the taxes paid or saved. Thus where the Total Taxes Paid figure is negative, this amount is added to the Pre-tax Cash Flow; where the Total Taxes Paid figure is positive, this amount is subtracted from the Pre-tax Cash Flow.

Once the after-tax cash flows have been calculated, the after-tax rate of return—often referred to as the after-tax yield—can be found by finding the interest rate that will discount the after-tax cash flows back to the cost of the computer, $1 million. Here, the lessor will receive an after-tax yield equal to 8.00%.

2.   A Lessor's Leveraged Lease Analysis

While the prospective lessor's goal in analyzing a leveraged lease is the same as with a nonleveraged lease, the addition of the loan makes the analysis much more complex. As a result, the investment analysis is frequently done on a computer.

▶ **Recommendation:**   Prospective lessees should consider using a lessor/computer software analysis program to estimate a proposing lessor's yield on a transaction. Such a program will also enable prospective lessees to compute other lease-related information. Stipulated loss values, for example, are based on the lessor's anticipated return, and so a program will enable lessees reasonably to verify those values. Unless this is done, there is no way to know if they have been properly computed. Because a prospective lessee will typically not have access to a lessor's computer yield analysis input information and, thus, a simulated lessor "run" may not be exact, a fair approximation can be obtained that will be helpful in negotiations.

To show the lessor's analysis in a leveraged lease, this section will use an illustrative example. Because a computer run is often used, the example's assumed facts will be set out in the manner of a computer run that is typical of one a prospective lessor would receive.

SUMMARY REPORT

--------------CASH FLOWS---------------

Asset Cost	$1,000,000.00	100.000000%
Nonrecourse loans	700,000.00	70.000000
Total equity	300,000.00	30,000.00
Rent	1,444,118.06	144.411806
Total cash in	1,444,118.06	144.411806
Equity	300,000.00	30.000000
Nonrecourse loans	700,000.00	70.000000
Total interest	306,486.95	30.648695
Total cash out	1,306,486.95	130.648695
Pre-tax cash flow	137,631.11	13.763111
Taxes paid	46,794.58	4.679458
After-tax cash flow	90,836.53	9.083653
Sinking fund earnings	0.00	0.000000
ATCF w/ fund earnings	$ 90,836.53	9.083653

------------------------- STATISTICS -------------------------

Composite Tax Rate . . . . .34.0000%   Finance Lease

	Pre - tax		After - tax	
	Effective	Nominal	Effective	Nominal
MIY - composite				
	20.48401	19.31459	13.51945	12.74763
MIY monthly				
	20.63656	19.45035	13.02013	12.00720
FAS 13 accounting				
	20.63656	19.45035	13.62013	12.83723

Present value at   10.0000%   of Rent
  on Jan 1, 1987 . . . . 100.436736   1,004,367.36

Payback from Jan 1, 1987 . . . . 3 yrs   0 mos   0 days
Effective cost (without residual) 10.1325
                    (with residual) 10.1325
Implicit cost (without residual) 10.1325
        (with residual) 10.1325

SUMMARY REPORT (Cont.)

──────── Asset(s) ────────

#	Cost	Delivery	Funding	Residual	ITC		Start Date		Basis	Method	Term	Sal/Pt	Convention
								Depreciation					
1	$1,000,000.00	Jan 1, 1987	Jan 1, 1987	$0.0000	0.00	Fed	Jan 1, 1987		100.00	DB / SL 200%	5.000	00.000	half-yr

──────── Rent(s) ────────

Commencement Date ...... Jan 1, 1987

#	Amount	Start Date	Tax Method	#	Timing	End of Period	Adv Arr	Rate	Method	Amount	% of Cost
1	$1,000,000.00	Jan 1, 1987	Default	7	annual	Jan 1, 1994	Arr	10.1325	Specify Amt	$206,302.58	20.630250

──────── Loan(s) - Fixed ────────

#	Amount	Start Date	Rec /Non	Tax Method	#	Timing	End of Period	Adv Arr	Rate	Method	Amount	% of cost
1	$700,000.00	Jan 1, 1987	Non	Default			Jan 1, 1987			Funding	($700,000.00)	(70.0000)
					7	annual	Jan 1, 1994	Arr	10.0000	Specify Amt	$143,783.85	14.378385

──────── Owner/Lessor ────────

Sinking fund rate 0.0000
Month fiscal year ends . . . . Dec
Tax calculation method . . . . cash
Tax estimation method . . . . annualize
Day of month taxes are paid 15

──── Federal ────

Start Date	Rate	Thru	Paid	Percent
Jan 1, 1987	34.000	Dec	Dec	100.0000

──── Federal ────

Start Date	Rate	Thru	Paid	Percent
Jan 1, 1987	34.000	Dec	Dec	100.0000

First year of analysis:
  tax payments . . . . rolled up into first date
  depreciation . . . . rolled up into first date
ITC recognition . . . . spread with "current" method
Residual is taxed over . . . . remaining tax payment dates

The preceding Summary Report presents the transactions facts:

- The Cash Flow section shows the equipment's total cost is $1 million ("Asset cost"). The funds to buy the equipment will come from a $300,000 equity investment ("Total equity") representing 30% of the total cost, and a $700,000 third-party loan ("Nonrecourse loans"). This section also sets out other relevant information, such as pre-tax and after-tax cash flows.
- The Statistics section list various investment return information, on a pre-tax and an after-tax basis. It indicates the method of lease analysis used as the multiple investment yield or MIY method.
- The Asset(s) section specifies the equipment delivery date as January 1, 1987 ("Delivery"), and that a $0 residual value ("Residual") was assumed. It also shows that there was no ITC claimed ("ITC").
- The Depreciation section shows that depreciation was assumed to begin on January 1, 1987 ("Start date") and that the asset will be depreciated over a period of five years ("Term"). It also shows that the method of depreciation, 200% declining-balance method with a switch to the straight-line method ("Method"). A half-year depreciation convention was assumed ("Convention").
- The Rent(s) section provides the fundamental lease structure information. The lease will begin on January 1, 1987 ("Commencement date"). The rent is due annually in arrears and is payable in seven installments ("Adv/Arr") of $206,302.58 each. The annual rent as a percentage of equipment cost is also listed ("% of Cost"). The implicit lease interest rate is 10.1325% ("Rate")
- The Loan section describes the assumed third-party loan. The principal amount of the loan is $700,000 ("Amount") and the annual loan interest rate is 10% ("Rate"). The analysis further anticipates that the loan funding date is January 1, 1987 ("Start date") and that the loan is payable in seven installments ("#") in arrears ("Adv/Arr"). The final payment is due January 1, 1994 ("End of Period").

The prospective lessor's investment presentation often includes an amortization schedule, an example of which follows, as Table 10-8.

For each debt service payment due date, the schedule shows the beginning loan principal outstanding ("Starting Balance"), the total annual payment amount ("Debt Service"), the interest component of each payment ("Interest"), the principal component of each payment ("Principal"), and the principal amount outstanding after each payment ("Remaining Balance").

TABLE 10-8

AMORTIZATION SCHEDULE

Date	Starting Balance	Loan Take Down	Debt Service	Interest	Principal	Remaining Balance
Jan 1, 1987	$ 0.00	$700,000.00				$700,000.00
Jan 1, 1988	700,000.00		$143,783.85	$70,000.00	$73,783.85	626,216.15
Jan 1, 1989	626,216.15		143,783.85	62,621.62	81,162.23	545,053.92
Jan 1, 1990	545,053.92		143,783.85	54,505.39	89,278.46	455,775.46
Jan 1, 1991	455,775.46		143,783.85	45,577.55	98,206.30	357,569.15
Jan 1, 1992	357,569.15		143,783.85	35,756.92	108,026.93	249,542.22
Jan 1, 1993	249,542.22		143,783.85	24,954.22	118,829.63	130,712.59
Jan 1, 1994	130,712.59		143,783.85	13,071.26	130,712.59	0.00
Total		$700,000.00	$1,006,486.95	$306,486.95	$700,000.00	

The next component in the prospective lessor's analysis is the federal tax consequences of the proposed transaction. A lessor's lease investment presentation will typically include a tax analysis in the form of Table 10-9 on next page.

TABLE 10-9

FEDERAL TAX STATEMENT

Period Ending	Revenue	Interest	Depreciation	Taxable Income	Federal Tax Due w/o ITC	Federal Tax Paid
Dec 30, 1987	$ 0	$ 0	$200,000	$(200,000)	$(68,000)	$(68,000)
Dec 30, 1988	206,303	70,000	320,000	(183,697)	(62,457)	(62,457)
Dec 30, 1989	206,303	62,622	192,000	(48,319)	(16,428)	(16,428)
Dec 30, 1990	206,303	54,505	115,200	36,597	12,443	12,443
Dec 30, 1991	206,303	45,578	115,200	45,525	15,479	15,479
Dec 30, 1992	206,303	35,757	57,600	112,946	38,402	38,402
Dec 30, 1993	206,303	24,954	0	181,348	61,658	61,658
Dec 30, 1994	206,303	13,071	0	193,231	65,699	65,699
Total	$1,444,121	$306,487	$1,000,000	$137,631	$46,796	$46,796

The preceding shows the steps involved in determining the tax consequences:

- The Revenue column shows when the lessor must include the rent payments in income. Because the rent is payable annually in arrears, there is no payment until January 1, 1988, and no reportable income until that year.
- The Interest column shows when the interest part of the third-party loan is deductible. As the loan is repayable annually in arrears, the first payment is not due until January 1, 1988, and there is no deduction until 1988.
- The Depreciation column shows when the prospective lessor may take his depreciation deduction. As the equipment will be placed in service in 1987, he is entitled to a $200,000 deduction for 1987. In years 1993 and 1994, the depreciation expense is $0 because the asset has, through 1992, been fully depreciated.
- The amounts in the Taxable Income column are computed by subtracting interest and depreciation deductions from the rent revenue.
- The Federal Tax Due column shows the amount of tax savings or additional tax payable for each year of the lease. It assumes that the prospective lessor is in the 34% tax bracket. During the first three years, the transaction will reduce the lessor's overall tax liability, after that it crosses over and no longer produces a loss because the depreciation and interest deductions are less than the rental income.

Another frequently included part of an investor presentation is a cash flow report. Table 10-10 presents the lease's cash-flow on an annual basis.

TABLE 10-10

CASH-FLOW REPORT

Period Ending	Rent & Income & Residual	Equity & Fees & Expenses	Debt Service	Pre-tax Cash-flow	Taxes Paid	After-tax Cash-flow	Cumulative After-tax Cash-flow
Dec 30, 1987	$ 0	$300,000	0	$(300,000)	$(68,000)	$(232,000)	$(232,000)
Dec 30, 1988	206,303	0	143,784	62,519	(62,457)	124,976	(107,024)
Dec 30, 1989	206,303	0	143,784	62,519	(16,428)	78,947	(28,077)
Dec 30, 1990	206,303	0	143,784	62,519	12,443	50,076	21,999
Dec 30, 1991	206,303	0	143,784	62,519	15,479	47,040	69,039
Dec 30, 1992	206,303	0	143,784	62,519	38,402	24,117	93,156
Dec 30, 1993	206,303	0	143,784	62,519	61,658	860	94,016
Dec 30, 1994	206,303	0	143,784	62,519	65,699	(3,180)	90,837
Total	$1,444,121	$300,000	$1,006,488	$137,633	$46,796	$90,836	

The after-tax cash-flows are arrived at as follows:

- The Rent and Income and Residual shows the total amount of income received each year.
- The Equity, Fees, and Expenses column reflects the lessor's initial $300,000 investment in 1987.
- The Debt Service shows the annual amount of the payment on the third-party loan.
- The Pre-tax Cash-Flow reflects the cumulative rent inflow, offset by the equity and loan payment outflows. In 1987, the lessor made no rent or loan payment, so the only amount in that column is the initial $300,000 equity payment.
- The Taxes Paid column comes from the Table 10-9 (see "Federal Tax Due").
- The After-tax Cash-Flow column is the result of adjusting the Pre-tax Cash-Flow by the Taxes Paid. Where the amount in the Taxes Paid column is negative (in the first three years), it is added to the pre-tax cash-flow because the tax savings are an inflow of cash that year. Where the taxes paid amount is positive, this amount is subtracted from the pre-tax cash-flow.

After the after-tax cash-flows are determined, the investment yields are computed in the same manner as they are in the nonleveraged lease example.

CHAPTER 11

Understanding the Lease Accounting Rules

A. Background

During the early years of the equipment leasing business, the accounting profession devoted considerable time and effort discussing how leases should be accounted for, both from the standpoint of the lessor and the lessee. There were many inconsistencies and substantive disagreements. Finally, in 1973, the subject of accounting for leases was addressed by the accounting profession's standard setting body, the Financial Accounting Standards Board (FASB), with the firm intent of resolving the many problems. After issuing several exposure drafts and considering a multitude of letters of comments, position papers, and oral presentations from interested parties, they adopted, in November 1976, the "Statement of Financial Accounting Standards No. 13—Accounting for Leases." FASB No. 13 established the standards to be followed by lessors and lessees in accounting for and reporting lease transactions. The problems were not over, however. Since FASB No. 13 was issued, the FASB has been called on to address a wide variety of issues raised by these financial accounting and reporting guidelines. As a result, various amendments and interpretations have been put out in an effort to clarify or handle many of the guideline's complex issues.

The lease accounting rules generally apply to lease transactions and certain lease revisions that were entered into on or after January 1, 1977. For calendar or fiscal years beginning after 1980, however, the rules generally must be retroactively applied to all leases reported.

▶ **Observation:** Keep in mind that FASB No. 13 is saying that a lease that transfers substantially all of an asset's ownership benefits and risks to the lessee must be treated by the lessee in the same way an asset bought with borrowed money is treated (capital lease treatment). The lessor must account for the lease as a sale or a financing. All other types of leases should be treated as the rental of property (operating lease treatment).

Because of the scope and detail of the lease accounting rules and because the intent of this chapter is to provide the reader with an awareness of the most relevant concepts, every aspect of the rules will not be explained. The material will, however, point out and generally explain the fundamental issues that have an impact on the everyday decisions involved in leasing equipment.

B. Lease Classifications for a Lessee Vary Significantly—A Careful Analysis Is Essential

Under the FASB No. 13, a lessee must account for and report a lease in its financial statements as either a "capital" lease or an "operating" lease, depending on how the transaction is structured. The way the two types of leases are treated varies significantly. In certain cases, it may not be advisable for a company to lease equipment because of the accounting treatment impact.

The criteria for determining whether a lease from the lessee's viewpoint must be classified as capital lease or an operating lease have been well defined in FASB No. 13. A lease must be treated as a capital lease if, at its inception, it meets one or more of the following criteria:

- The lease arrangement provides for a transfer of the property's ownership to the lessee by the end of the lease term.
- There is a bargain purchase option in the lease. A bargain purchase option is basically one in which the lessee has a right to buy the property for a price that is so far below its anticipated fair value, at the time it can be exercised, that it is likely the lessee will elect to buy the property.
- The term of the lease is for a period equal to or greater than 75% of the property's estimated economic useful life.
- The present value of the "minimum lease payments" at the lease inception (excluding any executory costs included in the payments such as insurance, maintenance, and taxes that the lessor will pay and any profits on those costs) is equal to or greater than 90% of the excess of the fair value of the leased property (determined at the beginning of the lease) over any investment tax credit (ITC) claimed and expected to be realized by the lessor. The present value computation is calculated by discounting the payments at the lower of the lessor's implicit lease interest rate or the interest rate the lessee would have to pay for a loan running the length of the lease term (the lessee's "incremental borrowing rate"). If it is not practicable for the lessee to learn the lessor's implicit lease rate of interest, the lessee must use its borrowing

rate to make the present value computation. FASB No. 13 defines "minimum lease payments" as those payments that the lessee must make or can be required to make. This includes minimum rent payments, residual value guarantees, and payments for failure to renew or extend the lease.

If the lease does not meet any of the above criteria, it is classified as an operating lease.

Illustrative Example—_The Present Value Test:_ Company Able is considering leasing a new truck from Company Baker. Will the present value test for capital lease classification be met? Here are the facts:

Noncancelable lease term	5 years
Monthly rent (in arrears)	$180
Fair market value (FMV) at lease inception	$10,000
Executory costs	To be paid by Company Able
ITC	0%
Company Able's borrowing rate	10%
Company Baker's Implicit Lease Rate	Company Able unable to determine

In this example, the minimum lease payments are the rental payments. The present value of the monthly rental payments computed by discounting the future rent payment stream by 10% per annum is equal to $8,472. Ninety percent of the truck's FMV at the beginning of the lease is $9,000. Because the present value of the rental stream is less than $9,000, the present value test for capital lease classification is not met.

C.   The Accounting Requirements Have an Impact on a Lessee

The way a lessee must account for a lease in its financial statements depends on its classification, that is, whether it falls within the capital or operating lease category. If a lease is classified as a capital lease, the lessee must record it both as an asset and an obligation at an amount equal to the present value of the minimum lease payments. Executory costs included in the payments, such as insurance, maintenance, and taxes that the lessor must pay, and any profit on these costs, must be excluded before making the present value computation. If, however, the minimum lease payment present value amount turns out to be greater than the property's "fair value" (generally the property's purchase cost) determined at the beginning of the lease, then the fair value is to be recorded.

The lease payment present value calculation is to be made in the same manner as it is when determining whether a lease meets the present value criteria for capital lease classification. In other words, the payment stream is to be discounted at the lower of the lessee's incremental borrowing rate for a loan of a similar term or the lessor's implicit lease interest rate. If it is not practicable for the lessee to learn the lessor's implicit interest rate, the incremental borrowing rate must be used.

A lessee must write off (amortize) a capital lease under certain specific rules. Which rule must be followed depends on which of the four capital lease classification criteria is met. If the lease meets the first or second criterion (that is, if the ownership of the property is transferred to the lessee at the end of the lease term or the lessee has a bargain purchase option), the lessee must write it off in a manner consistent with its usual depreciation practice for assets it owns. If the lease does not meet either of these two criteria, the lessee must amortize the property, over a period equal to the lease term, in a manner consistent with its normal depreciation practice down to a value it expects the property to be worth at the end of the lease.

A lessee must account for a lease categorized as an operating lease in a different manner than one that is classified as a capital lease. Generally, the rental payments will be charged to expense as they become due on a straight-line basis, whether they are in fact payable on a straight-line basis. There is, however, an exception to the straight-line reporting rule. If another systematic and rational time pattern method for reflecting the property's use benefit is more representative, that method must be used in reporting the rent expense.

▶ **Recommendation:** The difference in reporting impact between a capital lease and an operating lease is significant. If a prospective lessee does not want a lease obligation to appear as a long-term liability, he or she must make sure that it will be classified as an operating lease. If it cannot be so treated, and there are no other compelling reasons to lease, the possibility of buying the asset must be carefully considered in view of the effect on its financial picture.

D. The Lease Classification Categories for a Lessor Are Extensive

From the standpoint of lessor accounting, FASB No. 13 provides that all leases must be categorized as either sales-type leases, direct-financing leases, leveraged leases, or operating leases. Each category has certain attributes that the lessor must carefully take into account when making the classification determination.

A lease will be classified as a sales-type lease if all the following tests are met:

- The lease gives rise to a dealer's or manufacturer's profit, or loss, to the lessor.
- One or more of the lessee criteria for capital lease classification are met.
- The minimum lease payment collectibility is reasonably predictable.
- There are no important uncertainties as to the amount of any unreimbursable costs that the lessor has not yet incurred.

A dealer's or manufacturer's profit, or loss, will exist if the fair value of the leased equipment at the beginning of the lease is greater—or less, as the case may be—than the lessor's cost, or carrying amount if different than the cost. This test is usually met when an equipment manufacturer or dealer leases, instead of sells, his equipment to a lessee. In this case, the fair value of the equipment will typically be greater than his cost or carrying amount.

▶ **Observation:**   There are situations under FASB No. 13 when a lessor could accrue a dealer's or manufacturer's type of profit, or loss, without actually being a dealer or manufacturer. The lease accounting rules provide that a sales-type lease can exist if the equipment's fair value at the lease inception is greater, or less, than the lessor's cost or carrying amount if this amount is different from the cost.

The criteria for determining whether a lease will be classified as a direct-financing lease is much easier to understand once the governing rules for a sales-type lease and a lessee capital lease have been mastered. Very simply, a lease will be a direct-financing lease if, at its inception, all of the following five tests are satisfied:

- One or more of the criteria for lessee capital lease classification has been met.
- The lease does not fall within the category of leveraged lease.
- The lease does not give rise to a dealer's or manufacturer's profit, or loss, to the lessor.
- The collectibility of the minimum lease payments is reasonably predictable.
- There are no important uncertainties as to the amount of any unreimbursable costs that the lessor has yet to incur under the lease.

Ascertaining whether a lease will be categorized as a leveraged lease is more complex than determining whether it is a sales-type lease or a direct-financing lease. Basically, if a lease is a direct-financing lease *and* meets all of the following criteria it will be considered a leveraged lease.

- No less than three participants, a lessee, a lessor, and a long-term lender, are involved.
- The long-term debt is nonrecourse as to the lessor's general credit.
- The principal amount of the long-term debt will substantially leverage the lessor's investment.
- The lessor's net investment goes down in the early lease years after it has been completed and goes up in the later lease years before it is entirely eliminated.
- Any available ITC that the lessor retains is accounted for as one of the lease cash flow components.

The definition of an operating lease is straightforward. It is simply a lease that does not qualify as a direct-financing lease, a sales-type lease, or a leveraged lease.

E. The Lessor's Accounting Requirements Are Complex

FASB No. 13 carefully details how lessors must account for sales-type, direct financing, leveraged, and operating leases. The rules are complex, and a lessor must make sure they are clearly understood before committing to a lease transaction, to avoid an undesirable accounting treatment.

1. For a Sales-Type Lease

If a lease fits within the sales-type lease category, a lessor must determine his gross investment in the lease. The lessor's gross investment is the sum of the lease rents and other minimum lease payments and the equipment's unguaranteed residual value that will accrue to the lessor's benefit. The minimum lease payment sum must be computed net of any executory costs included in the payments, such as insurance, maintenance, and taxes, which the lessor must pay, and any profit on such costs.

The lessor must record the lease's unearned income. Unearned income is the difference between the lessor's gross investment and the sum of the present values of the minimum lease payments, adjusted for certain executory costs and the equipment's unguaranteed residual value that will accrue to the lessor's benefit. The present value computations are to be made using the lessor's implicit lease interest rate as the discount rate. Generally, the lease's unearned income must be amortized to income over the lease term in such a manner so as to produce a constant periodic rate of return on the lessor's net investment in the lease. Net investment is the difference between the gross investment and the unearned income. The accounting rules require that the lessor's net investment in a lease be treated in the same way as other current or noncurrent assets in a classified balance sheet.

The equipment's sales price, defined as the present value of the minimum lease payments, net of certain executory costs and any profits on those costs, must also be computed. The equipment's cost (or carrying amount if different), increased by any initial negotiation and consummation expenses, such as legal fees and reduced by the present value of the lessor's unguaranteed residual value, must be charged against income for the same period. The present value computation is to be made using a discount rate equal to the lessor's implicit lease interest rate.

The leased equipment's residual value is given special attention. The rules require a lessor to review the estimated value used in the required computations on an annual basis. If the value experiences a permanent decline, the reporting criteria must be adjusted accordingly. If, on the other hand, there has been an increase in the expected residual value no adjustments are permitted.

2.   For a Direct Financing Lease

A lessor must account for a direct financing lease in somewhat the same manner as a sales-type lease. As with a sales-type lease, he must determine his gross investment in the lease. Gross investment is defined in the same way as it is for a sales-type lease. Unearned income, defined for a direct financing lease as simply the difference between the lessor's gross investment and the equipment's cost, must be recorded. In the event the carrying amount of the equipment is different from its cost, the carrying amount must instead be used in making this computation.

The lessor's net investment in the lease is recorded and is to be classified in the same way as other current or noncurrent assets in a classified balance sheet. Net investment is defined as the gross investment minus the unearned income.

The rules require the initial direct costs of putting a lease transaction together, such as commissions or legal fees, to be expensed against income when they are incurred. The lessor must also recognize, as income for that period against any such charge, an amount of unearned income equal to the initial direct costs. The amount of unearned income remaining must be treated in the same manner as unearned income is in a sales-type lease situation, that is, generally amortized "to income" over the remaining term in such a way as to show a constant periodic return rate on the lessor's net investment.

The equipment's estimated residual value must be annually reviewed. If a permanent decrease in the value estimate has occurred, the computations incorporating the value must be adjusted accordingly. No adjustments are allowed to reflect an increase in the value estimate.

3.   For an Operating Lease

If a lease is deemed to be an operating lease, the accounting treatment is somewhat simpler for a lessor than if the lease is a sales-type or direct financing lease. Equipment subject to such a lease must be recorded on the lessor's balance sheet in or near the "property, plant, and equipment" category. Also, the equipment must be depreciated under the lessor's usual depreciation policy. The investment in the equipment must be shown reduced by the accumulated depreciation.

The rent received under an operating lease is handled in a straight-forward manner. It is reported as income when and as due and is taken in on a straight-line basis, regardless of how the rent is actually to be paid. There is, however, an exception to this reporting method. If any other systematic method for reporting the rent income would more accurately reflect the time pattern reduction in the property's use benefit, then that method must be used.

Any initial direct costs incurred by the lessor in connection with putting the transaction together cannot, in general, be treated as they are in a direct financing lease situation. They must be written off over the term of the lease in proportion to how the rent income is recognized. They may, however, be expensed when incurred if the effect would not be materially different than it would be under the deferred treatment.

4.   For a Leveraged Lease

The lessor's investment in a leveraged lease must be stated net of the transaction's nonrecourse debt. The lessor's investment at any point in time is determined by computing (1) the rents receivable, minus the portion going to pay the debt service on the nonrecourse debt; (2) a receivable for any ITC amount to be realized; (3) the equipment's estimated residual value; and (4) the transaction's unearned and deferred income. The unearned and deferred income at any point is defined as the sum of the lease's estimated remaining and unallocated pre-tax income or loss, adjusted by subtracting any initial direct costs, and any ITC that has not yet been allocated to income over the lease term.

The lessor must also determine the rate of return on his net investment during the years it is positive. The rate of return is defined as the rate that, when applied to the net investment during the years it is positive, will distribute the net income to these years. The lessor's net investment in a leveraged lease is simply the lessor's investment reduced by the deferred taxes arising from the difference between the lessor's pretax accounting income and taxable income.

As with a sales-type lease and a direct financing lease, the lessor must review the estimated residual value of the equipment each year and adjust it downward if it appears to have undergone a permanent reduction over that originally estimated. If an adjustment is necessary, certain other recalculations are necessary using the new residual assumption. No upward adjustment is permitted if there has been an estimated increase in the residual value.

F. Accounting Rules Governing Sale-Leaseback Situations

Because many leases arise through sale-leaseback transactions, it is worthwhile mentioning the governing lease accounting rules. A "sale-leaseback" is defined as a transaction in which an owner sells equipment to a third party and leases it back. The buyer will then be the lessor and the original owner will become the lessee.

From the lessee's viewpoint, the lease accounting rules are the same as in any lease situation. That is, if the lease would otherwise have to be classified as a capital lease, it will still be considered as a capital lease. If it qualifies as an operating lease, it will still be accounted for as an operating lease. The reporting of the profit or loss from the equipment's sale, however, is specially treated. If the lease is a capital lease, the seller-lessee must defer any profit or loss resulting from the sale to the lessor-buyer and amortize it in proportion to the amortization of the leased equipment. If the lease is classified as an operating lease, generally any profit or loss must be amortized in proportion to the rents charged to expense over the term of the lease.

If the lease would qualify for a lessee as a capital lease, the collectibility of the minimum lease payments is reasonably predictable, and there are no important uncertainties as to the amount of any unreimbursable costs that the lessor has yet to incur under the lease, the transaction must be treated by the lessor as a purchase and a direct financing lease. If it does not, it must be accounted for as a purchase and an operating lease.

G. A Lease Classification Checklist for Lessees

The lessee can use the following checklist as general guidelines in classifying its leases for accounting and reporting purposes.

■ If a lease meets one or more of the following criteria, has it been classified as a capital-lease?

- Does the lease transfer the equipment's ownership to the lessee by the end of the lease?

- Does the lessee have the right to buy the leased equipment at a price well below its value at the time the right can be exercised?

- Does the lease run for a term that is equal to or greater than 75% of the equipment's estimated economic useful life? (This rule does not apply if at the time the lease is signed the equipment has a remaining useful life of only 25% or less of its original life.)

- Is the present value of the rent and other minimum lease payments, net of certain executory costs and profits on such costs, equal to or greater than 90% of the equipment's fair value as of the lease inception, minus any investment tax credit to be retained by the lessor?

■ If it is practicable for the lessee to learn the implicit lease rate computed by the lessor and it is lower than the lessee's incremental borrowing rate, has the present value test been computed using this rate?

- If it is not lower, has the value been calculated using the lessee's incremental borrowing rate?

■ If a lease does not meet *any* of the tests above, has it been classified as an operating lease?

H. A Lease Classification Checklist for Lessors

The lessor can use the following checklist as general guidelines in classifying its leases for accounting and reporting purposes.

■ A lease must be classified as a sales-type lease if it meets all of the following:

- The lessor incurs a manufacturer's or dealer's type of profit or loss.

- The lease meets at least one of the following criteria:

  (1) The lease transfers the equipment's ownership to the lessee by the end of the lease.

  (2) The lessee has the right to buy the leased equipment at a price well below its expected fair value at the time the right can be exercised.

(3) The lease runs for a term that is equal to or greater than 75% of the equipment's estimated economic useful life. (This rule does not apply if at the time the lease is signed the equipment has a remaining useful life of only 25% or less of its original life.)

(4) The present value of the rent and other minimum lease payments, net of certain executory costs and profits on such costs, is equal to or greater than 90% of the equipment's fair value as of the lease inception, minus any ITC to be retained by the lessor.

- The collectibility of the rent and other minimum lease payments is reasonably predictable.

- There are no important uncertainties concerning the lessor's yet-to-be-incurred unreimbursable costs.

■ A lease (other than a leveraged lease) must be classified as a direct financing lease if it meets all of the following:

- The lessor does not incur a manufacturer's or dealer's type of profit or loss.

- The lease meets at least one of the following criteria:

(1) The lease transfers the equipment's ownership to the lessee by the end of the lease.

(2) The lessee has the right to buy the leased equipment at a price well below its expected fair value at the time the right can be exercised.

(3) The lease runs for a term that is equal to or greater than 75% of the equipment's estimated economic useful life. (This rule does not apply if at the time the lease is signed the equipment has a remaining useful life of only 25% or less of its original life.)

(4) The present value of the rent and other minimum lease payments, net of certain executory costs and profits on such costs, is equal to or greater than 90% of the equipment's fair value as of the lease inception, minus any ITC to be retained by the lessor.

- The collectibility of the rent and other minimum lease payments is reasonably predictable.

- There are no important uncertainties concerning the lessor's yet to be incurred unreimbursable costs.

■ A lease must be classified as a leveraged lease if all of the following criteria are met:

- The lease qualifies as a direct financing lease.
- The lease involves at least three parties—a lessee, a long-term lender, and a lessor.
- The long term debt financing is nonrecourse to the general credit of the lessor.
- The amount of long-term debt will substantially leverage the lessor's invested funds.
- The lessor's "net investment" goes down in the early lease years once made, and rises during the later lease years before eliminated.
- Any available ITC that the lessor retains is accounted for as one of the lease cash flow components.

■ If the lease does not qualify as a sales-type lease, a direct financing lease, or a leveraged lease, it must be classified as an operating lease.

■ If the lease arises out of a sales-leaseback transaction, have the governing rules been checked?

CHAPTER 12

Equipment Lease Terminology— The Definitions

When entering into a leasing transaction, a prospective lessor or lessee may encounter unfamiliar terms that have developed along with the leasing industry. This chapter defines terms according to their industry usage.

Accelerated cost recovery system (ACRS). The method prescribed by the Internal Revenue Code (IRC) that an equipment owner must use in computing depreciation deductions on most equipment placed in service after 1980 and before 1987. Under ACRS, the owner writes off the equipment's cost over a 3-year, 5-year, 10-year, or 15-year period, depending on the recovery period designated for the equipment type.

Acceptance certificate. A document in which a lessee acknowledges that certain specified equipment is acceptable for lease. Generally used in transactions where the parties enter into the lease document well in advance of the equipment's delivery date, it serves to notify the lessor that the equipment has been delivered, inspected, and accepted for lease as of a specified date. The typical form requires the lessee to list certain pertinent information, including the equipment manufacturer, purchase price, serial number, and location.

Acceptance supplement. The same as an Acceptance certificate.

ADR indemnity. A type of tax indemnification given by the lessee to the lessor relating to leased equipment depreciated under the Asset depreciation range system method. The lessee, in effect, guarantees the lessor against loss of, or inability to claim, anticipated ADR tax benefits under certain conditions.

Advance rental. Any payment in the form of rent made before the start of the lease term. The term is also sometimes used to describe a rental payment arrangement in which the lessee pays all rentals, on a per period basis, at the start of each rental payment period.

For example, a quarterly, in advance, rental program requires the lessee to pay one-fourth of the annual rental at the start of each consecutive three-month period during the lease term.

Alternative minimum tax (AMT). A system for taxing individuals and corporations that, in effect, prevents a taxpayer from otherwise reducing its tax below a formulated level. If the tax liability calculated under the AMT rules is greater than the taxpayer's regular tax, the excess amount has to be paid along with the regular tax. The AMT is basically an attempt to dampen a taxpayer's typical motivation to reduce excessively his tax liability.

Antichurning. A concept under the federal tax laws that prevents a taxpayer from taking advantage of more favorable equipment depreciation tax benefits through equipment transaction manipulations that violate the spirit of the tax laws.

Asset depreciation range system (ADR). A method prescribed by the IRC that could be used in computing depreciation deductions for certain assets placed in service after 1970 and before 1981. ADR provides a range of useful lives for specified assets that serve as the period over which the asset is depreciated. The lives listed are generally shorter than the period over which an asset may be depreciated under the "facts and circumstances" method of depreciation.

Balloon payment. Commonly found in mortgage financings, a balloon payment is a final payment that is larger than the periodic term payments. Usually it results because the debt has not been fully amortized during the repayment period. For example, a one-year financing arrangement providing for interest-only monthly payments during the year, with the principal plus the last interest payment due on the final payment date, is said to have a "balloon payment" or simply a "balloon" due at the end of the term.

Bareboat charter party. A form of net financial lease relating to vessels. Also sometimes referred to simply as a "bareboat charter."

Base lease term. The primary period of time that the lessee is entitled to use the leased equipment, without regard to any interim or renewal lease terms. The base lease term of a five-year lease is five years.

Base rental. The rental that the lessee must pay during the base, sometimes called primary, lease term.

Beneficial interest holder. Refers to a beneficial, as opposed to legal (title), owner. For example, when a trust has been created by the equity participants to act as the lessor, the equity participants are deemed the beneficial interest holders. They hold interests in the trust that has title to the equipment.

Bond. An instrument that represents a long-term debt obligation. The debt instruments, sometimes referred to as loan certificates, issued in a leveraged lease transaction, are referred to as bonds or notes.

Book reporting. The reporting of income or loss for financial, as opposed to tax, purposes on the financial records of a corporation or other reporting entity.

Book residual value. An estimate of the equipment's residual value that a lessor uses, or "books," to calculate his economic return on a lease transaction.

Broker. A person or entity who, for compensation, arranges lease transactions for another's account. A broker is also referred to as a syndicator or underwriter.

Call. The right a lessee may have to buy specified leased equipment for a predetermined fixed price, usually expressed as a percentage of original cost. Commonly, if given, such an option does not become exercisable until the end of the lease term, and it lapses if the lessee fails to give the lessor timely notice of its intention to exercise it. For example, a lessee may have a right to buy equipment at the end of the lease term for 30% of original cost, notice of intention to exercise the option to be given not less than 90 days before the lease term's end.

Capital lease. Under the guidelines set out in FASB 13 by the Financial Accounting Standards Board, a lessee must classify certain long-term leases as capital leases for accounting and reporting purposes. Capital leases are accounted for in a manner that reflects the long-term repayment obligation of such leases.

Cash flow. In a lease transaction, the amount of cash a lease generates for a lessor.

Casualty value. A predetermined amount of money that a lessee guarantees the lessor will receive in the event of an equipment casualty loss during the lease term. Generally, expressed as a percentage of original cost, the value varies depending on when during the lease term the loss occurs. It is also referred to as a "stipulated loss value."

Certificate of delivery and acceptance. The same as Acceptance certificate.

Charter party. A document that provides for the lease (charter) of a vessel or vessels. While the format is basically the same as any other lease, there are certain additions and modifications reflecting the requirements dictated by a vessel transaction.

Charterer. The lessee of a vessel.

Chattel mortgage. A mortgage relating to personal property. Thus, a mortgage on equipment is a chattel mortgage.

Collateral. Assets used as security for the repayment of a debt obligation. In a typical leveraged lease, the collateral is the leased equipment.

Commencement date. The date the base, or primary, lease term begins.

Commission agreement. An agreement between a lease broker and a prospective equity participant providing for the payment of a fee to the broker for services in arranging a lease transaction.

Commitment fee. Compensation paid to a lender in return for an agreement to make a future loan or to a lessor for its commitment to lease equipment to a lessee in the future.

Conditional sales agreement. A contract—also referred to as CSA—that provides for the time financing of asset purchases. The seller retains title to the asset until the buyer fulfills all specified conditions, such as installment payments. At that time, title automatically vests in the buyer.

Cost of money. Commonly, the cost that a lessor incurs to borrow money. This includes the interest rate and any additional costs related to such borrowing, such as fees or compensating balances. In pricing a lease transaction, a lessor factors this cost into the computation.

Cost-to-customer. The simple interest rate on a lease transaction.

DDB/SYD/TAN. A technique of switching methods of depreciation to maximize early depreciation writeoffs used on property not covered by ACRS or MACRS. Depreciation deductions are initially computed using the double-declining balance (DDB) method with an appropriately timed change to the sum-of-the-years-digits (SYD) method followed by another appropriately timed change to the straight-line method.

Debt participant. A long-term lender in a leveraged lease transaction. Frequently, those transactions have more than one debt participant.

Debt service. The aggregate periodic repayment amount, including principal and interest, due on a loan.

Default. In a lease transaction, when a party breaches certain material lease obligations.

Deficiency guarantee. A guarantee given to a lessor by a third party, such as an equipment vendor or manufacturer, to induce a lessor to enter into a lease that it would not otherwise enter into usually because the prospective lessee may be a poor credit risk, or the future value of equipment may be highly speculative. For example, a deficiency guarantor may agree to pay the lessor for any shortfall below a designated amount, say 20% of original cost, incurred when the equipment is sold at the end of the lease.

Delivery and acceptance certificate. The same as an Acceptance certificate.

Depreciation indemnity. A tax indemnification given by a lessee against the lessor's loss of anticipated depreciation tax benefits on leased equipment.

Direct financing lease. A classification prescribed under the lease accounting guidelines set out by the FASB in FASB 13, applicable to lessors. Those guidelines tell lessors how to report direct financing leases for accounting purposes.

Discounted cash flow analysis. The process of determining the present value of future cash flows.

DRA. The 1984 Deficit Reduction Act.

Equipment certificate of acceptance. The same as an Acceptance certificate.

Equity participant. The equity investor in a leveraged lease. Frequently, a leveraged lease transaction has more than one equity participant, who jointly own and lease the equipment. An equity participant is also sometimes referred to as an "owner participant."

ERTA. The 1981 Economic Recovery Tax Act.

Event of default. An event that provides the basis for the declaration of a default. For example, the nonpayment of rent under a lease agreement is typically prescribed as an event of default that gives the lessor the right to declare the lease in default and to pursue permitted remedies, such as terminating the lease and reclaiming the equipment.

Facts and circumstances depreciation. A method of determining the depreciable life of an asset generally usable on assets placed in service before 1981. Under the facts and circumstances method, the useful life determination is based on the owner's experience with similar property, giving due consideration to current and anticipated future conditions, such as wear and tear; normal progress of the art; economic changes, inventions, and current developments within the industry and the taxpayer's trade or business; climatic and other relevant local conditions that can affect the taxpayer's repair, renewal, and replacement program.

Fair market purchase value. An asset's value as determined in the open market in an arm's length transaction under normal selling conditions. It is also referred to simply as the "fair market value."

Fair market rental value. The rental rate that an asset would command in the open market in an arm's length transaction under normal renting conditions. It is also referred to simply as the "fair rental value."

FASB. The Financial Accounting Standards Board.

FASB Statement No. 13, Accounting for Leases. FASB No. 13 sets out the standards for financial lease accounting for lessors and lessees. FASB 13 was initially issued by the FASB, Stamford, Connecticut, in November 1976.

Finance lease. (1) The same as a Full payout lease. (2) A statutory lease category that would have permitted leases that otherwise would not have qualified as true leases for tax purposes to be so treated. Although enacted by TEFRA in 1982, the finance lease's effective date was postponed, and it was repealed by the 1986 TRA before having ever gone into effect, with limited exceptions.

Financing agreement. An agreement commonly entered into by the principal parties to a leveraged lease before equipment delivery. The agreement identifies each party's obligation to the transaction and any conditions that must be satisfied before the obligations are fixed. Typically, it will involve the debt and equity participants, their representatives, and the lessee. It is also referred to as a "participation agreement."

Floating rental rate. A form of periodic rental payments that change or "float" upward and downward over a lease's term with changes in a specified interest rate. Frequently, a designated bank's prime rate is the measuring interest rate.

Full payout lease. A form of lease that will provide the lessor with a cash flow generally sufficient to return his equipment investment; pay the principal, interest, and other financing costs on related debt; cover his related sales and administration expenses; and generate a profit. The cash flow is determined from the rental payments, the ownership tax benefits, and the equipment residual value. The lessee typically has the right to use the leased equipment for most of its actual useful life.

Gross income tax. A tax imposed by a state or local taxing authority on gross income generated from sources within its jurisdiction. The tax is deductible by the taxpayer for federal income tax purposes.

Grossing up. A concept that reimbursement for a monetary loss will include sufficient additional monies so that the after-tax amount will equal the loss. The recipient is said to be made whole for his loss because the amount paid must take into account any taxes he will have to pay as a result of the receipt of the payments from the payor.

Guaranteed residual value. An arrangement in which, for example, a broker or equipment manufacturer guarantees that a lessor will receive not less than a certain amount for specified equipment when it is disposed of at the end of the lease term. It is also sometimes referred to simply as a "guaranteed residual."

Guideline lease. A leveraged lease that meets with the IRS's guidelines set out in Revenue Procedures 75-21, 75-28, 76-30, and 79-48. While the guidelines specifically address only private ruling requests, generally a Guideline lease should qualify as a true lease for federal income tax purposes.

Half-year convention. A concept under the income tax rules for depreciating equipment under which all equipment placed in service during a tax year is treated as having been placed in service at the mid-point of that year, regardless of when during the year it was in fact placed in service.

Hell or high water clause. A lease provision that commits a lessee to pay the rent unconditionally. The lessee waives any right that exists or may arise to withhold any rent from the lessor or any assignee of the lessor for any reason whatsoever, including any setoff, counterclaim, recoupment, or defense.

High-low rental. A rental structure in which the rent payments are reduced from a higher to a lower rate at a prescribed point in the lease term.

Implicit lease rate. The annual interest rate that, when applied to the lease rental payments, will discount those payments to an amount equal to the cost of the equipment leased.

Indemnity agreement. A contract in which one party commits to insure another party against anticipated and specified losses.

Indenture. In a leveraged lease transaction, an agreement entered into by an owner trustee (the lessor's representative) and an indenture trustee (the lender's representative) in which the owner trustee grants a lien on the leased equipment, the lease rents, and other lessor contract rights as security for repayment of the outstanding equipment loan. It is also referred to as an indenture trust.

Indenture trustee. Where, in a leveraged lease transaction, the debt is provided through a trust arrangement, the representative of the lenders. As the lender's representative, the indenture trustee may, for example, have to file and maintain a security interest in the leased equipment, receive rentals from the lessee, pay out the proper amounts to the lenders and the lessor, and take certain action to protect the outstanding loan in the event of a loan default.

Institutional investors. Institutions that invest in lease transactions. They can be, for example, insurance companies, pension funds, banks, and trusts.

Insured value. The same as Casualty value.

Interim lease rental. The equipment rental due for the interim lease term. Typically, for each day during the interim lease term, a lessee must pay as interim lease rent an amount equal to the daily equivalent of the primary lease term rent. In a leveraged lease transaction, the lease sometimes instead permits the lessee to pay an amount equal to the daily equivalent of the long-term debt interest.

Interim lease term. The lease term period between the lessee's acceptance of the equipment for lease and the beginning of the primary, or base, lease term.

Investment tax credit (ITC). A credit allowed against federal income tax liability that can be claimed by a taxpayer for certain "Section 38 property" acquired and placed in service by a taxpayer during a tax year. ITC is generally not available for property placed in service after 1985.

ITC. The investment tax credit.

ITC indemnity. A type of indemnification in which the lessee commits to reimburse the lessor for any financial loss incurred through the loss of, or inability to claim, any or all of the anticipated ITC. If the lessor has "passed through" the ITC to the lessee, the lessor may have to give the indemnity.

ITC 'pass-through.' An election made by the lessor to treat, for ITC purposes, the lessee as the owner of the leased equipment. After the election, a lessee can claim the ITC on the equipment covered by the election.

Layoff. The sale by a lessor of his interest in the lease agreement, including the ownership of the leased equipment and the right to receive the rent payments.

Lease agreement. A contract in which an equipment owner, the lessor, transfers the equipment's use, subject to the specified terms and conditions, to another, the lessee, for a prescribed period of time and rental rate.

Lease line. A present commitment by a lessor to lease specified equipment to be delivered in the future. A lease line can cover a variety of types of equipment, at varying rental rates and lease terms. It is also referred to as a lease line of credit.

Lease underwriting. The process in which a lease broker arranges a lease transaction for the account of third parties—a prospective lessor and a prospective lessee. This can be on a best efforts basis or on a firm commitment basis. In a best efforts underwriting the broker only offers to attempt diligently to arrange the financing on certain proposed terms. In a firm commitment underwriting the broker in effect guarantees to arrange the financing as proposed.

Lessee. The user of equipment that is the subject of a lease agreement.

Lessor. The owner of equipment that is the subject of a lease agreement.

Level payments. Payments that are the same for each payment period during the payment term. Frequently, rent and debt service payments are paid in level payments over the payment period.

Leveraged lease. A lease in which a portion, generally 60% to 80%, of the equipment acquisition cost is borrowed from a bank or other lending institution, with the lessor paying the balance. The debt is commonly on a nonrecourse basis, and the rental payments are usually sufficient to cover the loan debt service.

Limited use property. Leased property that will be economically usable only by the lessee, or a member of the lessee group, at the lease term's end because, for example, of its immobility or unique aspects. The IRS will not rule that a lease is a true lease where the leased equipment is limited use property.

Loan certificate. A certificate that evidences a debt obligation.

Loan participant. A debt participant.

Low-high rental. The reverse of a high-low rental.

Management agreement. A contract in which one party agrees to manage a lease transaction during its term, including, for example, rental payment processing and equipment disposal.

Management fee. A fee that a lease transaction manager receives for services performed under a management agreement.

Master lease agreement. A lease agreement designed to permit future equipment not contemplated when the lease is executed to be added to the lease later. The document is set up in two parts. The main body contains the general, or boiler plate provisions, such as the maintenance and indemnification provisions. An annex, or schedule, contains the type of items that usually vary with a transaction, such as rental rates and options.

Mid-quarter convention. A concept under the income tax rules for depreciating equipment in which all equipment placed in service during a quarter of a tax year is treated as placed in service at the mid-point of such quarter, regardless of when it was in fact placed in service during the quarter.

Modified accelerated cost recovery system (MACRS). A method prescribed for depreciating assets that was introduced by the 1986 TRA. It applies to most equipment placed in service after 1986.

Mortgage. An arrangement whereby a lender (mortgagee) acquires a lien on property owned by a taxpayer (mortgagor) as security for the loan repayment. Once the debt obligation has been fully satisfied, the mortgage lien is terminated.

Negative spread. The amount by which a value is below a certain prescribed amount. Generally, in a leveraged lease, a negative spread is the amount by which the transaction's simple interest rate is below the leveraged debt interest rate.

Net lease. A lease arrangement in which the lessee pays all costs, such as maintenance, certain taxes, and insurance, related to using the leased equipment. Those costs are not included as part of the rental payments. Typically, finance leases are net leases.

1986 TRA. The 1986 Tax Reform Act.

Nonpayout lease. A lease arrangement that does not, over the primary term of the lease, generate enough cash flow to return substantially all the lessor's investment, debt financing costs, and sales and administration expenses.

Nonrecourse debt financing. A loan as to which the lender agrees to look solely to the lessee, the lease rents, and the leased equipment for the loan's repayment. As security for the loan repayment, the lender receives an assignment of the lessor's rights under the lease agreement and a grant of a first lien on the equipment. Although the lessor has no obligation to repay the debt in the event of a lessee default, his equity investment in the equipment is usually subordinated to the lender's rights.

Nonutilization fee. A fee that a lessor may impose in return for its present commitment to buy and lease specified equipment in the future. The fee is generally expressed as a percentage of the aggregate unused portion of the initial dollar commitment, for example, 1% of the unused balance of a $1 million lease line of credit. Thus, if all the commitment is used, no fee is payable.

Operating lease. A form of lease arrangement in which the lessor generally commits to provide certain additional equipment related services, other than the straight financing, such as maintenance, repairs, or technical advice. Generally, operating leases are nonpayout in nature. The term also refers to a lease classification under FASB 13.

Option. A contractual right that can be exercised under the granting terms. For example, a fair market value purchase option in a lease is the right to buy the equipment covered by it for its fair market value.

Packager. A person or entity who arranges a lease transaction for third parties. Also referred to as an underwriter, syndicator, or sometimes, a broker.

Participation agreement. The same as a Financing Agreement.

Payout lease. The same as a Full Payout Lease.

Portfolio lease. The term commonly refers to a lease that is entered into by a "professional" lessor for his own account and investment.

Present value. The term refers to the present worth of a future stream of payments calculated by discounting the future payments at a desired interest rate.

Primary lease term. The same as Base Lease Term.

Private letter ruling. A written opinion that the IRS issues in response to a taxpayer's request. The letter sets out the IRS's position on the tax treatment of a proposed transaction. In leveraged lease transactions, for the IRS to issue a favorable private letter ruling, the request must comply with the IRS Guidelines.

Progress payments. Payments that may be required by an equipment manufacturer or builder during the construction period toward the purchase price. Frequently required for costly equipment with a long construction period, the payments are designed to lessen the manufacturer's or builder's need to tie up his own funds during construction.

Purchase option. The right to buy agreed-on equipment at the times and the amounts specified in the option. Frequently, these options are only exercisable for at the end of the primary lease term, although they sometimes can be exercised during the primary lease term or at the end of any renewal term.

Put. A right that a lessor may have to sell specified leased equipment to the lessee at a fixed price at the end of the initial lease term. It is usually imposed to protect the lessor's residual value assumption.

Recourse debt financing. A loan under which the lender may look to the general credit of the lessor, in addition to the lessee and the equipment, for repayment of any outstanding loan obligation. The lender is said to have "recourse" against the lessor.

Recovery property. Property that can be depreciated under ACRS.

Renewal option. An option frequently given to a lessee to renew the lease term for a specified rental and time period.

Residual sharing. A compensation technique sometimes used by syndicators for arranging a lease transaction. Under this, the equity participants must pay a predetermined percentage of what the equipment is sold for at the end of the lease. For example, a syndicator may get 50% of any amount realized exceeding 20% of the equipment's original cost on sale.

Residual value. The value of leased equipment at the end of the lease term.

Right of first refusal. The right of the lessee to buy the leased equipment, or renew the lease, at the end of the lease term, for an amount equal to that offered by an unaffiliated third party.

Safe harbor lease. A statutory lease category enacted as part of ERTA that permitted a lease to qualify as a true lease for federal income tax purposes although it would not otherwise ordinarily qualify. It was repealed by the 1984 DRA, with limited exceptions. Under a safe harbor lease, an equipment owner could essentially sell the ownership tax benefits without giving up other ownership rights.

Sale-leaseback. An arrangement in which an equipment buyer buys equipment for the purpose of leasing it back to the seller.

Sales tax. A tax imposed on selling equipment.

Sales-type lease. A classification prescribed under the lease accounting guidelines that the FASB set out in FASB 13, applicable to lessors.

Salvage value. The amount, estimated for federal income tax purposes, that an asset is expected to be worth at the end of its useful life.

Section 38 property. Tangible personal property and certain other tangible property, as defined by IRC Section 38.

Security agreement. An agreement that evidences an assignment by the lessor to the lender, as security for the equipment loan, of the lessor's rights under the lease agreement and a granting of a security interest in the leased equipment.

Sinking fund. A fund frequently established in leveraged lease transactions by the lessor to accumulate funds to pay for future taxes.

Sinking fund rate. The interest rate that a sinking fund is deemed to earn on accumulated funds.

Special purpose equipment. The same as Limited use property.

Spread. The difference between two values. In lease transactions, the term is generally used to describe the difference between the lease interest rate and the interest rate on the debt.

Stipulated loss value. The same as Casualty value.

Sublease. The re-lease by a lessee of equipment that is on lease to the lessee.

Take or pay contract. An agreement in which one party commits to buy an agreed-on quantity of goods or material from another at a pre-determined price. If the goods or material are not bought, the party making the purchase commitment must pay the party an amount of money equal to the cost of goods or materials it had committed to buy. For example, a public utility can agree to buy 100 tons of coal annually from a mining company, and if it does not buy this amount in any year it will pay an amount of money equal to its sale price.

Tax benefit transfer lease. The same as a Safe harbor lease.

Tax lease. The same as a True lease.

Tax Reform Act. The 1986 Tax Reform Act.

TBT. A Tax benefit transfer lease.

TEFRA. The 1982 Tax Equity and Fiscal Responsibility Act.

Termination option. An option entitling a lessee to terminate the lease during the lease term for a predetermined value, termination value, if the equipment becomes obsolete or surplus to the lessee's needs. The lessor usually requires the lessee to sell the equipment to an unaffiliated third party, and the lessee must pay the lessor any amount by which the sale proceeds are less than the termination value. Typically, any excess sale proceeds go to the lessor.

Termination value. The amount that the lessee must pay the lessor if he exercises a termination option. Typically, the termination value is set as of each rental payment period and is generally expressed as a percentage of equipment cost. For example, the lessee may be permitted to terminate the lease at the end of the third year of a seven-year lease for an amount equal to 60% of cost.

Time sale. An installment sale.

Total earnings. The amount by which the aggregate rentals due the lessor over the entire lease term exceed the total equipment costs, including equity investment and debt financing costs. This concept does not consider the time value of money.

TRAC Lease. A lease of motor vehicles or trailers that contains what is referred to as a terminal rental adjustment clause (TRAC). The clause permits or requires the rent amount to be adjusted based on the proceeds the lessor receives from the sale of the leased equipment. TRAC leases qualify as true leases.

Transition rules. Statutory rules enacted when there is a change in the tax laws. The transition rules allow certain transactions to be exempted from the law change. For example, transition rules permit ITC to be claimed on certain equipment placed in service after 1985.

True lease. An arrangement that qualifies for lease treatment for federal income tax purposes. Under a true lease, the lessee may deduct the rental payments and the lessor may claim the tax benefits accruing to an equipment owner.

Trust. An arrangement in which property is held by one party for the benefit of another. It is frequently used in leveraged lease transactions.

Trust certificate. A trust document issued on behalf of a trust to evidence the beneficial ownership in the trust estate.

Trustee. The person or entity appointed, or designated, to carry out a trust's terms. In leveraged lease transactions, the trustee is generally a bank or trust company.

Trustee fees. Fees payable to a trustee as compensation for services performed.

Trustor. An individual or entity who causes the creation of a trust and for whose benefit it is established.

Unleveraged lease. A lease in which the lessor puts up 100% of the equipment's acquisition cost from its own funds.

Use tax. A tax imposed upon the use, storage, or consumption of tangible personal property within a taxing jurisdiction.

Useful life. Commonly, the economic usable life of an asset.

Vendor. A seller of property. Commonly, the manufacturer or distributor of equipment.

Vendor program. A program in which an equipment lessor provides a lease financing service to customers of an equipment manufacturer.

APPENDIXES: SAMPLE DOCUMENTS

The following sample equipment lease documents have been included in these appendixes:

The documents are reproduced merely as guidelines to give you an idea of the various format approaches. They should not be used without expert guidance.

Depreciation Tables are reproduced beginning at Page 313.

Request for Lease Quotation

THE MIDEASTERN RAILWAY CORPORATION

Lessee:	The Mideastern Railway Corporation.
Equipment:	Model 6 RD-10, 23,000 h.p. diesel locomotives (est. unit cost–$525,000), manufactured by Arcane Locomotive Corp.
Estimated Total Cost:	$3,150,000.
Equipment Delivery:	February, 19X9–Two units. March, 19X9–Two units. April, 19X9–Two units.
Equity Contribution & Commitment:	Not less than 20% of cost. The equity investor(s) must agree to buy equipment with a maximum equipment cost up to $3.5 million.
Interest Rate Assumptions:	8 3/4%, 9%, 9 1/4%.
Agent for Debt Placement:	Samon & Smith Co.
Attorney for Long-Term Lenders:	Carr, Swift & Moore, subject to agreement of the long-term lenders.
Structuring of the Transaction:	15-year net finance leveraged lease with semiannual, in arrears, level payments. Any other proposal format will be considered provided a bid as requested has been submitted.
	The lessee must have three two-year fair market rental renewal options. A fair market purchase option at the end of the initial term and each renewal term should also be provided. The lessee will give a letter stating that, in its opinion, the locomotives will have a useful life exceeding 18 years and a residual value equal to 20% of the original cost at the end of 15 years.
Delivery Cutoff Date:	The cutoff date for the equipment deliveries will be July 1, 19X9. All equipment not delivered before this date will be excluded from the transaction unless the lessor and the lessee agree to extend such date.

Expenses: All expenses of the transaction, including rating fees and the investment banking fees, will be borne by the lessor.

Security: The lessee's lease obligations will be unconditionally guaranteed by The Eastern Railway Company. The Mideastern Railway Company is a wholly owned subsidiary of The Eastern Railway Company.

                                The long-term debt will be secured by an assignment of the lease. An agent bank will be selected by The Eastern Railway Company and Samon & Smith Co. after the long-term debt is placed. The long-term debt will be noncallable except for casualty occurrences.

Indemnification: Preference will be given to bids with minimum indemnification. All indemnification requirements must be precisely stated in the proposal.

Interim Rentals: All quotations must assume not more than three equity closing dates and provide interim rents from such dates to July 1, 19X9, the beginning of the primary lease term. Interim rentals will be equal to the daily equivalent of the long-term debt interest rate.

Casualty Values: All bidders must provide a schedule of casualty values, expressed as a percentage of original cost, both for the primary lease term and any extensions thereafter. The method of calculating the casualty values must also be supplied.

Insurance: The equipment will be self-insured.

Please mail us your proposal in writing postmarked no later than April 15, 19X9. Your proposal must be on a "firm" basis and at the time of submission you must be prepared to identify the investor source(s) so that they may be contacted immediately by telephone for verification in the event you are the successful bidder.

Nonunderwriting Proposal Letter

December 5, 19X8

Secour Corporation
800 Second Avenue
New York, New York 10017

Attention: Mr. R. Babcox
            President

Gentlemen:

Able Leasing Corporation ("ALC") offers to purchase and lease to Secour Corporation ("Secour") an item of newly manufactured computer equipment on the following terms and conditions:

1. Equipment Description:	The equipment will consist of one (1) new computer, model no. EA-1, manufactured by IXT Computer Corp.
2. Equipment Cost:	Approximately $1 million.
3. Delivery and Payment:	Delivery of the Equipment is anticipated on January 1, 19X9, but in no event shall be later than March 1, 19X9. ALC shall pay for the Equipment on delivery and acceptance.
4. Lease Term:	Eight years, beginning on delivery and acceptance of the Equipment.
5. Rental Program:	Secour shall remit 32 consecutive, level, quarterly payments, in advance, each equal to 4.4000% of Equipment Cost.
6. Options:	At the conclusion of the Lease Term, Secour may (with at least 120 days' prior written notice):

A. Buy the Equipment for an amount equal to its then fair market value.

B. Renew the lease with respect to the Equipment for its then fair rental value.

7. Tax Benefits: The rent is calculated based on the assump-
                                tion that ALC will be entitled to:

                                A. Five-year MACRS depreciation on the full
                                   Equipment Cost, 200% declining-bal-
                                   ance switching to straight-line, and

                                B. A corporate income tax rate equal to
                                   34%.

8. Fixed Expenses: This is a net financial lease proposal and all
                                fixed expenses such as insurance, mainte-
                                nance, and personal property taxes shall be
                                for the account of Secour.

9. Conditions Precedent: This offer is subject to the approval of the
                                Board of Directors of ALC and to the execu-
                                tion of lease documentation mutually accept-
                                able to Secour and ALC.

If the foregoing is satisfactory to you, please indicate your acceptance of this
offer by signing the duplicate copy of this letter in the space provided therefor
and returning it directly to the undersigned.

This offer expires as of the close of business on December 19, 19X8.

Very truly yours,

ABLE LEASING CORPORATION

By _____
   Vice President

Accepted and Agreed to on this
_____ day of _____ , 19X8.
SECOUR CORPORATION

By _____

Its _____

Underwriting Proposal Letter

October 8, 19X8

White Airline Corporation
200 Park Avenue
New York, New York 10017

Attention: E. Rosset
Assistant Treasurer

Gentlemen:

Able Leasing Corporation ("ALC"), on behalf of its nominees, proposes to use its best efforts to arrange a lease for one new Martin RC-75 aircraft for use by White Airline Corporation under the following terms and conditions:

Lessee:	The Lessee shall be White Airline Corporation.
Lessor:	The Lessor will be a commercial bank or trust company acting as owner trustee ("Owner Trustee") pursuant to one or more owners' trusts (the "Trust") for the benefit of one or more commercial banks or other corporate investors (the "Owner Participant"). The Trust shall acquire the Equipment and lease it to the Lessee.
Equipment:	One new Martin RC-75 aircraft.
Cost:	For purposes of this proposal, a total cost of $28 million, plus or minus 5% has been assumed.
Delivery Date:	Delivery of the Equipment is anticipated as of November 1, 19X8, however, shall be no later than December 30, 19X8.
Interim Lease Term:	The interim lease term shall extend from the Delivery Date until the Commencement Date. For the purposes of this proposal the Commencement Date is assumed to be January 1, 19X9.
Interim Rent:	The Lessee shall pay interim rent equal to interest-only on the total cost of the Equip-

	ment at an interest rate equal to the Long-Term Debt Interest Rate.
Primary Lease Term:	The primary lease term shall be 20 years from the Commencement Date.
Primary Rent:	From the Commencement Date, the Lessee shall make 40 consecutive, level, semiannual payments, in arrears, each equal to 4.400% of Cost.
Debt Financing:	An investment banker acceptable to ALC and the Lessee shall arrange for the private placement of secured notes or similar instruments ("Indebtedness") to be issued by the Lessor for a principal amount equal to 80% of total Equipment cost to certain institutional investors ("Lenders") who may be represented by an indenture trustee or agent bank ("Agent"). This proposal assumes that the Indebtedness shall be amortized in semiannual payments of principal and interest at an 8% per annum interest rate ("Long-Term Debt Interest Rate"), payable in arrears over the term of the lease. In the event that the Long-Term Debt Interest Rate varies from that assumed, the rent shall be adjusted, upward or downward, so that the Owner Participant's after-tax yield and after-tax cash flows will be maintained. The Indebtedness shall be secured by an assignment of the lease and a security interest in the Equipment but otherwise shall be without recourse to the Owner Participant and the Lessor.
Insurance:	The Lessee may self-insure the Equipment.
Purchase & Renewal Options:	At the end of the Primary Lease Term, the Lessee may (with 180 days' written notice prior to the end of the term):

A. Renew the lease on the Equipment for its then fair rental value for one five-year period.

B. Buy the Equipment for an equivalent price and under similar conditions as rendered by a third party approached by the Lessor and agreed to by the Lessor prior to sale to that third party.

If the Lessee does not elect to exercise any of the above options, the Lessee shall return the Equipment to the Lessor at the end of the term at a mutually agreeable location.

Termination Option:

At any time during the Primary Lease Term, on or after 10 years from the Commencement Date, the Lessee may (with 180 days' prior written notice) terminate the lease in the event the Equipment becomes obsolete or surplus to its needs, on paying a mutually agreed on termination value.

Fixed Expenses:

This is a net financial lease proposal with all fixed expenses, such as maintenance, insurance, taxes (other than net income taxes) for the account of the Lessee.

Expenses of Transaction:

ALC shall pay all transaction expenses, including:

1. fees and disbursements of special counsel for the Agent and the Lenders;

2. acceptance and annual fees and expenses of the Agent;

3. fees and disbursements of special counsel for the Owner Trustee and the Trustor;

4. acceptance and annual fees and expenses of the Owner Trustee;

5. fees and disbursements in connection with obtaining a ruling from the Internal Revenue Service;

6. expenses of documentation, including printing and reproduction; and

7. fees and disbursements in connection with the private placement of the Indebtedness.

If the transaction is not consummated for any reason, the Lessee shall pay all of the above fees and expenses.

Nonutilization Fee:

Once ALC has obtained equity investor commitments satisfactory to the Lessee, the Lessee shall be liable to ALC for a nonutilization fee equal to 0.5% of the Equipment cost in the event it does not lease the Equipment in accordance with intent of this proposal.

Commitment Fee:

A commitment fee of 0.5% per annum shall be paid by the Lessee to the equity investors on the outstanding equity investor commitment. The fee shall accrue as of the date investor commitments satisfactory to White Airline Corporation have been obtained, shall run up to the Commencement Date, and shall be payable quarterly, in arrears.

Tax Assumptions:

A. The Rent is calculated based on the assumptions that:
1. the organization created by the Trust will be treated as a partnership for Federal income tax purposes;
2. the Lessor will be entitled to seven-year MACRS depreciation on 100% of the Equipment Cost, 200% declining- balance switching to straight-line;
3. the Lessor will be entitled to deduct interest on the Indebtedness under Section 163 of the 1986 Internal Revenue Code;
4. the Lessor will be entitled to amortize the transaction expenses over the Interim and Primary Lease Terms using a straight-line method;
5. the effective Federal income tax rate of the Owner Participant is 34%; and
6. the Lessor will not recognize any income from the transaction other than from Lessee rental, termination value, stipulated loss value, and indemnity payments payable to the Lessor.

B. The Lessee shall provide necessary representation relating to the estimated economic life and residual value of the Equipment.

Tax Ruling:

The Lessor plans to obtain a Internal Revenue Service ruling with respect to the tax assumptions stated above. The Lessee shall agree to indemnify for the tax assumptions above. Such indemnity shall remain in effect until a favorable ruling has been obtained.

If the foregoing proposal is satisfactory to you, please indicate your acceptance by signing the duplicate copy of this letter in the space provided therefor, and returning it directly to the undersigned.

This offer expires at the close of business on October 28, 19X8 and is subject to the approval of the Owner Participant's Board of Directors and mutually satisfactory lease documentation.

Very truly yours,

ABLE LEASING CORPORATION

By _____
Vice President

Accepted and Agreed to on this
_____ day of _____ , 19X8.
WHITE AIRLINE CORPORATION

By _____

Its _____

Net Finance Lease

MASTER LEASE

of

COMPUTER EQUIPMENT

dated as of _____ , 198 ____

between

[   ]

Lessor

and

[   ]

Lessee

Form Of Net Finance Lease When The Lessor Is
Not Also The Vendor

Master Lease of Computer Equipment

TABLE OF CONTENTS

MASTER LEASE OF COMPUTER EQUIPMENT, dated as of _____ , 19_____ , between _____ , a _____ corporation, with a principal place of business located at _____ (the "Lessor", such term to include, to the extent permitted hereunder, its successors and assigns), and _____ , a _____ corporation, with a principal place of business located at _____ (the "Lessee", such term to include, to the extent permitted hereunder, its successors and assigns).

SECTION 1. *DEFINITIONS*

The following terms shall have the respective meanings set forth below for all purposes of this Lease.

1.1 "Acceptance Date" as to each Item of Equipment shall mean the date on which Lessee determines that such Item of Equipment is acceptable for lease pursuant to the terms and conditions of this Lease, as specified by Lessee in the applicable Certificate of Acceptance.

1.2 "Appraiser" shall mean a qualified independent computer equipment appraiser selected in accordance with the provisions of Section 14 of this Lease.

1.3 "Basic Lease Commencement Date" as to each Unit shall mean the date on which the Primary Term shall begin, as specified in the applicable Equipment Schedule.

1.4 "Basic Lease Rate Factor" as to each Unit shall mean the percentage rental set forth in the applicable Equipment Schedule.

1.5 "Basic Rent" as to each Unit shall mean the rent due and payable on each Rent Date during the Primary Term, as specified in the applicable Equipment Schedule.

1.6 "Business Day" shall mean a calendar day, excluding Saturdays, Sundays, and all days on which banking institutions in [insert jurisdiction(s) of Lessee's and/or Lessor's principal place(s) of business] shall be closed.

1.7 "Casualty Occurrence" shall have the meaning set forth in Section 9 of this Lease.

1.8 "Casualty Value" as to each Unit shall be the amount calculated in accordance with the Casualty Value provisions of the applicable Equipment Schedule.

1.9 "Certificate of Acceptance" shall mean a certificate substantially in the form attached as Annex A to the form of Equipment Schedule attached hereto as Exhibit A.

1.10 "Code" shall mean the United States Internal Revenue Code of 1986, as amended and in effect from time to time [if appropriate, insert other relevant governing tax law].

1.11 "Cut-off Date" as to each Item of Equipment shall mean the date specified in the applicable Equipment Schedule after which Lessor shall not be obligated to purchase and lease such Item of Equipment to Lessee in accordance with the terms and conditions of this Lease.

1.12 "Discount Rate" shall mean the per annum interest charge (calculated on the basis of a 360-day year and 30-day month) specified in the applicable Equipment Schedule.

1.13 "Equipment Schedule" shall mean each schedule, substantially in the form of Exhibit A attached hereto, which shall refer to this Lease and which shall become a part hereof as executed from time to time by the parties hereto, covering one or more Items of Equipment that may be leased by Lessee from Lessor hereunder.

1.14 "Event of Default" shall mean any of the events specified in Section 13.1 of this Lease.

1.15 "Fair Market Rental" shall mean the rental value of a Unit determined in accordance with the provisions of Section 14 of this Lease.

1.16 "Fair Market Value" shall mean the sale value of a Unit determined in accordance with the provisions of Section 14 of this Lease.

1.17 "Impositions" shall have the meaning set forth in Section 7.1 of this Lease.

1.18 "Interim Rent" as to each Unit shall mean the rent payable with respect to any Interim Term, as specified in the applicable Equipment Schedule.

1.19 "Interim Term" as to each Unit shall mean the period of time, if any, commencing on the Acceptance Date and ending on the day immediately preceding the Basic Lease Commencement Date.

1.20 "Item of Equipment" shall mean an item of electronic data processing equipment described in an Equipment Schedule. When an "Item of Equipment" becomes subject to this Lease it is thereafter for all purposes of this Lease referred to and defined as a "Unit".

1.21 "Invoice Purchase Price" as to each Unit shall mean the aggregate amount payable by Lessor to Manufacturer for such Unit, as specified in one or more Manufacturer's invoices for such Unit.

1.22 "Lease" shall mean this Master Lease of Computer Equipment between Lessor and Lessee, including without limitation all Equipment Schedules and all exhibits to this Lease and to all Equipment Schedules. The words "herein," "hereof," "hereunder," and other words of similar import used in this Lease refer to this Lease as a whole and not to any particular Section, Subsection, or other portion of this Lease.

1.23 "Lessor's Cost" as to each Unit shall mean the Invoice Purchase Price plus additional costs and expenses that are assumed and subsequently paid by Lessor pursuant to the applicable Equipment Schedule.

1.24 "Lessor's Lien" shall have the meaning set forth in Section 15.3 of this Lease.

1.25 "Lien" shall have the meaning set forth in Section 15.3 of this Lease.

1.26 "Loss Payment Date" as to a Unit suffering a Casualty Occurrence shall mean the date on which Lessee shall be obligated to pay Lessor the Casualty Value in accordance with provisions of Section 9.1 of this Lease.

1.27 "Manufacturer" as to each Unit shall mean the manufacturer or vendor thereof specified by Lessee in the applicable Equipment Schedule.

1.28 "Overdue Rate" shall mean the per annum interest charge (calculated on the basis of a 360-day year and 30-day month) pursuant to Section 18 as specified in the applicable Equipment Schedule.

1.29 "Primary Term" as to each Unit shall mean that period of time commencing on, and including, the Basic Lease Commencement Date and ending that period of time thereafter, as designated in the applicable Equipment Schedule, unless earlier terminated pursuant to the provisions of this Lease.

1.30 "Purchase Documents" shall mean those documents relating to the purchase of a Unit or Units by Lessor from Manufacturer.

1.31 "Purchase Right" as to each Unit shall have the meaning specified in Section 16.1 of this Lease.

1.32 "Renewal Rent" as to each Unit shall mean the rent due and payable on each Rent Date during a Renewal Term, as specified in the applicable Equipment Schedule.

1.33 "Renewal Right" as to each Unit shall have the meaning specified in Section 16.2 of this Lease.

1.34 "Renewal Term" as to each Unit shall mean that aggregate period of time following the end of the Primary Term for which this Lease is extended.

1.35 "Rent" as to each Unit shall mean and include Basic Rent and any Interim Rent and Renewal Rent payable or to become payable, by Lessee to Lessor.

1.36 "Rent Date" as to each Unit shall mean each date during the Term on which Rent is due and payable, as specified in the applicable Equipment Schedule.

1.37 "Term" as to each Unit shall mean the Primary Term and any Interim Term and Renewal Term.

1.38 "Termination Right" as to each Unit shall have the meaning specified in Section 16.3 of this Lease.

1.39 "Termination Value" as to each Unit shall be the amount calculated in accordance with the Termination Value provisions of the applicable Equipment Schedule.

1.40 "Unit" shall mean an Item of Equipment, and any modifications thereof, or improvements or additions thereto, which is leased by Lessor to Lessee pursuant to the terms and provisions of this Lease.

1.41 "Upgrade Right" shall have the meaning specified in Section 16.4 of this Lease.

SECTION 2. *EQUIPMENT ACQUISITION AND ACCEPTANCE*

2.1 *Lease Commitment.* In consideration of the Rent to be paid by Lessee and the other covenants contained in this Lease to be kept and performed by Lessee, Lessor hereby agrees to lease to Lessee each Item of Equipment described in each Equipment Schedule in accordance with the terms and conditions of this Lease.

2.2 *Lessor Payment.* Lessor shall purchase each Unit from Manufacturer solely for its own investment and account as a principal and not as a broker and promptly pay to Manufacturer the full Invoice Purchase Price for each Unit. In no event shall Lessor make such payment later than the earlier of the due date specified by Manufacturer or thirty (30) days after the Acceptance Date. Lessor shall, immediately upon making such payment, deliver to Lessee reasonably satisfactory evidence of such payment. If the full Invoice Purchase Price for any such Unit is not so paid to Manufacturer as provided in this Section 2.2, Lessee shall have the absolute right, in its discretion, (a) to make such payment to Manufacturer whereupon all of Lessor's rights in, and title to, such Unit shall automatically vest in Lessee and (b) to withhold any Rent and/or (c) terminate this Lease as to such Unit. In addition to paying the Invoice Purchase Price for each Unit, Lessor shall also pay, no later than the due date, such other costs and expenses as to a Unit as specified as part of the Lessor's Cost for such Unit in the applicable Equipment Schedule.

2.3 *Cut-Off Date.* Lessor shall have no obligation to purchase and lease any Item of Equipment hereunder which has not been accepted by Lessee in accordance with the provisions of Section 2.5 on or before the Cut-Off Date.

2.4 *Installation Location.* Each Unit shall be installed at the address set forth in the applicable Equipment Schedule. Lessee may, without Lessor's consent, move any such Unit from such address, or any relocated address, to any other address in the[United States of America/Dominion of Canada—as appropriate], provided Lessee has notified Lessor in writing at least thirty (30) days prior to effecting any change of location.

2.5 *Lessee Acceptance.* Lessee shall acknowledge its acceptance of each Item of Equipment for lease hereunder by executing and delivering to Lessor a Certificate of Acceptance as to each such Item of Equipment, whereupon each such Item of Equipment shall become subject to this Lease as of the Acceptance Date.

SECTION 3. *LEASE TERM*

3.1 *Term of Lease.* The Term for each Unit shall be as specified in the applicable Equipment Schedule.

3.2 *Lease Termination.* This Lease shall not be terminated by Lessor or Lessee with respect to any Unit for any reason whatsoever, except as expressly provided herein.

SECTION 4. *NET LEASE*

This Lease is a net lease and Lessee, subject to the provisions of Section 2.2, shall not be entitled to any abatement or reduction of Rent, or set-off against Rent, including without limitation abatements, reductions, or set-offs due or alleged to be due by reason of any past, present, or future claims of Lessee against Lessor under this Lease. Notwithstanding the foregoing, however, nothing shall preclude Lessee from otherwise enforcing any and all other rights it may have against Lessor under this Lease or otherwise.

SECTION 5. *RENT AND USAGE*

5.1 *Rent Payment.* Lessee agrees to pay Lessor Rent for each Unit in accordance with the provisions of this Lease. The Rent for each Unit shall be paid on each Rent Date in the amount set forth in the applicable Equipment Schedule. In accordance with Section 23.1 hereof, if any date on which a Rent payment is due is not a Business Day, the Rent payment otherwise payable on such date shall be payable on the next succeeding Business Day.

5.2 *Unlimited Usage.* Lessor agrees that there shall be no limit on the number of hours for which any Unit may be used.

SECTION 6. *IDENTIFICATION MARKS*

Lessee, at its own cost and expense, will cause each Unit to be legibly and permanently marked, in a reasonably prominent location, with the following legend evidencing the fact that such Unit is owned by Lessor and subject to this Lease:

"[Name and Address of Lessor],
Owner, Lessor."

Lessee shall, upon at least thirty (30) Business Days prior written notice from Lessor, make such changes and/or additions in such markings specified by Lessor as may be required by law in order to protect Lessor's ownership of such Unit and the rights of Lessor under this Lease. Lessee will promptly replace or cause to be replaced any such markings that are removed, defaced, or destroyed.

SECTION 7. *GENERAL TAX INDEMNIFICATION*

7.1 *General Tax Indemnity.* All Rent and other payments required to be made by Lessee hereunder shall be net of any deductions, charges, costs, expenses, and Impositions with respect to collection or otherwise. Lessee agrees to pay, on written demand by Lessor specifying such Impositions in reasonable detail, any and all Impositions and shall keep and save harmless and indemnify Lessor from and against all such Impositions. "Impositions" shall mean the amount of any local, state [replace "state" with "provincial" for Canada], federal, or foreign taxes of any nature whatsoever, assessments, license fees, governmental charges, duties, fines, interest charges, or penalties with respect to any Unit or any part thereof, or with respect to the purchase, ownership, delivery, leasing, possession, use, or operation thereof. The term "Impositions" shall not include (a) federal, state [replace "state" with "provincial" for Canada], local, and foreign tax on, or measured by, the net income of Lessor; (b) any tax based on, or measured by, gross income or gross receipts of Lessor as a substitute for and not in addition to taxes based on net income of Lessor; (c) [U.S. only] any tax imposed by Section 531 [Accumulated Earnings Tax] or Section 541 [Personal Holding Company Tax] of the Code; (d) taxes, fees, or other charges included in Lessor's Cost; (e) the aggregate of all franchise taxes or other similar taxes up to the amount in the aggregate of any such taxes which would be payable to the states [replace "states" with "provinces" for Canada] and cities in which Lessor maintains or has maintained places of, or otherwise does, business during the Term of this Lease, except any such tax which is in substitution for or relieves Lessee from the payment of taxes which it would otherwise be obligated to pay or reimburse Lessor for as herein provided; (f) any fines or penalties that are imposed as a result of (A) the misconduct or negligence of Lessor or (B) a failure by Lessor to take reasonable action or to furnish reasonable cooperation to Lessee as a result of which Lessee is unable to diligently fulfill its obligations under this Section 7; (g) any claim made against Lessor for any Imposition that Lessee is obligated to pay hereunder with respect to which Lessor has not notified Lessee in writing pursuant to Section 7.2; (h) any tax imposed on the purchase of a Unit or Units from Manufacturer; and (i) any sales or use tax imposed upon (A) the voluntary transfer or other disposition by Lessor, or any assignee of Lessor, of all or any of the Units, or (B) another obtaining any interest in a Unit by, through or under Lessor. In this regard it is understood that any transfer or disposition (A) that occurs in the Lessor's exercise of the remedies provided in Section 13.2 after an Event of Default has occurred and while the same is continuing or (B) of a Unit which has suffered a Casualty Occurrence, shall not be deemed to be a voluntary transfer or disposition.

7.2 *Claim Notification.* If a claim is made against Lessor for any Imposition that Lessee is obligated to pay hereunder, Lessor shall promptly notify Lessee in writing.

7.3 *Right to Contest.* Lessee shall be under no obligation to pay any Imposition so long as Lessee is contesting such Imposition in good faith. Lessor hereby agrees to fully cooperate with Lessee, including providing any information Lessee shall request, in connection with any such contest. So long as Lessee is so contesting such Imposition and no final, unreviewable judgment adverse to Lessee has been entered by a court of competent jurisdiction, Lessee shall not be in default hereunder with respect to the nonpayment of any such Imposition.

7.4 *Lessor Payment Reimbursement.* If any Imposition shall have been charged or levied against Lessor directly and paid by Lessor, Lessee shall reimburse Lessor on presentation of reasonably satisfactory evidence of payment; provided, however, Lessor has obtained Lessee's prior written approval for the payment thereof, which approval shall not be unreasonably withheld.

7.5 *Lessor Refund Reimbursement.* If Lessee has reimbursed Lessor for any Imposition pursuant to this Section 7 (or if Lessee has made a payment to the appropriate taxing authority for an Imposition which it is required to pay hereunder), Lessee may take such steps (in the name of Lessee or in the name of Lessor) as are necessary or appropriate to seek a refund of such Imposition, and Lessor shall fully cooperate with Lessee in seeking such refund. In the event of a refund of any Imposition for which Lessor has received a payment from Lessee, the amount of such refund shall be immediately paid over to or retained by Lessee, as appropriate.

SECTION 8. *GENERAL INDEMNIFICATION*

8.1 *Conflict.* The provisions of this Section 8 are in addition to, and not in limitation of, the provisions of Section 7 hereof; provided, however, that in the event of a conflict between the provisions of this Section 8 and the provisions of Section 7, the provisions of Section 7 shall be controlling.

8.2 *General Indemnity.* Lessee hereby agrees to assume liability for, and does hereby agree to indemnify, protect, save, and keep Lessor harmless from and against any and all liabilities, obligations, losses, damages, penalties, claims, actions, suits, costs, expenses, or disbursements arising out of Lessee's actions that may be imposed on, incurred by, or asserted against Lessor relating to or arising out of this Lease or the manufacture, purchase, acceptance, rejection, return, lease, ownership, possession, use, condition, operation, or sale of each Unit or any accident in connection therewith. Lessor hereby expressly authorizes Lessee to contest, and agrees to cooperate fully with Lessee in contesting, in the name of Lessee or Lessor as Lessee shall deem appropriate for the benefit of Lessee, any such liability, obligation, penalty, or claim asserted against either Lessee or Lessor. Lessee shall not be required to indemnify Lessor except as specifically set forth in the preceding sentence, including without limitation as to (a) loss or liability in respect of any Unit arising from any act or event which occurs after such Unit has been returned to Lessor pursuant to the provisions of this Lease; (b) loss or liability resulting from the breach of any covenant, representation or warranty made by Lessor in this Lease or in any document relating to the transactions contemplated by this Lease; (c) loss or liability resulting from the negligence or misconduct of Lessor (including acts by employees, agents or other representatives of Lessor); (d) any legal or accounting fees or other expenses incurred by Lessor in connection with this Lease and the other documents referred to herein and any amendments or other modifications or additions to this Lease or such other documents; (e) any brokerage fees or similar fees or commissions incurred by Lessor in connection with any transactions contemplated hereby; or (f) any liability, obligation, penalty, or claim indemnified against herein so long as the validity or amount thereof is being contested by Lessee in good faith.

SECTION 9. *PAYMENT FOR CASUALTY OCCURRENCE*

9.1 *Casualty Occurrence.* In the event that any Unit becomes damaged or otherwise inoperable so as to preclude its use for the purpose intended by Lessee, as determined by Lessee in good faith, or in the event any Unit is lost or stolen or is permanently returned by Lessee to Manufacturer pursuant to the Purchase Documents [*Author's Note*: This relates to when a Unit is permitted to be returned to the manufacturer because it is defective or otherwise fails to meet requirements set forth in the Purchase Documents], or for ninety (90) consecutive days or more is taken or requisitioned by condemnation or other-wise in such a manner as to result in Lessee's loss of possession or use, excluding any permitted sublease (any such occurrence being hereinafter referred to as a "Casualty Occurrence") during the Term of this Lease, Lessee shall promptly so notify Lessor. On the Rent Date next succeeding a Casualty Occurrence (the "Loss Payment Date"), Lessee shall pay to Lessor an amount equal to the Casualty Value of such Unit applicable on the date of such Casualty Occurrence. [*Author's Note*: Casualty Value payments vary in ar-rangement—each situation must be looked at independently.] Upon, but not prior to, the time when such payment is made by Lessee as to any Unit, Lessee's obligation to pay Rent for such Unit, including without limitation any Rent that would be attributable to any Rent payment period subsequent to the Loss Payment Date, shall cease and the Term of this Lease as to such Unit shall automatically terminate. Lessor hereby appoints Lessee as its sole agent to dispose of any Unit or any part thereof suffering a Casualty Occurrence in the best manner and at the best price obtainable, as determined by Lessee in its sole discretion, on an "as is, where is" basis. If Lessee shall have so paid the Casualty Value to Lessor, unless an Event of Default shall have occurred and be continuing, Lessee shall be entitled to the proceeds of such sale up to an amount equal to the sum of the Casualty Value of such Unit plus all costs, expenses, and damages incurred by Lessee in connection with such Casualty Occurrence and the disposition of such Unit. Lessor shall be entitled to any excess. In the case of the taking or requisition of any Unit by any governmental authority, any payments received from such governmental authority as com-pensation for such taking or requisition shall, if Lessee has therefore paid the Casualty Value, be immediately paid over to or retained by Lessee, as appropri-ate, up to an amount equal to the sum of the Casualty Value of such Unit plus all costs, expenses, and damages incurred by Lessee in connection with such Casualty Occurrence, and Lessor shall be entitled to any excess. Lessor shall have no duty to Lessee to pursue any claim against any governmental authority, but Lessee may at its own cost and expense pursue the same on its own behalf and on behalf of Lessor, and Lessor shall cooperate fully in Lessee's pursuit of such claim.

9.2 *Manufacturer Returned Unit.* As to each Unit returned to Manufacturer in the manner described in the first sentence of Section 9.1, Lessee shall be entitled to immediately receive and retain all amounts paid or payable to Lessor by Manufacturer with respect to the return of such Unit, up to the Casualty Value paid by Lessee hereunder plus all costs, expenses, and damages incurred by Lessee in connection therewith. Any excess shall immediately be paid over to or retained by Lessor, as appropriate.

9.3 *Return After Requisition.* In the event of the taking or requisition for use by any governmental authority of any Unit during the Term of this Lease as to such Unit, unless such taking or requisition shall constitute a Casualty Occurrence, all of Lessee's obligations under this Lease with respect to such Unit shall continue to the same extent as if such taking or requisition had not occurred, except that if such Unit is returned by such governmental authority to Lessee at any time after the end of the Term of this Lease as to such Unit, anything to the contrary contained in this Lease notwithstanding, Lessee shall only be required to promptly return such Unit to Lessor upon such return by such governmental authority, rather than at the end of the Term of this Lease as to such Unit. All payments received by Lessor or Lessee from any governmental authority for the use during the Term of this Lease of such Unit as provided in this Section 9.3 shall be immediately paid over to or retained by Lessee, as appropriate, unless an Event of Default shall have occurred and be continuing in which case the amount otherwise payable to Lessee may be retained by Lessor and applied to discharge the liabilities of Lessee under Section 13.

SECTION 10. *INSURANCE*

10.1 *Insurance Maintenance.* Lessee will, at all times during the Term of this Lease as to each Unit prior to the return of such Unit to Lessor in accordance with Section 17 of this Lease, at its own expense, cause to be carried and maintained with insurers of recognized responsibility (a) property and casualty insurance for such Unit and (b) public liability insurance against claims for personal injury, death, or property damage resulting from the ownership, possession, maintenance, use, or operation of such Unit, in both cases in at least such amounts and against such risks as are customarily insured against by Lessee on similar equipment; provided, however, that in no event shall (a) the amount of such property and casualty insurance be less than the Casualty Value of such Unit from time to time (except that Lessee may self-insure in an amount up to _____) and (b) the amount of such public liability insurance be less than [$ _____] as to any one occurrence. The benefits under such insurance shall be payable to Lessor and Lessee, as their respective interests may appear. Any policy of insurance carried in accordance with this Section 10 shall (a) require thirty (30) days prior written notice to Lessor of a material change or cancellation or nonrenewal; (b) name Lessor as an additional insured, as its interest may appear, and provide that all provisions of such policy, except the limits of liability, will operate in the same manner as if there were a separate policy governing such additional insured; and (c) provide that, as to Lessor's interest, such insurance shall not be invalidated by reason of any breach of representation or violation of warranty made by Lessee to the insurer in connection with obtaining such policy of insurance or maintaining the same in full force and effect. Lessee shall deliver to Lessor together with each Certificate of Acceptance a copy of each such policy (or a certificate of insurance relating thereto) with respect to each Unit covered by such Certificate of Acceptance.

10.2 *Insurance Proceeds.* Any insurance proceeds resulting from insurance carried by Lessee or condemnation payments received by Lessor for each Unit suffering a Casualty Occurrence shall be deducted from the amounts payable by Lessee for a Casualty Occurrence pursuant to Section 9. If Lessor shall receive any such insurance proceeds or condemnation payments after Lessee shall have made payment to Section 9 without deduction for such insurance proceeds or such condemnation payments, Lessor shall immediately pay such insurance proceeds or condemnation payments to Lessee, up to the sum of the Casualty Value amount paid by Lessee plus all costs, expenses, and damages incurred by Lessee in connection with the disposition of each Unit suffering a Casualty Occurrence, unless an Event of Default shall have occurred and be continuing, in which case the amount otherwise payable to Lessee may be retained by Lessor and applied to discharge the liabilities of Lessee under Section 13. The balance of such insurance proceeds or condemnation payments shall be retained by Lessor. All property damage insurance proceeds received by Lessor or Lessee with respect to a damaged Unit not suffering a Casualty Occurrence shall be applied toward the payment, when due, of the cost of repairing such Unit. Any condemnation payments received with respect to a Unit not suffering a Casualty Occurrence shall be the property of Lessee unless an Event of Default shall have occurred and be continuing, in which case the amount otherwise payable to Lessee shall be paid to or retained by Lessor, as appropriate, and applied to discharge the liabilities of Lessee under Section 13.

SECTION 11. *INSPECTION*

Lessor shall have the right during the Term of this Lease upon not less than ten (10) Business Days prior written notice to Lessee to inspect any Unit for the purpose of confirming its existence, condition, and proper maintenance, at mutually agreeable times during Lessee's regular business hours. Notwithstanding the foregoing, Lessor may not inspect any Units if it would unreasonably interfere with Lessee's business operations, violate any applicable governmental security laws, regulations or rules, or violate the reasonable security regulations or procedures of Lessee.

SECTION 12. *DISCLAIMER OF WARRANTIES; COMPLIANCE WITH LAWS AND RULES; MAINTENANCE; ADDITIONS*

12.1 *Warranty Disclaimer.* LESSOR MAKES NO WARRANTY OR REPRESENTATION, EITHER EXPRESS OR IMPLIED, AS TO THE DESIGN OR CONDITION, OR QUALITY OF THE MATERIAL, EQUIPMENT OR WORKMANSHIP OF THE UNITS LEASED TO LESSEE HEREUNDER, AND LESSOR MAKES NO WARRANTY OF MERCHANTABILITY OR FITNESS OF THE UNITS FOR ANY PARTICULAR PURPOSE [*Author's Note*: This warranty disclaimer should be given to a lessor *only* when the lessor is not also the vendor], it being agreed that all such risks, as between Lessor and Lessee, are to be borne by Lessee; but Lessor hereby assigns and transfers to Lessee, and hereby irrevocably appoints and constitutes Lessee as its agent and attorney-in-fact to assert and enforce from time to time as Lessee shall deem appropriate, in the name of and for the account of Lessor and/or Lessee, as their respective interests may appear, at Lessee's sole cost and expense, whatever claims and rights Lessor may have as owner of each Unit against Manufacturer (or any subcontractor or supplier of Manufacturer) under the Purchase Documents or otherwise. Lessor agrees to cooperate fully at Lessee's request in Lessee's pursuit of any such claims or rights. If for any reason Lessee is prevented from asserting such claims or rights in the name of and for the account of Lessor and/or Lessee, as their respective interests may appear, Lessor will, at Lessee's expense, promptly upon Lessee's request enforce such claims or rights as directed from time to time by Lessee.

12.2 *Compliance With Laws.* Lessee agrees to use its best efforts to comply in all material respects with all applicable laws (including without limitation laws with respect to Lessee's use, maintenance, and operation of each Unit) of each jurisdiction in which a Unit is located; provided, however, Lessee shall not be required to comply with any such law so long as Lessee is, in good faith, contesting the validity or application of any such law. Lessor agrees to cooperate fully at Lessee's request in Lessee's contest of any such law or its applicability.

12.3 *Maintenance.* Lessee shall pay all costs, expenses, fees, and charges (other than those included in Lessor's Cost) incurred in connection with Lessee's use and operation of the Units. Subject to the provisions of Section 9, Lessee, at its own cost and expense, shall maintain, repair, and service, or cause to be maintained, repaired, and serviced, each Unit so as to keep it in the same operating condition and repair as it was when it first became subject to this Lease, ordinary wear and tear for the use intended by Lessee excepted, and within a resonable period of time shall replace all parts of any Unit that may have become worn out, stolen, confiscated, destroyed, or otherwise rendered permanently unfit for use with appropriate replacement parts, which shall be free and clear from all Liens, other than any Lessor's Lien. Upon replacement, title to the replacement parts shall automatically be vested in Lessee.

12.4 *Maintenance Agreement.* Lessee shall, upon expiration of the Manufacturer's warranty period applicable to each Unit, enter into and maintain in force for the longest possible period obtainable by Lessee during the Term of this Lease as to such Unit a maintenance agreement (the "Maintenance Agreement") with Manufacturer or with another qualified party covering at least the prime shift maintenance of such Unit; provided, however, if Lessee is unable to obtain a Maintenance Agreement reasonably satisfactory to it as to any Unit, Lessee shall have the right to maintain such Unit itself. Charges under the Maintenance Agreement and all other maintenance and service charges, including installation and dismantling charges, shall be borne by Lessee.

12.5 *Additions.* Lessee may, at its option and at its own cost and expense, make additions, modifications, and improvements to any Unit provided such additions, modifications, and improvements are readily removable without causing material damage to such Unit. All such additions, modifications, and improvements shall remain the property of Lessee and shall be removed by Lessee before such Unit is returned to Lessor. Lessee shall repair all damage to any such Unit resulting from such installation and removal. Lessee shall not, without the prior written consent of Lessor, which consent shall not be unreasonably withheld, alter any Unit, or affix or install any accessories or devices on any Unit, if the same shall materially impair the function or use of such Unit. Except to the extent otherwise provided in the first sentence of this Section 12.5, any and all other additions or modifications and improvements to any Unit shall constitute accessions to such Unit and title thereto, free from any Lien (except for any Lessor's Lien), shall immediately be vested in Lessor, any and all warranties of Manufacturer with respect thereto shall thereupon automatically be assigned to Lessee and Lessor shall cooperate fully with Lessee in their enforcement to the same extent and on the same basis as provided in Section 12.1.

SECTION 13. *EVENTS OF DEFAULT AND REMEDIES*

13.1 *Events of Default.* During the Term of this Lease the occurrence of any of the following events shall constitute an "Event of Default:"

(a) Nonpayment of all or any part of the Rent provided for in Section 5 (except as otherwise expressly provided in Section 2.2), if such nonpayment shall continue for ten (10) Business Days after Lessee's receipt from Lessor of written notice of such nonpayment;

(b) Lessee shall make or permit any unauthorized assignment or transfer of this Lease or any interest herein or any unauthorized transfer of the right to possession of any Unit;

(c) Lessee shall fail or refuse to comply with any other covenant, agreement, term, or provision of this Lease required to be kept or performed by Lessee or to make reasonable provision for such compliance within thirty (30) days after Lessee's receipt from Lessor of a written demand for the performance thereof which demand shall specify in reasonable detail the nonperformance;

(d) [U.S. only] Any proceedings shall be commenced by or against Lessee for any relief under any bankruptcy or insolvency law, or any law relating to the relief of debtors, readjustment of indebtedness, reorganization, arrangement, composition, or extension, and, unless such proceedings shall have been dismissed, nullified, stayed, or otherwise rendered ineffective (but then only so long as such stay shall continue in force or such ineffectiveness shall continue), all of the obligations of Lessee hereunder shall not have been and shall not continue to be duly assumed in writing, pursuant to a court order or decree, by a trustee or trustees or receiver or receivers appointed (whether or not subject to ratification) for Lessee or its property in connection with any such proceedings in such manner that such obligations shall have the same status as obligations incurred by such trustee or trustees or receiver or receivers, within thirty (30) days after such appointment, if any, or thirty (30) days after such proceedings shall have been commenced, whichever is earlier, or Lessee shall make a general assignment for the benefit of creditors or shall admit in writing its inability to pay its debts generally as they become due;

(e) any representation or warranty made by Lessee in this Lease, or in any certificate or other document delivered by Lessee pursuant hereto, shall be incorrect in any material respect as of the date made and shall remain uncorrected for a period of thirty (30) days after receipt by Lessee of written notice from Lessor specifying in reasonable detail the incorrect representation or warranty.

13.2 *Remedies*. Upon the occurrence of an Event of Default, and so long as such Event of Default shall be continuing, Lessor may, at its option, declare this Lease to be in default and may exercise in its sole discretion any one or more of the following remedies:

(a) proceed by appropriate court action or actions, either at law or in equity, to enforce performance by Lessee of the applicable covenants of this Lease or to recover damages for the breach thereof; or

(b) by notice in writing to Lessee terminate this Lease with respect to any or all of the Units, whereupon all rights of Lessee to the possession and use of such Unit or units shall absolutely cease and terminate as though this Lease had never been made, but Lessee shall remain liable as hereinafter provided; and thereupon Lessor may, by its agent or agents, enter upon the premises of Lessee or any other premises where any of such Units may be located and take possession of all or any of such Units and thenceforth hold, possess, operate, sell, lease, and enjoy such Unit or Units free from any right of Lessee to use such Unit or Units for any purpose whatsoever and without any duty to account to Lessee for any action or inaction or for any proceeds arising therefrom, but Lessor shall, nevertheless, have a right to recover from Lessee any and all amounts that under the provisions of this Lease and any applicable Equipment Schedule may then be due or which may have accrued to the date of such termination (computing the Rent for any number of days less than a full Rent payment period by multiplying the Rent for such full Rent payment period by a fraction the numerator of which is such number of days and the denominator of which is the total number of days in the full Rent payment period) and also to recover from Lessee (i) as damages for loss of the bargain and not as a penalty, whichever of the following sums, with respect to each such Unit, Lessor, in its sole discretion, shall specify by written notice to Lessee: (a) an amount equal to the excess, if any, computed as of the Rent Date immediately succeeding the date of the Event of Default, of the Casualty Value for such Unit over the present value of the Fair Market Rental of such Unit for the remainder of the Term of this Lease following such Rent Date, such present value to be computed in each case using the Discount Rate specified in the applicable Equipment Schedule [*Author's Note*: This is for an "in advance" rental structure]; or (B) an amount equal to the excess, if any, computed as of the Rent Date immediately succeeding the date of the Event of Default, of the Casualty Value for such Unit over the Fair Market Value of such Unit [*Author's Note*: This is for an "in advance" rental structure]; and any reasonable costs and expenses (including legal and accounting fees) incurred in connection with the recovery, repair, repainting, return, and remarketing of such Unit or other exercise of Lessor's remedies hereunder.

The remedies in this Lease provided in favor of Lessor shall not be deemed exclusive, but shall be cumulative and shall be in addition to all other remedies existing in its favor at law or in equity.

Lessor shall use its best efforts to mitigate any damages suffered by it. IN NO EVENT SHALL LESSEE BE LIABLE FOR ANY INDIRECT, SPECIAL, OR CONSE-QUENTIAL DAMAGES OF ANY KIND UNDER THIS LEASE.

SECTION 14. *FAIR MARKET VALUE AND FAIR MARKET RENTAL*

"Fair Market Value" and "Fair Market Rental," as to each Unit for all purposes in connection with this Lease, shall have the respective meanings and shall be determined in accordance with the procedure set forth in this Section 14. Fair Market Value and Fair Market Rental shall be determined on the basis of, and be equal in amount to, the value which would obtain in an arm's-length transaction between an informed and willing buyer-user (or lessee, if determining Fair Market Rental), other than a lessee currently in possession or a used equipment dealer, under no compulsion to buy (or lease), and an informed and willing seller (or lessor, if determining Fair Market Rental) under no compulsion to sell (or lease), and, in such determination, costs of removal from the location of current use shall not be a deduction from such value.

In the event that a determination of Fair Market Value or Fair Market Rental of a Unit shall be made under any provision of this Lease, the party requesting the determination shall deliver a written notice to the other party so indicating and appointing an Appraiser selected by the requesting party to determine the Fair Market Value or Fair Market Rental. Within fifteen (15) days after the receipt of such written notice the party receiving such notice shall deliver to the requesting party a written notice appointing an Appraiser of its selection to make such determination. The two Appraisers appointed in such written notices shall meet promptly to determine the Fair Market Value or Fair Market Rental of such Unit as of the applicable date. If within thirty (30) days after the initial written notice the two Appraisers so appointed by Lessor and Lessee shall be unable to agree upon the Fair Market Value or the Fair Market Rental of such Unit, whichever is applicable, such Appraisers shall within five (5) days thereaf-ter appoint a third Appraiser. The decision of the three Appraisers so appointed shall be given within a period of ten (10) days after the appointment of such third Appraiser. Any decision in which any two Appraisers so appointed and acting hereunder concur shall in all cases be binding and conclusive upon Lessor and Lessee. The fees and expenses of the Appraisers shall be borne equally by Lessee and Lessor, unless the Lease shall have been terminated pursuant to Section 13 hereof, in which case Lessee shall pay all such fees and expenses.

SECTION 15. *ASSIGNMENT, POSSESSION, LIENS, SUBLEASE, AND MERGER*

15.1 *Lessor Assignment.* Lessor agrees that it will not assign all or any portion of its rights under, or interests in, this Lease or any of the Units unless such assignment is made pursuant to a security agreement relating to any borrowing by Lessor from one or more institutional lenders. Notwithstanding the foregoing, Lessor agrees that it will not make any such assignment to any entities listed on an Annex to any Equipment Schedule. Lessor agrees that if such a security interest in any Unit is granted, the security agreement covering such Unit shall expressly provide that the rights and interests of Lessee in and to such Unit as provided in this Lease shall remain paramount so long as no Event of Default shall have occurred and be continuing. Lessor shall give Lessee prompt written notice of any such assignment by Lessor. All the rights of Lessor hereunder (including without limitation the right to receive Rent payable under this Lease) shall inure to the benefit of Lessor's permitted assigns to the extent of such assignment. Any payment of Rent or other payment by Lessee to such assignee shall be in full satisfaction of Lessee's obligation to make such payment under this Lease and Lessor hereby indemnifies Lessee against any damages, claims, costs, or expenses incurred by Lessee in connection therewith, but Lessee shall be under no obligation to make any payment to any such assignee until Lessor shall give Lessee written notice to make such payment to such assignee. Notwithstanding anything to the contrary herein, any permitted assignee of Lessor can declare an Event of Default hereunder only with respect to one or more Units subject to such assignee's security interest.

15.2 *Lessee Possession and Assignment.* So long as an Event of Default under this Lease shall not have occurred and be continuing, Lessee shall be entitled to the quiet enjoyment and peaceful possession and use of the Units in accordance with and subject to all the terms and conditions of this Lease, but without the prior written consent of Lessor, which consent shall not be unreasonably withheld, Lessee shall not, except as otherwise permitted herein, lease, assign, or transfer its leasehold interest in any or all of the Units.

15.3 *Liens.* Except as otherwise provided herein, Lessee, at its own expense, shall promptly pay or discharge any and all sums claimed by, or liabilities in favor of, any person that, if unpaid, would become a mortgage, lien, charge, security interest, or other encumbrance (any of the foregoing being herein referred to as a "Lien"), other than a Lien by, through or under Lessor on or with respect to any Unit, including any accession thereto, or the interest of Lessor or Lessee therein, which shall include without limitation any Lien resulting from a breach of Lessor's covenant in Section 2.2 or resulting from claims against Lessor not related to the ownership or leasing of any Unit (any of the foregoing being herein referred to as a "Lessor's Lien"), and shall promptly discharge any such Lien that arises. Lessee shall not be required to pay or discharge any such Lien so long as the validity thereof is being contested in good faith. The existence of any Lessor's Lien or any Lien for taxes, assessments, or governmental charges, or levies (in each case so long as not due and delinquent), or inchoate materialmen's, mechanics', workmen's, repairmen's, employees', or other like Liens arising in the ordinary course of business and in each case not delinquent shall not constitute a breach of this covenant.

15.4 *Lessee Sublease.* So long as no Event of Default under this Lease shall have occurred and be continuing, Lessee shall be entitled without Lessor's consent to sublease any or all of the Units, or any part thereof, to, or permit their use by, any person or entity, including without limitation any subsidiary, affiliate or parent corporation of Lessee, incorporated in [the United States of America/Dominion of Canada—as appropriate] [or any (state/province as appropriate) thereof] [or the District of Columbia—U.S. only], but in all cases only upon and subject to all the terms and conditions of this Lease. No such sublease or other assignment of use by Lessee shall relieve Lessee of its obligations hereunder.

15.5 *Merger or Consolidation.* Notwithstanding anything herein to the contrary, Lessee may assign or transfer this Lease and its leasehold interest in the Units to any corporation incorporated under the laws of any [state/province—as appropriate] of the [United States of America/Dominion of Canada—as appropriate] [or the District of Columbia—U.S. only] into or with which Lessee shall have merged or consolidated or which shall have acquired all or substantially all of the property of Lessee, provided that such assignee or transferee will not, upon the effectiveness of such merger, consolidation, or acquisition and the assignment or transfer of this Lease to it, be in default under any provision of this Lease.

SECTION 16. *LESSEE RIGHTS*

16.1 *Purchase Right.* Lessee shall have the right to purchase any Unit as provided in the applicable Equipment Schedule.

16.2 *Renewal Right.* Lessee shall have the right to renew this Lease as to any Unit as provided in the applicable Equipment Schedule.

16.3 *Termination Right.* Lessee shall have the right to terminate this Lease as to any Unit as provided in the applicable Equipment Schedule.

16.4 *Upgrade Right.* Lessee shall have the right to upgrade any Unit as provided in the applicable Equipment Schedule.

SECTION 17. *RETURN OF EQUIPMENT*

As soon as practicable on or after the expiration of the Term of this Lease as to each Unit, Lessee shall prepare the Unit for return to Lessor and deliver possession of such Unit to Lessor at the location of such Unit on the final day of the Term of this Lease. The Units shall be returned in the condition in which they are required to be maintained by Lessee under Section 12.3.

SECTION 18. *INTEREST ON OVERDUE PAYMENTS*

Anything herein to the contrary notwithstanding, any nonpayment of Rent or any other payment obligation with respect to any Unit after the due date shall result in the obligation on the part of Lessee promptly to pay with respect to such Unit, to the extent legally enforceable, interest on such Rent or other payment obligation for the period of time during which it is overdue at the Overdue Rate as specified in the applicable Equipment Schedule, or such lesser amount as may be legally enforceable.

SECTION 19. *CONFIDENTIAL INFORMATION*

Lessor agrees that it will not, without first obtaining Lessee's written consent, disclose to any person, firm, or enterprise, or use for its benefit, any information not generally available to the public relating to Lessee's business, including without limitation any pricing methods, processes, financial data, lists, apparatus, statistics, programs, research, development, or related information concerning past, present, or future business activities of Lessee.

SECTION 20. *ADVERTISING OR PUBLICITY*

Neither Lessor nor Lessee shall use the name of the other in publicity releases or advertising without securing the prior written consent of the other.

SECTION 21. *REPRESENTATIONS AND WARRANTIES*

Each of Lessor and Lessee represents and warrants to the other that:

(a) It is a corporation duly organized, validly existing, and in good standing under the laws of the jurisdiction of its incorporation. It has full power and authority to carry on its business as presently conducted, to own or hold under lease its properties, and to enter into and perform its obligations under this Lease, and it is duly qualified to do business as a foreign corporation and is in good standing in each jurisdiction in which the location of any Unit requires such qualification.

(b) Its execution, delivery, and performance of this Lease have been duly authorized by all necessary corporate action on its part, do not contravene its corporate charter or by-laws or any law, governmental rule, or regulation, or any order, writ, injunction, decree, judgment, award, determination, direction, or demand (collectively "Order") of which it is aware binding on it or its properties and do not and will not contravene the provisions of, or constitute a default under, or result in the creation of any Lien upon any Unit under, any material indenture, mortgage, contract, or other instrument to which it is a party or by which it or its property is bound.

(c) No consent or approval of, giving of notice to, registration with, or taking of any other action by, any [state/province—as appropriate], federal or other governmental commission, agency, or regulatory authority is required for the performance by it of the transactions contemplated by this Lease, or if any such approval, registration, or giving of notice is required it has been obtained, so registered, or given, as the case may be.

(d) This Lease has been duly entered into and delivered by it and constitutes a legal, valid, and binding agreement of it enforceable against it in accordance with its terms, except as limited by (i) any bankruptcy, insolvency, reorganization, or other similar laws of general application affecting the enforcement of creditors' or lessors' rights generally, (ii) emergency powers lawfully conferred upon any governmental agency, and (iii) laws or judicial decisions limiting the right to specific performance or other equitable remedies.

(e) To the best of its knowledge there are no actions, suits, or proceedings pending or threatened against or affecting it or any of its property in any court or before any arbitrator or before or by any federal [state/provincial— as appropriate], municipal or other governmental department, commission, board, bureau, agency, or instrumentality, domestic or foreign (collectively "Governmental Body"), except actions, suits, or proceedings of the character normally incident to the kind of business conducted by it as to which any adverse determination in excess of any accruals to reflect potential liability would not materially adversely affect its business, assets, operations, or condition, financial or otherwise, taken as a whole, or materially adversely affect its ability to perform its obligations under this Lease, and it is not in material default with respect to any material Order of any court, arbitrator, or Governmental Body.

(f) As to Lessee only, its consolidated balance sheet as of _____ , and its related consolidated statements of income, retained earnings and changes in financial position for the two years then ended, heretofore delivered to Lessor, fairly present its consolidated financial position as of such date and its consolidated results of operations and consolidated changes in financial position for the two years then ended, all in conformity with generally accepted accounting principles consistently applied during the periods. Since the date of such balance sheet there has not been any material adverse change in its business, assets, liabilities, results of operations, or condition, financial or otherwise.

(g) It is not a party to any agreement or instrument or subject to any charter or other corporate restriction that, so far as it is now aware, materially adversely affects or will, so far as it can now foresee, materially adversely affect, its business, operations, or properties or its ability to perform its obligations under this Lease.

(h) To the best of its knowledge it has filed all required tax returns in all jurisdictions in which such returns were required to be filed and has paid, or made provision for, all material taxes shown to be due and payable on such returns and all other material taxes and assessments that are payable by it, except for any taxes and assessments of which the amount, applicability, or validity is currently being contested in good faith and as to which any adverse determination in excess of any accruals to reflect potential liability would not materially adversely affect its ability to perform its obligations under this Lease.

SECTION 22. *FINANCIAL INFORMATION*

During the term of this Lease, Lessee agrees to provide Lessor with its consolidated quarterly and annual financial statements promptly as they become available and such other financial information as may be provided to Lessee's shareholders from time to time.

SECTION 23. *PAYMENTS*

23.1 *Postponement of Payment Date.* If any date on which a Rent or other payment is due and payable is not a Business Day, the payment otherwise payable on such date shall be due and payable on the next succeeding Business Day.

23.2 *Payment Address.* All Rent and other payments required to be made by Lessee to Lessor shall be made to Lessor at the address of Lessor set forth in Section 24 or at such other address as may be specified in writing by Lessor at least thirty (30) Business Days prior to the date such notice is intended to become effective.

23.3 *Method of Payment.* All Rent and other payments under this Lease shall be made in lawful money of the [United States of America]/[Dominion of Canada].

SECTION 24. *NOTICES*

Any notice or document or payment to be delivered hereunder to any of the persons designated below, except as otherwise expressly provided herein, shall be deemed to have been properly delivered if delivered personally or deposited with the [United States/Canadian—as appropriate] Postal Service, registered or certified mail, return receipt requested, postage prepaid, to the following respective addresses:

If To Lessor: _____

_____

Attn:_____

If To Lessee: _____

_____

Attn: _____

or such other address as may be furnished from time to time by any of the parties hereto upon at least thirty (30) days prior written notice.

SECTION 25. *STATEMENT OF LEASE*

It is expressly understood and agreed by and between the parties hereto that this instrument constitutes a lease of the Units, and nothing herein shall be construed as conveying to Lessee any right, title, or interest in the Units except as a lessee only. Neither the execution nor the filing of any financing statement with respect to any of the Units or the execution or filing of any financing statement with respect to this Lease or the recording hereof shall in any manner imply that the relationship between Lessor and Lessee is anything other than that of lessor and lessee. Any such filing of financing statements or recordation of this Lease is solely to protect the interests of Lessor and Lessee in the event of any unwarranted assertions by any person not a party to this Lease transaction.

SECTION 26. *SEVERABILITY, EFFECT, AND INTERPRETATION OF LEASE*

26.1 *Severability.* Any provision of this Lease that is prohibited or unenforceable by any applicable law of any jurisdiction shall as to such jurisdiction be ineffective to the extent of such prohibition or unenforceability without invalidating the remaining provisions hereof, and any such prohibition or unenforceability in any jurisdiction shall not invalidate or render unenforceable such provision in any other jurisdiction.

26.2 *Complete Statement of Rights.* This Lease exclusively and completely states the rights of Lessor and Lessee with respect to the leasing of the Units and supersedes all other agreements, oral or written, with respect thereto.

26.3 *Section Headings.* All Section headings are inserted for convenience only and shall not affect any construction or interpretation of this Lease.

SECTION 27. *LAW GOVERNING*

The terms and provisions of this Lease and all rights and obligations hereunder shall be governed in all respects by the laws of [_____].

SECTION 28. *FURTHER ASSURANCES*

Each of Lessor and Lessee agrees that at any time and from time to time, after the execution and delivery of this Lease, it shall, upon request of the other party, promptly execute and deliver such further documents and do such further acts and things the requesting party may reasonably request in order fully to effectuate the purposes of this Lease.

SECTION 29. *MODIFICATION, WAIVER, AND CONSENT*

Any modification or waiver of any provision of this Lease, or any consent to any departure by Lessee or Lessor, as the case may be, therefrom, shall not be effective in any event unless the same is in writing and signed by the party to be charged, and then such modification, waiver, or consent shall be effective only in the specific instance and for the specific purpose given.

SECTION 30. *BINDING EFFECT*

This Lease shall be binding upon and shall inure to the benefit of the respective successors and permitted assigns of Lessee and Lessor.

SECTION 31. *EXECUTION IN COUNTERPARTS*

This Lease may be executed in any number of counterparts, each of which shall constitute an original and which taken together shall constitute one and the same Lease.

IN WITNESS WHEREOF, the parties, pursuant to due authority, have caused this Lease to be signed in their respective names by duly authorized officers or representatives as of the date first above written.

_____

as Lessor

By _____   _____

Title _____

_____

as Lessee

By _____

Title _____

Equipment Schedule   EXHIBIT A

Equipment Schedule No. _____ ("Schedule")

Dated as of _____ , 19 _____

to Master Lease of Computer Equipment ("Lease")

Dated as of _____ , 19 _____

between

_____ ("Lessor")

and

_____ ("Lessee")

1. *EQUIPMENT DESCRIPTION*

					Estimated Invoice Purchase Price	
Quantity	Manufacturer	Model	New/ Used	Description	Per Unit	Aggregate

TOTAL ESTIMATED INVOICE PURCHASE PRICE _____

2. *BASIC LEASE COMMENCEMENT DATE*

The Basic Lease Commencement Date for each Unit shall commence on [insert relevant time—such as the 1st day of the month immediately following the Unit's Acceptance Date if the Acceptance Date does not fall on the 1st day of a month].

3. *CUTOFF DATE*

Lessor shall be obligated to purchase and lease each Item of Equipment specified in Section 1 of this Schedule to Lessee provided such Item of Equipment has been accepted by Lessee for lease in accordance with the provisions of Section 2.5 of the Lease on or before _____ , 19 _____ .

4. *DISCOUNT RATE*

The Discount Rate applicable to each Unit shall be equal to an interest charge of _____ % per annum.

5. *LESSOR'S COST*

The Lessor's Cost for each Item of Equipment subject to this Schedule shall be an amount equal to the Invoice Purchase Price for such Item of Equipment plus all sales taxes in connection with the purchase from Manufacturer of such Item of Equipment, transportation charges in connection with the delivery of such Item of Equipment from the Manufacturer to Lessee and [Insert other relevant charges which are to be included].

6. *OVERDUE RATE*
The Overdue Rate for each Unit shall be equal to an interest charge of _____ % per annum.

7. *RENT DATE*
The Rent Date as to each Unit shall be the _____ day of each _____ during the Primary Term and the _____ day of each _____ during any Renewal Term.

8. *UNIT LOCATION*
Each Unit shall be located at Lessee's place of business at _____ .

9. *LESSOR COMMITMENT*
Lessor shall be obligated to purchase and lease Items of Equipment pursuant to the terms of the Lease and this Schedule with an aggregate Lessor's Cost of not less than $ _____ . [*Author's Note*: This amount should have a minimum + 10% leeway above the anticipated aggregate Lessor's Cost.]

10. *LEASE TERM*
(a) The Primary Term for each Unit shall commence on the Basic Lease Commencement Date of such Unit and shall end on the anniversary date thereof that number of years indicated below opposite the relevant Unit thereafter.

Unit Description	*Primary Term In Years*

(b) The Renewal Term for each Unit shall be as specified in Section 13 of this Schedule.

11. *UNIT RENT*
(a) The Interim Rent for each Unit as to any Interim Term shall be payable on the Basic Lease Commencement Date of such Unit and shall be an amount equal to the Basic Rent multiplied by a fraction, the numerator of which is that number of days in the Interim Term and the denominator of which is that number of days in a Primary Term Rent payment period. [*Author's Note*: This can vary from transaction to transaction.] (b) The Basic Rent shall be an amount equal to the product of the Basic Lease Rate Factor indicated below for the relevant Unit times the Lessor's Cost of such Unit.

Unit Description	*Basic Lease Rate Factor As A % Of Lessor's Cost*

(c) The Renewal Rent for each Unit shall be payable on each Rent Date during the Renewal Term in the amounts specified in Section 13 of this Schedule.

12. CASUALTY VALUE

The Casualty Value of each Unit shall be that percentage of the Lessor's Cost for such Unit as specified on Annex B attached hereto opposite the Rent Date through which Lessee has paid Rent.

13. PURCHASE AND RENEWAL RIGHT

Provided that the Lease has not been terminated earlier and no Event of Default has occurred and is continuing, not earlier than one hundred eighty (180) days and not later than ninety (90) days before the end of the Primary Term or each year of any Renewal Term of each Unit, Lessee may deliver to Lessor a written notice (a) tentatively electing either to purchase such Unit at the end of the Primary Term or each year of any Renewal Term for an amount equal to the Fair Market Value of such Unit at the end of such Term, or to extend the Term of this Lease at the end of the Primary Term or each year of any Renewal Term as to such Unit on a year-to-year basis (but such aggregate Renewal Term shall not exceed _____ years) at the Fair Market Rental at the end of such Term; and (b) appointing an Appraiser selected by Lessee to determine the Fair Market Value or the Fair Market Rental thereof, whichever is applicable, in accordance with the provisions of Section 14 of the Lease. If no such written notice is delivered by Lessee to Lessor within such period, Lessee shall be deemed to have waived any right to purchase or extend the Term with respect to such Unit. At any time within the fifteen (15) day period following the determination of Fair Market Value or Fair Market Rental, as appropriate, of such Unit, Lessee may deliver to Lessor a further written notice finally electing to purchase or extend the Term with respect to such Unit. If no such further notice is delivered by Lessee to Lessor within such fifteen (15) day period, Lessee, shall be deemed to have waived any right to purchase or extend the Term with respect to such Unit. At the end of the Term, if Lessee has finally elected to purchase such Unit, Lessee shall purchase from Lessor, and Lessor shall sell to Lessee, such Unit for a cash consideration equal to the Fair Market Value of such Unit, and Lessor shall transfer title to such Unit to Lessee without recourse or warranty, except that Lessor shall represent and warrant that it owns such Unit free and clear of any Lessor's Lien.

14. EARLY TERMINATION RIGHT

(a) Provided an Event of Default shall not have occurred and be continuing, Lessee shall have the right at its option at any time on not less than ninety (90) days prior written notice to Lessor to terminate the Lease with respect to any or all of the Units on the _____ Primary Term Rent Date or any Primary Term Rent Date thereafter for any one or more of such Units (hereinafter called the "Termination Date"), provided that Lessee shall have made a good faith determination that such Unit or Units are obsolete or surplus to Lessee's requirements. During the period from the giving of such notice until the Termination Date Lessee, as agent for Lessor, shall use its best efforts to obtain bids for the purchase of such Unit or Units by a person other than Lessee or an affiliate of Lessee. Lessee shall promptly certify in writing to Lessor the amount and terms of each bid received by Lessee and the name and address of the party submitting such bid. Subject to Lessor's right to retain such Unit or Units as provided in Subsection (b) below, on the Termination Date Lessor shall sell such Unit or Units for cash to the bidder or bidders who shall have submitted the highest bid for each such Unit prior to such date and shall transfer title to such Unit or Units to such purchaser or purchasers without recourse or warranty, except that Lessor shall represent and warrant that it owns such Unit or Units free and clear of any Lessor's Lien. The total sale price realized upon such sale shall be retained by Lessor and, in addition, on the Termination Date, Lessee shall pay to Lessor the amount, if any, by which the Termination Value of such Unit or Units as provided in Subsection (d) below, computed as of the Termination Date, exceeds the proceeds of such sale, whereupon the Lease shall terminate as to such Unit or Units except as herein otherwise expressly provided. Subject to the provisions of Subsection (c) below, in the event no bids are received by Lessee, Lessee shall pay to Lessor the Termination Value of such Unit or Units, computed as of the Termination Date, and deliver such Unit or Units to the Lessor in accordance with the provisions of Section 17 of the Lease, whereupon the Lease shall terminate as to such Unit or Units, except as herein otherwise expressly provided.

(b) Notwithstanding the provisions of Subsection (a) above but subject to the provisions of Subsection (c) below, Lessor shall have the right at any time up to and including thirty (30) days prior to the Termination Date, within its sole discretion, to elect not to sell such Unit or Units to any prospective purchaser obtained by Lessee ("Third Party Purchaser"). In the event Lessor elects not to sell such Unit or Units to the Third Party Purchaser, Lessee shall return such Unit or Units to Lessor in accordance with the provisions of Section 17 of the Lease, and Lessor thereupon may retain such Unit or Units for its own account without further obligation under the Lease. If no sale shall have occurred on or as of the Termination Date because the Third Party Purchaser fails to consummate a proposed sale and Lessor shall not have requested the return of such Unit or Units pursuant hereto, the Lease shall continue in full force and effect as to such Unit or Units. In the event of any such sale or the return of such Unit or Units to Lessor pursuant hereto, and provided no Event of Default has occurred and is continuing, all obligations of Lessee to pay Rent and otherwise with respect to such Unit or Units for any period subsequent to the Termination Date shall cease.

(c) If the Termination Value exceeds the highest bid or in the event no bids are received by Lessee, or if Lessor should exercise its election under Subsection (b) above, Lessee may, at its option, upon written notice given to Lessor not less than fifteen (15) days prior to the Termination Date, elect to (i) rescind and cancel Lessee's notice of termination with respect to any one or more of such Units, whereupon the Lease shall not terminate with respect to such Unit or Units pursuant to this Section 14 but shall continue in full force and effect as though no notice of termination had been given by Lessee with respect to such Unit or Units, or (ii) pay Lessor the applicable Termination Value with respect to any one or more of such Units, whereupon Lessor shall transfer title to such Unit or Units to Lessee without recourse or warranty, except that Lessor shall represent and warrant that it owns such Unit or Units free and clear of any Lessor's Lien. In the event Lessee fails to pay Lessor an amount of money equal to the applicable Termination Value on the Termination Date, the Lease as to such Unit or Units shall continue in full force and effect.

(d) The Termination Value of any Unit shall be that percentage described on Annex C attached hereto of Lessor's Cost set forth opposite the Rent Date through which the Lessee has paid Rent.

15. *UPGRADE RIGHT*
[*Author's Note*: This must be negotiated on a case-by-case basis. There is no one standard form.]

16. *REPRESENTATIONS AND WARRANTIES*
Each of Lessor and Lessee represents and warrants to the other that:

(a) Its representations and warranties contained in Section 21 of the Lease are true and accurate on and as of the date of this Schedule as though made on and as of such date.

(b) It is not in default under any of the terms, covenants, agreements, or other provisions of the Lease.

(c) Simultaneously with the execution and delivery hereof it has delivered to the other its Incumbency Certificate, Certified Resolutions, and Opinion of Counsel substantially in the respective forms of Annexes D, E, and F attached hereto, with such changes as the receiving party shall reasonably request.

17. *TERM DEFINITIONS*
The terms used in this Schedule, where not defined in this Schedule to the contrary, shall have the same meanings as defined in the Lease.

_____

as Lessor

By _____

Title _____

_____

as Lessee

By _____

Title _____

Certificate of Acceptance   ANNEX A

Date _____

Certificate of Acceptance No. _____
to Equipment Schedule No. _____ ("Schedule")
dated as of, _____ 19 _____
to Master Lease of Computer Equipment ("Lease")
dated as of _____ , 19 _____
between
_____ ("Lessor")
and
_____ ("Lessee")

Lessee hereby confirms that the Acceptance Date of the Unit or Units described in Exhibit A attached hereto shall be the date of this Certificate.

Lessee confirms that (a) such Unit or Units have been examined by duly appointed and authorized representatives of Lessee, (b) such Unit or Units have been duly accepted by Lessee as Units for leasing under the Lease, (c) such Unit or Units have become subject to and governed by the terms of the Lease, and (d) Lessee has become obligated to pay to Lessor the Rent provided for in the Lease and the Schedule with respect to such Unit or Units.

The terms used herein shall have the respective meanings given to such terms In the Lease.

_____

as Lessee

By _____

Title _____

Basic Lease Commencement Date _____

Exhibit A to Certificate of Acceptance No. _____ dated
_____ 19 _____ to Equipment Schedule No. _____ dated
_____, 19 _____ to Master Lease of Computer Equipment
dated _____, 19 _____ between

_____
and
_____

Description of Unit	Manufacturer	Installation Location Address	I.D. or Serial #

Total Lessor's Cost of
Units Included in this Certificate of Acceptance $ _____

ANNEX B

Casualty Values

<u>*After Rent Date No.*</u>   <u>*Percentage of Per Unit Cost*</u>

ANNEX C

Termination Values

<u>*After Rent Date No.*</u>   <u>*Percentage of Lessor's Cost*</u>

ANNEX D

Incumbency Certificate

This Certificate is delivered by the undersigned pursuant to the Master Lease of Computer Equipment (the "Lease") dated as of _____ between _____ (the "Lessor"), and _____ (the "Lessee"):

The undersigned hereby certifies that the following persons are on the date hereof, and have been at all times since _____ , duly elected or appointed, qualified and acting officers of the undersigned holding the offices set forth opposite their respective names below and that the signatures set forth opposite their respective names and offices below are their genuine signatures:

Name	*Title*	*Signature*
		_____
		_____
		_____
		_____

By _____

Title _____

Certified Resolutions

The undersigned, being the _____ of _____ . a
_____ corporation (" _____ "), does hereby certify
that the following is a true and correct copy of certain resolutions duly adopted
by the _____ of _____ on _____ , 19 _____ ,
and that such resolutions have not been modified or rescinded and remain in
full force and effect on the date hereof:

"RESOLVED, that the proposed Master Lease of Computer Equipment
(the "Lease"), including the proposed Equipment Schedule attached as
Annex A thereto (the "Schedule"), between _____ as
_____ and this Corporation as _____ , in the form
of the draft of _____ , 19 _____ filed with the records of this Corporation, be, and it hereby is, approved in all respects; and further

"RESOLVED", that the officers of this Corporation be, and each and any
of them hereby is, authorized and empowered, in the name and on behalf of
this Corporation, to execute and deliver the Lease and any Schedule substantially in the form approved in the preceding resolution, together with
such changes therein as such officers or any of them, in conjunction with
counsel to this Corporation, shall from time to time in their discretion deem
necessary or desirable and shall approve, such approval to be conclusively
evidenced by their execution and delivery thereof, and to enforce all rights
and perform all obligations of this Corporation thereunder; provided, however, that without further action by this Board of Directors the aggregate cost
of equipment to become subject to the Lease and all Schedules shall not
exceed $ _____ ; and further

"RESOLVED, that the officers of this Corporation be, and each and any of
them hereby is, authorized and empowered, in the name and on behalf of
this Corporation, to execute, deliver, file, and record any and all such further
agreements, undertakings, instruments, certificates, letters, and other documents, and to perform any and all such further actions, as such officers or
any of them, in conjunction with counsel to this Corporation, shall from time
to time in their discretion deem necessary or desirable to fully effectuate the
Lease and the purposes of the foregoing resolutions."

IN WITNESS WHEREOF, the undersigned has made and executed this
Certificate as of this _____ day of _____ , 19 _____ .

_____

By _____

Title _____

ANNEX F

Opinion of Counsel

_____ , 19, _____

Gentlemen:

As counsel to _____ (" _____ ") I have examined the Master Lease of Computer Equipment dated as of _____ 19 _____ (the "Lease"), between _____ and _____ and Equipment Schedule No. _____ to the Lease dated of even date herewith, such other documents and corporate records, and such questions of law as I have deemed relevant for purposes of the opinions expressed below. The terms used herein have the same meanings as defined in the Lease. Based on such examination, I am of the opinion that:

1. _____ is a corporation duly organized, validly existing, and in good standing under the laws of the _____ ; has full power and authority to carry on its business as presently conducted, to own or hold under lease its properties and to enter into and perform its obligations under the Lease; and is duly qualified to do business as a foreign corporation and is in good standing in each jurisdiction in which the location of any (Unit) requires such qualification.

2. The execution, delivery, and performance by _____ of the Lease have been duly authorized by all necessary corporate action on the part of _____ , do not materially contravene any law, governmental rule, regulation, or Order binding on _____ or its properties or the corporate charter or By-laws of _____ , and to the best of my knowledge do not contravene the provisions of, or constitute a material default under, or result in the creation of any lien upon the (Units) under, any material indenture, mortgage, contract, or other instrument to which _____ is a party or by which _____ or its property is bound.

3. No consent or approval of, giving of notice to, registration with or taking of any other action by, any [state/provincial—as appropriate], federal or other governmental commission, agency or regulatory authority is required for the performance by _____ of the transactions contemplated by the Lease; or, if any such action is required, it has been obtained, performed or registered.

4. The Lease has been duly entered into and delivered by _____ , and constitutes a legal, valid and binding agreement of _____ enforceable against _____ in accordance with its terms, except as limited by (a) bankruptcy, insolvency, reorganization, or other similar laws of general application affecting the enforcement of creditors' or lessors' rights, (b) emergency powers lawfully conferred upon any governmental agency, and (c) laws or judicial decisions limiting the right to specific performance or other equitable remedies, and the Lease creates a valid leasehold interest in the (Units).

5. To the best of my knowledge there are no actions, suits or proceedings pending or threatened before any court, administrative agency, arbitrator or Governmental Body which would, if determined adversely to _____ , have a material adverse effect on the business, assets, operations or condition, financial or otherwise, of _____ , or materially adversely affect the ability of _____ to perform its obligations under the Lease; and to the best of my knowledge _____ is not in material default with respect to any material Order of any court, arbitrator or Governmental Body.

6. No recorded Lien other than the Lease of any nature whatsoever which now covers or affects, or which will hereafter cover or affect, any property (or interests therein) of _____ now attaches or hereafter will attach to any of the (Units,) or materially adversely affects or will affect _____ right, title and interest in or to any of the (Units.)

Very truly yours,

ANNEX G

Prohibited Lender Assignees

MACRS Depreciation Tables

Reproduced below, from Revenue Procedure 87-57 [1987-42 IRB 17], are those tables that set out the annual deduction rates under the Modified Accelerated Cost Recovery System (MACRS) for equipment. (Tables pertaining only to real property are omitted.) Tables 1-5 set out rates under the general MACRS system; Tables 8-12 provide rates under the MACRS Alternative Depreciation System; and Tables 14-18 set out rates when the Alternative Minimum Tax applies.

Table 1.   General Depreciation System
Applicable Depreciation Method: 200 or 150 Percent
Declining Balance Switching to Straight Line
Applicable Recovery Periods: 3, 5, 7, 10, 15, 20 years
Applicable Convention: Half-year

If the Recovery Year is:	3-year	and the Recovery Period is:				
		5-year	7-year	10-year	15-year	20-year
		the Depreciation Rate is:				
1	33.33	20.00	14.29	10.00	5.00	3.750
2	44.45	32.00	24.49	18.00	9.50	7.219
3	14.81	19.20	17.49	14.40	8.55	6.677
4	7.41	11.52	12.49	11.52	7.70	6.177
5		11.52	8.93	9.22	6.93	5.713
6		5.76	8.92	7.37	6.23	5.285
7			8.93	6.55	5.90	4.888
8			4.46	6.55	5.90	4.522
9				6.56	5.91	4.462
10				6.55	5.90	4.461
11				3.28	5.91	4.462
12					5.90	4.461
13					5.91	4.462
14					5.90	4.461
15					5.91	4.462
16					2.95	4.461
17						4.462
18						4.461
19						4.462
20						4.461
21						2.231

Table 2.   General Depreciation System
            Applicable Depreciation Method: 200 or 150 Percent
            Declining Balance Switching to Straight Line
            Applicable Recovery Periods: 3, 5, 7, 10, 15, 20 years
            Applicable Convention: Mid-quarter (property placed in
            service in first quarter)

If the Recovery Year is:	3-year	5-year	7-year	10-year	15-year	20-year
			the Depreciation Rate is:			
1	58.33	35.00	25.00	17.50	8.75	6.563
2	27.78	26.00	21.43	16.50	9.13	7.000
3	12.35	15.60	15.31	13.20	8.21	6.482
4	1.54	11.01	10.93	10.56	7.39	5.996
5		11.01	8.75	8.45	6.65	5.546
6		1.38	8.74	6.76	5.99	5.130
7			8.75	6.55	5.90	4.746
8			1.09	6.55	5.91	4.459
9				6.56	5.90	4.459
10				6.55	5.91	4.459
11				0.82	5.90	4.459
12					5.91	4.460
13					5.90	4.459
14					5.91	4.460
15					5.90	4.459
16					0.74	4.460
17						4.459
18						4.460
19						4.459
20						4.460
21						0.557

Table 3. General Depreciation System
          Applicable Depreciation Method: 200 or 150 Percent
          Declining Balance Switching to Straight Line
          Applicable Recovery Periods: 3, 5, 7, 10, 15, 20 years
          Applicable Convention: Mid-quarter (property placed in
          service in second quarter)

If the Recovery Year is:	3-year	and the Recovery Period is				
		5-year	7-year	10-year	15-year	20-year
		the Depreciation Rate is:				
1	41.67	25.00	17.85	12.50	6.25	4.688
2	38.89	30.00	23.47	17.50	9.38	7.148
3	14.14	18.00	16.76	14.00	8.44	6.612
4	5.30	11.37	11.97	11.20	7.59	6.116
5		11.37	8.87	8.96	6.83	5.658
6		4.26	8.87	7.17	6.15	5.233
7			8.87	6.55	5.91	4.841
8			3.33	6.55	5.90	4.478
9				6.56	5.91	4.463
10				6.55	5.90	4.463
11				2.46	5.91	4.463
12					5.90	4.463
13					5.91	4.463
14					5.90	4.463
15					5.91	4.462
16					2.21	4.463
17						4.462
18						4.463
19						4.462
20						4.463
21						1.673

Table 4. General Depreciation System
          Applicable Depreciation Method: 200 or 150 Percent
          Declining Balance Switching to Straight Line
          Applicable Recovery Periods: 3, 5, 7, 10, 15, 20 years
          Applicable Convention: Mid-quarter (property placed in
          service in third quarter)

If the Recovery Year is:	and the Recovery Period is:					
	3-year	5-year	7-year	10-year	15-year	20-year
	the Depreciation Rate is:					
1	25.00	15.00	10.71	7.50	3.75	2.813
2	50.00	34.00	25.51	18.50	9.63	7.289
3	16.67	20.40	18.22	14.80	8.66	6.742
4	8.33	12.24	13.02	11.84	7.80	6.237
5		11.30	9.30	9.47	7.02	5.769
6		7.06	8.85	7.58	6.31	5.336
7			8.86	6.55	5.90	4.936
8			5.53	6.55	5.90	4.566
9				6.56	5.91	4.460
10				6.55	5.90	4.460
11				4.10	5.91	4.460
12					5.90	4.460
13					5.91	4.461
14					5.90	4.460
15					5.91	4.461
16					3.69	4.460
17						4.461
18						4.460
19						4.461
20						4.460
21						2.700

Table 5.   General Depreciation System
            Applicable Depreciation Method: 200 or 150 Percent
            Declining Balance Switching to Straight Line
            Applicable Recovery Periods: 3, 5, 7, 10, 15, 20 years
            Applicable Convention: Mid-quarter (property placed in
            service in fourth quarter)

If the Recovery Year is:	and the Recovery Period is:					
	3-year	5-year	7-year	10-year	15-year	20-year
	the Depreciation Rate is:					
1	8.33	5.00	3.57	2.50	1.25	0.938
2	61.11	38.00	27.55	19.50	9.88	7.430
3	20.37	22.80	19.68	15.60	8.89	6.872
4	10.19	13.68	14.06	12.48	8.00	6.357
5		10.94	10.04	9.98	7.20	5.880
6		9.58	8.73	7.99	6.48	5.439
7			8.73	6.55	5.90	5.031
8			7.64	6.55	5.90	4.654
9				6.56	5.90	4.458
10				6.55	5.91	4.458
11				5.74	5.90	4.458
12					5.91	4.458
13					5.90	4.458
14					5.91	4.458
15					5.90	4.458
16					5.17	4.458
17						4.458
18						4.459
19						4.458
20						4.459
21						3.901

TABLE 8   General and Alternative Depreciation Systems
Applicable Depreciation Method: Straight Line
Applicable Recovery Periods: 2.5 - 50 years
Applicable Convention: Half-year

and the Recovery Period is:

If the Recovery Year is:	2.5	3.0	3.5	4.0	4.5	5.0	5.5	6.0	6.5	7.0	7.5	8.0	8.5	9.0	9.5
						the Depreciation Rate is:									
1	20.00	16.67	14.29	12.50	11.11	10.00	9.09	8.33	7.69	7.14	6.67	6.25	5.88	5.56	5.26
2	40.00	33.33	28.57	25.00	22.22	20.00	18.18	16.67	15.39	14.29	13.33	12.50	11.77	11.11	10.53
3	40.00	33.33	28.57	25.00	22.22	20.00	18.18	16.67	15.38	14.29	13.33	12.50	11.76	11.11	10.53
4		16.67	28.57	25.00	22.23	20.00	18.18	16.67	15.38	14.28	13.33	12.50	11.77	11.11	10.53
5				12.50	22.22	20.00	18.19	16.66	15.38	14.29	13.34	12.50	11.76	11.11	10.52
6						10.00	18.18	16.67	15.39	14.28	13.33	12.50	11.77	11.11	10.53
7								8.33	15.38	14.29	13.34	12.50	11.76	11.11	10.52
8										7.14	13.33	12.50	11.77	11.11	10.53
9												6.25	11.76	11.11	10.52
10														5.56	10.53

and the Recovery Period is:

If the Recovery Year is:	10.0	10.5	11.0	11.5	12.0	12.5	13.0	13.5	14.0	14.5	15.0	15.5	16.0	16.5	17.0
						the Depreciation Rate is:									
1	5.00	4.76	4.55	4.35	4.17	4.00	3.85	3.70	3.57	3.45	3.33	3.23	3.13	3.03	2.94
2	10.00	9.52	9.09	8.70	8.33	8.00	7.69	7.41	7.14	6.90	6.67	6.45	6.25	6.06	5.88
3	10.00	9.52	9.09	8.70	8.33	8.00	7.69	7.41	7.14	6.90	6.67	6.45	6.25	6.06	5.88
4	10.00	9.53	9.09	8.69	8.33	8.00	7.69	7.41	7.14	6.90	6.67	6.45	6.25	6.06	5.88
5	10.00	9.52	9.09	8.70	8.33	8.00	7.69	7.41	7.14	6.90	6.67	6.45	6.25	6.06	5.88
6	10.00	9.53	9.09	8.70	8.33	8.00	7.69	7.41	7.14	6.90	6.67	6.45	6.25	6.06	5.88
7	10.00	9.53	9.09	8.70	8.34	8.00	7.69	7.41	7.15	6.89	6.66	6.45	6.25	6.06	5.88
8	10.00	9.53	9.09	8.70	8.33	8.00	7.69	7.41	7.14	6.90	6.67	6.45	6.25	6.06	5.88
9	10.00	9.53	9.09	8.70	8.34	8.00	7.70	7.40	7.15	6.89	6.66	6.45	6.25	6.06	5.89
10	10.00	9.53	9.09	8.69	8.33	8.00	7.69	7.41	7.15	6.89	6.66	6.45	6.25	6.06	5.88
11	5.00	9.52	9.09	8.70	8.34	8.00	7.69	7.41	7.14	6.90	6.67	6.45	6.25	6.06	5.88
12			4.55	8.69	8.33	8.00	7.70	7.40	7.15	6.89	6.66	6.45	6.25	6.06	5.89
13					4.17	8.00	7.69	7.41	7.14	6.90	6.67	6.46	6.25	6.06	5.88
14							3.85	7.40	7.15	6.89	6.66	6.45	6.25	6.06	5.89
15									3.57	6.89	6.67	6.46	6.25	6.06	5.88
16											3.33	6.45	6.25	6.06	5.89
17													3.12	6.07	5.88
18															2.94

and the Recovery Period is:

the Depreciation Rate is:

If the Recovery Year is:	17.5	18.0	18.5	19.0	19.5	20.0	20.5	21.0	21.5	22.0	22.5	23.0	23.5	24.0	24.5
1	2.86	2.78	2.70	2.63	2.56	2.500	2.439	2.381	2.326	2.273	2.222	2.174	2.128	2.083	2.041
2	5.71	5.56	5.41	5.26	5.13	5.000	4.878	4.762	4.651	4.545	4.444	4.348	4.255	4.167	4.082
3	5.71	5.56	5.41	5.26	5.13	5.000	4.878	4.762	4.651	4.545	4.445	4.348	4.255	4.167	4.082
4	5.71	5.55	5.41	5.26	5.13	5.000	4.878	4.762	4.651	4.545	4.444	4.348	4.255	4.167	4.082
5	5.72	5.56	5.40	5.26	5.13	5.000	4.878	4.762	4.651	4.546	4.445	4.348	4.255	4.167	4.082
6	5.71	5.55	5.41	5.26	5.13	5.000	4.878	4.762	4.651	4.545	4.444	4.348	4.255	4.167	4.082
7	5.72	5.56	5.40	5.26	5.13	5.000	4.878	4.762	4.651	4.546	4.445	4.348	4.255	4.167	4.082
8	5.71	5.55	5.41	5.26	5.13	5.000	4.878	4.762	4.651	4.545	4.444	4.348	4.255	4.167	4.081
9	5.72	5.56	5.40	5.27	5.13	5.000	4.878	4.762	4.651	4.546	4.445	4.348	4.255	4.167	4.082
10	5.71	5.55	5.41	5.26	5.13	5.000	4.878	4.762	4.651	4.545	4.444	4.348	4.256	4.166	4.081
11	5.72	5.56	5.40	5.27	5.13	5.000	4.878	4.762	4.651	4.546	4.445	4.348	4.255	4.167	4.082
12	5.71	5.55	5.41	5.26	5.13	5.000	4.878	4.762	4.651	4.545	4.444	4.348	4.256	4.166	4.081
13	5.72	5.56	5.40	5.27	5.13	5.000	4.878	4.762	4.651	4.546	4.445	4.348	4.255	4.167	4.082
14	5.71	5.55	5.41	5.26	5.13	5.000	4.878	4.762	4.651	4.545	4.444	4.348	4.256	4.166	4.081
15	5.72	5.56	5.40	5.27	5.12	5.000	4.878	4.762	4.651	4.546	4.445	4.348	4.255	4.167	4.082
16	5.71	5.55	5.41	5.26	5.13	5.000	4.878	4.762	4.651	4.545	4.444	4.348	4.256	4.166	4.081
17	5.72	5.56	5.40	5.27	5.13	5.000	4.878	4.762	4.652	4.546	4.445	4.347	4.255	4.167	4.082
18	5.71	5.55	5.41	5.26	5.12	5.000	4.878	4.762	4.651	4.545	4.444	4.347	4.256	4.166	4.081
19		2.78	5.40	5.27	5.13	5.000	4.878	4.761	4.652	4.546	4.445	4.348	4.255	4.167	4.082
20				2.63	5.12	5.000	4.878	4.762	4.651	4.545	4.444	4.347	4.256	4.166	4.081
21						2.500	4.879	4.761	4.652	4.546	4.445	4.348	4.255	4.167	4.082
22							4.878	2.381	4.651	4.545	4.444	4.347	4.256	4.166	4.081
23										2.273	4.444	4.348	4.255	4.167	4.082
24												2.174	4.255	4.166	4.081
25														2.083	4.082

and the Recovery Period is:

If the Recovery Year is:	25.0	25.5	26.0	26.5	27.0	27.5	28.0	28.5	29.0	29.5	30.0	30.5	31.0	31.5	32.0
			the Depreciation Rate is:												
1	2.000	1.961	1.923	1.887	1.852	1.818	1.786	1.754	1.724	1.695	1.667	1.639	1.613	1.587	1.563
2	4.000	3.922	3.846	3.774	3.704	3.636	3.571	3.509	3.448	3.390	3.333	3.279	3.226	3.175	3.125
3	4.000	3.922	3.846	3.774	3.704	3.636	3.571	3.509	3.448	3.390	3.333	3.279	3.226	3.175	3.125
4	4.000	3.922	3.846	3.774	3.704	3.636	3.571	3.509	3.448	3.390	3.333	3.279	3.226	3.175	3.125
5	4.000	3.922	3.846	3.774	3.704	3.636	3.571	3.509	3.448	3.390	3.333	3.279	3.226	3.175	3.125
6	4.000	3.921	3.846	3.773	3.704	3.636	3.572	3.509	3.448	3.390	3.333	3.279	3.226	3.175	3.125
7	4.000	3.922	3.846	3.774	3.704	3.636	3.571	3.509	3.448	3.390	3.333	3.279	3.226	3.175	3.125
8	4.000	3.921	3.846	3.773	3.704	3.636	3.572	3.509	3.448	3.390	3.333	3.279	3.226	3.175	3.125
9	4.000	3.922	3.846	3.774	3.704	3.637	3.571	3.509	3.448	3.390	3.333	3.279	3.226	3.175	3.125
10	4.000	3.921	3.846	3.773	3.704	3.636	3.572	3.509	3.448	3.390	3.333	3.279	3.226	3.174	3.125
11	4.000	3.922	3.846	3.774	3.704	3.637	3.571	3.509	3.448	3.390	3.333	3.279	3.226	3.175	3.125
12	4.000	3.921	3.846	3.773	3.703	3.636	3.572	3.509	3.448	3.390	3.334	3.279	3.226	3.174	3.125
13	4.000	3.922	3.846	3.774	3.704	3.637	3.571	3.509	3.448	3.390	3.333	3.279	3.226	3.175	3.125
14	4.000	3.921	3.846	3.773	3.703	3.636	3.572	3.509	3.448	3.390	3.334	3.279	3.226	3.174	3.125
15	4.000	3.922	3.846	3.774	3.704	3.637	3.571	3.509	3.449	3.390	3.333	3.278	3.226	3.175	3.125
16	4.000	3.921	3.846	3.773	3.703	3.636	3.572	3.509	3.448	3.390	3.334	3.279	3.226	3.174	3.125
17	4.000	3.922	3.846	3.774	3.704	3.637	3.571	3.509	3.449	3.390	3.333	3.278	3.226	3.175	3.125
18	4.000	3.921	3.846	3.773	3.703	3.636	3.572	3.508	3.448	3.390	3.334	3.279	3.226	3.174	3.125
19	4.000	3.922	3.846	3.774	3.704	3.637	3.572	3.509	3.449	3.390	3.333	3.278	3.226	3.175	3.125
20	4.000	3.921	3.847	3.773	3.703	3.636	3.571	3.508	3.448	3.390	3.334	3.279	3.226	3.174	3.125
21	4.000	3.922	3.846	3.774	3.703	3.637	3.572	3.509	3.449	3.389	3.334	3.278	3.225	3.175	3.125
22	4.000	3.921	3.847	3.773	3.704	3.636	3.571	3.508	3.448	3.390	3.333	3.279	3.226	3.174	3.125
23	4.000	3.922	3.846	3.774	3.703	3.637	3.572	3.509	3.449	3.389	3.334	3.278	3.225	3.175	3.125
24	4.000	3.921	3.847	3.773	3.703	3.636	3.571	3.508	3.448	3.390	3.333	3.279	3.226	3.174	3.125
25	4.000	3.922	3.846	3.774	3.704	3.637	3.572	3.509	3.449	3.389	3.334	3.278	3.225	3.175	3.125
26	2.000	3.921	3.847	3.773	3.703	3.636	3.571	3.508	3.448	3.390	3.333	3.279	3.226	3.174	3.125
27			1.923	3.774	3.704	3.637	3.572	3.509	3.449	3.389	3.334	3.278	3.226	3.175	3.125
28					1.852	3.636	3.571	3.508	3.448	3.390	3.333	3.279	3.225	3.174	3.125
29							1.786	3.509	3.449	3.389	3.334	3.278	3.226	3.175	3.125
30									1.724	3.390	3.334	3.279	3.226	3.174	3.125
31											1.667	3.278	3.226	3.175	3.125
32													1.613	3.174	3.125
33															1.562

and the Recovery Period is:

the Depreciation Rate is:

If the Recovery Year is:	32.5	33.0	33.5	34.0	34.5	35.0	35.5	36.0	36.5	37.0	37.5	38.0	38.5	39.0	39.5
1	1.538	1.515	1.493	1.471	1.449	1.429	1.408	1.389	1.370	1.351	1.333	1.316	1.299	1.282	1.266
2	3.077	3.030	2.985	2.941	2.899	2.857	2.817	2.778	2.740	2.703	2.667	2.632	2.597	2.564	2.532
3	3.077	3.030	2.985	2.941	2.899	2.857	2.817	2.778	2.740	2.703	2.667	2.632	2.597	2.564	2.532
4	3.077	3.030	2.985	2.941	2.899	2.857	2.817	2.778	2.740	2.703	2.667	2.632	2.597	2.564	2.532
5	3.077	3.030	2.985	2.941	2.899	2.857	2.817	2.778	2.740	2.703	2.667	2.632	2.597	2.564	2.532
6	3.077	3.030	2.985	2.941	2.899	2.857	2.817	2.778	2.740	2.703	2.667	2.632	2.597	2.564	2.532
7	3.077	3.030	2.985	2.941	2.898	2.857	2.817	2.778	2.740	2.703	2.667	2.631	2.597	2.564	2.532
8	3.077	3.030	2.985	2.941	2.899	2.857	2.817	2.778	2.740	2.703	2.667	2.632	2.597	2.564	2.532
9	3.077	3.030	2.985	2.941	2.899	2.857	2.817	2.778	2.740	2.703	2.667	2.631	2.598	2.564	2.532
10	3.077	3.030	2.985	2.941	2.899	2.857	2.817	2.778	2.740	2.703	2.667	2.632	2.598	2.564	2.532
11	3.077	3.030	2.985	2.941	2.898	2.857	2.817	2.778	2.740	2.703	2.667	2.631	2.597	2.564	2.532
12	3.077	3.030	2.985	2.941	2.899	2.857	2.817	2.778	2.740	2.703	2.667	2.632	2.597	2.564	2.532
13	3.077	3.030	2.985	2.941	2.898	2.857	2.817	2.778	2.740	2.703	2.667	2.631	2.598	2.564	2.531
14	3.077	3.030	2.985	2.941	2.899	2.857	2.817	2.778	2.740	2.703	2.667	2.632	2.597	2.564	2.532
15	3.077	3.031	2.985	2.941	2.899	2.857	2.817	2.778	2.740	2.703	2.667	2.631	2.597	2.564	2.532
16	3.077	3.031	2.985	2.941	2.898	2.857	2.817	2.778	2.739	2.703	2.666	2.632	2.598	2.564	2.531
17	3.077	3.030	2.985	2.941	2.899	2.857	2.817	2.778	2.740	2.703	2.667	2.631	2.597	2.564	2.532
18	3.077	3.031	2.985	2.941	2.899	2.857	2.817	2.778	2.739	2.702	2.666	2.632	2.598	2.564	2.531
19	3.077	3.031	2.985	2.941	2.898	2.857	2.817	2.778	2.740	2.703	2.667	2.631	2.597	2.564	2.532
20	3.077	3.030	2.985	2.941	2.899	2.857	2.817	2.778	2.739	2.702	2.666	2.632	2.598	2.564	2.531
21	3.077	3.030	2.985	2.941	2.899	2.857	2.817	2.778	2.740	2.703	2.667	2.631	2.597	2.564	2.532
22	3.077	3.030	2.985	2.941	2.899	2.857	2.817	2.777	2.740	2.702	2.666	2.632	2.598	2.564	2.532
23	3.077	3.031	2.985	2.941	2.899	2.857	2.817	2.778	2.739	2.703	2.667	2.631	2.597	2.564	2.531
24	3.077	3.030	2.985	2.941	2.898	2.857	2.817	2.777	2.740	2.702	2.666	2.632	2.598	2.564	2.532
25	3.077	3.031	2.985	2.942	2.899	2.857	2.817	2.778	2.739	2.703	2.667	2.631	2.597	2.564	2.531
26	3.077	3.030	2.985	2.941	2.898	2.857	2.817	2.777	2.740	2.702	2.666	2.632	2.598	2.564	2.532
27	3.077	3.031	2.985	2.942	2.899	2.857	2.817	2.778	2.739	2.702	2.667	2.631	2.597	2.564	2.531
28	3.077	3.031	2.985	2.941	2.899	2.858	2.817	2.777	2.740	2.702	2.666	2.632	2.597	2.564	2.532
29	3.077	3.031	2.985	2.942	2.898	2.857	2.817	2.778	2.739	2.702	2.667	2.631	2.598	2.564	2.531
30	3.077	3.030	2.985	2.941	2.899	2.858	2.817	2.777	2.740	2.703	2.666	2.632	2.597	2.564	2.532
31	3.076	3.031	2.986	2.942	2.899	2.857	2.816	2.778	2.739	2.702	2.667	2.631	2.598	2.564	2.531
32	3.077	3.030	2.985	2.941	2.898	2.858	2.817	2.777	2.740	2.702	2.666	2.632	2.597	2.564	2.532
33	3.077	3.031	2.986	2.942	2.899	2.857	2.816	2.778	2.739	2.702	2.667	2.631	2.598	2.564	2.531
34		1.515	2.985	2.941	2.898	2.858	2.817	2.777	2.740	2.703	2.666	2.632	2.597	2.565	2.532
35				1.471	2.899	2.857	2.816	2.778	2.739	2.702	2.667	2.631	2.598	2.564	2.531
36						1.429	2.816	2.777	2.739	2.703	2.666	2.632	2.597	2.564	2.532
37								1.389	2.739	2.702	2.667	2.631	2.598	2.565	2.531
38										1.351	2.667	2.632	2.597	2.565	2.532
39												1.316	2.597	2.564	2.531
40														1.282	2.531

and the Recovery Period is:

If the Recovery Year is:	40.0	40.5	41.0	41.5	42.0	42.5	43.0	43.5	44.0	44.5	45.0	45.5	46.0	46.5	47.0
	the Depreciation Rate is:														
1	1.250	1.235	1.220	1.205	1.190	1.176	1.163	1.149	1.136	1.124	1.111	1.099	1.087	1.075	1.064
2	2.500	2.469	2.439	2.410	2.381	2.353	2.326	2.299	2.273	2.247	2.222	2.198	2.174	2.151	2.128
3	2.500	2.469	2.439	2.410	2.381	2.353	2.326	2.299	2.273	2.247	2.222	2.198	2.174	2.151	2.128
4	2.500	2.469	2.439	2.410	2.381	2.353	2.326	2.299	2.273	2.247	2.222	2.198	2.174	2.151	2.128
5	2.500	2.469	2.439	2.410	2.381	2.353	2.326	2.299	2.273	2.247	2.222	2.198	2.174	2.151	2.128
6	2.500	2.469	2.439	2.410	2.381	2.353	2.326	2.299	2.273	2.247	2.222	2.198	2.174	2.151	2.128
7	2.500	2.469	2.439	2.410	2.381	2.353	2.326	2.299	2.273	2.247	2.222	2.198	2.174	2.151	2.128
8	2.500	2.469	2.439	2.410	2.381	2.353	2.326	2.299	2.273	2.247	2.222	2.198	2.174	2.151	2.128
9	2.500	2.469	2.439	2.410	2.381	2.353	2.325	2.299	2.273	2.247	2.222	2.198	2.174	2.150	2.128
10	2.500	2.469	2.439	2.410	2.381	2.353	2.326	2.299	2.273	2.247	2.222	2.198	2.174	2.150	2.128
11	2.500	2.469	2.439	2.410	2.381	2.353	2.325	2.299	2.273	2.247	2.222	2.198	2.174	2.151	2.128
12	2.500	2.469	2.439	2.410	2.381	2.353	2.326	2.299	2.273	2.247	2.222	2.198	2.174	2.150	2.128
13	2.500	2.469	2.439	2.410	2.381	2.353	2.325	2.299	2.273	2.247	2.222	2.198	2.174	2.151	2.128
14	2.500	2.469	2.439	2.410	2.381	2.353	2.326	2.293	2.273	2.247	2.222	2.198	2.174	2.150	2.128
15	2.500	2.469	2.439	2.410	2.381	2.353	2.325	2.293	2.273	2.247	2.222	2.198	2.174	2.151	2.128
16	2.500	2.469	2.439	2.409	2.381	2.353	2.326	2.293	2.273	2.247	2.222	2.198	2.174	2.150	2.127
17	2.500	2.469	2.439	2.410	2.381	2.353	2.325	2.293	2.273	2.247	2.222	2.198	2.174	2.151	2.128
18	2.500	2.469	2.439	2.410	2.381	2.353	2.326	2.293	2.273	2.247	2.222	2.198	2.174	2.150	2.128
19	2.500	2.469	2.439	2.409	2.381	2.353	2.325	2.293	2.273	2.247	2.222	2.198	2.174	2.151	2.127
20	2.500	2.469	2.439	2.410	2.381	2.353	2.326	2.299	2.273	2.247	2.222	2.198	2.174	2.150	2.128
21	2.500	2.469	2.439	2.410	2.381	2.353	2.325	2.295	2.273	2.247	2.222	2.198	2.174	2.151	2.128
22	2.500	2.469	2.439	2.409	2.381	2.353	2.326	2.295	2.273	2.247	2.222	2.198	2.174	2.150	2.128
23	2.500	2.469	2.439	2.410	2.381	2.353	2.325	2.295	2.273	2.247	2.222	2.198	2.174	2.151	2.128
24	2.500	2.469	2.439	2.410	2.381	2.353	2.326	2.295	2.272	2.247	2.222	2.198	2.174	2.150	2.127
25	2.500	2.469	2.439	2.409	2.381	2.353	2.325	2.295	2.273	2.247	2.222	2.198	2.174	2.151	2.128
26	2.500	2.469	2.439	2.410	2.381	2.353	2.326	2.299	2.273	2.247	2.222	2.198	2.174	2.150	2.127
27	2.500	2.469	2.439	2.409	2.381	2.353	2.325	2.299	2.273	2.247	2.223	2.198	2.174	2.151	2.128
28	2.500	2.469	2.439	2.410	2.381	2.353	2.326	2.299	2.272	2.248	2.223	2.198	2.174	2.150	2.128
29	2.500	2.469	2.439	2.409	2.381	2.353	2.325	2.299	2.273	2.247	2.222	2.197	2.174	2.151	2.128
30	2.500	2.469	2.439	2.410	2.381	2.353	2.326	2.299	2.273	2.248	2.223	2.198	2.174	2.150	2.127
31	2.500	2.470	2.439	2.410	2.381	2.353	2.325	2.298	2.273	2.247	2.222	2.198	2.174	2.151	2.128
32	2.500	2.469	2.439	2.409	2.381	2.353	2.326	2.299	2.272	2.247	2.223	2.197	2.174	2.150	2.128
33	2.500	2.469	2.439	2.410	2.381	2.353	2.325	2.298	2.273	2.248	2.222	2.198	2.174	2.151	2.127
34	2.500	2.470	2.439	2.409	2.381	2.353	2.326	2.299	2.273	2.247	2.223	2.197	2.174	2.150	2.128
35	2.500	2.469	2.439	2.410	2.381	2.353	2.325	2.298	2.272	2.248	2.222	2.198	2.174	2.151	2.127
36	2.500	2.470	2.439	2.409	2.381	2.353	2.326	2.299	2.273	2.247	2.223	2.197	2.174	2.150	2.128
37	2.500	2.469	2.439	2.410	2.381	2.353	2.325	2.258	2.272	2.248	2.222	2.198	2.174	2.151	2.127
38	2.500	2.470	2.439	2.409	2.381	2.353	2.326	2.259	2.273	2.248	2.223	2.197	2.174	2.150	2.128
39	2.500	2.469	2.439	2.410	2.381	2.353	2.325	2.259	2.273	2.248	2.222	2.197	2.173	2.151	2.128
40	2.500	2.470	2.439	2.409	2.381	2.353	2.326	2.293	2.272	2.247	2.223	2.198	2.174	2.150	2.127
41	1.250	2.469	2.439	2.410	2.330	2.353	2.326	2.299	2.273	2.248	2.223	2.197	2.173	2.151	2.128
42		1.235	1.220	2.409	2.381	2.353	2.325	2.299	2.273	2.248	2.223	2.197	2.174	2.151	2.127
43				2.410	1.190	2.353	2.326	2.299	2.273	2.247	2.223	2.198	2.174	2.150	2.127
44						2.352	1.163	2.299	2.273	2.248	2.223	2.198	2.173	2.150	2.128
45								2.299	1.136	2.247	2.222	2.198	2.173	2.151	2.127
46										1.124	1.111	2.198	2.174	2.151	2.127
47												2.197	1.087	2.151	2.128
48														2.150	1.064

and the Recovery Period is:

the Depreciation Rate is:

If the Recovery Year is:	47.5	48.0	48.5	49.0	49.5	50.0
1	1.053	1.042	1.031	1.020	1.010	1.000
2	2.105	2.083	2.062	2.041	2.020	2.000
3	2.105	2.083	2.062	2.041	2.020	2.000
4	2.105	2.083	2.062	2.041	2.020	2.000
5	2.105	2.083	2.062	2.041	2.020	2.000
6	2.105	2.083	2.062	2.041	2.020	2.000
7	2.105	2.083	2.062	2.041	2.020	2.000
8	2.105	2.083	2.062	2.041	2.020	2.000
9	2.105	2.083	2.062	2.041	2.020	2.000
10	2.105	2.083	2.062	2.041	2.020	2.000
11	2.105	2.083	2.062	2.041	2.020	2.000
12	2.105	2.083	2.062	2.041	2.020	2.000
13	2.105	2.083	2.062	2.041	2.020	2.000
14	2.105	2.083	2.062	2.041	2.020	2.000
15	2.105	2.083	2.062	2.041	2.020	2.000
16	2.105	2.083	2.062	2.041	2.020	2.000
17	2.105	2.083	2.062	2.041	2.020	2.000
18	2.105	2.083	2.062	2.041	2.020	2.000
19	2.105	2.084	2.062	2.041	2.020	2.000
20	2.105	2.083	2.062	2.041	2.020	2.000
21	2.105	2.084	2.062	2.041	2.020	2.000
22	2.105	2.083	2.062	2.041	2.020	2.000
23	2.105	2.084	2.062	2.041	2.020	2.000
24	2.105	2.083	2.062	2.041	2.020	2.000
25	2.105	2.084	2.062	2.041	2.020	2.000
26	2.106	2.083	2.062	2.041	2.020	2.000

and the Recovery Period is:

the Depreciation Rate is:

47.5	48.0	48.5	49.0	49.5	50.0	If the Recovery Year is:
2.105	2.084	2.062	2.041	2.020	2.000	27
2.106	2.083	2.062	2.041	2.020	2.000	28
2.105	2.084	2.062	2.041	2.020	2.000	29
2.106	2.083	2.062	2.041	2.020	2.000	30
2.105	2.084	2.062	2.041	2.021	2.000	31
2.106	2.083	2.062	2.041	2.020	2.000	32
2.105	2.084	2.062	2.041	2.021	2.000	33
2.106	2.083	2.062	2.040	2.020	2.000	34
2.105	2.084	2.062	2.041	2.021	2.000	35
2.106	2.083	2.062	2.040	2.020	2.000	36
2.105	2.084	2.061	2.041	2.021	2.000	37
2.106	2.083	2.062	2.040	2.020	2.000	38
2.105	2.084	2.061	2.041	2.021	2.000	39
2.106	2.083	2.062	2.040	2.020	2.000	40
2.105	2.084	2.061	2.041	2.021	2.000	41
2.106	2.083	2.062	2.040	2.020	2.000	42
2.105	2.084	2.061	2.041	2.021	2.000	43
2.106	2.083	2.062	2.040	2.020	2.000	44
2.105	2.084	2.061	2.041	2.021	2.000	45
2.106	2.083	2.062	2.040	2.020	2.000	46
2.105	2.084	2.061	2.041	2.021	2.000	47
2.106	2.083	2.062	2.040	2.020	2.000	48
	1.042	2.061	2.041	2.021	2.000	49
			1.020	2.020	2.000	50
					1.000	51

TABLE 9

General and Alternative Depreciation Systems
Applicable Depreciation Method: Straight Line
Applicable Recovery Periods: 2.5 - 50 years
Applicable Convention: Mid-quarter (property placed in service in first quarter)

and the Recovery Period is:

the Depreciation Rate is:

If the Recovery Year is:	2.5	3.0	3.5	4.0	4.5	5.0	5.5	6.0	6.5	7.0	7.5	8.0	8.5	9.0	9.5
1	35.00	29.17	25.00	21.88	19.44	17.50	15.91	14.58	13.46	12.50	11.67	10.94	10.29	9.72	9.21
2	40.00	33.33	28.57	25.00	22.22	20.00	18.18	16.67	15.38	14.29	13.33	12.50	11.77	11.11	10.53
3	25.00	33.33	28.57	25.00	22.22	20.00	18.18	16.67	15.39	14.28	13.33	12.50	11.76	11.11	10.53
4	4.17	4.17	17.86	25.00	22.23	20.00	18.18	16.65	15.39	14.28	13.34	12.50	11.77	11.11	10.53
5				3.12	13.89	20.00	18.18	16.67	15.38	14.29	13.33	12.50	11.76	11.11	10.52
6						2.50	11.37	2.03	9.62	14.28	13.34	12.50	11.77	11.11	10.53
7										1.79	8.33	12.50	11.76	11.11	10.52
8												1.56	7.35	11.12	10.53
9														1.39	10.52
10															6.58

and the Recovery Period is:

the Depreciation Rate is:

If the Recovery Year is:	10.0	10.5	11.0	11.5	12.0	12.5	13.0	13.5	14.0	14.5	15.0	15.5	16.0	16.5	17.0
1	8.75	8.33	7.95	7.61	7.29	7.00	6.73	6.48	6.25	6.03	5.83	5.65	5.47	5.30	5.15
2	10.00	9.52	9.09	8.70	8.33	8.00	7.69	7.41	7.14	6.90	6.67	6.45	6.25	6.06	5.88
3	10.00	9.52	9.09	8.70	8.33	8.00	7.69	7.41	7.14	6.90	6.67	6.45	6.25	6.06	5.88
4	10.00	9.53	9.09	8.69	8.33	8.00	7.69	7.41	7.14	6.90	6.67	6.45	6.25	6.06	5.88
5	10.00	9.52	9.09	8.70	8.34	8.00	7.69	7.41	7.14	6.90	6.67	6.45	6.25	6.06	5.88
6	10.00	9.53	9.09	8.69	8.33	8.00	7.69	7.41	7.14	6.90	6.67	6.45	6.25	6.06	5.88
7	10.00	9.52	9.09	8.70	8.34	8.00	7.69	7.41	7.15	6.89	6.66	6.45	6.25	6.06	5.88
8	10.00	9.53	9.09	8.59	8.33	8.00	7.69	7.40	7.14	6.90	6.67	6.45	6.25	6.06	5.88
9	10.00	9.52	9.09	8.70	8.33	8.00	7.69	7.41	7.14	6.89	6.66	6.45	6.25	6.06	5.88
10	10.00	9.53	9.09	8.59	8.34	8.00	7.70	7.41	7.15	6.90	6.67	6.45	6.25	6.06	5.88
11	1.25	5.95	9.10	8.70	8.33	8.00	7.70	7.41	7.14	6.89	6.66	6.45	6.25	6.06	5.89
12			1.14	5.43	8.34	8.00	7.70	7.41	7.15	6.90	6.67	6.45	6.25	6.06	5.88
13					1.04	8.00	7.70	7.40	7.14	6.89	6.66	6.46	6.25	6.06	5.89
14						5.00	0.96	4.63	7.15	6.90	6.67	6.45	6.25	6.06	5.88
15									0.89	6.89	6.66	6.46	6.25	6.06	5.89
16										4.31	6.67	6.46	6.25	6.06	5.88
17											0.83	4.03	6.25	6.07	5.88
18													0.78	3.79	0.74

and the Recovery Period is:

If the Recovery Year is:

the Depreciation Rate is:

Recovery Year	17.5	18.0	18.5	19.0	19.5	20.0	20.5	21.0	21.5	22.0	22.5	23.0	23.5	24.0	24.5
1	5.00	4.86	4.73	4.61	4.49	4.375	4.268	4.167	4.070	3.977	3.889	3.804	3.723	3.646	3.571
2	5.71	5.56	5.41	5.26	5.13	5.000	4.878	4.762	4.651	4.545	4.444	4.348	4.255	4.167	4.082
3	5.71	5.56	5.41	5.26	5.13	5.000	4.878	4.762	4.651	4.545	4.444	4.348	4.255	4.167	4.082
4	5.71	5.56	5.40	5.26	5.13	5.000	4.878	4.762	4.651	4.546	4.444	4.348	4.255	4.167	4.082
5	5.72	5.56	5.41	5.26	5.13	5.000	4.878	4.762	4.651	4.545	4.445	4.348	4.255	4.167	4.082
6	5.71	5.56	5.40	5.26	5.13	5.000	4.878	4.762	4.651	4.546	4.444	4.348	4.255	4.167	4.082
7	5.72	5.55	5.41	5.26	5.13	5.000	4.878	4.762	4.651	4.545	4.444	4.348	4.255	4.167	4.082
8	5.71	5.56	5.40	5.26	5.13	5.000	4.878	4.762	4.651	4.546	4.444	4.348	4.255	4.167	4.082
9	5.72	5.55	5.41	5.26	5.13	5.000	4.878	4.762	4.651	4.545	4.445	4.348	4.255	4.167	4.082
10	5.71	5.55	5.40	5.27	5.13	5.000	4.878	4.762	4.651	4.546	4.444	4.348	4.256	4.166	4.082
11	5.72	5.55	5.41	5.26	5.13	5.000	4.878	4.762	4.651	4.545	4.445	4.348	4.255	4.167	4.081
12	5.71	5.56	5.40	5.27	5.13	5.000	4.878	4.762	4.651	4.546	4.444	4.348	4.256	4.166	4.082
13	5.72	5.56	5.41	5.26	5.12	5.000	4.878	4.762	4.651	4.545	4.444	4.348	4.255	4.167	4.081
14	5.71	5.55	5.40	5.27	5.13	5.000	4.878	4.762	4.651	4.546	4.445	4.348	4.256	4.166	4.082
15	5.72	5.56	5.41	5.26	5.12	5.000	4.878	4.762	4.651	4.545	4.444	4.348	4.255	4.167	4.081
16	5.71	5.56	5.40	5.27	5.13	5.000	4.878	4.762	4.651	4.545	4.444	4.348	4.256	4.166	4.082
17	5.72	5.55	5.41	5.26	5.13	5.000	4.878	4.762	4.651	4.546	4.445	4.348	4.255	4.167	4.081
18	5.71	5.56	5.40	5.27	5.12	5.000	4.878	4.762	4.652	4.545	4.444	4.348	4.256	4.166	4.082
19	5.72	5.56	5.40	5.26	5.13	5.000	4.878	4.761	4.651	4.546	4.445	4.347	4.255	4.167	4.081
20	3.57	5.56	3.38	5.26	5.13	5.000	4.878	4.762	4.652	4.545	4.444	4.348	4.256	4.166	4.082
21		0.69		0.66	3.20	0.625	4.879	4.761	4.651	4.546	4.445	4.347	4.255	4.166	4.081
22							3.049	4.762	4.652	4.545	4.444	4.348	4.256	4.167	4.082
23								0.595	4.651	4.546	4.445	4.347	4.255	4.167	4.081
24									2.907	4.546	4.444	4.348	4.255	4.166	4.082
25										0.568	2.778	0.543	2.660	0.521	2.551

and the Recovery Period is:

the Depreciation Rate is:

If the Recovery Year is:	25.0	25.5	26.0	26.5	27.0	27.5	28.0	28.5	29.0	29.5	30.0	30.5	31.0	31.5	32.0
1	3.500	3.431	3.365	3.302	3.241	3.182	3.125	3.070	3.017	2.966	2.917	2.869	2.823	2.778	2.734
2	4.000	3.922	3.846	3.774	3.704	3.636	3.571	3.509	3.448	3.390	3.333	3.279	3.226	3.175	3.125
3	4.000	3.922	3.846	3.774	3.704	3.636	3.571	3.509	3.448	3.390	3.333	3.279	3.226	3.175	3.125
4	4.000	3.922	3.846	3.774	3.704	3.636	3.571	3.509	3.448	3.390	3.333	3.279	3.226	3.175	3.125
5	4.000	3.922	3.846	3.774	3.704	3.636	3.572	3.509	3.448	3.390	3.333	3.279	3.226	3.175	3.125
6	4.000	3.922	3.846	3.774	3.704	3.636	3.571	3.509	3.448	3.390	3.333	3.279	3.226	3.175	3.125
7	4.000	3.921	3.846	3.773	3.704	3.636	3.572	3.509	3.448	3.390	3.333	3.279	3.226	3.174	3.125
8	4.000	3.922	3.846	3.774	3.704	3.636	3.571	3.509	3.448	3.390	3.333	3.279	3.226	3.175	3.125
9	4.000	3.921	3.846	3.773	3.704	3.636	3.572	3.509	3.448	3.390	3.333	3.279	3.226	3.174	3.125
10	4.000	3.922	3.846	3.774	3.704	3.637	3.571	3.509	3.448	3.390	3.333	3.279	3.226	3.175	3.125
11	4.000	3.921	3.846	3.773	3.704	3.636	3.572	3.509	3.448	3.390	3.333	3.279	3.226	3.174	3.125
12	4.000	3.922	3.846	3.774	3.704	3.637	3.572	3.509	3.448	3.390	3.333	3.278	3.226	3.175	3.125
13	4.000	3.921	3.346	3.773	3.703	3.636	3.571	3.509	3.448	3.390	3.334	3.279	3.226	3.174	3.125
14	4.000	3.922	3.846	3.774	3.704	3.637	3.572	3.509	3.448	3.390	3.333	3.279	3.226	3.175	3.125
15	4.000	3.921	3.846	3.773	3.703	3.636	3.571	3.509	3.449	3.390	3.333	3.278	3.226	3.174	3.125
16	4.000	3.922	3.846	3.774	3.704	3.637	3.572	3.509	3.448	3.390	3.334	3.279	3.226	3.175	3.125
17	4.000	3.921	3.846	3.773	3.703	3.636	3.571	3.509	3.449	3.390	3.333	3.278	3.226	3.174	3.125
18	4.000	3.922	3.846	3.774	3.704	3.636	3.572	3.508	3.448	3.390	3.334	3.279	3.226	3.175	3.125
19	4.000	3.921	3.847	3.773	3.703	3.637	3.571	3.509	3.449	3.390	3.334	3.278	3.226	3.174	3.125
20	4.000	3.922	3.846	3.774	3.704	3.636	3.572	3.508	3.448	3.390	3.333	3.279	3.225	3.175	3.125
21	4.000	3.921	3.847	3.773	3.703	3.637	3.571	3.509	3.449	3.390	3.334	3.278	3.226	3.174	3.125
22	4.000	3.922	3.846	3.774	3.704	3.636	3.572	3.508	3.448	3.389	3.333	3.279	3.225	3.175	3.125
23	4.000	3.921	3.847	3.773	3.703	3.637	3.571	3.509	3.449	3.390	3.334	3.278	3.226	3.175	3.125
24	4.000	3.922	3.846	3.774	3.704	3.636	3.572	3.508	3.448	3.390	3.333	3.279	3.226	3.174	3.125
25	4.000	3.921	3.847	3.773	3.703	3.637	3.571	3.509	3.449	3.390	3.334	3.278	3.226	3.175	3.125
26	0.500	2.451	3.846	3.774	3.704	3.636	3.572	3.508	3.448	3.389	3.333	3.279	3.226	3.174	3.125
27			0.481	2.358	3.704	3.636	3.571	3.509	3.448	3.390	3.334	3.278	3.226	3.175	3.125
28					0.463	2.273	3.571	3.508	3.449	3.390	3.333	3.279	3.226	3.174	3.125
29							0.446	2.193	3.448	3.390	3.334	3.278	3.226	3.175	3.125
30									0.431	2.118	3.333	3.279	3.226	3.174	3.125
31											0.417	2.049	3.226	3.175	3.125
32													0.403	1.984	3.125
33															0.391

and the Recovery Period is:

the Depreciation Rate is:

If the Recovery Year is:	32.5	33.0	33.5	34.0	34.5	35.0	35.5	36.0	36.5	37.0	37.5	38.0	38.5	39.0	39.5
1	2.692	2.652	2.612	2.574	2.536	2.500	2.465	2.431	2.397	2.365	2.333	2.303	2.273	2.244	2.215
2	3.077	3.030	2.985	2.941	2.899	2.857	2.817	2.778	2.740	2.703	2.667	2.632	2.597	2.564	2.532
3	3.077	3.030	2.985	2.941	2.899	2.857	2.817	2.778	2.740	2.703	2.667	2.632	2.597	2.564	2.532
4	3.077	3.030	2.985	2.941	2.899	2.857	2.817	2.778	2.740	2.703	2.667	2.632	2.597	2.564	2.532
5	3.077	3.030	2.985	2.941	2.898	2.857	2.817	2.778	2.740	2.703	2.667	2.632	2.597	2.564	2.532
6	3.077	3.030	2.985	2.941	2.899	2.857	2.817	2.778	2.740	2.703	2.667	2.632	2.597	2.564	2.532
7	3.077	3.030	2.985	2.941	2.898	2.857	2.817	2.778	2.740	2.703	2.667	2.631	2.597	2.564	2.532
8	3.077	3.030	2.985	2.941	2.899	2.857	2.817	2.778	2.740	2.703	2.667	2.632	2.597	2.564	2.532
9	3.077	3.030	2.985	2.941	2.899	2.857	2.817	2.778	2.740	2.703	2.667	2.632	2.597	2.564	2.532
10	3.077	3.030	2.985	2.941	2.899	2.857	2.817	2.778	2.740	2.703	2.667	2.631	2.598	2.564	2.532
11	3.077	3.030	2.985	2.941	2.899	2.857	2.817	2.778	2.740	2.703	2.667	2.632	2.597	2.564	2.532
12	3.077	3.030	2.985	2.941	2.899	2.857	2.817	2.778	2.740	2.703	2.667	2.632	2.597	2.564	2.532
13	3.077	3.030	2.985	2.941	2.898	2.857	2.817	2.778	2.740	2.703	2.666	2.631	2.598	2.564	2.532
14	3.077	3.030	2.985	2.941	2.898	2.857	2.817	2.778	2.740	2.703	2.667	2.631	2.598	2.564	2.531
15	3.077	3.030	2.985	2.941	2.898	2.857	2.817	2.778	2.740	2.703	2.667	2.632	2.598	2.564	2.532
16	3.077	3.030	2.985	2.941	2.898	2.857	2.817	2.778	2.740	2.703	2.667	2.631	2.597	2.564	2.531
17	3.077	3.031	2.985	2.941	2.899	2.857	2.817	2.778	2.740	2.703	2.667	2.632	2.598	2.564	2.532
18	3.077	3.031	2.985	2.941	2.899	2.857	2.817	2.778	2.740	2.702	2.666	2.632	2.597	2.564	2.532
19	3.077	3.030	2.985	2.941	2.898	2.857	2.817	2.778	2.740	2.703	2.667	2.631	2.598	2.564	2.531
20	3.077	3.030	2.985	2.941	2.898	2.857	2.817	2.778	2.740	2.703	2.667	2.631	2.597	2.564	2.532
21	3.077	3.031	2.985	2.941	2.899	2.857	2.817	2.778	2.739	2.702	2.666	2.632	2.598	2.564	2.532
22	3.077	3.030	2.985	2.941	2.898	2.857	2.817	2.777	2.739	2.702	2.666	2.631	2.597	2.564	2.531
23	3.077	3.031	2.985	2.941	2.899	2.857	2.817	2.778	2.740	2.702	2.666	2.632	2.598	2.564	2.532
24	3.077	3.030	2.985	2.941	2.898	2.857	2.817	2.777	2.739	2.703	2.667	2.631	2.597	2.564	2.532
25	3.077	3.030	2.985	2.942	2.899	2.858	2.817	2.777	2.740	2.703	2.666	2.631	2.598	2.564	2.531
26	3.077	3.030	2.985	2.941	2.898	2.857	2.817	2.778	2.739	2.702	2.667	2.632	2.598	2.564	2.532
27	3.077	3.031	2.985	2.942	2.899	2.858	2.817	2.777	2.739	2.702	2.666	2.631	2.598	2.564	2.532
28	3.077	3.030	2.985	2.941	2.898	2.858	2.817	2.777	2.740	2.702	2.666	2.631	2.597	2.564	2.531
29	3.076	3.031	2.985	2.942	2.899	2.858	2.817	2.777	2.739	2.703	2.667	2.632	2.598	2.564	2.532
30	3.077	3.030	2.985	2.941	2.899	2.857	2.816	2.778	2.740	2.703	2.666	2.631	2.598	2.564	2.531
31	3.077	3.030	2.986	2.941	2.898	2.857	2.817	2.777	2.739	2.702	2.667	2.631	2.597	2.564	2.531
32	3.076	3.031	2.985	2.942	2.899	2.858	2.816	2.777	2.739	2.702	2.666	2.632	2.597	2.564	2.532
33	3.076	3.030	2.986	2.941	2.898	2.858	2.816	2.778	2.740	2.703	2.666	2.631	2.598	2.565	2.531
34	1.923	0.379	2.985	2.941	2.899	2.858	2.817	2.778	2.740	2.702	2.667	2.632	2.597	2.564	2.532
35			1.866	0.368	1.812	0.357	1.760	0.347	1.712	0.338	2.666	2.631	2.598	2.564	2.531
36											1.667	0.329	1.623	2.565	2.532
37														2.564	2.531
38														0.321	2.564
39															2.532
40															1.582

and the Recovery Period is:

If the Recovery Year is:

the Depreciation Rate is:

Recovery Year	40.0	40.5	41.0	41.5	42.0	42.5	43.0	43.5	44.0	44.5	45.0	45.5	46.0	46.5	47.0
1	2.188	2.150	2.134	2.103	2.083	2.059	2.015	2.011	1.989	1.956	1.944	1.923	1.902	1.882	1.862
2	2.500	2.469	2.439	2.410	2.381	2.353	2.326	2.299	2.273	2.247	2.222	2.193	2.174	2.151	2.128
3	2.500	2.469	2.439	2.413	2.381	2.353	2.326	2.299	2.273	2.247	2.222	2.198	2.174	2.150	2.128
4	2.500	2.469	2.439	2.413	2.381	2.353	2.326	2.299	2.273	2.247	2.222	2.198	2.174	2.151	2.128
5	2.500	2.469	2.439	2.410	2.381	2.353	2.326	2.299	2.273	2.247	2.222	2.198	2.174	2.151	2.128
6	2.500	2.469	2.439	2.410	2.381	2.353	2.326	2.299	2.273	2.247	2.222	2.198	2.174	2.150	2.128
7	2.500	2.469	2.439	2.410	2.381	2.353	2.326	2.299	2.273	2.247	2.222	2.198	2.174	2.151	2.128
8	2.500	2.469	2.439	2.410	2.381	2.353	2.326	2.299	2.273	2.247	2.222	2.198	2.174	2.150	2.128
9	2.500	2.469	2.439	2.410	2.381	2.353	2.325	2.299	2.273	2.247	2.222	2.198	2.174	2.151	2.128
10	2.500	2.469	2.439	2.410	2.381	2.353	2.326	2.299	3.273	2.247	2.222	2.198	2.174	2.150	2.128
11	2.500	2.469	2.439	2.410	2.381	2.353	2.325	2.299	2.273	2.247	2.222	2.198	2.174	2.151	2.128
12	2.500	2.469	2.439	2.410	2.381	2.353	2.326	2.299	2.273	2.247	2.222	2.198	2.174	2.150	2.128
13	2.500	2.469	2.439	2.410	2.381	2.353	2.325	2.293	2.273	2.247	2.222	2.198	2.174	2.150	2.128
14	2.500	2.469	2.439	2.410	2.381	2.353	2.325	2.293	2.273	2.247	2.222	2.198	2.174	2.151	2.128
15	2.500	2.470	2.439	2.409	2.381	2.353	2.325	2.299	2.273	2.247	2.222	2.198	2.174	2.150	2.128
16	2.500	2.469	2.439	2.409	2.381	2.353	2.326	2.299	2.273	2.247	2.222	2.138	2.174	2.151	2.127
17	2.500	2.469	2.439	2.4.0	2.381	2.353	2.325	2.299	2.273	2.247	2.222	2.198	2.174	2.151	2.128
18	2.500	2.469	2.439	2.409	2.381	2.353	2.326	2.299	2.273	2.247	2.222	2.198	2.174	2.150	2.128
19	2.500	2.469	2.439	2.4.0	2.381	2.353	2.326	2.299	2.273	2.247	2.222	2.198	2.174	2.151	2.127
20	2.500	2.469	2.439	2.439	2.381	2.353	2.326	2.299	2.273	2.247	2.222	2.198	2.174	2.150	2.128
21	2.500	2.469	2.439	2.410	2.381	2.353	2.326	2.299	2.272	2.247	2.222	2.198	2.174	2.151	2.127
22	2.500	2.469	2.439	2.409	2.381	2.353	2.326	2.299	2.273	2.247	2.222	2.198	2.174	2.150	2.128
23	2.500	2.469	2.439	2.410	2.381	2.353	2.326	2.299	2.273	2.247	2.222	2.198	2.174	2.151	2.128
24	2.500	2.469	2.439	2.410	2.381	2.353	2.326	2.299	2.272	2.247	2.222	2.198	2.174	2.150	2.128
25	2.500	2.469	2.439	2.409	2.381	2.353	2.325	2.299	2.273	2.247	2.222	2.198	2.174	2.151	2.127
26	2.500	2.469	2.439	2.409	2.381	2.353	2.325	2.299	2.272	2.247	2.223	2.198	2.174	2.150	2.128
27	2.500	2.469	2.439	2.410	2.381	2.353	2.326	2.299	2.273	2.247	2.223	2.198	2.174	2.151	2.127
28	2.500	2.469	2.439	2.409	2.381	2.353	2.325	2.299	2.272	2.247	2.223	2.198	2.174	2.150	2.127
29	2.500	2.470	2.439	2.410	2.381	2.353	2.325	2.299	2.273	2.248	2.222	2.198	2.174	2.150	2.127
30	2.500	2.470	2.439	2.409	2.381	2.353	2.325	2.299	2.273	2.247	2.223	2.197	2.174	2.151	2.128
31	2.500	2.469	2.439	2.410	2.381	2.353	2.325	2.299	2.273	2.248	2.222	2.198	2.174	2.150	2.127
32	2.500	2.470	2.439	2.409	2.381	2.353	2.325	2.299	2.272	2.247	2.223	2.197	2.174	2.151	2.128
33	2.500	2.469	2.439	2.410	2.381	2.353	2.325	2.298	2.273	2.248	2.222	2.198	2.174	2.150	2.127
34	2.500	2.470	2.439	2.409	2.381	2.353	2.326	2.299	2.272	2.247	2.223	2.197	2.174	2.151	2.128
35	2.500	2.469	2.439	2.410	2.381	2.353	2.325	2.298	2.272	2.248	2.223	2.198	2.174	2.151	2.127
36	2.500	2.470	2.439	2.409	2.381	2.353	2.325	2.298	2.272	2.248	2.223	2.197	2.174	2.151	2.128
37	2.500	2.469	2.439	2.410	2.381	2.353	2.325	2.298	2.272	2.248	2.223	2.198	2.174	2.150	2.127
38	2.500	2.470	2.439	2.409	2.381	2.353	2.326	2.298	2.273	2.248	2.222	2.198	2.174	2.150	2.128
39	2.500	2.470	2.439	2.410	2.381	2.352	2.325	2.299	2.272	2.247	2.223	2.197	2.174	2.151	2.127
40	2.500	2.470	2.440	2.409	2.380	2.353	2.326	2.298	2.273	2.248	2.223	2.197	2.174	2.150	2.128
41	2.500	2.469	2.439	2.410	2.381	2.353	2.326	2.299	2.273	2.247	2.222	2.198	2.174	2.151	2.128
42	2.500	2.469	2.439	2.410	2.381	2.352	2.325	2.298	2.272	2.248	2.223	2.197	2.174	2.150	2.127
43	0.312	2.470	2.439	2.409	2.380	2.353	2.326	2.299	2.272	2.247	2.222	2.198	2.173	2.151	2.128
44		0.305	2.410	2.381	2.352	2.325	2.298	2.273	2.247	2.223	2.197	2.174	2.151	2.127	
45			2.409	2.380	2.352	2.326	2.299	2.273	2.248	2.222	2.198	2.174	2.150	2.128	
46				2.410	2.381	2.353	2.325	2.298	2.273	2.248	2.223	2.197	2.173	2.150	2.128
47				2.409		2.353	2.325	2.299	2.273	2.247	2.222	2.198	2.174	2.151	2.127
48		1.543	0.305	1.506	0.298	1.470	0.291	1.437	0.284	1.405	0.278	1.373	0.272	1.344	0.266

Note: Because of the extreme density and small print of this numeric table, some least-significant digits may not be read with full certainty.

and the Recovery Period is:

the Depreciation Rate is:

If the Recovery Year is:	47.5	48.0	48.5	49.0	49.5	50.0
1	1.842	1.823	1.804	1.786	1.768	1.750
2	2.105	2.083	2.062	2.041	2.020	2.000
3	2.105	2.083	2.062	2.041	2.020	2.000
4	2.105	2.083	2.062	2.041	2.020	2.000
5	2.105	2.083	2.062	2.041	2.020	2.000
6	2.105	2.083	2.062	2.041	2.020	2.000
7	2.105	2.083	2.062	2.041	2.020	2.000
8	2.105	2.083	2.062	2.041	2.020	2.000
9	2.105	2.083	2.062	2.041	2.020	2.000
10	2.105	2.083	2.062	2.041	2.020	2.000
11	2.105	2.083	2.062	2.041	2.020	2.000
12	2.105	2.083	2.062	2.041	2.020	2.000
13	2.105	2.083	2.062	2.041	2.020	2.000
14	2.105	2.083	2.062	2.041	2.020	2.000
15	2.105	2.083	2.062	2.041	2.020	2.000
16	2.105	2.083	2.062	2.041	2.020	2.000
17	2.105	2.083	2.062	2.041	2.020	2.000
18	2.105	2.084	2.062	2.041	2.020	2.000
19	2.105	2.083	2.062	2.041	2.020	2.000
20	2.105	2.084	2.062	2.041	2.020	2.000
21	2.105	2.083	2.062	2.041	2.020	2.000
22	2.105	2.084	2.062	2.041	2.020	2.000
23	2.105	2.083	2.062	2.041	2.020	2.000
24	2.106	2.084	2.062	2.041	2.020	2.000
25	2.105	2.083	2.062	2.041	2.020	2.000
26	2.106	2.084	2.062	2.041	2.020	2.000
27	2.105	2.083	2.062	2.041	2.020	2.000
28	2.106	2.084	2.062	2.041	2.020	2.000
29	2.105	2.083	2.062	2.041	2.020	2.000
30	2.106	2.084	2.062	2.041	2.020	2.000
31	2.105	2.083	2.062	2.041	2.020	2.000
32	2.106	2.084	2.062	2.040	2.021	2.000
33	2.105	2.083	2.062	2.041	2.020	2.000
34	2.106	2.084	2.062	2.040	2.021	2.000
35	2.105	2.083	2.062	2.041	2.020	2.000
36	2.106	2.084	2.062	2.040	2.021	2.000
37	2.105	2.083	2.061	2.041	2.020	2.000
38	2.106	2.084	2.062	2.040	2.021	2.000
39	2.105	2.083	2.061	2.041	2.020	2.000
40	2.106	2.084	2.062	2.040	2.021	2.000
41	2.105	2.083	2.061	2.041	2.020	2.000
42	2.106	2.084	2.062	2.040	2.021	2.000
43	2.105	2.083	2.061	2.041	2.020	2.000
44	2.106	2.084	2.062	2.040	2.021	2.000
45	2.105	2.083	2.061	2.041	2.020	2.000
46	2.106	2.084	2.062	2.040	2.021	2.000
47	2.105	2.083	2.061	2.041	2.020	2.000
48	1.316	2.084	2.062	2.040	2.021	2.000
49		0.260	2.062	0.255	2.020	2.000
50			1.288		1.263	2.000
51						0.250

TABLE 10

General and Alternative Depreciation Systems
Applicable Depreciation Method: Straight Line
Applicable Recovery Periods: 2.5 – 50 years
Applicable Convention: Mid-quarter (property placed in service in second quarter)

and the Recovery Period is:

the Depreciation Rate is:

If the Recovery Year is:	2.5	3.0	3.5	4.0	4.5	5.0	5.5	6.0	6.5	7.0	7.5	8.0	8.5	9.0	9.5
1	25.00	20.83	17.86	15.63	13.89	12.50	11.36	10.42	9.62	8.93	8.33	7.81	7.35	6.94	6.58
2	40.00	33.33	28.57	25.00	22.22	20.00	18.18	16.67	15.38	14.29	13.33	12.50	11.77	11.11	10.53
3	35.00	33.34	28.57	25.00	22.22	20.00	18.18	16.67	15.38	14.28	13.33	12.50	11.76	11.11	10.53
4		12.50	25.00	25.00	22.22	20.00	18.18	16.67	15.39	14.29	13.33	12.50	11.77	11.11	10.52
5				9.37	19.45	20.00	18.19	16.67	15.38	14.28	13.33	12.50	11.76	11.11	10.53
6						7.50	15.91	16.67	15.39	14.29	13.33	12.50	11.77	11.11	10.52
7								6.25	13.46	14.28	13.33	12.50	11.76	11.11	10.53
8										5.36	11.67	12.50	11.77	11.12	10.53
9												4.69	10.29	11.11	10.52
10														4.17	9.21

and the Recovery Period is:

the Depreciation Rate is:

If the Recovery Year is:	10.0	10.5	11.0	11.5	12.0	12.5	13.0	13.5	14.0	14.5	15.0	15.5	16.0	16.5	17.0
1	6.25	5.95	5.68	5.43	5.21	5.00	4.81	4.63	4.46	4.31	4.17	4.03	3.91	3.79	3.68
2	10.00	9.52	9.09	8.70	8.33	8.00	7.69	7.41	7.14	6.90	6.67	6.45	6.25	6.06	5.88
3	10.00	9.52	9.09	8.70	8.33	8.00	7.69	7.41	7.14	6.90	6.67	6.45	6.25	6.06	5.88
4	10.00	9.53	9.09	8.70	8.33	8.00	7.69	7.41	7.14	6.90	6.67	6.45	6.25	6.06	5.88
5	10.00	9.52	9.09	8.70	8.33	8.00	7.59	7.41	7.14	6.90	6.67	6.45	6.25	6.06	5.88
6	10.00	9.53	9.09	8.69	8.34	8.00	7.69	7.41	7.14	6.90	6.67	6.45	6.25	6.06	5.88
7	10.00	9.52	9.09	8.70	8.33	8.00	7.69	7.41	7.15	6.89	6.67	6.45	6.25	6.06	5.88
8	10.00	9.53	9.09	8.69	8.34	8.00	7.69	7.40	7.14	6.90	6.66	6.45	6.25	6.06	5.88
9	10.00	9.52	9.09	8.70	8.34	8.00	7.69	7.41	7.15	6.89	6.67	6.45	6.25	6.06	5.88
10	10.00	9.53	9.10	8.69	8.33	8.00	7.70	7.40	7.14	6.90	6.66	6.45	6.25	6.06	5.88
11	3.75	8.33	3.41	7.61	8.34	8.00	7.69	7.41	7.15	6.89	6.67	6.46	6.25	6.06	5.88
12					8.33	8.00	7.70	7.40	7.14	6.90	6.66	6.45	6.25	6.06	5.89
13					1.13	7.00	7.69	6.48	2.68	6.03	6.66	6.46	6.25	6.06	5.88
14							2.89				6.67	6.45	6.25	6.06	5.89
15											2.50	6.45	6.25	6.06	5.88
16												5.65	6.25	6.06	5.89
17													2.34	5.31	5.88
18															2.21

and the Recovery Period is:

the Depreciation Rate is:

If the Recovery Year is:	17.5	18.0	18.5	19.0	19.5	20.0	20.5	21.0	21.5	22.0	22.5	23.0	23.5	24.0	24.5
1	3.57	3.47	3.38	3.29	3.21	3.125	3.049	2.976	2.907	2.841	2.778	2.717	2.660	2.604	2.551
2	5.71	5.56	5.41	5.26	5.13	5.000	4.878	4.762	4.651	4.545	4.444	4.348	4.255	4.167	4.082
3	5.71	5.56	5.41	5.26	5.13	5.000	4.878	4.762	4.651	4.545	4.444	4.348	4.255	4.167	4.082
4	5.71	5.55	5.40	5.26	5.13	5.000	4.878	4.762	4.651	4.545	4.444	4.348	4.255	4.167	4.082
5	5.72	5.56	5.41	5.26	5.13	5.000	4.878	4.762	4.651	4.546	4.445	4.348	4.255	4.167	4.082
6	5.71	5.56	5.40	5.26	5.13	5.000	4.878	4.762	4.651	4.545	4.444	4.348	4.255	4.167	4.082
7	5.72	5.55	5.41	5.26	5.13	5.000	4.878	4.762	4.651	4.546	4.444	4.348	4.255	4.167	4.082
8	5.71	5.56	5.40	5.26	5.13	5.000	4.878	4.762	4.651	4.545	4.444	4.348	4.255	4.167	4.082
9	5.72	5.55	5.41	5.27	5.13	5.000	4.878	4.762	4.651	4.546	4.445	4.348	4.255	4.167	4.081
10	5.71	5.56	5.40	5.26	5.13	5.000	4.878	4.762	4.651	4.545	4.444	4.348	4.255	4.167	4.082
11	5.72	5.55	5.41	5.27	5.13	5.000	4.878	4.762	4.651	4.546	4.445	4.348	4.255	4.166	4.081
12	5.71	5.56	5.40	5.26	5.13	5.000	4.878	4.762	4.651	4.545	4.444	4.348	4.256	4.167	4.082
13	5.72	5.55	5.41	5.27	5.13	5.000	4.878	4.762	4.651	4.546	4.445	4.348	4.255	4.166	4.081
14	5.71	5.56	5.40	5.26	5.12	5.000	4.878	4.762	4.651	4.545	4.444	4.348	4.256	4.167	4.082
15	5.72	5.55	5.41	5.27	5.13	5.000	4.878	4.762	4.651	4.546	4.445	4.348	4.255	4.166	4.081
16	5.71	5.56	5.40	5.26	5.12	5.000	4.878	4.762	4.651	4.545	4.444	4.348	4.256	4.167	4.082
17	5.72	5.56	5.40	5.27	5.13	5.000	4.878	4.762	4.652	4.546	4.445	4.348	4.255	4.166	4.081
18	5.71	5.55	5.41	5.26	5.12	5.000	4.878	4.762	4.651	4.545	4.444	4.347	4.256	4.167	4.082
19	5.00	5.56	5.40	5.27	5.13	5.000	4.878	4.762	4.652	4.546	4.445	4.348	4.255	4.166	4.081
20		2.08	4.73	1.97	5.13	5.000	4.878	4.762	4.651	4.545	4.444	4.347	4.256	4.167	4.082
21					4.48	1.875	4.878	4.762	4.652	4.546	4.445	4.347	4.255	4.167	4.081
22							4.269	1.786	4.070	4.545	4.444	4.348	4.255	4.167	4.082
23										1.705	3.889	4.347	4.256	4.167	4.081
24												1.630	3.724	4.166	4.082
25														1.562	3.571

and the Recovery Period is:

the Depreciation Rate is:

If the Recovery Year is:	25.0	25.5	26.0	26.5	27.0	27.5	28.0	28.5	29.0	29.5	30.0	30.5	31.0	31.5	32.0
1	2.500	2.451	2.404	2.358	2.315	2.273	2.232	2.193	2.155	2.119	2.083	2.049	2.016	1.984	1.953
2	4.000	3.922	3.846	3.774	3.704	3.636	3.571	3.509	3.448	3.390	3.333	3.279	3.226	3.175	3.125
3	4.000	3.922	3.846	3.774	3.704	3.636	3.571	3.509	3.448	3.390	3.333	3.279	3.226	3.175	3.125
4	4.000	3.922	3.846	3.774	3.704	3.636	3.571	3.509	3.448	3.390	3.333	3.279	3.226	3.175	3.125
5	4.000	3.922	3.846	3.774	3.704	3.636	3.572	3.509	3.448	3.390	3.333	3.279	3.226	3.175	3.125
6	4.000	3.921	3.846	3.774	3.704	3.636	3.571	3.509	3.448	3.390	3.333	3.279	3.226	3.175	3.125
7	4.000	3.922	3.846	3.773	3.704	3.636	3.572	3.509	3.448	3.390	3.333	3.279	3.226	3.175	3.125
8	4.000	3.921	3.846	3.774	3.704	3.636	3.571	3.509	3.448	3.390	3.333	3.279	3.226	3.175	3.125
9	4.000	3.922	3.846	3.773	3.704	3.637	3.572	3.509	3.448	3.390	3.333	3.279	3.226	3.175	3.125
10	4.000	3.921	3.846	3.774	3.704	3.636	3.571	3.509	3.448	3.390	3.333	3.279	3.226	3.174	3.125
11	4.000	3.922	3.846	3.773	3.704	3.637	3.572	3.509	3.448	3.390	3.333	3.279	3.226	3.175	3.125
12	4.000	3.921	3.846	3.773	3.703	3.636	3.571	3.509	3.448	3.390	3.334	3.279	3.226	3.175	3.125
13	4.000	3.922	3.846	3.773	3.704	3.637	3.572	3.509	3.448	3.390	3.333	3.278	3.226	3.175	3.125
14	4.000	3.921	3.846	3.774	3.703	3.637	3.571	3.509	3.448	3.390	3.334	3.279	3.226	3.175	3.125
15	4.000	3.922	3.846	3.773	3.704	3.636	3.572	3.509	3.449	3.390	3.333	3.278	3.226	3.174	3.125
16	4.000	3.921	3.846	3.773	3.704	3.637	3.571	3.509	3.448	3.390	3.334	3.279	3.226	3.175	3.125
17	4.000	3.922	3.846	3.774	3.703	3.636	3.572	3.509	3.449	3.390	3.333	3.279	3.226	3.175	3.125
18	4.000	3.921	3.846	3.773	3.704	3.637	3.571	3.508	3.448	3.390	3.334	3.278	3.226	3.174	3.125
19	4.000	3.922	3.846	3.774	3.703	3.636	3.572	3.509	3.449	3.390	3.333	3.279	3.226	3.175	3.125
20	4.000	3.921	3.847	3.773	3.704	3.637	3.571	3.508	3.448	3.390	3.334	3.278	3.226	3.175	3.125
21	4.000	3.922	3.846	3.774	3.703	3.636	3.572	3.509	3.449	3.389	3.333	3.279	3.225	3.174	3.125
22	4.000	3.921	3.847	3.773	3.704	3.637	3.571	3.508	3.448	3.390	3.334	3.278	3.226	3.175	3.125
23	4.000	3.922	3.846	3.774	3.703	3.636	3.572	3.509	3.449	3.389	3.333	3.279	3.226	3.174	3.125
24	4.000	3.921	3.847	3.773	3.704	3.637	3.571	3.508	3.448	3.390	3.334	3.278	3.225	3.175	3.125
25	4.000	3.922	3.846	3.774	3.703	3.636	3.572	3.509	3.449	3.389	3.333	3.279	3.226	3.174	3.125
26	1.500	3.431	3.847	3.773	3.704	3.637	3.571	3.509	3.449	3.390	3.333	3.279	3.226	3.175	3.125
27			1.442	3.302	3.703	3.636	3.572	3.508	3.448	3.389	3.334	3.278	3.226	3.174	3.125
28					1.389	3.182	3.571	3.509	3.449	3.390	3.333	3.279	3.226	3.175	3.125
29							1.339	3.070	3.448	3.389	3.334	3.278	3.225	3.174	3.125
30									1.293	2.966	3.333	3.279	3.225	3.175	3.125
31											1.250	2.869	3.226	3.174	3.125
32													1.210	2.778	3.125
33															1.172

and the Recovery Period is:

the Depreciation Rate is:

If the Recovery Year is:	39.5	39.0	38.5	38.0	37.5	37.0	36.5	36.0	35.5	35.0	34.5	34.0	33.5	33.0	32.5
1	1.582	1.603	1.623	1.645	1.667	1.689	1.712	1.736	1.761	1.786	1.812	1.838	1.866	1.894	1.923
2	2.532	2.564	2.597	2.632	2.667	2.703	2.740	2.778	2.817	2.857	2.899	2.941	2.985	3.030	3.077
3	2.532	2.564	2.597	2.632	2.667	2.703	2.740	2.778	2.817	2.857	2.899	2.941	2.985	3.030	3.077
4	2.532	2.564	2.597	2.632	2.667	2.703	2.740	2.778	2.817	2.857	2.899	2.941	2.985	3.030	3.077
5	2.532	2.564	2.597	2.632	2.667	2.703	2.740	2.778	2.817	2.857	2.898	2.941	2.985	3.030	3.077
6	2.532	2.564	2.597	2.632	2.667	2.703	2.740	2.778	2.817	2.857	2.899	2.941	2.985	3.030	3.077
7	2.532	2.564	2.597	2.632	2.667	2.703	2.740	2.778	2.817	2.857	2.899	2.941	2.985	3.030	3.077
8	2.532	2.564	2.598	2.632	2.667	2.703	2.740	2.778	2.817	2.857	2.899	2.941	2.985	3.030	3.077
9	2.532	2.564	2.597	2.631	2.667	2.703	2.740	2.778	2.817	2.857	2.898	2.941	2.985	3.030	3.077
10	2.532	2.564	2.597	2.632	2.667	2.703	2.740	2.778	2.817	2.857	2.898	2.941	2.985	3.030	3.077
11	2.532	2.564	2.598	2.632	2.667	2.703	2.740	2.778	2.817	2.857	2.899	2.941	2.985	3.030	3.077
12	2.532	2.564	2.597	2.632	2.667	2.703	2.740	2.778	2.817	2.857	2.898	2.941	2.985	3.030	3.077
13	2.532	2.564	2.598	2.632	2.666	2.703	2.740	2.778	2.817	2.857	2.898	2.941	2.985	3.030	3.077
14	2.531	2.564	2.597	2.632	2.666	2.703	2.740	2.778	2.817	2.857	2.899	2.941	2.985	3.031	3.077
15	2.532	2.564	2.597	2.631	2.667	2.703	2.740	2.778	2.817	2.857	2.898	2.941	2.985	3.030	3.077
16	2.532	2.564	2.597	2.632	2.666	2.703	2.740	2.778	2.817	2.857	2.899	2.941	2.985	3.031	3.077
17	2.532	2.564	2.598	2.632	2.667	2.702	2.740	2.778	2.817	2.857	2.898	2.941	2.985	3.031	3.077
18	2.532	2.564	2.597	2.631	2.666	2.703	2.740	2.778	2.817	2.857	2.899	2.941	2.985	3.030	3.077
19	2.532	2.564	2.598	2.632	2.667	2.702	2.739	2.778	2.817	2.857	2.898	2.941	2.985	3.031	3.077
20	2.532	2.564	2.597	2.631	2.666	2.703	2.740	2.778	2.817	2.857	2.899	2.941	2.985	3.030	3.077
21	2.531	2.564	2.597	2.632	2.667	2.703	2.740	2.778	2.817	2.857	2.898	2.941	2.985	3.031	3.077
22	2.532	2.564	2.597	2.631	2.666	2.702	2.739	2.778	2.817	2.857	2.899	2.941	2.985	3.031	3.077
23	2.532	2.564	2.598	2.632	2.666	2.703	2.740	2.778	2.817	2.857	2.898	2.941	2.985	3.030	3.077
24	2.532	2.564	2.597	2.631	2.667	2.702	2.739	2.778	2.817	2.857	2.899	2.942	2.985	3.031	3.077
25	2.531	2.564	2.598	2.632	2.666	2.703	2.740	2.778	2.817	2.857	2.899	2.941	2.985	3.030	3.077
26	2.532	2.564	2.597	2.631	2.667	2.702	2.739	2.778	2.817	2.857	2.898	2.942	2.985	3.031	3.077
27	2.532	2.564	2.598	2.632	2.666	2.703	2.740	2.778	2.817	2.857	2.899	2.941	2.985	3.030	3.077
28	2.532	2.564	2.597	2.631	2.667	2.702	2.739	2.778	2.817	2.857	2.898	2.941	2.985	3.031	3.077
29	2.532	2.564	2.598	2.632	2.666	2.703	2.740	2.778	2.817	2.858	2.899	2.941	2.985	3.031	3.077
30	2.531	2.564	2.597	2.631	2.667	2.702	2.739	2.777	2.817	2.857	2.898	2.942	2.985	3.030	3.077
31	2.532	2.564	2.598	2.632	2.666	2.703	2.740	2.778	2.817	2.857	2.899	2.941	2.986	3.031	3.076
32	2.532	2.564	2.597	2.631	2.666	2.702	2.739	2.777	2.816	2.858	2.898	2.942	2.985	3.030	3.076
33	2.531	2.564	2.597	2.632	2.667	2.703	2.740	2.778	2.817	2.857	2.899	2.942	2.986	3.031	2.692
34	2.532	2.564	2.598	2.631	2.666	2.702	2.739	2.777	2.816	2.857	2.899	2.942	2.612	1.136	
35	2.531	2.564	2.597	2.631	2.667	2.703	2.740	2.778	2.817	2.858	2.536	1.103			
36	2.532	2.565	2.598	2.632	2.666	2.702	2.739	2.778	2.464	1.072					
37	2.531	2.565	2.597	2.631	2.667	2.703	2.397	1.042							
38	2.531	2.565	2.597	2.631	2.333	1.013									
39	2.532	2.564	2.273	0.987											
40	2.215	0.962													

and the Recovery Period is:

the Depreciation Rate is:

If the Recovery Year is:	40.0	40.5	41.0	41.5	42.0	42.5	43.0	43.5	44.0	44.5	45.0	45.5	46.0	46.5	47.0
1	1.563	1.543	1.524	1.506	1.488	1.471	1.453	1.437	1.420	1.404	1.389	1.374	1.359	1.344	1.330
2	2.500	2.469	2.439	2.410	2.381	2.353	2.326	2.299	2.271	2.247	2.222	2.198	2.174	2.151	2.128
3	2.500	2.469	2.439	2.410	2.381	2.353	2.326	2.299	2.273	2.247	2.222	2.198	2.174	2.151	2.128
4	2.500	2.469	2.439	2.410	2.381	2.353	2.326	2.299	2.273	2.247	2.222	2.198	2.174	2.151	2.128
5	2.500	2.469	2.439	2.410	2.381	2.353	2.326	2.299	2.273	2.247	2.222	2.198	2.174	2.150	2.128
6	2.500	2.469	2.439	2.410	2.381	2.353	2.326	2.299	2.273	2.247	2.222	2.198	2.174	2.150	2.128
7	2.500	2.469	2.439	2.410	2.381	2.353	2.326	2.299	2.273	2.247	2.222	2.198	2.174	2.151	2.128
8	2.500	2.469	2.439	2.410	2.381	2.353	2.326	2.299	2.273	2.247	2.222	2.198	2.174	2.150	2.128
9	2.500	2.469	2.439	2.410	2.381	2.353	2.326	2.299	2.273	2.247	2.222	2.198	2.171	2.150	2.128
10	2.500	2.469	2.439	2.410	2.381	2.353	2.325	2.299	2.273	2.247	2.222	2.198	2.174	2.150	2.128
11	2.500	2.469	2.439	2.410	2.381	2.353	2.325	2.299	2.273	2.247	2.222	2.198	2.171	2.150	2.128
12	2.500	2.469	2.439	2.410	2.381	2.353	2.325	2.299	2.273	2.247	2.222	2.198	2.174	2.150	2.128
13	2.500	2.469	2.439	2.410	2.381	2.353	2.336	2.299	2.273	2.247	2.222	2.198	2.174	2.150	2.128
14	2.500	2.469	2.439	2.409	2.381	2.353	2.325	2.299	2.273	2.247	2.222	2.198	2.174	2.150	2.128
15	2.500	2.469	2.439	2.410	2.381	2.353	2.336	2.299	2.273	2.247	2.222	2.198	2.174	2.150	2.127
16	2.500	2.469	2.439	2.409	2.381	2.353	2.335	2.299	2.273	2.247	2.222	2.198	2.174	2.150	2.128
17	2.500	2.469	2.439	2.410	2.381	2.353	2.326	2.299	2.273	2.247	2.222	2.198	2.174	2.150	2.128
18	2.500	2.469	2.439	2.405	2.381	2.353	2.325	2.299	2.273	2.247	2.222	2.198	2.174	2.150	2.128
19	2.500	2.469	2.439	2.410	2.381	2.353	2.326	2.299	2.273	2.247	2.222	2.198	2.174	2.150	2.128
20	2.500	2.469	2.439	2.409	2.381	2.353	2.325	2.299	2.273	2.247	2.222	2.198	2.174	2.150	2.127
21	2.500	2.469	2.439	2.410	2.381	2.353	2.326	2.299	2.273	2.247	2.222	2.198	2.174	2.151	2.128
22	2.500	2.469	2.439	2.410	2.381	2.353	2.326	2.299	2.273	2.247	2.222	2.198	2.174	2.150	2.127
23	2.500	2.469	2.439	2.409	2.381	2.353	2.325	2.299	2.272	2.247	2.222	2.198	2.174	2.150	2.128
24	2.500	2.469	2.439	2.410	2.381	2.353	2.326	2.299	2.273	2.247	2.222	2.198	2.174	2.150	2.127
25	2.500	2.465	2.439	2.409	2.381	2.353	2.326	2.299	2.273	2.247	2.222	2.198	2.174	2.151	2.128
26	2.500	2.469	2.439	2.410	2.381	2.353	2.325	2.299	2.273	2.247	2.222	2.198	2.174	2.150	2.128
27	2.500	2.469	2.439	2.403	2.381	2.353	2.326	2.299	2.272	2.247	2.223	2.198	2.174	2.151	2.127
28	2.500	2.469	2.439	2.410	2.381	2.353	2.325	2.299	2.272	2.248	2.223	2.197	2.174	2.150	2.128
29	2.500	2.469	2.439	2.410	2.381	2.353	2.326	2.299	2.273	2.247	2.222	2.198	2.174	2.151	2.127
30	2.500	2.470	2.439	2.409	2.381	2.353	2.326	2.299	2.272	2.248	2.223	2.198	2.174	2.150	2.128
31	2.500	2.469	2.439	2.410	2.381	2.353	2.326	2.298	2.273	2.247	2.222	2.197	2.174	2.151	2.128
32	2.500	2.469	2.439	2.409	2.381	2.353	2.325	2.299	2.273	2.247	2.223	2.198	2.174	2.150	2.127
33	2.500	2.469	2.439	2.410	2.381	2.353	2.326	2.299	2.272	2.248	2.222	2.197	2.174	2.151	2.128
34	2.500	2.470	2.439	2.409	2.381	2.353	2.326	2.299	2.273	2.247	2.223	2.198	2.174	2.150	2.127
35	2.500	2.469	2.439	2.410	2.381	2.353	2.325	2.298	2.272	2.248	2.222	2.197	2.174	2.151	2.128
36	2.500	2.470	2.439	2.409	2.381	2.353	2.326	2.299	2.272	2.247	2.223	2.198	2.174	2.150	2.128
37	2.500	2.470	2.439	2.410	2.381	2.353	2.325	2.298	2.273	2.247	2.222	2.197	2.173	2.150	2.127
38	2.500	2.469	2.439	2.409	2.381	2.353	2.326	2.299	2.272	2.248	2.223	2.198	2.174	2.151	2.127
39	2.500	2.470	2.440	2.410	2.381	2.352	2.326	2.299	2.273	2.247	2.222	2.197	2.174	2.150	2.128
40	2.500	2.470	2.439	2.409	2.380	2.353	2.325	2.299	2.272	2.248	2.223	2.198	2.174	2.150	2.128
41	0.937	2.469	2.439	2.410	2.380	2.353	2.326	2.298	2.273	2.247	2.222	2.198	2.173	2.151	2.127
42		2.161	2.440	2.409	2.380	2.353	2.325	2.299	2.272	2.248	2.223	2.197	2.174	2.150	2.127
43			0.915	2.108	2.380	2.353	2.326	2.299	2.273	2.247	2.222	2.198	2.174	2.151	2.128
44					0.893	2.058	0.872	2.299	2.272	2.248	2.223	2.197	2.173	2.150	2.127
45								2.011	0.852	1.967	2.222	2.198	2.174	2.150	2.128
46											0.833	1.923	0.815	2.151	2.128
47														1.882	2.127
48															0.798

and the Recovery Period is:

the Depreciation Rate is:

If the Recovery Year is:	47.5	48.0	48.5	49.0	49.5	50.0
1	1.316	1.302	1.289	1.276	1.263	1.250
2	2.105	2.083	2.062	2.041	2.020	2.000
3	2.105	2.083	2.062	2.041	2.020	2.000
4	2.105	2.083	2.062	2.041	2.020	2.000
5	2.105	2.083	2.062	2.041	2.020	2.000
6	2.105	2.083	2.062	2.041	2.020	2.000
7	2.105	2.083	2.062	2.041	2.020	2.000
8	2.105	2.083	2.062	2.041	2.020	2.000
9	2.105	2.083	2.062	2.041	2.020	2.000
10	2.105	2.083	2.062	2.041	2.020	2.000
11	2.105	2.083	2.062	2.041	2.020	2.000
12	2.105	2.083	2.062	2.041	2.020	2.000
13	2.105	2.083	2.062	2.041	2.020	2.000
14	2.105	2.083	2.062	2.041	2.020	2.000
15	2.105	2.083	2.062	2.041	2.020	2.000
16	2.105	2.083	2.062	2.041	2.020	2.000
17	2.105	2.083	2.062	2.041	2.020	2.000
18	2.105	2.084	2.062	2.041	2.020	2.000
19	2.105	2.083	2.062	2.041	2.020	2.000
20	2.105	2.084	2.062	2.041	2.020	2.000
21	2.105	2.083	2.062	2.041	2.020	2.000
22	2.105	2.084	2.062	2.041	2.020	2.000
23	2.105	2.083	2.062	2.041	2.020	2.000
24	2.105	2.084	2.062	2.041	2.020	2.000
25	2.106	2.083	2.062	2.041	2.020	2.000
26	2.105	2.084	2.062	2.041	2.020	2.000

and the Recovery Period is:

the Depreciation Rate is:

If the Recovery Year is:	47.5	48.0	48.5	49.0	49.5	50.0
27	2.106	2.083	2.062	2.041	2.020	2.000
28	2.105	2.084	2.062	2.041	2.020	2.000
29	2.106	2.083	2.062	2.041	2.020	2.000
30	2.105	2.083	2.062	2.041	2.020	2.000
31	2.106	2.083	2.062	2.041	2.020	2.000
32	2.105	2.084	2.062	2.040	2.021	2.000
33	2.106	2.083	2.062	2.041	2.020	2.000
34	2.105	2.084	2.061	2.040	2.021	2.000
35	2.106	2.083	2.062	2.041	2.020	2.000
36	2.105	2.084	2.061	2.040	2.021	2.000
37	2.106	2.083	2.062	2.041	2.020	2.000
38	2.105	2.084	2.061	2.040	2.020	2.000
39	2.106	2.083	2.062	2.041	2.020	2.000
40	2.105	2.084	2.061	2.040	2.021	2.000
41	2.106	2.083	2.062	2.041	2.020	2.000
42	2.105	2.084	2.061	2.040	2.021	2.000
43	2.106	2.083	2.062	2.041	2.020	2.000
44	2.105	2.084	2.061	2.041	2.020	2.000
45	2.106	2.083	2.062	2.041	2.020	2.000
46	2.105	2.084	2.061	2.040	2.021	2.000
47	2.106	2.083	2.062	2.041	2.020	2.000
48	1.842	2.084	2.061	2.040	2.021	2.000
49		0.781	1.804	2.041	2.020	2.000
50				0.765	1.768	2.000
51						0.750

TABLE 11   General and Alternative Depreciation Systems
Applicable Depreciation Method: Straight Line
Applicable Recovery Periods: 2.5 - 50 years
Applicable Convention: Mid-quarter (property placed
in service in third quarter)

and the Recovery Period is:
the Depreciation Rate is:

If the Recovery Year is:	2.5	3.0	3.5	4.0	4.5	5.0	5.5	6.0	6.5	7.0	7.5	8.0	8.5	9.0	9.5
1	15.00	12.50	10.71	9.38	8.33	7.50	6.82	6.25	5.77	5.36	5.00	4.69	4.41	4.17	3.95
2	40.00	33.33	28.57	25.00	22.22	20.00	18.18	16.67	15.38	14.29	13.33	12.50	11.76	11.11	10.53
3	40.00	33.34	28.57	25.00	22.22	20.00	18.18	16.67	15.39	14.28	13.33	12.50	11.77	11.11	10.53
4	5.00	20.83	28.58	25.00	22.23	20.00	18.18	16.67	15.39	14.29	13.34	12.50	11.76	11.11	10.52
5			3.57	15.62	22.22	20.00	18.18	16.67	15.38	14.28	13.33	12.50	11.77	11.11	10.53
6					2.78	12.50	18.19	16.65	15.38	14.29	13.33	12.50	11.76	11.11	10.52
7							2.27	10.42	15.39	14.28	13.34	12.50	11.76	11.11	10.53
8									1.92	8.93	13.33	12.50	11.77	11.11	10.52
9											1.67	7.81	11.76	11.11	10.53
10													1.47	6.95	10.52
11															1.32

and the Recovery Period is:
the Depreciation Rate is:

If the Recovery Year is:	10.0	10.5	11.0	11.5	12.0	12.5	13.0	13.5	14.0	14.5	15.0	15.5	16.0	16.5	17.0
1	3.75	3.57	3.41	3.26	3.13	3.00	2.88	2.78	2.68	2.59	2.50	2.42	2.34	2.27	2.21
2	10.00	9.52	9.09	8.70	8.33	8.00	7.69	7.41	7.14	6.90	6.67	6.45	6.25	6.06	5.88
3	10.00	9.52	9.09	8.70	8.33	8.00	7.69	7.41	7.14	6.90	6.67	6.45	6.25	6.06	5.88
4	10.00	9.52	9.09	8.69	8.33	8.00	7.69	7.41	7.14	6.90	6.67	6.45	6.25	6.06	5.88
5	10.00	9.53	9.09	8.70	8.33	8.00	7.69	7.41	7.14	6.83	6.67	6.45	6.25	6.06	5.88
6	10.00	9.52	9.09	8.70	8.34	8.00	7.69	7.41	7.14	6.90	6.67	6.45	6.25	6.06	5.88
7	10.00	9.53	9.09	8.69	8.33	8.00	7.70	7.40	7.14	6.89	6.66	6.45	6.25	6.06	5.88
8	10.00	9.52	9.09	8.70	8.34	8.00	7.69	7.41	7.15	6.90	6.67	6.45	6.25	6.06	5.88
9	10.00	9.53	9.09	8.69	8.33	8.00	7.70	7.40	7.14	6.89	6.66	6.45	6.25	6.06	5.88
10	10.00	9.53	9.09	8.70	8.34	8.00	7.69	7.40	7.15	6.90	6.67	6.45	6.25	6.06	5.88
11	6.25	9.53	9.10	8.70	8.34	8.00	7.70	7.41	7.11	6.90	6.66	6.45	6.25	6.06	5.89
12		1.19	5.68	8.69	8.33	8.00	7.69	7.41	7.15	6.89	6.67	6.46	6.25	6.06	5.88
13				1.09	5.21	8.00	7.70	7.40	7.14	6.90	6.66	6.45	6.25	6.06	5.89
14						1.00	4.81	7.40	7.14	6.90	6.67	6.45	6.25	6.06	5.88
15								0.93	4.47	6.89	6.66	6.46	6.25	6.07	5.89
16										0.86	4.17	6.45	6.25	6.06	5.88
17												0.81	3.91	6.06	5.88
18														0.76	3.68

and the Recovery Period is:

the Depreciation Rate is:

If the Recovery Year is:	17.5	18.0	18.5	19.0	19.5	20.0	20.5	21.0	21.5	22.0	22.5	23.0	23.5	24.0	24.5
1	2.14	2.08	2.03	1.97	1.92	1.875	1.829	1.786	1.744	1.705	1.667	1.630	1.596	1.563	1.531
2	5.71	5.56	5.41	5.26	5.13	5.000	4.878	4.762	4.651	4.545	4.444	4.348	4.255	4.167	4.082
3	5.71	5.56	5.40	5.26	5.13	5.000	4.878	4.762	4.651	4.545	4.444	4.348	4.255	4.167	4.082
4	5.72	5.56	5.41	5.26	5.13	5.000	4.878	4.762	4.651	4.545	4.444	4.348	4.255	4.167	4.082
5	5.71	5.55	5.40	5.26	5.13	5.000	4.878	4.762	4.651	4.546	4.444	4.348	4.255	4.167	4.082
6	5.72	5.56	5.41	5.26	5.13	5.000	4.878	4.762	4.651	4.545	4.445	4.348	4.255	4.167	4.082
7	5.71	5.55	5.40	5.26	5.13	5.000	4.878	4.762	4.651	4.545	4.445	4.348	4.255	4.167	4.082
8	5.72	5.56	5.41	5.27	5.13	5.000	4.878	4.762	4.651	4.545	4.444	4.348	4.255	4.166	4.081
9	5.71	5.55	5.40	5.26	5.13	5.000	4.878	4.762	4.651	4.546	4.444	4.348	4.255	4.167	4.082
10	5.72	5.56	5.41	5.27	5.13	5.000	4.878	4.762	4.651	4.545	4.445	4.348	4.256	4.166	4.081
11	5.71	5.55	5.40	5.26	5.13	5.000	4.878	4.762	4.651	4.546	4.444	4.348	4.255	4.167	4.082
12	5.72	5.56	5.41	5.26	5.13	5.000	4.878	4.762	4.651	4.545	4.445	4.348	4.256	4.166	4.081
13	5.71	5.55	5.40	5.27	5.13	5.000	4.878	4.762	4.651	4.546	4.444	4.348	4.256	4.167	4.082
14	5.72	5.56	5.41	5.26	5.13	5.000	4.878	4.762	4.651	4.545	4.445	4.348	4.255	4.166	4.081
15	5.71	5.55	5.40	5.27	5.12	5.000	4.878	4.762	4.651	4.546	4.444	4.348	4.256	4.166	4.082
16	5.72	5.56	5.41	5.26	5.13	5.000	4.878	4.762	4.651	4.545	4.444	4.348	4.255	4.167	4.081
17	5.71	5.55	5.40	5.27	5.12	5.000	4.878	4.762	4.652	4.546	4.445	4.348	4.256	4.166	4.082
18	5.72	5.56	5.41	5.26	5.13	5.000	4.878	4.762	4.651	4.545	4.444	4.348	4.255	4.167	4.081
19	0.71	3.47	5.40	5.27	5.12	5.000	4.879	4.761	4.652	4.546	4.445	4.347	4.256	4.166	4.082
20			0.68	3.29	5.13	5.000	4.878	4.762	4.651	4.545	4.444	4.348	4.255	4.167	4.081
21					0.64	3.125	0.610	4.761	4.652	4.546	4.445	4.347	4.256	4.166	4.082
22								2.976	4.651	4.545	4.444	4.348	4.255	4.166	4.081
23									0.581	2.841	4.445	2.717	4.256	4.167	4.082
24											0.556		4.255	4.167	4.081
25													0.532	2.604	4.082
26															0.510

and the Recovery Period is:

the Depreciation Rate is:

If the Recovery Year is:	25.0	25.5	26.0	26.5	27.0	27.5	28.0	28.5	29.0	29.5	30.0	30.5	31.0	31.5	32.0
1	1.500	1.471	1.442	1.415	1.389	1.364	1.339	1.316	1.293	1.271	1.250	1.230	1.210	1.190	1.172
2	4.000	3.922	3.846	3.774	3.704	3.636	3.571	3.509	3.448	3.390	3.333	3.279	3.226	3.175	3.125
3	4.000	3.922	3.846	3.774	3.704	3.636	3.571	3.509	3.448	3.390	3.333	3.279	3.226	3.175	3.125
4	4.000	3.921	3.846	3.774	3.704	3.636	3.571	3.509	3.448	3.390	3.333	3.279	3.226	3.175	3.125
5	4.000	3.922	3.846	3.774	3.704	3.636	3.572	3.509	3.448	3.390	3.333	3.279	3.226	3.175	3.125
6	4.000	3.921	3.846	3.773	3.704	3.636	3.571	3.509	3.448	3.390	3.333	3.279	3.226	3.175	3.125
7	4.000	3.922	3.846	3.774	3.704	3.636	3.572	3.509	3.448	3.390	3.333	3.279	3.226	3.175	3.125
8	4.000	3.921	3.846	3.773	3.704	3.636	3.571	3.509	3.448	3.390	3.333	3.279	3.226	3.175	3.125
9	4.000	3.922	3.846	3.774	3.704	3.636	3.572	3.509	3.448	3.390	3.333	3.279	3.226	3.174	3.125
10	4.000	3.921	3.846	3.773	3.704	3.636	3.571	3.509	3.448	3.390	3.333	3.279	3.226	3.175	3.125
11	4.000	3.922	3.846	3.774	3.704	3.637	3.572	3.509	3.448	3.390	3.333	3.279	3.226	3.174	3.125
12	4.000	3.921	3.846	3.773	3.704	3.636	3.571	3.509	3.448	3.390	3.333	3.278	3.226	3.175	3.125
13	4.000	3.922	3.846	3.774	3.703	3.637	3.572	3.509	3.448	3.390	3.333	3.279	3.226	3.174	3.125
14	4.000	3.921	3.846	3.773	3.704	3.636	3.571	3.509	3.449	3.390	3.334	3.278	3.226	3.175	3.125
15	4.000	3.922	3.846	3.774	3.703	3.637	3.572	3.509	3.448	3.390	3.333	3.279	3.226	3.174	3.125
16	4.000	3.921	3.846	3.773	3.704	3.636	3.571	3.509	3.449	3.390	3.333	3.279	3.226	3.175	3.125
17	4.000	3.922	3.846	3.774	3.703	3.637	3.572	3.508	3.448	3.390	3.334	3.278	3.226	3.174	3.125
18	4.000	3.921	3.846	3.773	3.703	3.636	3.571	3.509	3.449	3.390	3.333	3.279	3.226	3.175	3.125
19	4.000	3.922	3.847	3.774	3.703	3.637	3.572	3.508	3.448	3.390	3.334	3.279	3.225	3.175	3.125
20	4.000	3.922	3.846	3.773	3.704	3.636	3.571	3.509	3.449	3.390	3.333	3.279	3.226	3.175	3.125
21	4.000	3.921	3.847	3.774	3.703	3.637	3.572	3.508	3.448	3.389	3.334	3.278	3.225	3.175	3.125
22	4.000	3.922	3.846	3.774	3.704	3.636	3.571	3.509	3.449	3.390	3.333	3.279	3.226	3.174	3.125
23	4.000	3.921	3.847	3.773	3.703	3.637	3.572	3.508	3.448	3.390	3.334	3.278	3.226	3.175	3.125
24	4.000	3.922	3.846	3.774	3.704	3.636	3.571	3.509	3.449	3.389	3.333	3.279	3.225	3.174	3.125
25	4.000	3.921	3.847	3.773	3.703	3.637	3.572	3.508	3.448	3.390	3.334	3.278	3.225	3.175	3.125
26	2.500	3.922	3.846	3.774	3.703	3.636	3.571	3.509	3.449	3.389	3.333	3.279	3.226	3.174	3.125
27		0.490	2.404	3.773	3.704	3.637	3.572	3.508	3.448	3.390	3.333	3.279	3.225	3.175	3.125
28				0.472	2.315	3.636	3.571	3.509	3.449	3.389	3.334	3.278	3.226	3.174	3.125
29						0.455	2.232	3.508	3.448	3.390	3.333	3.279	3.225	3.175	3.125
30								0.439	2.155	3.389	3.334	3.279	3.225	3.175	3.125
31										0.424	2.083	3.278	3.225	3.174	3.125
32												0.410	2.016	3.175	3.125
33														0.397	1.953

and the Recovery Period is:

If the Recovery Year is: / the Depreciation Rate is:

Recovery Year	32.5	33.0	33.5	34.0	34.5	35.0	35.5	36.0	36.5	37.0	37.5	38.0	38.5	39.0	39.5
1	1.154	1.136	1.119	1.103	1.087	1.071	1.056	1.042	1.027	1.014	1.000	0.987	0.974	0.962	0.949
2	3.077	3.030	2.985	2.941	2.899	2.857	2.817	2.778	2.740	2.703	2.667	2.632	2.597	2.564	2.532
3	3.077	3.030	2.985	2.941	2.899	2.857	2.817	2.778	2.740	2.703	2.667	2.632	2.597	2.564	2.532
4	3.077	3.030	2.985	2.941	2.899	2.857	2.817	2.778	2.740	2.703	2.667	2.632	2.597	2.564	2.532
5	3.077	3.030	2.985	2.941	2.899	2.857	2.817	2.778	2.740	2.703	2.667	2.632	2.597	2.564	2.532
6	3.077	3.030	2.985	2.941	2.899	2.857	2.817	2.778	2.740	2.703	2.667	2.632	2.597	2.564	2.532
7	3.077	3.030	2.985	2.941	2.899	2.857	2.817	2.778	2.740	2.703	2.667	2.632	2.597	2.564	2.532
8	3.077	3.030	2.985	2.941	2.898	2.857	2.817	2.778	2.740	2.703	2.667	2.631	2.597	2.564	2.532
9	3.077	3.030	2.985	2.941	2.899	2.857	2.817	2.778	2.740	2.703	2.667	2.632	2.597	2.564	2.532
10	3.077	3.030	2.985	2.941	2.899	2.857	2.817	2.778	2.740	2.703	2.667	2.632	2.598	2.564	2.532
11	3.077	3.030	2.985	2.941	2.899	2.857	2.817	2.778	2.740	2.703	2.667	2.632	2.597	2.564	2.532
12	3.077	3.030	2.985	2.941	2.899	2.857	2.817	2.778	2.740	2.703	2.667	2.632	2.598	2.564	2.532
13	3.077	3.030	2.985	2.941	2.899	2.857	2.817	2.778	2.740	2.703	2.667	2.632	2.597	2.564	2.532
14	3.077	3.030	2.985	2.941	2.899	2.857	2.817	2.778	2.740	2.703	2.667	2.631	2.598	2.564	2.532
15	3.077	3.031	2.985	2.941	2.899	2.857	2.817	2.778	2.740	2.703	2.666	2.632	2.597	2.564	2.531
16	3.077	3.030	2.985	2.941	2.898	2.857	2.817	2.778	2.740	2.702	2.667	2.631	2.598	2.564	2.532
17	3.077	3.031	2.985	2.941	2.899	2.857	2.817	2.778	2.740	2.703	2.666	2.632	2.597	2.564	2.531
18	3.077	3.030	2.985	2.941	2.899	2.857	2.817	2.778	2.740	2.702	2.666	2.632	2.597	2.564	2.532
19	3.077	3.031	2.985	2.941	2.899	2.857	2.817	2.778	2.740	2.703	2.666	2.631	2.598	2.564	2.531
20	3.077	3.030	2.985	2.941	2.899	2.857	2.817	2.778	2.740	2.703	2.667	2.632	2.597	2.564	2.532
21	3.077	3.031	2.985	2.941	2.899	2.857	2.817	2.778	2.740	2.703	2.666	2.632	2.597	2.564	2.532
22	3.077	3.030	2.985	2.941	2.899	2.857	2.817	2.778	2.740	2.703	2.666	2.632	2.598	2.564	2.531
23	3.077	3.031	2.985	2.941	2.898	2.857	2.817	2.778	2.739	2.702	2.667	2.631	2.597	2.564	2.532
24	3.077	3.030	2.985	2.941	2.899	2.857	2.817	2.778	2.740	2.702	2.667	2.631	2.598	2.564	2.532
25	3.077	3.031	2.985	2.942	2.899	2.857	2.817	2.778	2.739	2.703	2.666	2.632	2.597	2.564	2.531
26	3.077	3.030	2.985	2.941	2.899	2.857	2.817	2.778	2.740	2.703	2.666	2.631	2.598	2.564	2.532
27	3.077	3.031	2.985	2.941	2.899	2.857	2.817	2.778	2.739	2.703	2.667	2.632	2.597	2.564	2.531
28	3.077	3.031	2.985	2.942	2.899	2.858	2.817	2.778	2.740	2.703	2.666	2.631	2.598	2.564	2.532
29	3.076	3.031	2.985	2.941	2.899	2.857	2.817	2.778	2.739	2.702	2.667	2.632	2.597	2.564	2.531
30	3.077	3.030	2.986	2.942	2.898	2.858	2.817	2.777	2.739	2.702	2.667	2.631	2.598	2.564	2.532
31	3.076	3.031	2.985	2.941	2.899	2.857	2.816	2.778	2.739	2.703	2.666	2.631	2.598	2.564	2.531
32	3.077	3.030	2.986	2.942	2.898	2.858	2.817	2.777	2.740	2.702	2.667	2.632	2.597	2.564	2.532
33	3.077	3.030	2.986	2.942	2.898	2.857	2.816	2.778	2.739	2.702	2.666	2.631	2.598	2.565	2.531
34	3.076	3.031	2.985	2.941	2.899	2.858	2.817	2.778	2.740	2.703	2.667	2.632	2.597	2.564	2.532
35	0.385	1.894	2.986	2.942	2.899	2.857	2.816	2.777	2.739	2.703	2.666	2.631	2.598	2.564	2.531
36			0.373	1.838	2.899	2.857	2.817	2.778	2.740	2.703	2.667	2.632	2.597	2.564	2.532
37					0.362	1.786	2.817	2.778	2.740	2.703	2.667	2.631	2.598	2.564	2.531
38							0.352	1.736	2.739	2.703	2.666	2.632	2.597	2.564	2.532
39									0.342	1.689	2.666	2.631	2.598	2.565	2.531
40											0.333	1.645	2.597	2.564	2.532
41													0.325	1.603	0.316

and the Recovery Period is:

If the Recovery Year is:	40.0	40.5	41.0	41.5	42.0	42.5	43.0	43.5	44.0	44.5	45.0	45.5	46.0	46.5	47.0
	the Depreciation Rate is:														
1	0.938	0.926	0.915	0.904	0.893	0.882	0.872	0.862	0.852	0.843	0.833	0.824	0.815	0.806	0.798
2	2.500	2.469	2.439	2.410	2.381	2.353	2.326	2.299	2.273	2.247	2.222	2.198	2.174	2.151	2.128
3	2.500	2.469	2.439	2.410	2.381	2.353	2.326	2.299	2.273	2.247	2.222	2.198	2.174	2.151	2.128
4	2.500	2.469	2.439	2.410	2.381	2.353	2.326	2.299	2.273	2.247	2.222	2.198	2.174	2.151	2.128
5	2.500	2.469	2.439	2.410	2.381	2.353	2.326	2.299	2.273	2.247	2.222	2.198	2.174	2.151	2.128
6	2.500	2.469	2.439	2.410	2.381	2.353	2.326	2.299	2.273	2.247	2.222	2.198	2.174	2.151	2.128
7	2.500	2.469	2.439	2.410	2.381	2.353	2.326	2.299	2.273	2.247	2.222	2.198	2.174	2.151	2.128
8	2.500	2.469	2.439	2.410	2.381	2.353	2.326	2.299	2.273	2.247	2.222	2.198	2.174	2.151	2.128
9	2.500	2.469	2.439	2.410	2.381	2.353	2.326	2.299	2.273	2.247	2.222	2.198	2.174	2.151	2.128
10	2.500	2.469	2.439	2.410	2.381	2.353	2.326	2.299	2.273	2.247	2.222	2.198	2.174	2.151	2.128
11	2.500	2.469	2.439	2.410	2.381	2.353	2.324	2.299	2.273	2.247	2.222	2.198	2.174	2.151	2.128
12	2.500	2.469	2.439	2.410	2.381	2.353	2.325	2.299	2.273	2.247	2.222	2.198	2.174	2.150	2.128
13	2.500	2.469	2.439	2.410	2.381	2.353	2.325	2.299	2.273	2.247	2.222	2.198	2.174	2.151	2.128
14	2.500	2.469	2.439	2.410	2.381	2.353	2.325	2.299	2.273	2.247	2.222	2.198	2.174	2.151	2.128
15	2.500	2.469	2.439	2.409	2.381	2.353	2.325	2.299	2.273	2.247	2.222	2.198	2.174	2.150	2.127
16	2.500	2.469	2.439	2.410	2.381	2.353	2.325	2.299	2.273	2.247	2.222	2.198	2.174	2.150	2.128
17	2.500	2.469	2.439	2.409	2.331	2.353	2.325	2.299	2.273	2.247	2.222	2.198	2.174	2.151	2.128
18	2.500	2.469	2.439	2.410	2.331	2.353	2.325	2.299	2.273	2.247	2.222	2.198	2.174	2.150	2.128
19	2.500	2.469	2.439	2.409	2.381	2.353	2.325	2.299	2.273	2.247	2.222	2.198	2.174	2.151	2.127
20	2.500	2.469	2.439	2.410	2.381	2.353	2.325	2.299	2.273	2.247	2.222	2.198	2.174	2.150	2.127
21	2.500	2.469	2.439	2.410	2.381	2.353	2.326	2.299	2.273	2.247	2.222	2.198	2.174	2.150	2.128
22	2.500	2.469	2.439	2.410	2.381	2.353	2.325	2.299	2.272	2.247	2.222	2.198	2.174	2.151	2.128
23	2.500	2.469	2.439	2.409	2.381	2.353	2.326	2.299	2.272	2.247	2.222	2.198	2.174	2.150	2.127
24	2.500	2.469	2.439	2.410	2.381	2.353	2.325	2.299	2.272	2.247	2.222	2.198	2.174	2.151	2.128
25	2.500	2.469	2.439	2.410	2.381	2.353	2.326	2.299	2.273	2.247	2.222	2.198	2.174	2.150	2.127
26	2.500	2.459	2.439	2.410	2.381	2.353	2.325	2.299	2.273	2.247	2.222	2.198	2.174	2.151	2.128
27	2.500	2.469	2.439	2.409	2.381	2.353	2.326	2.299	2.272	2.247	2.223	2.198	2.174	2.150	2.127
28	2.500	2.159	2.439	2.409	2.381	2.353	2.325	2.299	2.273	2.247	2.222	2.198	2.174	2.151	2.128
29	2.500	2.469	2.439	2.409	2.381	2.353	2.326	2.299	2.272	2.248	2.223	2.198	2.174	2.150	2.128
30	2.500	2.469	2.439	2.410	2.381	2.353	2.325	2.299	2.272	2.247	2.223	2.198	2.174	2.151	2.127
31	2.500	2.469	2.439	2.409	2.381	2.353	2.326	2.299	2.273	2.248	2.222	2.198	2.174	2.150	2.128
32	2.500	2.470	2.439	2.409	2.381	2.353	2.325	2.298	2.273	2.247	2.222	2.198	2.174	2.151	2.128
33	2.500	2.469	2.439	2.410	2.381	2.353	2.326	2.299	2.272	2.247	2.223	2.198	2.173	2.150	2.128
34	2.500	2.470	2.439	2.410	2.381	2.353	2.325	2.298	2.273	2.248	2.222	2.197	2.174	2.151	2.128
35	2.500	2.469	2.439	2.409	2.381	2.353	2.326	2.299	2.273	2.247	2.223	2.198	2.174	2.150	2.127
36	2.500	2.469	2.439	2.410	2.381	2.353	2.325	2.299	2.272	2.248	2.222	2.197	2.174	2.151	2.128
37	2.500	2.470	2.439	2.409	2.381	2.353	2.325	2.299	2.273	2.247	2.223	2.198	2.174	2.150	2.127
38	2.500	2.469	2.439	2.410	2.381	2.353	2.326	2.298	2.273	2.248	2.222	2.198	2.174	2.151	2.128
39	2.500	2.469	2.439	2.409	2.381	2.353	2.325	2.238	2.273	2.248	2.223	2.198	2.174	2.150	2.127
40	2.500	2.470	2.439	2.410	2.380	2.352	2.326	2.298	2.272	2.247	2.223	2.198	2.174	2.151	2.128
41	1.562	2.469	2.439	2.409	2.381	2.352	2.325	2.299	2.272	2.248	2.222	2.197	2.174	2.150	2.127
42		0.309	1.525	2.410	2.380	2.353	2.326	2.298	2.272	2.247	2.222	2.198	2.173	2.151	2.128
43				0.301	1.488	2.353	2.325	2.299	2.273	2.247	2.223	2.198	2.174	2.150	2.128
44						0.294	1.453	2.298	2.272	2.248	2.222	2.197	2.174	2.151	2.127
45								0.287	1.420	2.247	2.223	2.198	2.173	2.150	2.128
46										0.281	1.389	2.198	2.174	2.151	2.128
47												0.275	1.358	2.151	2.127
48														0.269	1.330

If the Recovery Year is:	and the Recovery Period is: the Depreciation Rate is:					
	47.5	48.0	48.5	49.0	49.5	50.0
1	0.789	0.781	0.773	0.765	0.758	0.750
2	2.105	2.083	2.062	2.041	2.020	2.000
3	2.105	2.083	2.062	2.041	2.020	2.000
4	2.105	2.083	2.062	2.041	2.020	2.000
5	2.105	2.083	2.062	2.041	2.020	2.000
6	2.105	2.083	2.062	2.041	2.020	2.000
7	2.105	2.083	2.062	2.041	2.020	2.000
8	2.105	2.083	2.062	2.041	2.020	2.000
9	2.105	2.083	2.062	2.041	2.020	2.000
10	2.105	2.083	2.062	2.041	2.020	2.000
11	2.105	2.083	2.062	2.041	2.020	2.000
12	2.105	2.083	2.062	2.041	2.020	2.000
13	2.105	2.083	2.062	2.041	2.020	2.000
14	2.105	2.083	2.062	2.041	2.020	2.000
15	2.105	2.083	2.062	2.041	2.020	2.000
16	2.105	2.083	2.062	2.041	2.020	2.000
17	2.105	2.083	2.062	2.041	2.020	2.000
18	2.105	2.083	2.062	2.041	2.020	2.000
19	2.105	2.083	2.062	2.041	2.020	2.000
20	2.105	2.083	2.062	2.041	2.020	2.000
21	2.105	2.083	2.062	2.041	2.020	2.000
22	2.105	2.084	2.062	2.041	2.020	2.000
23	2.105	2.083	2.062	2.041	2.020	2.000
24	2.106	2.084	2.062	2.041	2.020	2.000
25	2.105	2.083	2.062	2.041	2.020	2.000
26	2.106	2.084	2.062	2.041	2.020	2.000
27	2.105	2.083	2.062	2.041	2.020	2.000
28	2.106	2.084	2.062	2.041	2.020	2.000
29	2.105	2.083	2.062	2.041	2.020	2.000
30	2.106	2.084	2.062	2.041	2.020	2.000
31	2.105	2.083	2.062	2.041	2.020	2.000
32	2.106	2.084	2.062	2.041	2.020	2.000
33	2.105	2.083	2.062	2.041	2.020	2.000
34	2.106	2.084	2.062	2.040	2.020	2.000
35	2.105	2.083	2.062	2.041	2.020	2.000
36	2.106	2.084	2.062	2.040	2.020	2.000
37	2.105	2.083	2.061	2.041	2.021	2.000
38	2.106	2.084	2.062	2.040	2.020	2.000
39	2.105	2.083	2.061	2.041	2.021	2.000
40	2.106	2.084	2.062	2.040	2.020	2.000
41	2.105	2.083	2.061	2.041	2.021	2.000
42	2.106	2.084	2.062	2.040	2.020	2.000
43	2.105	2.083	2.061	2.041	2.021	2.000
44	2.106	2.084	2.062	2.040	2.020	2.000
45	2.105	2.083	2.061	2.041	2.021	2.000
46	2.106	2.084	2.062	2.040	2.020	2.000
47	2.105	2.083	2.061	2.041	2.021	2.000
48	2.106	2.084	2.062	2.040	2.020	2.000
49	0.263	1.302	2.061	2.041	2.020	2.000
50			0.258	1.275	2.020	2.000
51					0.253	1.250

TABLE 12

General and Alternative Depreciation Systems
Applicable Depreciation Method: Straight Line
Applicable Recovery Periods: 2.5 – 50 years
Applicable Convention: Mid-quarter (property placed in service in fourth quarter)

and the Recovery Period is:

the Depreciation Rate is:

If the Recovery Year is:	2.5	3.0	3.5	4.0	4.5	5.0	5.5	6.0	6.5	7.0	7.5	8.0	8.5	9.0	9.5
1	5.00	4.17	3.57	3.13	2.78	2.50	2.27	2.08	1.92	1.79	1.67	1.56	1.47	1.39	1.32
2	40.00	33.33	28.57	25.00	22.22	20.00	18.18	16.67	15.39	14.29	13.33	12.50	11.76	11.11	10.53
3	40.00	33.33	28.57	25.00	22.22	20.00	18.18	16.67	15.38	14.28	13.33	12.50	11.77	11.11	10.53
4	15.00	29.17	28.57	25.00	22.22	20.00	18.18	16.67	15.39	14.29	13.33	12.50	11.76	11.11	10.52
5			10.72	21.87	22.23	20.00	18.19	16.66	15.38	14.28	13.33	12.50	11.77	11.11	10.53
6					8.33	17.50	18.18	16.67	15.39	14.29	13.33	12.50	11.77	11.11	10.52
7							6.82	14.58	15.38	14.28	13.34	12.50	11.76	11.11	10.53
8									5.77	12.50	13.34	12.50	11.77	11.11	10.52
9											5.00	10.94	4.41	9.73	10.53
10															10.52

and the Recovery Period is:

the Depreciation Rate is:

If the Recovery Year is:	10.0	10.5	11.0	11.5	12.0	12.5	13.0	13.5	14.0	14.5	15.0	15.5	16.0	16.5	17.0
1	1.25	1.19	1.14	1.09	1.04	1.00	0.96	0.93	0.89	0.86	0.83	0.81	0.78	0.76	0.74
2	10.00	9.52	9.09	8.73	8.33	8.00	7.69	7.41	7.14	6.90	6.67	6.45	6.25	6.06	5.88
3	10.00	9.52	9.09	8.69	8.33	8.00	7.69	7.41	7.14	6.90	6.67	6.45	6.25	6.06	5.88
4	10.00	9.52	9.09	8.73	8.33	8.00	7.69	7.41	7.14	6.93	6.67	6.45	6.25	6.06	5.88
5	10.00	9.53	9.09	8.69	8.34	8.00	7.69	7.41	7.14	6.90	6.67	6.45	6.25	6.06	5.88
6	10.00	9.52	9.09	8.70	8.33	8.00	7.69	7.41	7.14	6.90	6.67	6.45	6.25	6.06	5.88
7	10.00	9.53	9.09	8.69	8.34	8.00	7.69	7.41	7.15	6.90	6.66	6.45	6.25	6.06	5.88
8	10.00	9.52	9.09	8.70	8.33	8.00	7.69	7.40	7.14	6.89	6.67	6.45	6.25	6.06	5.88
9	10.00	9.53	9.09	8.69	8.33	8.00	7.69	7.41	7.15	6.90	6.67	6.45	6.25	6.06	5.88
10	10.00	9.52	9.09	8.70	8.34	8.00	7.69	7.40	7.14	6.89	6.66	6.45	6.25	6.06	5.88
11	8.75	9.53	9.09	8.69	8.33	8.00	7.69	7.41	7.15	6.90	6.67	6.45	6.25	6.06	5.88
12		3.57	7.96	8.70	8.34	8.00	7.70	7.40	7.14	6.89	6.67	6.46	6.25	6.06	5.89
13				3.26	7.29	8.00	7.69	7.41	7.14	6.90	6.66	6.45	6.25	6.06	5.88
14						3.00	6.73	7.40	7.15	6.89	6.67	6.46	6.25	6.06	5.89
15								2.73	6.25	6.90	6.67	6.45	6.25	6.06	5.88
16										2.59	5.83	6.46	6.25	6.06	5.89
17												2.42	5.47	6.07	5.88
18														2.21	5.15

and the Recovery Period is:

the Depreciation Rate is:

If the Recovery Year is:	17.5	18.0	18.5	19.0	19.5	20.0	20.5	21.0	21.5	22.0	22.5	23.0	23.5	24.0	24.5
1	0.71	0.69	0.68	0.66	0.64	0.625	0.610	0.595	0.581	0.568	0.556	0.543	0.532	0.521	0.510
2	5.71	5.56	5.41	5.26	5.13	5.000	4.878	4.762	4.651	4.545	4.444	4.348	4.255	4.167	4.082
3	5.71	5.56	5.40	5.26	5.13	5.000	4.878	4.762	4.651	4.545	4.444	4.348	4.255	4.167	4.082
4	5.72	5.56	5.41	5.26	5.13	5.000	4.878	4.762	4.651	4.546	4.444	4.348	4.255	4.167	4.082
5	5.71	5.55	5.40	5.26	5.13	5.000	4.878	4.762	4.651	4.545	4.444	4.348	4.255	4.167	4.082
6	5.72	5.56	5.41	5.26	5.13	5.000	4.878	4.762	4.651	4.546	4.445	4.348	4.255	4.167	4.082
7	5.71	5.55	5.41	5.26	5.13	5.000	4.878	4.762	4.651	4.545	4.444	4.348	4.255	4.167	4.082
8	5.72	5.56	5.41	5.26	5.13	5.000	4.878	4.762	4.651	4.546	4.445	4.348	4.255	4.167	4.082
9	5.71	5.55	5.40	5.26	5.13	5.000	4.878	4.762	4.651	4.545	4.444	4.348	4.255	4.167	4.081
10	5.72	5.56	5.41	5.27	5.13	5.000	4.878	4.762	4.651	4.546	4.445	4.348	4.255	4.166	4.082
11	5.71	5.55	5.40	5.26	5.13	5.000	4.878	4.762	4.651	4.545	4.444	4.348	4.256	4.167	4.081
12	5.72	5.56	5.41	5.27	5.13	5.000	4.878	4.762	4.651	4.546	4.445	4.348	4.255	4.166	4.082
13	5.71	5.55	5.40	5.26	5.13	5.000	4.878	4.762	4.651	4.545	4.444	4.348	4.256	4.167	4.082
14	5.72	5.56	5.41	5.27	5.12	5.000	4.878	4.762	4.651	4.546	4.444	4.348	4.255	4.167	4.081
15	5.71	5.55	5.40	5.26	5.13	5.000	4.878	4.762	4.651	4.545	4.445	4.348	4.256	4.166	4.082
16	5.72	5.56	5.41	5.27	5.12	5.000	4.878	4.762	4.652	4.546	4.444	4.348	4.255	4.167	4.082
17	5.71	5.55	5.40	5.26	5.13	5.000	4.878	4.762	4.651	4.545	4.445	4.347	4.256	4.167	4.081
18	5.72	5.56	5.41	5.27	5.12	5.000	4.878	4.762	4.652	4.546	4.444	4.348	4.255	4.166	4.082
19	5.71	5.55	5.40	5.26	5.13	5.000	4.878	4.762	4.651	4.545	4.445	4.347	4.256	4.167	4.081
20	2.14	4.86	5.40	5.26	5.13	5.000	4.878	4.761	4.652	4.546	4.444	4.348	4.255	4.166	4.082
21			2.03	4.61	1.92	4.375	4.879	4.762	4.651	4.545	4.445	4.347	4.256	4.167	4.081
22							1.829	4.166	4.652	4.546	4.444	4.348	4.255	4.166	4.082
23									1.744	3.977	4.445	4.347	4.256	4.167	4.081
24											1.667	3.804	4.255	4.166	4.082
25													1.596	3.646	4.081
26															1.531

and the Recovery Period is:

the Depreciation Rate is:

If the Recovery Year is:	25.0	25.5	26.0	26.5	27.0	27.5	28.0	28.5	29.0	29.5	30.0	30.5	31.0	31.5	32.0
1	0.500	0.490	0.481	0.472	0.463	0.455	0.446	0.439	0.431	0.424	0.417	0.410	0.403	0.397	0.391
2	4.000	3.922	3.846	3.774	3.704	3.636	3.571	3.509	3.448	3.390	3.333	3.279	3.226	3.175	3.125
3	4.000	3.922	3.846	3.774	3.704	3.636	3.571	3.509	3.448	3.390	3.333	3.279	3.226	3.175	3.125
4	4.000	3.922	3.846	3.774	3.704	3.636	3.571	3.509	3.448	3.390	3.333	3.279	3.226	3.175	3.125
5	4.000	3.922	3.846	3.774	3.704	3.636	3.571	3.509	3.448	3.390	3.333	3.279	3.226	3.175	3.125
6	4.000	3.921	3.846	3.773	3.704	3.636	3.571	3.509	3.448	3.390	3.333	3.279	3.226	3.175	3.125
7	4.000	3.922	3.846	3.774	3.704	3.636	3.572	3.509	3.448	3.390	3.333	3.279	3.226	3.175	3.125
8	4.000	3.921	3.846	3.774	3.704	3.636	3.571	3.509	3.448	3.390	3.333	3.279	3.226	3.175	3.125
9	4.000	3.922	3.846	3.773	3.704	3.636	3.572	3.509	3.448	3.390	3.333	3.279	3.226	3.174	3.125
10	4.000	3.921	3.846	3.774	3.704	3.636	3.571	3.509	3.448	3.390	3.333	3.279	3.226	3.175	3.125
11	4.000	3.922	3.846	3.773	3.704	3.636	3.572	3.509	3.448	3.390	3.333	3.279	3.226	3.174	3.125
12	4.000	3.922	3.846	3.774	3.704	3.637	3.571	3.509	3.448	3.390	3.333	3.279	3.226	3.175	3.125
13	4.000	3.921	3.846	3.773	3.703	3.636	3.572	3.509	3.448	3.390	3.334	3.279	3.226	3.174	3.125
14	4.000	3.921	3.846	3.773	3.704	3.636	3.571	3.509	3.448	3.390	3.333	3.278	3.226	3.175	3.125
15	4.000	3.922	3.846	3.774	3.703	3.637	3.572	3.509	3.449	3.390	3.334	3.279	3.226	3.174	3.125
16	4.000	3.921	3.846	3.773	3.704	3.636	3.572	3.509	3.448	3.390	3.333	3.278	3.226	3.175	3.125
17	4.000	3.922	3.847	3.774	3.703	3.637	3.571	3.509	3.449	3.390	3.334	3.279	3.226	3.174	3.125
18	4.000	3.921	3.846	3.773	3.704	3.636	3.572	3.508	3.449	3.390	3.333	3.278	3.226	3.175	3.125
19	4.000	3.922	3.847	3.774	3.703	3.637	3.571	3.508	3.448	3.390	3.334	3.279	3.226	3.174	3.125
20	4.000	3.921	3.846	3.773	3.704	3.636	3.572	3.509	3.448	3.390	3.333	3.278	3.226	3.175	3.125
21	4.000	3.922	3.847	3.774	3.703	3.637	3.571	3.508	3.449	3.389	3.334	3.279	3.226	3.174	3.125
22	4.000	3.921	3.846	3.773	3.704	3.636	3.572	3.509	3.448	3.390	3.333	3.278	3.225	3.175	3.125
23	4.000	3.922	3.847	3.774	3.703	3.637	3.571	3.509	3.449	3.389	3.334	3.279	3.226	3.174	3.125
24	4.000	3.921	3.845	3.773	3.704	3.636	3.572	3.508	3.448	3.390	3.333	3.278	3.225	3.175	3.125
25	4.000	3.922	3.847	3.774	3.703	3.637	3.571	3.509	3.449	3.389	3.334	3.279	3.226	3.174	3.125
26	3.500	3.921	3.846	3.773	3.704	3.636	3.572	3.508	3.448	3.390	3.333	3.278	3.225	3.175	3.125
27		3.921	3.366	3.774	3.703	3.636	3.571	3.509	3.449	3.389	3.334	3.279	3.226	3.174	3.125
28		1.471		1.415	3.241	3.636	3.572	3.508	3.448	3.390	3.333	3.278	3.225	3.175	3.125
29						1.364	3.125	3.509	3.449	3.389	3.334	3.279	3.226	3.174	3.125
30								1.316	3.017	3.390	3.333	3.278	3.225	3.175	3.125
31										1.271	2.917	3.279	3.226	3.174	3.125
32												1.229	2.822	3.175	3.125
33														1.190	2.734

and the Recovery Period is:

the Depreciation Rate is:

If the Recovery Year is:	32.5	33.0	33.5	34.0	34.5	35.0	35.5	36.0	36.5	37.0	37.5	38.0	38.5	39.0	39.5
1	0.385	0.379	0.373	0.368	0.362	0.357	0.352	0.347	0.342	0.338	0.333	0.329	0.325	0.321	0.316
2	3.077	3.030	2.985	2.941	2.899	2.857	2.817	2.778	2.740	2.703	2.667	2.632	2.597	2.564	2.532
3	3.077	3.030	2.985	2.941	2.899	2.857	2.817	2.778	2.740	2.703	2.667	2.632	2.597	2.564	2.532
4	3.077	3.030	2.985	2.941	2.899	2.857	2.817	2.778	2.740	2.703	2.667	2.632	2.597	2.564	2.532
5	3.077	3.030	2.985	2.941	2.899	2.857	2.817	2.778	2.740	2.703	2.667	2.632	2.597	2.564	2.532
6	3.077	3.030	2.985	2.941	2.898	2.857	2.817	2.778	2.740	2.703	2.667	2.632	2.597	2.564	2.532
7	3.077	3.030	2.985	2.941	2.899	2.857	2.817	2.778	2.740	2.703	2.667	2.631	2.597	2.564	2.532
8	3.077	3.030	2.985	2.941	2.898	2.857	2.817	2.778	2.740	2.703	2.667	2.631	2.597	2.564	2.532
9	3.077	3.030	2.985	2.941	2.899	2.857	2.817	2.778	2.740	2.703	2.667	2.631	2.597	2.564	2.532
10	3.077	3.030	2.985	2.941	2.899	2.857	2.817	2.778	2.740	2.703	2.667	2.632	2.597	2.564	2.532
11	3.077	3.030	2.985	2.941	2.898	2.857	2.817	2.778	2.740	2.703	2.667	2.632	2.598	2.564	2.532
12	3.077	3.030	2.985	2.941	2.899	2.857	2.817	2.778	2.740	2.703	2.667	2.631	2.597	2.564	2.532
13	3.077	3.030	2.985	2.941	2.898	2.857	2.817	2.778	2.740	2.703	2.667	2.631	2.598	2.564	2.532
14	3.077	3.030	2.985	2.941	2.899	2.857	2.817	2.778	2.740	2.703	2.667	2.631	2.597	2.564	2.532
15	3.077	3.030	2.985	2.941	2.898	2.857	2.817	2.778	2.740	2.703	2.667	2.632	2.598	2.564	2.532
16	3.077	3.031	2.985	2.941	2.899	2.857	2.817	2.778	2.740	2.703	2.666	2.631	2.597	2.564	2.532
17	3.077	3.030	2.985	2.941	2.898	2.857	2.817	2.778	2.740	2.702	2.667	2.632	2.598	2.564	2.531
18	3.077	3.031	2.985	2.941	2.899	2.857	2.817	2.778	2.740	2.703	2.667	2.632	2.597	2.564	2.531
19	3.077	3.030	2.985	2.941	2.898	2.857	2.817	2.778	2.740	2.703	2.666	2.631	2.598	2.564	2.531
20	3.077	3.031	2.985	2.941	2.899	2.857	2.817	2.778	2.739	2.703	2.666	2.632	2.597	2.564	2.532
21	3.077	3.030	2.985	2.941	2.898	2.857	2.817	2.778	2.740	2.703	2.667	2.631	2.597	2.564	2.532
22	3.077	3.031	2.985	2.941	2.899	2.857	2.817	2.778	2.739	2.703	2.666	2.632	2.598	2.564	2.532
23	3.077	3.031	2.985	2.941	2.898	2.857	2.817	2.777	2.739	2.702	2.667	2.632	2.598	2.564	2.531
24	3.077	3.030	2.985	2.941	2.899	2.857	2.817	2.778	2.740	2.702	2.667	2.631	2.597	2.564	2.531
25	3.077	3.031	2.985	2.942	2.898	2.857	2.817	2.777	2.739	2.703	2.666	2.632	2.598	2.564	2.531
26	3.077	3.030	2.985	2.941	2.899	2.857	2.817	2.778	2.740	2.703	2.667	2.631	2.597	2.564	2.532
27	3.077	3.030	2.985	2.941	2.899	2.858	2.817	2.777	2.740	2.702	2.667	2.632	2.598	2.564	2.532
28	3.077	3.031	2.985	2.941	2.898	2.857	2.817	2.778	2.739	2.703	2.666	2.631	2.597	2.564	2.531
29	3.076	3.030	2.985	2.942	2.899	2.858	2.817	2.777	2.739	2.703	2.667	2.632	2.598	2.564	2.532
30	3.077	3.031	2.985	2.941	2.898	2.857	2.817	2.778	2.739	2.702	2.666	2.632	2.597	2.564	2.532
31	3.077	3.030	2.986	2.942	2.898	2.858	2.817	2.777	2.740	2.702	2.667	2.631	2.598	2.564	2.532
32	3.076	3.031	2.985	2.941	2.899	2.857	2.816	2.777	2.739	2.703	2.667	2.632	2.598	2.564	2.531
33	3.077	3.030	2.986	2.942	2.898	2.858	2.816	2.777	2.740	2.702	2.667	2.632	2.598	2.564	2.532
34	1.154	2.652	2.985	2.941	2.899	2.857	2.817	2.778	2.739	2.702	2.666	2.631	2.597	2.564	2.531
35			1.120	2.574	2.898	2.858	2.816	2.777	2.740	2.703	2.667	2.632	2.597	2.565	2.531
36					2.898	2.858	2.817	2.777	2.740	2.702	2.666	2.631	2.598	2.564	2.531
37					1.087	2.500	2.817	2.778	2.739	2.703	2.667	2.631	2.597	2.565	2.532
38							1.056	2.430	2.740	2.702	2.666	2.303	2.598	2.564	2.532
39									1.027	2.365	1.000		0.974	2.244	2.531
40															2.532
41															0.949

and the Recovery Period is:

the Depreciation Rate is:

If the Recovery Year is:	47.0	46.5	46.0	45.5	45.0	44.5	44.0	43.5	43.0	42.5	42.0	41.5	41.0	40.5	40.0
1	0.266	0.269	0.272	0.275	0.278	0.281	0.284	0.287	0.291	0.294	0.298	0.301	0.305	0.309	0.313
2	2.128	2.151	2.174	2.198	2.222	2.247	2.273	2.299	2.326	2.353	2.381	2.410	2.439	2.469	2.500
3	2.128	2.151	2.174	2.198	2.222	2.247	2.273	2.299	2.326	2.353	2.381	2.410	2.439	2.469	2.500
4	2.128	2.151	2.174	2.198	2.222	2.247	2.273	2.299	2.326	2.353	2.381	2.410	2.439	2.469	2.500
5	2.128	2.150	2.174	2.198	2.222	2.247	2.273	2.299	2.326	2.353	2.381	2.410	2.439	2.469	2.500
6	2.128	2.150	2.174	2.198	2.222	2.247	2.273	2.299	2.326	2.353	2.381	2.410	2.439	2.469	2.500
7	2.128	2.151	2.174	2.198	2.222	2.247	2.273	2.299	2.326	2.353	2.381	2.413	2.439	2.469	2.500
8	2.128	2.150	2.174	2.198	2.222	2.247	2.273	2.295	2.326	2.353	2.381	2.410	2.439	2.469	2.500
9	2.128	2.151	2.174	2.198	2.222	2.247	2.273	2.295	2.325	2.353	2.381	2.410	2.439	2.469	2.500
10	2.128	2.150	2.174	2.198	2.222	2.247	2.273	2.295	2.326	2.353	2.381	2.410	2.439	2.469	2.500
11	2.128	2.151	2.174	2.198	2.222	2.247	2.273	2.299	2.325	2.353	2.381	2.410	2.439	2.469	2.500
12	2.128	2.150	2.174	2.198	2.222	2.247	2.273	2.299	2.326	2.353	2.381	2.410	2.439	2.469	2.500
13	2.128	2.151	2.174	2.198	2.222	2.247	2.273	2.299	2.325	2.353	2.381	2.410	2.439	2.469	2.500
14	2.128	2.150	2.174	2.198	2.222	2.247	2.273	2.299	2.326	2.353	2.381	2.409	2.439	2.469	2.500
15	2.128	2.151	2.174	2.196	2.222	2.247	2.273	2.299	2.325	2.353	2.381	2.409	2.439	2.469	2.500
16	2.128	2.150	2.174	2.198	2.222	2.247	2.273	2.299	2.326	2.353	2.381	2.430	2.439	2.469	2.500
17	2.127	2.151	2.174	2.198	2.222	2.247	2.273	2.299	2.325	2.353	2.381	2.409	2.439	2.469	2.500
18	2.128	2.150	2.174	2.198	2.222	2.247	2.273	2.293	2.326	2.353	2.381	2.410	2.439	2.469	2.500
19	2.128	2.151	2.174	2.198	2.222	2.247	2.273	2.293	2.325	2.353	2.381	2.409	2.439	2.469	2.500
20	2.128	2.150	2.174	2.198	2.222	2.247	2.273	2.293	2.326	2.353	2.381	2.410	2.439	2.469	2.500
21	2.128	2.151	2.174	2.198	2.222	2.247	2.273	2.293	2.325	2.353	2.381	2.410	2.439	2.469	2.500
22	2.128	2.150	2.174	2.198	2.222	2.247	2.272	2.299	2.326	2.353	2.381	2.409	2.439	2.469	2.500
23	2.127	2.151	2.174	2.198	2.222	2.247	2.272	2.299	2.325	2.353	2.381	2.410	2.439	2.469	2.500
24	2.127	2.150	2.174	2.198	2.222	2.247	2.373	2.299	2.326	2.353	2.381	2.410	2.439	2.469	2.500
25	2.128	2.151	2.174	2.198	2.222	2.247	2.372	2.299	2.325	2.353	2.381	2.410	2.439	2.469	2.500
26	2.127	2.150	2.174	2.198	2.222	2.247	2.273	2.299	2.326	2.353	2.381	2.409	2.439	2.469	2.500
27	2.128	2.151	2.174	2.198	2.222	2.247	2.273	2.299	2.325	2.353	2.381	2.410	2.439	2.469	2.500
28	2.128	2.150	2.174	2.198	2.222	2.247	2.273	2.259	2.326	2.353	2.381	2.439	2.439	2.469	2.500
29	2.127	2.151	2.174	2.197	2.223	2.247	2.272	2.259	2.325	2.353	2.381	2.410	2.439	2.469	2.500
30	2.128	2.150	2.174	2.198	2.223	2.248	2.273	2.259	2.326	2.353	2.381	2.409	2.439	2.469	2.500
31	2.127	2.151	2.174	2.197	2.222	2.247	2.272	2.259	2.325	2.353	2.381	2.410	2.439	2.469	2.500
32	2.128	2.150	2.174	2.198	2.223	2.248	2.273	2.299	2.326	2.353	2.381	2.409	2.439	2.469	2.500
33	2.127	2.151	2.174	2.198	2.222	2.247	2.272	2.299	2.325	2.353	2.381	2.410	2.439	2.469	2.500
34	2.128	2.150	2.174	2.197	2.222	2.248	2.273	2.298	2.326	2.353	2.381	2.409	2.439	2.470	2.500
35	2.128	2.150	2.174	2.198	2.223	2.248	2.272	2.299	2.325	2.353	2.381	2.410	2.439	2.469	2.500
36	2.127	2.150	2.174	2.197	2.223	2.247	2.273	2.298	2.326	2.353	2.381	2.409	2.439	2.470	2.500
37	2.128	2.151	2.174	2.197	2.222	2.247	2.272	2.299	2.325	2.353	2.381	2.410	2.439	2.470	2.500
38	2.128	2.150	2.174	2.198	2.248	2.238	2.272	2.239	2.326	2.352	2.381	2.409	2.439	2.469	2.500
39	2.127	2.151	2.174	2.197	2.223	2.247	2.272	2.239	2.325	2.353	2.381	2.410	2.439	2.470	2.500
40	2.128	2.150	2.173	2.198	2.223	2.248	2.273	2.238	2.326	2.352	2.380	2.409	2.439	2.469	2.500
41	2.127	2.151	2.174	2.197	2.222	2.247	2.272	2.239	2.325	2.353	2.381	2.410	2.439	2.470	2.187
42	2.128	2.150	2.173	2.198	2.223	2.248	2.273	2.298	2.326	2.352	2.381	2.409	2.439	2.470	
43	2.127	2.151	2.173	2.197	2.222	2.247	2.272	2.299	2.326	2.353	2.381	2.410	2.439	2.470	
44	2.128	2.150	2.173	2.198	2.223	2.248	2.273	2.298	2.325	2.353	2.381	2.409	2.439	2.470	
45	2.127	2.151	2.174	2.197	2.223	2.247	2.273	2.298	2.326	2.353	2.380	2.410	2.439	0.926	
46	2.128	2.150	2.173	2.198	2.222	2.247	2.272	2.298	2.325	2.353	2.083	0.904	2.135		
47	2.128	2.151	2.174	2.197	2.222	2.247	2.273	2.298	2.035	0.882					
48	1.862	0.806	1.902	0.824	1.945	0.843	1.988	0.862							

If the Recovery Year is:	and the Recovery Period is:					
	47.5	48.0	48.5	49.0	49.5	50.0
	the Depreciation Rate is:					
1	0.263	0.260	0.258	0.255	0.253	0.250
2	2.105	2.083	2.062	2.041	2.020	2.000
3	2.105	2.083	2.062	2.041	2.020	2.000
4	2.105	2.083	2.062	2.041	2.020	2.000
5	2.105	2.083	2.062	2.041	2.020	2.000
6	2.105	2.083	2.062	2.041	2.020	2.000
7	2.105	2.083	2.062	2.041	2.020	2.000
8	2.105	2.083	2.062	2.041	2.020	2.000
9	2.105	2.083	2.062	2.041	2.020	2.000
10	2.105	2.083	2.062	2.041	2.020	2.000
11	2.105	2.083	2.062	2.041	2.020	2.000
12	2.105	2.083	2.062	2.041	2.020	2.000
13	2.105	2.083	2.062	2.041	2.020	2.000
14	2.105	2.083	2.062	2.041	2.020	2.000
15	2.105	2.083	2.062	2.041	2.020	2.000
16	2.105	2.083	2.062	2.041	2.020	2.000
17	2.105	2.083	2.062	2.041	2.020	2.000
18	2.105	2.084	2.062	2.041	2.020	2.000
19	2.105	2.083	2.062	2.041	2.020	2.000
20	2.105	2.084	2.062	2.041	2.020	2.000
21	2.105	2.083	2.062	2.041	2.020	2.000
22	2.105	2.084	2.062	2.041	2.020	2.000
23	2.105	2.083	2.062	2.041	2.020	2.000
24	2.105	2.084	2.062	2.041	2.020	2.000
25	2.106	2.083	2.062	2.041	2.020	2.000
26	2.105	2.084	2.062	2.041	2.020	2.000

If the Recovery Year is:	and the Recovery Period is:					
	47.5	48.0	48.5	49.0	49.5	50.0
	the Depreciation Rate is:					
27	2.106	2.083	2.062	2.041	2.020	2.000
28	2.105	2.084	2.062	2.041	2.020	2.000
29	2.106	2.083	2.062	2.041	2.020	2.000
30	2.105	2.084	2.062	2.041	2.020	2.000
31	2.105	2.084	2.062	2.041	2.020	2.000
32	2.105	2.084	2.062	2.041	2.020	2.000
33	2.106	2.083	2.062	2.041	2.020	2.000
34	2.105	2.084	2.062	2.040	2.020	2.000
35	2.106	2.083	2.062	2.041	2.021	2.000
36	2.105	2.084	2.061	2.040	2.020	2.000
37	2.106	2.083	2.062	2.041	2.021	2.000
38	2.105	2.084	2.061	2.040	2.020	2.000
39	2.106	2.083	2.062	2.041	2.021	2.000
40	2.105	2.084	2.061	2.040	2.020	2.000
41	2.106	2.083	2.062	2.041	2.021	2.000
42	2.105	2.084	2.061	2.040	2.020	2.000
43	2.106	2.083	2.062	2.041	2.021	2.000
44	2.105	2.084	2.061	2.040	2.020	2.000
45	2.105	2.083	2.062	2.041	2.021	2.000
46	2.105	2.084	2.061	2.040	2.020	2.000
47	2.106	2.083	2.062	2.041	2.021	2.000
48	2.105	2.084	2.061	2.040	2.020	2.000
49	2.105	2.083	2.062	2.041	2.021	2.000
50	0.790	1.823	0.773	1.785	2.020	2.000
51					0.758	1.750

TABLE 14   Alternative Minimum Tax (see section 7 of this revenue procedure)

Applicable Depreciation Method: 150 Percent Declining Balance
Switching to Straight Line
Applicable Recovery Periods: 2.5 – 50 years
Applicable Convention: Half-year

and the Recovery Period is:

the Depreciation Rate is:

If the Recovery Year is:	2.5	3.0	3.5	4.0	4.5	5.0	5.5	6.0	6.5	7.0	7.5	8.0	8.5	9.0	9.5
1	30.00	25.00	21.43	18.75	16.67	15.00	13.64	12.50	11.54	10.71	10.00	9.38	8.82	8.33	7.89
2	42.00	37.50	33.67	30.47	27.78	25.50	23.55	21.88	20.41	19.13	18.00	16.99	16.09	15.28	14.54
3	28.00	25.00	22.45	20.31	18.52	17.35	17.13	16.41	15.70	15.03	14.40	13.81	13.25	12.73	12.25
4		12.50	22.45	20.31	18.52	16.66	15.23	14.06	13.09	12.25	11.52	11.22	10.91	10.61	10.31
5				10.16	18.51	16.66	15.23	14.06	13.09	12.25	11.52	10.80	10.19	9.65	9.17
6						8.33	15.22	14.06	13.09	12.25	11.52	10.80	10.19	9.64	9.17
7								7.03	13.08	12.25	11.52	10.80	10.18	9.65	9.17
8										6.13	11.52	10.80	10.19	9.64	9.17
9												5.40	10.18	9.65	9.17
10														4.82	9.16

and the Recovery Period is:

the Depreciation Rate is:

If the Recovery Year is:	10.0	10.5	11.0	11.5	12.0	12.5	13.0	13.5	14.0	14.5	15.0	15.5	16.0	16.5	17.0
1	7.50	7.14	6.82	6.52	6.25	6.00	5.77	5.56	5.36	5.17	5.00	4.84	4.69	4.55	4.41
2	13.88	13.27	12.71	12.19	11.72	11.28	10.87	10.49	10.14	9.81	9.50	9.21	8.94	8.68	8.43
3	11.79	11.37	10.97	10.60	10.25	9.93	9.62	9.33	9.05	8.80	8.55	8.32	8.10	7.89	7.69
4	10.02	9.75	9.48	9.22	8.97	8.73	8.51	8.29	8.08	7.88	7.70	7.51	7.34	7.17	7.01
5	8.74	8.35	8.18	8.02	7.85	7.69	7.53	7.37	7.22	7.07	6.93	6.79	6.65	6.52	6.39
6	8.74	8.35	7.98	7.64	7.33	7.05	6.79	6.55	6.44	6.34	6.23	6.13	6.03	5.93	5.83
7	8.74	8.35	7.97	7.64	7.33	7.05	6.79	6.55	6.32	6.10	5.90	5.72	5.55	5.39	5.32
8	8.74	8.35	7.98	7.63	7.33	7.05	6.73	6.55	6.32	6.10	5.90	5.72	5.55	5.39	5.23
9	8.74	8.35	7.97	7.64	7.33	7.04	6.73	6.55	6.32	6.10	5.91	5.72	5.55	5.39	5.23
10	8.74	8.35	7.98	7.63	7.33	7.05	6.73	6.55	6.32	6.10	5.90	5.72	5.55	5.39	5.23
11	4.37	8.36	7.97	7.64	7.32	7.04	6.73	6.55	6.32	6.11	5.91	5.72	5.55	5.39	5.23
12			3.99	7.63	7.33	7.05	6.78	6.55	6.32	6.10	5.90	5.72	5.55	5.39	5.23
13					3.66	7.04	6.79	6.56	6.32	6.11	5.91	5.72	5.54	5.38	5.23
14							3.39	6.55	6.31	6.10	5.90	5.72	5.55	5.39	5.23
15									3.16	6.10	5.91	5.72	5.54	5.38	5.23
16											2.95	5.72	5.55	5.39	5.23
17													2.77	5.38	5.23
18															2.62

and the Recovery Period is:

the Depreciation Rate is:

If the Recovery Year is:	17.5	18.0	18.5	19.0	19.5	20.0	20.5	21.0	21.5	22.0	22.5	23.0	23.5	24.0	24.5
1	4.29	4.17	4.05	3.95	3.85	3.750	3.659	3.571	3.488	3.409	3.333	3.261	3.191	3.125	3.061
2	8.20	7.99	7.78	7.58	7.40	7.219	7.049	6.888	6.733	6.586	6.444	6.309	6.179	6.055	5.935
3	7.50	7.32	7.15	6.98	6.83	6.677	6.534	6.396	6.264	6.137	6.015	5.898	5.785	5.676	5.572
4	6.86	6.71	6.57	6.43	6.30	6.177	6.055	5.939	5.827	5.718	5.614	5.513	5.416	5.322	5.231
5	6.27	6.15	6.04	5.93	5.82	5.713	5.612	5.515	5.420	5.328	5.240	5.153	5.070	4.989	4.910
6	5.73	5.64	5.55	5.46	5.37	5.285	5.202	5.121	5.042	4.965	4.890	4.817	4.746	4.677	4.610
7	5.24	5.17	5.10	5.03	4.96	4.888	4.821	4.755	4.690	4.627	4.564	4.503	4.443	4.385	4.327
8	5.08	4.94	4.81	4.69	4.57	4.522	4.468	4.415	4.363	4.311	4.260	4.210	4.160	4.111	4.062
9	5.08	4.94	4.81	4.69	4.58	4.462	4.354	4.252	4.155	4.063	3.976	3.935	3.894	3.854	3.814
10	5.08	4.94	4.81	4.69	4.57	4.461	4.354	4.252	4.155	4.063	3.976	3.890	3.808	3.729	3.655
11	5.08	4.94	4.81	4.69	4.58	4.462	4.354	4.252	4.155	4.063	3.976	3.890	3.808	3.729	3.655
12	5.08	4.95	4.81	4.69	4.57	4.461	4.354	4.252	4.155	4.063	3.976	3.890	3.808	3.729	3.655
13	5.09	4.94	4.82	4.69	4.58	4.462	4.354	4.252	4.155	4.064	3.976	3.890	3.808	3.730	3.655
14	5.08	4.95	4.81	4.69	4.57	4.461	4.354	4.252	4.155	4.063	3.976	3.890	3.808	3.729	3.655
15	5.09	4.94	4.82	4.69	4.58	4.462	4.354	4.252	4.155	4.064	3.976	3.890	3.808	3.730	3.655
16	5.08	4.95	4.81	4.69	4.57	4.461	4.354	4.252	4.155	4.063	3.976	3.890	3.808	3.729	3.655
17	5.09	4.94	4.82	4.69	4.58	4.462	4.354	4.252	4.155	4.064	3.976	3.889	3.808	3.730	3.655
18	5.08	4.95	4.81	4.70	4.57	4.461	4.354	4.252	4.156	4.063	3.976	3.890	3.807	3.729	3.655
19		2.47	4.82	4.69	4.58	4.462	4.353	4.251	4.155	4.064	3.976	3.889	3.808	3.730	3.655
20				2.35	4.57	4.461	4.354	4.252	4.156	4.063	3.976	3.890	3.807	3.729	3.655
21						2.231	4.353	4.251	4.155	4.064	3.976	3.889	3.808	3.730	3.655
22								2.126	4.156	4.063	3.976	3.890	3.807	3.729	3.655
23										2.032	3.976	3.889	3.808	3.730	3.654
24												1.945	3.807	3.729	3.655
25														1.865	3.654

and the Recovery Period is:

the Depreciation Rate is:

If the Recovery Year is:	25.0	25.5	26.0	26.5	27.0	27.5	28.0	28.5	29.0	29.5	30.0	30.5	31.0	31.5	32.0
1	3.000	2.941	2.885	2.830	2.778	2.727	2.679	2.632	2.586	2.542	2.500	2.459	2.419	2.381	2.344
2	5.820	5.709	5.603	5.500	5.401	5.306	5.214	5.125	5.039	4.955	4.875	4.797	4.722	4.649	4.578
3	5.471	5.374	5.280	5.189	5.101	5.016	4.934	4.855	4.778	4.704	4.631	4.561	4.493	4.427	4.363
4	5.143	5.057	4.975	4.895	4.818	4.743	4.670	4.599	4.531	4.464	4.400	4.337	4.276	4.216	4.159
5	4.834	4.760	4.688	4.618	4.550	4.484	4.420	4.357	4.297	4.237	4.180	4.124	4.069	4.016	3.964
6	4.544	4.480	4.417	4.357	4.297	4.239	4.183	4.128	4.074	4.022	3.971	3.921	3.872	3.824	3.778
7	4.271	4.216	4.163	4.110	4.059	4.008	3.959	3.911	3.864	3.817	3.772	3.728	3.685	3.642	3.601
8	4.015	3.968	3.922	3.877	3.833	3.790	3.747	3.705	3.664	3.623	3.584	3.545	3.506	3.469	3.432
9	3.774	3.735	3.696	3.658	3.620	3.583	3.546	3.510	3.474	3.439	3.404	3.370	3.337	3.304	3.271
10	3.584	3.515	3.483	3.451	3.419	3.387	3.356	3.325	3.294	3.264	3.234	3.204	3.175	3.146	3.118
11	3.583	3.515	3.448	3.383	3.321	3.262	3.205	3.150	3.124	3.098	3.072	3.047	3.022	2.996	2.971
12	3.584	3.515	3.448	3.383	3.321	3.262	3.205	3.150	3.096	3.044	2.994	2.945	2.899	2.854	2.832
13	3.583	3.515	3.448	3.383	3.321	3.262	3.205	3.150	3.096	3.044	2.994	2.945	2.899	2.854	2.809
14	3.584	3.515	3.448	3.383	3.321	3.262	3.205	3.150	3.096	3.044	2.994	2.945	2.899	2.854	2.809
15	3.583	3.515	3.448	3.383	3.321	3.262	3.205	3.150	3.096	3.044	2.994	2.945	2.899	2.854	2.809
16	3.584	3.515	3.448	3.383	3.322	3.262	3.205	3.150	3.096	3.044	2.994	2.945	2.899	2.854	2.809
17	3.583	3.515	3.448	3.383	3.321	3.262	3.205	3.150	3.096	3.044	2.994	2.945	2.899	2.854	2.809
18	3.584	3.516	3.448	3.383	3.322	3.262	3.205	3.150	3.096	3.044	2.994	2.946	2.899	2.854	2.809
19	3.583	3.515	3.448	3.383	3.321	3.262	3.205	3.150	3.096	3.044	2.994	2.945	2.899	2.854	2.809
20	3.584	3.515	3.447	3.384	3.322	3.262	3.205	3.150	3.096	3.044	2.993	2.946	2.899	2.854	2.809
21	3.583	3.516	3.448	3.383	3.321	3.262	3.205	3.150	3.096	3.044	2.994	2.945	2.899	2.854	2.809
22	3.584	3.516	3.447	3.384	3.322	3.262	3.205	3.150	3.096	3.044	2.993	2.946	2.898	2.854	2.809
23	3.583	3.515	3.448	3.383	3.321	3.262	3.205	3.150	3.096	3.044	2.994	2.945	2.899	2.854	2.809
24	3.584	3.516	3.447	3.384	3.322	3.262	3.205	3.151	3.096	3.044	2.993	2.946	2.898	2.854	2.809
25	3.583	3.515	3.447	3.383	3.321	3.262	3.205	3.150	3.096	3.044	2.994	2.946	2.899	2.854	2.810
26	1.792	3.516	3.447	3.384	3.322	3.262	3.205	3.151	3.096	3.044	2.993	2.945	2.898	2.853	2.809
27			1.724	3.383	3.322	3.262	3.205	3.150	3.096	3.044	2.994	2.946	2.899	2.854	2.810
28					1.661	3.263	3.205	3.151	3.096	3.044	2.993	2.945	2.898	2.853	2.809
29							1.602	3.150	3.096	3.044	2.994	2.946	2.899	2.854	2.809
30									1.548	3.043	2.993	2.945	2.898	2.853	2.809
31											1.497	2.945	2.899	2.854	2.810
32													1.449	2.853	2.809
33															1.405

and the Recovery Period is:

the Depreciation Rate is:

If the Recovery Year is:	32.5	33.0	33.5	34.0	34.5	35.0	35.5	36.0	36.5	37.0	37.5	38.0	38.5	39.0	39.5
1	2.308	2.273	2.239	2.206	2.174	2.143	2.113	2.083	2.055	2.027	2.000	1.974	1.948	1.923	1.899
2	4.509	4.442	4.377	4.314	4.253	4.194	4.136	4.080	4.025	3.972	3.920	3.869	3.820	3.772	3.725
3	4.301	4.240	4.181	4.124	4.068	4.014	3.961	3.910	3.860	3.811	3.763	3.717	3.671	3.627	3.584
4	4.102	4.048	3.994	3.942	3.892	3.842	3.794	3.747	3.701	3.656	3.613	3.570	3.528	3.488	3.448
5	3.913	3.864	3.815	3.768	3.722	3.677	3.634	3.591	3.549	3.508	3.468	3.429	3.391	3.353	3.317
6	3.732	3.688	3.645	3.602	3.560	3.520	3.480	3.441	3.403	3.366	3.329	3.294	3.259	3.225	3.191
7	3.560	3.520	3.481	3.443	3.406	3.369	3.333	3.298	3.263	3.229	3.196	3.164	3.132	3.100	3.070
8	3.396	3.360	3.325	3.291	3.258	3.225	3.192	3.160	3.129	3.099	3.068	3.039	3.010	2.981	2.953
9	3.239	3.208	3.177	3.146	3.116	3.086	3.057	3.029	3.001	2.973	2.946	2.919	2.893	2.867	2.841
10	3.090	3.062	3.034	3.007	2.980	2.954	2.928	2.903	2.877	2.852	2.828	2.804	2.780	2.756	2.733
11	2.947	2.923	2.898	2.875	2.851	2.828	2.804	2.782	2.759	2.737	2.715	2.693	2.671	2.650	2.629
12	2.811	2.790	2.769	2.748	2.727	2.706	2.686	2.666	2.646	2.626	2.606	2.587	2.567	2.548	2.529
13	2.766	2.725	2.685	2.646	2.608	2.590	2.572	2.555	2.537	2.519	2.502	2.485	2.467	2.450	2.433
14	2.766	2.725	2.685	2.646	2.608	2.571	2.535	2.500	2.466	2.434	2.402	2.386	2.371	2.356	2.341
15	2.766	2.725	2.685	2.646	2.608	2.571	2.535	2.500	2.466	2.434	2.402	2.370	2.340	2.310	2.281
16	2.766	2.725	2.685	2.646	2.608	2.571	2.535	2.500	2.466	2.434	2.402	2.370	2.340	2.310	2.281
17	2.766	2.725	2.685	2.646	2.608	2.571	2.535	2.500	2.467	2.434	2.402	2.370	2.340	2.310	2.281
18	2.766	2.725	2.685	2.646	2.609	2.571	2.535	2.500	2.466	2.434	2.402	2.370	2.340	2.310	2.281
19	2.766	2.725	2.685	2.646	2.608	2.571	2.535	2.500	2.467	2.434	2.402	2.370	2.340	2.310	2.281
20	2.766	2.725	2.685	2.646	2.609	2.571	2.535	2.500	2.466	2.434	2.402	2.370	2.340	2.310	2.281
21	2.766	2.725	2.685	2.646	2.608	2.571	2.535	2.500	2.467	2.434	2.402	2.370	2.340	2.310	2.281
22	2.767	2.725	2.685	2.646	2.609	2.571	2.535	2.500	2.466	2.434	2.402	2.370	2.340	2.310	2.281
23	2.766	2.725	2.685	2.646	2.608	2.571	2.535	2.500	2.467	2.433	2.402	2.370	2.340	2.310	2.281
24	2.767	2.724	2.685	2.646	2.609	2.571	2.535	2.500	2.466	2.434	2.402	2.370	2.340	2.310	2.281
25	2.766	2.725	2.685	2.646	2.608	2.571	2.535	2.500	2.467	2.433	2.402	2.370	2.339	2.310	2.281
26	2.767	2.724	2.685	2.646	2.609	2.571	2.535	2.500	2.466	2.434	2.402	2.370	2.340	2.310	2.281
27	2.766	2.724	2.684	2.646	2.608	2.571	2.536	2.500	2.467	2.433	2.402	2.370	2.339	2.310	2.281
28	2.767	2.724	2.685	2.646	2.609	2.572	2.535	2.501	2.466	2.434	2.402	2.370	2.340	2.310	2.281
29	2.766	2.725	2.684	2.646	2.608	2.571	2.536	2.500	2.467	2.433	2.402	2.370	2.339	2.310	2.281
30	2.767	2.724	2.685	2.646	2.609	2.572	2.535	2.501	2.466	2.434	2.402	2.371	2.340	2.310	2.281
31	2.766	2.725	2.684	2.646	2.608	2.571	2.536	2.500	2.467	2.433	2.401	2.370	2.339	2.310	2.281
32	2.767	2.724	2.685	2.646	2.609	2.572	2.535	2.501	2.466	2.434	2.402	2.371	2.340	2.310	2.281
33	2.766	2.725	2.684	2.645	2.608	2.571	2.536	2.500	2.467	2.433	2.401	2.370	2.339	2.310	2.281
34		1.362	2.685	2.645	2.609	2.572	2.535	2.501	2.466	2.434	2.402	2.371	2.340	2.310	2.281
35				1.323	2.608	2.571	2.536	2.500	2.467	2.433	2.401	2.370	2.339	2.310	2.281
36						1.286	2.535	2.500	2.467	2.433	2.402	2.371	2.340	2.310	2.281
37								1.250	2.466	2.434	2.401	2.370	2.339	2.310	2.281
38										1.217	2.402	2.371	2.340	2.310	2.281
39												1.185	2.339	2.310	2.282
40														1.155	2.281

the Depreciation Rate is:

If the Recovery Year is:	40.0	40.5	41.0	41.5	42.0	42.5	43.0	43.5	44.0	44.5	45.0	45.5	46.0	46.5	47.0
1	1.875	1.852	1.829	1.807	1.786	1.765	1.744	1.724	1.705	1.685	1.667	1.648	1.630	1.613	1.596
2	3.680	3.635	3.592	3.549	3.508	3.467	3.428	3.389	3.351	3.314	3.278	3.242	3.208	3.174	3.141
3	3.542	3.500	3.460	3.421	3.382	3.345	3.308	3.272	3.237	3.202	3.169	3.135	3.103	3.071	3.040
4	3.409	3.371	3.334	3.297	3.262	3.227	3.193	3.159	3.126	3.094	3.063	3.032	3.002	2.972	2.943
5	3.281	3.246	3.212	3.178	3.145	3.113	3.081	3.050	3.020	2.990	2.961	2.932	2.904	2.876	2.849
6	3.158	3.126	3.094	3.063	3.033	3.003	2.974	2.945	2.917	2.889	2.862	2.836	2.809	2.784	2.758
7	3.040	3.010	2.981	2.952	2.924	2.897	2.870	2.843	2.817	2.792	2.767	2.742	2.718	2.694	2.670
8	2.926	2.899	2.872	2.846	2.820	2.795	2.770	2.745	2.721	2.698	2.674	2.652	2.629	2.607	2.585
9	2.816	2.791	2.767	2.743	2.719	2.696	2.673	2.651	2.629	2.607	2.585	2.564	2.543	2.523	2.503
10	2.710	2.688	2.666	2.644	2.622	2.601	2.580	2.559	2.539	2.519	2.499	2.480	2.460	2.441	2.423
11	2.609	2.588	2.568	2.548	2.529	2.509	2.490	2.471	2.452	2.434	2.416	2.398	2.380	2.363	2.345
12	2.511	2.492	2.474	2.456	2.438	2.421	2.403	2.386	2.368	2.352	2.335	2.319	2.303	2.287	2.271
13	2.417	2.400	2.384	2.367	2.351	2.335	2.319	2.304	2.288	2.273	2.257	2.242	2.228	2.213	2.198
14	2.326	2.311	2.296	2.282	2.257	2.253	2.238	2.224	2.210	2.196	2.182	2.169	2.155	2.141	2.128
15	2.253	2.226	2.212	2.199	2.186	2.173	2.160	2.148	2.135	2.122	2.110	2.097	2.085	2.072	2.060
16	2.253	2.226	2.198	2.172	2.146	2.121	2.097	2.073	2.062	2.051	2.039	2.028	2.017	2.005	1.994
17	2.253	2.226	2.198	2.172	2.146	2.121	2.097	2.073	2.050	2.027	2.005	1.983	1.962	1.941	1.931
18	2.253	2.226	2.198	2.172	2.147	2.121	2.097	2.073	2.050	2.027	2.005	1.983	1.961	1.941	1.920
19	2.253	2.226	2.199	2.172	2.146	2.121	2.097	2.074	2.050	2.027	2.005	1.983	1.962	1.941	1.920
20	2.253	2.226	2.198	2.172	2.147	2.121	2.097	2.074	2.050	2.027	2.005	1.983	1.961	1.941	1.920
21	2.253	2.225	2.199	2.172	2.146	2.122	2.097	2.073	2.058	2.027	2.005	1.983	1.962	1.941	1.920
22	2.253	2.225	2.198	2.172	2.146	2.121	2.097	2.074	2.050	2.027	2.005	1.983	1.961	1.941	1.920
23	2.253	2.226	2.199	2.172	2.146	2.121	2.097	2.073	2.050	2.027	2.005	1.983	1.962	1.941	1.920
24	2.253	2.225	2.198	2.172	2.147	2.121	2.097	2.074	2.053	2.027	2.004	1.983	1.961	1.941	1.920
25	2.253	2.225	2.199	2.172	2.146	2.122	2.097	2.074	2.053	2.027	2.005	1.983	1.962	1.941	1.920
26	2.253	2.226	2.198	2.172	2.147	2.121	2.057	2.073	2.053	2.027	2.004	1.983	1.961	1.941	1.920
27	2.253	2.226	2.199	2.172	2.147	2.122	2.057	2.074	2.053	2.027	2.005	1.983	1.962	1.941	1.920
28	2.253	2.225	2.198	2.172	2.146	2.121	2.097	2.073	2.050	2.027	2.004	1.983	1.961	1.941	1.920
29	2.253	2.226	2.199	2.172	2.147	2.122	2.097	2.074	2.050	2.027	2.005	1.983	1.962	1.941	1.920
30	2.253	2.226	2.199	2.172	2.146	2.121	2.097	2.073	2.050	2.027	2.004	1.983	1.961	1.941	1.920
31	2.253	2.226	2.199	2.172	2.147	2.122	2.097	2.074	2.050	2.027	2.005	1.983	1.962	1.941	1.920
32	2.253	2.226	2.198	2.172	2.146	2.121	2.097	2.073	2.050	2.027	2.004	1.983	1.961	1.941	1.920
33	2.252	2.226	2.199	2.173	2.146	2.122	2.097	2.074	2.050	2.027	2.005	1.983	1.962	1.940	1.920
34	2.253	2.225	2.198	2.172	2.147	2.121	2.097	2.073	2.050	2.027	2.004	1.983	1.961	1.941	1.920
35	2.253	2.225	2.199	2.173	2.146	2.122	2.097	2.074	2.050	2.027	2.005	1.982	1.962	1.941	1.920
36	2.253	2.226	2.198	2.173	2.147	2.122	2.097	2.073	2.050	2.027	2.004	1.983	1.962	1.940	1.920
37	2.252	2.225	2.199	2.173	2.146	2.122	2.098	2.074	2.050	2.027	2.005	1.983	1.961	1.941	1.920
38	2.253	2.226	2.198	2.172	2.146	2.121	2.097	2.073	2.050	2.027	2.004	1.982	1.962	1.940	1.920
39	2.252	2.225	2.199	2.173	2.147	2.122	2.097	2.074	2.050	2.027	2.005	1.983	1.961	1.941	1.920
40	2.252	2.226	2.199	2.173	2.146	2.122	2.097	2.073	2.050	2.027	2.005	1.983	1.962	1.941	1.921
41	2.253	2.225	2.198	2.173	2.147	2.122	2.097	2.074	2.050	2.027	2.004	1.982	1.961	1.940	1.921
42	2.252	2.226	2.199	2.173	2.146	2.121	2.038	2.073	2.050	2.027	2.005	1.983	1.962	1.941	1.920
43	2.253	2.226	2.199	2.173	2.147	2.122	2.037	2.073	2.049	2.027	2.004	1.983	1.961	1.940	1.921
44	1.126	2.226	1.099	2.173	1.073	2.122	1.049	2.073	1.025	2.026	1.002	1.982	0.981	1.941	1.920
45														1.940	1.920
46														1.940	1.921
47														1.940	1.920
48														1.941	0.960

and the Recovery Period is:

the Depreciation Rate is:

If the Recovery Year is:	47.5	48.0	48.5	49.0	49.5	50.0
1	1.579	1.563	1.546	1.531	1.515	1.500
2	3.108	3.076	3.045	3.014	2.984	2.955
3	3.010	2.980	2.951	2.922	2.894	2.866
4	2.915	2.887	2.860	2.833	2.806	2.780
5	2.823	2.797	2.771	2.746	2.721	2.697
6	2.734	2.709	2.685	2.662	2.639	2.616
7	2.647	2.625	2.602	2.580	2.559	2.538
8	2.564	2.543	2.522	2.501	2.481	2.461
9	2.483	2.463	2.444	2.425	2.406	2.388
10	2.404	2.386	2.368	2.351	2.333	2.316
11	2.328	2.312	2.295	2.279	2.262	2.246
12	2.255	2.239	2.224	2.209	2.194	2.179
13	2.184	2.169	2.155	2.141	2.127	2.114
14	2.115	2.102	2.089	2.076	2.063	2.050
15	2.048	2.036	2.024	2.012	2.000	1.989
16	1.983	1.972	1.961	1.951	1.940	1.929
17	1.921	1.911	1.901	1.891	1.881	1.871
18	1.900	1.880	1.861	1.842	1.824	1.815
19	1.900	1.880	1.861	1.842	1.824	1.806
20	1.900	1.880	1.861	1.842	1.824	1.806
21	1.900	1.880	1.861	1.842	1.824	1.806
22	1.900	1.880	1.861	1.842	1.824	1.806
23	1.900	1.880	1.861	1.842	1.824	1.806
24	1.900	1.880	1.861	1.842	1.824	1.806
25	1.900	1.880	1.861	1.842	1.824	1.806
26	1.900	1.880	1.861	1.842	1.824	1.806

and the Recovery Period is:

the Depreciation Rate is:

If the Recovery Year is:	47.5	48.0	48.5	49.0	49.5	50.0
27	1.900	1.880	1.861	1.842	1.824	1.806
28	1.900	1.880	1.861	1.842	1.824	1.806
29	1.900	1.880	1.861	1.843	1.824	1.806
30	1.900	1.881	1.861	1.842	1.824	1.806
31	1.900	1.880	1.861	1.843	1.824	1.806
32	1.900	1.881	1.861	1.842	1.824	1.806
33	1.900	1.880	1.861	1.843	1.824	1.806
34	1.900	1.880	1.861	1.842	1.824	1.806
35	1.900	1.881	1.861	1.843	1.824	1.806
36	1.900	1.880	1.861	1.842	1.824	1.806
37	1.900	1.881	1.861	1.843	1.824	1.806
38	1.900	1.881	1.861	1.842	1.824	1.806
39	1.900	1.880	1.862	1.843	1.824	1.806
40	1.900	1.881	1.861	1.842	1.824	1.806
41	1.900	1.880	1.861	1.843	1.824	1.806
42	1.900	1.881	1.862	1.842	1.824	1.805
43	1.900	1.880	1.861	1.843	1.824	1.806
44	1.900	1.881	1.862	1.842	1.824	1.805
45	1.900	1.880	1.861	1.843	1.825	1.806
46	1.900	1.881	1.862	1.842	1.824	1.805
47	1.900	1.881	1.861	1.843	1.825	1.806
48	1.900	1.881	1.862	1.842	1.824	1.805
49	1.899	1.881	1.862	1.843	1.825	1.806
50		0.940	1.861	1.842	1.824	1.805
51				0.921		0.903

revenue procedure)
Applicable Depreciation Method: 150 Percent Declining Balance
Switching to Straight Line
Applicable Recovery Periods: 2.5 - 50 years
Applicable Convention: Mid-quarter (property placed in service in first quarter)

and the Recovery Period is:

the Depreciation Rate is:

If the Recovery Year is:	2.5	3.0	3.5	4.0	4.5	5.0	5.5	6.0	6.5	7.0	7.5	8.0	8.5	9.0	9.5
1	52.50	43.75	37.50	32.81	29.17	26.25	23.85	21.88	20.19	18.75	17.50	16.41	15.44	14.58	13.82
2	29.23	28.13	26.79	25.20	23.61	22.13	20.77	19.53	18.42	17.41	16.50	15.67	14.92	14.24	13.61
3	18.27	25.00	21.98	19.76	17.39	16.52	15.27	14.65	14.17	13.68	13.20	12.74	12.29	11.86	11.46
4		3.12	13.73	19.76	17.39	16.52	15.28	14.06	13.03	12.16	11.42	10.77	10.20	9.89	9.65
5				2.47	17.39	16.52	15.28	14.06	13.03	12.16	11.42	10.77	10.19	9.64	9.15
6					11.24	16.52	15.27	14.06	13.02	12.16	11.41	10.76	10.20	9.65	9.15
7						2.06	15.27	14.06	13.03	12.16	11.42	10.77	10.19	9.64	9.15
8							9.55	14.06	13.03	12.16	11.41	10.76	10.20	9.65	9.15
9								1.76	8.14	12.16	11.42	10.77	10.20	9.64	9.14
10										1.52	7.13	1.35	6.37	1.21	5.72

and the Recovery Period is:

the Depreciation Rate is:

If the Recovery Year is:	10.0	10.5	11.0	11.5	12.0	12.5	13.0	13.5	14.0	14.5	15.0	15.5	16.0	16.5	17.0
1	13.13	12.50	11.93	11.41	10.94	10.50	10.10	9.72	9.33	9.05	8.75	8.47	8.20	7.95	7.72
2	13.03	12.50	12.01	11.56	11.13	10.74	10.37	10.03	9.71	9.41	9.13	8.86	8.61	8.37	8.14
3	11.08	10.71	10.37	10.05	9.74	9.45	9.18	8.92	8.67	8.44	8.21	8.00	7.80	7.61	7.42
4	9.41	9.18	8.96	8.74	8.52	8.32	8.12	7.93	7.74	7.56	7.39	7.23	7.07	6.92	6.77
5	8.71	8.32	7.96	7.64	7.46	7.32	7.18	7.04	6.91	6.78	6.65	6.53	6.41	6.29	6.17
6	8.71	8.32	7.96	7.64	7.33	7.04	6.78	6.53	6.31	6.10	5.99	5.89	5.80	5.71	5.63
7	8.71	8.32	7.96	7.64	7.33	7.04	6.77	6.54	6.31	6.11	5.90	5.72	5.54	5.38	5.23
8	8.71	8.32	7.96	7.64	7.33	7.04	6.78	6.53	6.31	6.10	5.91	5.72	5.54	5.38	5.23
9	8.71	8.31	7.97	7.63	7.33	7.04	6.77	6.54	6.31	6.11	5.90	5.72	5.54	5.38	5.23
10	8.71	8.31	7.96	7.64	7.32	7.04	6.78	6.53	6.31	6.10	5.91	5.71	5.54	5.38	5.22
11	1.09	5.20	7.96	7.64	7.33	7.04	6.77	6.54	6.31	6.11	5.90	5.72	5.54	5.38	5.23
12			1.00	4.77	7.32	7.03	6.78	6.53	6.31	6.10	5.91	5.71	5.54	5.38	5.22
13					0.92	4.40	6.77	6.54	6.31	6.11	5.90	5.72	5.55	5.38	5.23
14							0.85	4.08	6.32	6.10	5.91	5.71	5.54	5.38	5.23
15									0.79	3.82	5.90	5.72	5.55	5.37	5.22
16											0.74	3.57	5.54	5.38	5.23
17													0.69	3.36	5.23
18															0.65

and the Recovery Period is:

the Depreciation Rate is:

If the Recovery Year is:	17.5	18.0	18.5	19.0	19.5	20.0	20.5	21.0	21.5	22.0	22.5	23.0	23.5	24.0	24.5
1	7.50	7.29	7.09	6.91	6.73	6.563	6.402	6.250	6.105	5.966	5.833	5.707	5.585	5.469	5.357
2	7.93	7.73	7.53	7.35	7.17	7.008	6.849	6.696	6.551	6.411	6.278	6.150	6.026	5.908	5.794
3	7.25	7.08	6.92	6.77	6.62	6.482	6.347	6.218	6.094	5.974	5.859	5.748	5.642	5.539	5.440
4	6.63	6.49	6.36	6.23	6.11	5.996	5.883	5.774	5.669	5.567	5.469	5.374	5.282	5.193	5.107
5	6.06	5.95	5.85	5.74	5.64	5.546	5.453	5.362	5.273	5.187	5.104	5.023	4.945	4.868	4.794
6	5.54	5.45	5.37	5.29	5.21	5.130	5.054	4.979	4.905	4.834	4.764	4.696	4.629	4.564	4.500
7	5.08	5.00	4.94	4.87	4.81	4.746	4.684	4.623	4.563	4.504	4.446	4.389	4.333	4.279	4.225
8	5.08	4.94	4.81	4.69	4.57	4.459	4.354	4.293	4.245	4.197	4.150	4.103	4.057	4.011	3.966
9	5.08	4.95	4.81	4.69	4.57	4.459	4.354	4.252	4.154	4.061	3.972	3.888	3.808	3.761	3.723
10	5.08	4.94	4.81	4.69	4.57	4.459	4.354	4.252	4.154	4.061	3.972	3.888	3.808	3.729	3.654
11	5.08	4.95	4.81	4.69	4.57	4.460	4.354	4.252	4.154	4.061	3.972	3.888	3.808	3.729	3.654
12	5.09	4.94	4.81	4.69	4.57	4.459	4.354	4.252	4.154	4.061	3.972	3.888	3.808	3.730	3.654
13	5.08	4.95	4.81	4.69	4.57	4.460	4.355	4.252	4.154	4.061	3.973	3.888	3.808	3.729	3.654
14	5.09	4.94	4.82	4.68	4.57	4.459	4.354	4.252	4.154	4.061	3.972	3.888	3.808	3.730	3.654
15	5.08	4.95	4.81	4.69	4.57	4.460	4.355	4.252	4.154	4.061	3.973	3.888	3.808	3.729	3.654
16	5.09	4.94	4.81	4.69	4.57	4.459	4.354	4.252	4.154	4.061	3.972	3.888	3.808	3.729	3.654
17	5.08	4.95	4.82	4.68	4.57	4.460	4.355	4.252	4.154	4.061	3.973	3.888	3.808	3.729	3.654
18	3.18	4.94	4.81	4.69	4.58	4.459	4.354	4.251	4.153	4.061	3.972	3.888	3.808	3.730	3.654
19		0.62	3.01	4.68	4.57	4.460	4.355	4.252	4.154	4.061	3.973	3.888	3.808	3.729	3.654
20				0.59	2.86	4.460	4.354	4.251	4.153	4.060	3.972	3.889	3.808	3.730	3.654
21						0.557	2.722	4.252	4.154	4.061	3.973	3.888	3.808	3.729	3.654
22								0.531	4.153	4.060	3.972	3.889	3.808	3.730	3.654
23									2.596	0.508	3.973	3.888	3.808	3.730	3.654
24											2.483	3.889	3.809	3.729	3.654
25												0.486	2.380	0.466	2.284

and the Recovery Period is:

the Depreciation Rate is:

If the Recovery Year is:	25.0	25.5	26.0	26.5	27.0	27.5	28.0	28.5	29.0	29.5	30.0	30.5	31.0	31.5	32.0
1	5.250	5.147	5.048	4.953	4.861	4.773	4.688	4.605	4.526	4.449	4.375	4.303	4.234	4.167	4.102
2	5.685	5.580	5.478	5.380	5.286	5.194	5.106	5.021	4.938	4.859	4.781	4.706	4.634	4.563	4.495
3	5.344	5.251	5.162	5.075	4.992	4.911	4.832	4.757	4.683	4.611	4.542	4.475	4.410	4.346	4.285
4	5.023	4.942	4.864	4.788	4.714	4.643	4.574	4.506	4.441	4.377	4.315	4.255	4.196	4.139	4.084
5	4.722	4.652	4.584	4.517	4.453	4.390	4.329	4.269	4.211	4.154	4.099	4.046	3.993	3.942	3.892
6	4.439	4.378	4.319	4.262	4.205	4.150	4.097	4.044	3.993	3.943	3.894	3.847	3.800	3.754	3.710
7	4.172	4.121	4.070	4.020	3.972	3.924	3.877	3.831	3.787	3.743	3.700	3.657	3.616	3.576	3.536
8	3.922	3.878	3.835	3.793	3.751	3.710	3.669	3.630	3.591	3.552	3.515	3.478	3.441	3.405	3.370
9	3.687	3.650	3.614	3.578	3.543	3.508	3.473	3.439	3.405	3.372	3.339	3.307	3.275	3.243	3.212
10	3.582	3.513	3.447	3.383	3.346	3.316	3.287	3.258	3.229	3.200	3.172	3.144	3.116	3.089	3.062
11	3.582	3.513	3.447	3.384	3.321	3.261	3.204	3.148	3.095	3.044	3.013	2.989	2.965	2.942	2.918
12	3.582	3.513	3.447	3.383	3.321	3.261	3.204	3.149	3.095	3.044	2.994	2.945	2.898	2.853	2.809
13	3.582	3.513	3.447	3.384	3.321	3.261	3.204	3.148	3.095	3.044	2.994	2.945	2.898	2.853	2.809
14	3.582	3.513	3.447	3.383	3.321	3.261	3.204	3.149	3.095	3.044	2.994	2.945	2.898	2.852	2.809
15	3.582	3.513	3.447	3.384	3.321	3.261	3.204	3.149	3.095	3.044	2.994	2.945	2.898	2.853	2.809
16	3.582	3.513	3.447	3.383	3.321	3.261	3.204	3.148	3.095	3.044	2.994	2.945	2.898	2.852	2.809
17	3.582	3.513	3.447	3.384	3.321	3.262	3.204	3.149	3.095	3.044	2.994	2.945	2.898	2.852	2.809
18	3.582	3.513	3.447	3.383	3.321	3.261	3.204	3.148	3.095	3.044	2.994	2.945	2.898	2.853	2.809
19	3.581	3.513	3.446	3.384	3.322	3.262	3.204	3.149	3.095	3.044	2.994	2.945	2.898	2.852	2.809
20	3.582	3.513	3.447	3.383	3.321	3.261	3.204	3.148	3.095	3.044	2.993	2.945	2.898	2.853	2.808
21	3.581	3.513	3.447	3.384	3.322	3.262	3.204	3.149	3.095	3.044	2.994	2.945	2.898	2.853	2.809
22	3.582	3.512	3.446	3.384	3.321	3.261	3.203	3.148	3.096	3.044	2.993	2.945	2.898	2.853	2.808
23	3.582	3.513	3.447	3.383	3.322	3.262	3.204	3.149	3.095	3.044	2.994	2.945	2.898	2.853	2.809
24	3.581	3.512	3.446	3.384	3.321	3.261	3.203	3.149	3.096	3.044	2.993	2.945	2.898	2.852	2.808
25	3.582	3.513	3.446	3.383	3.322	3.262	3.204	3.148	3.095	3.044	2.994	2.945	2.898	2.853	2.809
26	3.581	3.512	3.447	3.384	3.321	3.261	3.203	3.149	3.096	3.044	2.993	2.944	2.897	2.852	2.808
27	0.448	2.195	3.446	3.383	3.322	3.262	3.204	3.148	3.095	3.044	2.994	2.945	2.897	2.853	2.808
28			0.431	2.115	3.321	3.261	3.203	3.149	3.096	3.045	2.994	2.944	2.898	2.852	2.808
29					0.415	3.262	3.204	3.148	3.095	3.044	2.993	2.944	2.897	2.853	2.809
30						2.038	0.400	3.149	3.096	3.044	2.994	2.945	2.898	2.852	2.808
31								1.968	3.095	3.044	2.994	2.944	2.898	2.852	2.808
32									0.387	3.045	0.374	2.945	2.897	2.853	2.809
33										1.903		1.840	0.362	1.783	0.351

and the Recovery Period is:

the Depreciation Rate is:

If the Recovery Year is:	32.5	33.0	33.5	34.0	34.5	35.0	35.5	36.0	36.5	37.0	37.5	38.0	38.5	39.0	39.5
1	4.038	3.977	3.918	3.860	3.804	3.750	3.697	3.646	3.596	3.547	3.500	3.454	3.409	3.365	3.323
2	4.429	4.365	4.302	4.241	4.182	4.125	4.069	4.015	3.962	3.910	3.860	3.811	3.763	3.717	3.671
3	4.225	4.166	4.110	4.054	4.001	3.948	3.897	3.847	3.799	3.752	3.706	3.661	3.617	3.574	3.532
4	4.030	3.977	3.926	3.876	3.827	3.779	3.733	3.687	3.643	3.600	3.557	3.516	3.476	3.436	3.398
5	3.844	3.796	3.750	3.705	3.660	3.617	3.575	3.534	3.493	3.454	3.415	3.377	3.340	3.304	3.269
6	3.666	3.626	3.582	3.541	3.501	3.462	3.424	3.386	3.350	3.314	3.278	3.244	3.210	3.177	3.145
7	3.497	3.459	3.415	3.385	3.354	3.313	3.279	3.245	3.212	3.179	3.147	3.116	3.085	3.055	3.025
8	3.336	3.302	3.268	3.235	3.203	3.172	3.141	3.110	3.080	3.050	3.021	2.993	2.965	2.937	2.910
9	3.182	3.152	3.122	3.093	3.064	3.036	3.008	2.980	2.953	2.927	2.901	2.875	2.849	2.824	2.800
10	3.035	3.008	2.982	2.956	2.931	2.906	2.881	2.856	2.832	2.808	2.785	2.761	2.738	2.716	2.693
11	2.895	2.872	2.849	2.826	2.803	2.781	2.759	2.737	2.716	2.694	2.673	2.652	2.632	2.611	2.591
12	2.766	2.741	2.721	2.701	2.682	2.662	2.642	2.623	2.604	2.585	2.566	2.548	2.529	2.511	2.493
13	2.766	2.725	2.684	2.645	2.607	2.571	2.535	2.514	2.497	2.480	2.464	2.447	2.431	2.414	2.398
14	2.766	2.725	2.684	2.645	2.607	2.571	2.535	2.500	2.466	2.433	2.401	2.370	2.340	2.322	2.307
15	2.766	2.725	2.684	2.645	2.607	2.571	2.535	2.500	2.466	2.433	2.401	2.370	2.340	2.310	2.281
16	2.766	2.725	2.684	2.645	2.607	2.571	2.535	2.500	2.466	2.433	2.401	2.370	2.340	2.310	2.281
17	2.766	2.725	2.684	2.645	2.607	2.571	2.535	2.500	2.466	2.433	2.401	2.370	2.340	2.310	2.281
18	2.767	2.725	2.684	2.645	2.607	2.571	2.535	2.500	2.466	2.433	2.401	2.370	2.340	2.310	2.281
19	2.766	2.725	2.684	2.645	2.608	2.571	2.535	2.500	2.466	2.433	2.401	2.370	2.340	2.310	2.281
20	2.767	2.725	2.684	2.645	2.607	2.571	2.535	2.500	2.466	2.433	2.401	2.370	2.340	2.310	2.281
21	2.766	2.725	2.684	2.645	2.608	2.571	2.535	2.501	2.466	2.433	2.401	2.370	2.340	2.310	2.281
22	2.767	2.725	2.685	2.645	2.608	2.571	2.535	2.500	2.466	2.433	2.401	2.370	2.340	2.310	2.281
23	2.766	2.725	2.684	2.646	2.607	2.571	2.535	2.500	2.466	2.433	2.401	2.370	2.340	2.310	2.281
24	2.766	2.725	2.685	2.645	2.607	2.570	2.535	2.501	2.466	2.433	2.401	2.370	2.340	2.310	2.281
25	2.767	2.725	2.685	2.646	2.607	2.570	2.535	2.500	2.466	2.433	2.401	2.370	2.340	2.310	2.281
26	2.766	2.724	2.684	2.645	2.607	2.571	2.536	2.500	2.466	2.433	2.401	2.370	2.340	2.310	2.281
27	2.766	2.725	2.685	2.645	2.607	2.570	2.535	2.501	2.466	2.433	2.401	2.370	2.340	2.310	2.281
28	2.767	2.724	2.685	2.645	2.608	2.571	2.536	2.500	2.466	2.433	2.401	2.370	2.340	2.310	2.281
29	2.766	2.724	2.684	2.646	2.607	2.571	2.535	2.501	2.466	2.433	2.401	2.370	2.339	2.310	2.281
30	2.766	2.724	2.685	2.645	2.608	2.570	2.536	2.500	2.466	2.433	2.401	2.370	2.339	2.310	2.281
31	2.767	2.725	2.684	2.646	2.607	2.571	2.536	2.501	2.466	2.434	2.401	2.370	2.340	2.310	2.280
32	2.767	2.724	2.685	2.646	2.608	2.570	2.536	2.500	2.467	2.433	2.401	2.370	2.340	2.310	2.280
33	1.729	2.724	2.684	2.645	2.607	2.571	2.535	2.501	2.466	2.434	2.401	2.370	2.339	2.310	2.281
34		0.341	1.678	2.646	2.608	2.570	2.536	2.500	2.467	2.433	2.401	2.370	2.339	2.310	2.280
35				0.331	1.630	2.571	2.535	2.500	2.467	2.434	2.402	2.370	2.340	2.310	2.280
36						0.321	1.585	2.500	2.466	2.433	2.402	2.370	2.340	2.310	2.280
37								0.313	1.542	2.434	2.401	2.370	2.339	2.309	2.281
38										0.304	1.501	2.369	2.339	2.309	2.280
39												0.296	1.462	2.310	2.280
40														0.289	1.425

and the Recovery Period is:

the Depreciation Rate is:

If the Recovery Year is:	40.0	40.5	41.0	41.5	42.0	42.5	43.0	43.5	44.0	44.5	45.0	45.5	46.0	46.5	47.0
1	3.281	3.201	3.201	3.163	3.125	3.088	3.052	3.017	2.983	2.949	2.917	2.885	2.853	2.823	2.793
2	3.627	3.584	3.541	3.500	3.460	3.420	3.382	3.344	3.307	3.271	3.236	3.202	3.168	3.135	3.102
3	3.491	3.451	3.412	3.374	3.336	3.300	3.264	3.229	3.195	3.161	3.128	3.096	3.065	3.034	3.003
4	3.360	3.323	3.287	3.252	3.211	3.183	3.150	3.118	3.086	3.055	3.024	2.994	2.965	2.936	2.908
5	3.234	3.200	3.167	3.134	3.102	3.071	3.040	3.010	2.981	2.952	2.923	2.895	2.868	2.841	2.815
6	3.113	3.082	3.051	3.021	2.991	2.963	2.934	2.906	2.879	2.852	2.826	2.800	2.774	2.749	2.725
7	2.996	2.967	2.939	2.912	2.885	2.858	2.832	2.806	2.781	2.756	2.732	2.708	2.684	2.661	2.638
8	2.884	2.857	2.832	2.806	2.782	2.757	2.733	2.709	2.686	2.663	2.640	2.618	2.596	2.575	2.554
9	2.776	2.752	2.728	2.705	2.682	2.660	2.638	2.616	2.594	2.573	2.552	2.532	2.512	2.492	2.472
10	2.671	2.650	2.628	2.607	2.586	2.566	2.546	2.526	2.506	2.487	2.467	2.448	2.430	2.411	2.393
11	2.571	2.552	2.532	2.513	2.494	2.475	2.457	2.439	2.421	2.403	2.385	2.368	2.351	2.334	2.317
12	2.475	2.457	2.440	2.422	2.405	2.388	2.371	2.354	2.338	2.322	2.306	2.290	2.274	2.258	2.243
13	2.382	2.366	2.350	2.335	2.319	2.304	2.288	2.273	2.258	2.243	2.229	2.214	2.200	2.186	2.171
14	2.293	2.278	2.264	2.250	2.236	2.222	2.209	2.195	2.181	2.168	2.154	2.141	2.128	2.115	2.102
15	2.252	2.225	2.198	2.172	2.172	2.144	2.132	2.119	2.107	2.095	2.083	2.071	2.059	2.047	2.035
16	2.253	2.225	2.198	2.172	2.147	2.121	2.097	2.073	2.050	2.027	2.013	2.002	1.992	1.981	1.970
17	2.252	2.225	2.198	2.172	2.147	2.121	2.097	2.073	2.050	2.027	2.005	1.983	1.961	1.940	1.920
18	2.253	2.225	2.198	2.172	2.147	2.121	2.097	2.073	2.050	2.027	2.005	1.983	1.961	1.940	1.920
19	2.252	2.225	2.198	2.172	2.147	2.121	2.097	2.073	2.050	2.027	2.005	1.983	1.961	1.940	1.920
20	2.253	2.225	2.198	2.172	2.147	2.121	2.097	2.073	2.050	2.027	2.005	1.983	1.961	1.940	1.920
21	2.252	2.225	2.198	2.172	2.147	2.121	2.097	2.073	2.050	2.027	2.005	1.983	1.961	1.940	1.920
22	2.253	2.225	2.198	2.172	2.147	2.121	2.097	2.073	2.050	2.027	2.005	1.983	1.961	1.940	1.920
23	2.253	2.225	2.198	2.172	2.147	2.121	2.097	2.073	2.050	2.027	2.005	1.983	1.961	1.940	1.920
24	2.252	2.225	2.198	2.172	2.146	2.121	2.097	2.073	2.050	2.027	2.005	1.983	1.961	1.940	1.920
25	2.253	2.225	2.198	2.172	2.147	2.121	2.097	2.073	2.050	2.027	2.005	1.983	1.961	1.940	1.920
26	2.252	2.225	2.198	2.172	2.146	2.121	2.097	2.073	2.050	2.027	2.004	1.983	1.961	1.940	1.920
27	2.253	2.225	2.198	2.172	2.147	2.121	2.097	2.073	2.050	2.027	2.005	1.982	1.961	1.940	1.920
28	2.252	2.225	2.198	2.172	2.146	2.122	2.097	2.073	2.049	2.027	2.004	1.983	1.961	1.940	1.920
29	2.253	2.225	2.198	2.172	2.147	2.121	2.097	2.073	2.049	2.027	2.004	1.983	1.961	1.940	1.920
30	2.253	2.225	2.198	2.172	2.146	2.122	2.097	2.073	2.050	2.027	2.004	1.983	1.961	1.941	1.920
31	2.252	2.225	2.198	2.172	2.147	2.122	2.097	2.073	2.049	2.027	2.005	1.982	1.961	1.940	1.920
32	2.253	2.225	2.198	2.172	2.146	2.121	2.097	2.073	2.050	2.027	2.004	1.983	1.961	1.941	1.920
33	2.253	2.225	2.198	2.172	2.147	2.121	2.096	2.073	2.050	2.027	2.005	1.982	1.962	1.940	1.920
34	2.252	2.225	2.199	2.172	2.146	2.122	2.097	2.073	2.049	2.027	2.004	1.983	1.961	1.941	1.920
35	2.253	2.225	2.198	2.172	2.147	2.121	2.097	2.073	2.049	2.027	2.005	1.982	1.962	1.940	1.920
36	2.252	2.225	2.199	2.172	2.147	2.122	2.097	2.073	2.050	2.027	2.005	1.983	1.961	1.941	1.920
37	2.253	2.225	2.198	2.173	2.146	2.121	2.096	2.073	2.049	2.027	2.004	1.982	1.962	1.940	1.920
38	2.252	2.225	2.199	2.172	2.147	2.122	2.097	2.073	2.049	2.027	2.005	1.983	1.961	1.941	1.920
39	2.253	2.225	2.199	2.173	2.146	2.121	2.096	2.073	2.050	2.027	2.005	1.982	1.961	1.940	1.920
40	2.253	2.225	2.198	2.172	2.147	2.122	2.097	2.073	2.049	2.027	2.004	1.983	1.962	1.941	1.920
41	0.282	2.225	2.199	2.173	2.146	2.121	2.096	2.073	2.050	2.027	2.005	1.982	1.961	1.940	1.920
42		1.090	0.275	2.172	2.147	2.121	2.097	2.073	2.050	2.027	2.004	1.983	1.962	1.941	1.920
43				1.358	0.268	2.121	2.097	2.073	2.050	2.027	2.005	1.982	1.961	1.940	1.920
44						1.326	0.262	2.073	2.050	2.027	2.004	1.983	1.962	1.941	1.920
45								1.265	0.256	2.027	2.005	1.983	1.961	1.940	1.919
46										1.267	0.251	1.982	1.961	1.941	1.920
47												1.239	0.245	1.940	1.920
48														1.213	0.240

and the Recovery Period is:

the Depreciation Rate is:

If the Recovery Year is:	47.5	48.0	48.5	49.0	49.5	50.0
1	2.763	2.734	2.706	2.679	2.652	2.625
2	3.071	3.040	3.009	2.979	2.950	2.921
3	2.974	2.945	2.916	2.888	2.861	2.834
4	2.880	2.853	2.826	2.800	2.774	2.749
5	2.789	2.763	2.738	2.714	2.690	2.666
6	2.701	2.677	2.654	2.631	2.608	2.586
7	2.615	2.593	2.572	2.550	2.529	2.509
8	2.533	2.512	2.492	2.472	2.453	2.433
9	2.453	2.434	2.415	2.397	2.378	2.360
10	2.375	2.358	2.340	2.323	2.306	2.290
11	2.300	2.284	2.268	2.252	2.236	2.221
12	2.228	2.213	2.198	2.183	2.169	2.154
13	2.157	2.144	2.130	2.116	2.103	2.090
14	2.089	2.077	2.064	2.052	2.039	2.027
15	2.023	2.012	2.000	1.989	1.977	1.966
16	1.959	1.949	1.938	1.928	1.917	1.907
17	1.900	1.888	1.878	1.869	1.859	1.850
18	1.900	1.880	1.861	1.842	1.824	1.806
19	1.900	1.880	1.861	1.842	1.824	1.806
20	1.900	1.880	1.861	1.842	1.824	1.806
21	1.900	1.880	1.861	1.842	1.824	1.806
22	1.900	1.880	1.861	1.842	1.824	1.806
23	1.900	1.880	1.861	1.842	1.824	1.806
24	1.900	1.880	1.861	1.842	1.824	1.806
25	1.900	1.880	1.861	1.842	1.824	1.806
26	1.900	1.880	1.861	1.842	1.824	1.806

and the Recovery Period is:

the Depreciation Rate is:

If the Recovery Year is:	47.5	48.0	48.5	49.0	49.5	50.0
27	1.900	1.880	1.861	1.842	1.824	1.806
28	1.900	1.880	1.861	1.842	1.824	1.805
29	1.900	1.880	1.861	1.842	1.824	1.806
30	1.900	1.880	1.861	1.842	1.824	1.805
31	1.900	1.880	1.861	1.842	1.824	1.806
32	1.900	1.881	1.861	1.842	1.824	1.805
33	1.900	1.880	1.861	1.842	1.823	1.806
34	1.900	1.881	1.861	1.842	1.824	1.805
35	1.900	1.880	1.861	1.842	1.823	1.806
36	1.900	1.881	1.861	1.842	1.824	1.805
37	1.900	1.880	1.861	1.842	1.823	1.805
38	1.900	1.881	1.861	1.842	1.824	1.805
39	1.900	1.880	1.861	1.842	1.823	1.806
40	1.900	1.881	1.861	1.842	1.824	1.805
41	1.900	1.880	1.861	1.842	1.823	1.806
42	1.900	1.881	1.861	1.842	1.824	1.805
43	1.900	1.880	1.861	1.843	1.823	1.806
44	1.901	1.881	1.861	1.842	1.824	1.805
45	1.900	1.880	1.861	1.843	1.823	1.806
46	1.901	1.881	1.862	1.842	1.824	1.805
47	1.901	1.880	1.861	1.843	1.823	1.806
48	1.900	1.881	1.862	1.842	1.824	1.805
49	1.188	1.881	1.861	1.843	1.823	1.806
50		0.235	1.862	1.843	1.824	1.805
51			1.163	0.230	1.140	0.226

TABLE 16 Alternative Minimum Tax (see section 7 of this revenue procedure)

Applicable Depreciation Method: 150 Percent Declining Balance
Switching to Straight Line
Applicable Recovery Periods: 2.5 - 50 years
Applicable Convention: Mid-quarter (property placed in service in second quarter)

and the Recovery Period is:

If the Recovery Year is:	2.5	3.0	3.5	4.0	4.5	5.0	5.5	6.0	6.5	7.0	7.5	8.0	8.5	9.0	9.5
	the Depreciation Rate is:														
1	37.50	31.25	26.79	23.44	20.83	18.75	17.05	15.63	14.42	13.39	12.50	11.72	11.03	10.42	9.87
2	37.50	34.38	31.38	28.71	26.39	24.38	22.62	21.09	19.75	18.56	17.50	16.55	15.70	14.93	14.23
3	25.00	25.00	22.31	20.15	18.36	17.06	16.45	15.82	15.19	14.58	14.00	13.45	12.93	12.44	11.98
4		9.37	19.52	20.15	18.36	16.76	15.26	14.06	13.07	12.22	11.49	10.93	10.65	10.37	10.09
5				7.55	16.06	16.76	15.26	14.06	13.07	12.22	11.49	10.82	10.19	9.64	9.16
6						6.29	13.36	14.06	13.07	12.22	11.48	10.83	10.19	9.65	9.16
7								5.27	11.43	12.23	10.05	10.82	10.19	9.64	9.16
8										4.53		4.06	10.20	9.64	9.17
9													8.92	9.64	9.16
10														3.62	8.02

and the Recovery Period is:

If the Recovery Year is:	10.0	10.5	11.0	11.5	12.0	12.5	13.0	13.5	14.0	14.5	15.0	15.5	16.0	16.5	17.0
	the Depreciation Rate is:														
1	9.38	8.93	8.52	8.15	7.81	7.50	7.21	6.94	6.70	6.47	6.25	6.05	5.86	5.68	5.51
2	13.59	13.01	12.47	11.98	11.52	11.10	10.71	10.34	10.00	9.68	9.38	9.09	8.83	8.57	8.34
3	11.55	11.15	10.77	10.42	10.08	9.77	9.47	9.19	8.92	8.67	8.44	8.21	8.00	7.80	7.60
4	9.82	9.—	9.31	9.06	8.82	8.60	8.38	8.17	7.97	7.78	7.59	7.42	7.25	7.09	6.93
5	8.73	8.34	8.04	7.88	7.72	7.56	7.41	7.26	7.12	6.97	6.83	6.70	6.57	6.44	6.32
6	8.73	8.34	7.98	7.64	7.33	7.04	6.78	6.55	6.35	6.25	6.15	6.05	5.95	5.86	5.76
7	8.73	8.34	7.98	7.64	7.33	7.05	6.79	6.55	6.32	6.10	5.91	5.72	5.55	5.38	5.25
8	8.73	8.34	7.99	7.64	7.33	7.04	6.78	6.54	6.32	6.11	5.90	5.72	5.55	5.39	5.23
9	8.73	8.34	7.98	7.64	7.33	7.05	6.79	6.55	6.32	6.10	5.91	5.72	5.55	5.38	5.23
10	8.73	8.35	7.99	7.63	7.33	7.04	6.79	6.54	6.32	6.11	5.90	5.72	5.55	5.39	5.23
11	3.28	7.30	2.99	7.64	7.32	7.05	6.78	6.55	6.32	6.11	5.91	5.72	5.54	5.38	5.23
12				6.68	2.75	6.16	6.79	6.54	6.32	6.10	5.91	5.72	5.55	5.39	5.24
13							2.54	5.73	6.33	6.11	5.90	5.72	5.55	5.38	5.23
14									2.37	5.34	5.91	5.72	5.54	5.39	5.24
15											2.21	5.00	5.54	5.38	5.23
16													2.08	5.39	5.24
17														4.71	5.24
18															1.96

and the Recovery Period is:

the Depreciation Rate is:

If the Recovery Year is:	17.5	18.0	18.5	19.0	19.5	20.0	20.5	21.0	21.5	22.0	22.5	23.0	23.5	24.0	24.5
1	5.36	5.21	5.07	4.93	4.81	4.688	4.573	4.464	4.360	4.261	4.167	4.076	3.989	3.906	3.827
2	8.11	7.90	7.70	7.51	7.32	7.148	6.982	6.824	6.673	6.528	6.389	6.256	6.128	6.006	5.888
3	7.42	7.24	7.07	6.91	6.76	6.612	6.472	6.337	6.207	6.083	5.963	5.848	5.737	5.631	5.528
4	6.78	6.64	6.50	6.37	6.24	6.116	5.998	5.884	5.774	5.668	5.565	5.467	5.371	5.279	5.189
5	6.20	6.08	5.97	5.86	5.76	5.658	5.559	5.464	5.371	5.281	5.194	5.110	5.028	4.949	4.872
6	5.67	5.58	5.49	5.40	5.32	5.233	5.152	5.073	4.996	4.921	4.848	4.777	4.707	4.639	4.573
7	5.18	5.11	5.04	4.98	4.91	4.841	4.775	4.711	4.648	4.586	4.525	4.465	4.407	4.349	4.293
8	5.08	4.94	4.81	4.69	4.57	4.478	4.426	4.375	4.324	4.273	4.223	4.174	4.126	4.078	4.030
9	5.08	4.94	4.81	4.69	4.57	4.463	4.354	4.252	4.155	4.063	3.975	3.902	3.862	3.823	3.784
10	5.08	4.95	4.81	4.69	4.57	4.463	4.354	4.252	4.155	4.063	3.975	3.890	3.808	3.729	3.655
11	5.08	4.94	4.81	4.69	4.57	4.463	4.354	4.252	4.155	4.062	3.975	3.891	3.808	3.729	3.655
12	5.09	4.95	4.82	4.69	4.58	4.463	4.355	4.252	4.155	4.063	3.975	3.890	3.808	3.729	3.654
13	5.08	4.94	4.81	4.69	4.57	4.463	4.354	4.252	4.155	4.062	3.975	3.891	3.808	3.730	3.655
14	5.09	4.95	4.82	4.69	4.58	4.463	4.355	4.252	4.155	4.063	3.975	3.890	3.808	3.729	3.654
15	5.08	4.94	4.81	4.69	4.57	4.462	4.354	4.252	4.155	4.062	3.975	3.891	3.808	3.730	3.655
16	5.09	4.95	4.82	4.69	4.58	4.463	4.355	4.252	4.155	4.063	3.975	3.890	3.808	3.729	3.654
17	5.08	4.94	4.81	4.69	4.57	4.462	4.354	4.252	4.155	4.062	3.975	3.891	3.808	3.730	3.655
18	4.45	4.95	4.82	4.69	4.58	4.463	4.355	4.252	4.154	4.063	3.975	3.891	3.808	3.729	3.654
19		1.85	4.81	4.69	4.57	4.462	4.354	4.252	4.154	4.062	3.975	3.890	3.808	3.730	3.655
20			4.21	4.69	4.58	4.463	4.355	4.251	4.154	4.063	3.975	3.891	3.808	3.729	3.654
21				1.76	4.57	4.462	4.354	4.251	4.155	4.063	3.974	3.890	3.808	3.730	3.655
22					4.00	4.463	4.355	4.252	4.154	4.062	3.975	3.891	3.808	3.730	3.654
23						1.673	4.354	4.251	4.155	4.063	3.974	3.890	3.809	3.730	3.655
24							3.810	4.252	3.635	4.062	3.478	1.459	3.332	3.729	3.654
25								1.594		1.523				1.399	3.198

and the Recovery Period is:

the Depreciation Rate is:

If the Recovery Year is:	25.0	25.5	26.0	26.5	27.0	27.5	28.0	28.5	29.0	29.5	30.0	30.5	31.0	31.5	32.0
1	3.750	3.676	3.606	3.538	3.472	3.409	3.348	3.289	3.233	3.178	3.125	3.074	3.024	2.976	2.930
2	5.775	5.666	5.561	5.460	5.363	5.269	5.178	5.090	5.005	4.923	4.843	4.767	4.692	4.620	4.550
3	5.429	5.333	5.240	5.151	5.065	4.981	4.900	4.822	4.746	4.673	4.602	4.532	4.465	4.400	4.337
4	5.103	5.019	4.938	4.859	4.783	4.710	4.638	4.568	4.501	4.435	4.371	4.310	4.249	4.191	4.134
5	4.797	4.724	4.653	4.584	4.518	4.453	4.389	4.328	4.268	4.210	4.153	4.098	4.044	3.991	3.940
6	4.509	4.446	4.385	4.325	4.267	4.210	4.154	4.100	4.047	3.996	3.945	3.896	3.848	3.801	3.755
7	4.238	4.184	4.132	4.080	4.030	3.980	3.932	3.884	3.838	3.792	3.748	3.704	3.662	3.620	3.579
8	3.984	3.938	3.893	3.849	3.806	3.763	3.721	3.680	3.639	3.600	3.561	3.522	3.485	3.448	3.411
9	3.745	3.707	3.669	3.631	3.594	3.558	3.522	3.486	3.451	3.417	3.383	3.349	3.316	3.283	3.251
10	3.583	3.514	3.457	3.426	3.395	3.364	3.333	3.303	3.273	3.243	3.213	3.184	3.156	3.127	3.099
11	3.583	3.515	3.448	3.384	3.321	3.262	3.205	3.150	3.103	3.078	3.053	3.028	3.003	2.978	2.954
12	3.583	3.514	3.448	3.383	3.321	3.262	3.205	3.150	3.096	3.044	2.994	2.945	2.898	2.853	2.815
13	3.583	3.515	3.448	3.384	3.321	3.262	3.205	3.150	3.096	3.044	2.994	2.945	2.898	2.853	2.810
14	3.583	3.514	3.448	3.383	3.321	3.262	3.205	3.150	3.096	3.044	2.994	2.945	2.899	2.853	2.810
15	3.583	3.515	3.448	3.384	3.321	3.262	3.205	3.150	3.096	3.044	2.994	2.945	2.898	2.853	2.810
16	3.583	3.514	3.448	3.383	3.321	3.262	3.204	3.150	3.096	3.044	2.994	2.945	2.899	2.853	2.809
17	3.583	3.514	3.448	3.384	3.321	3.262	3.205	3.150	3.097	3.044	2.994	2.945	2.898	2.853	2.810
18	3.583	3.514	3.449	3.383	3.321	3.262	3.204	3.149	3.096	3.044	2.993	2.945	2.899	2.854	2.809
19	3.583	3.515	3.448	3.384	3.321	3.261	3.205	3.150	3.097	3.044	2.994	2.945	2.898	2.853	2.810
20	3.583	3.514	3.449	3.383	3.322	3.262	3.204	3.149	3.096	3.044	2.994	2.945	2.899	2.854	2.809
21	3.583	3.515	3.448	3.384	3.321	3.261	3.205	3.149	3.097	3.044	2.993	2.945	2.898	2.853	2.810
22	3.583	3.514	3.449	3.383	3.322	3.262	3.204	3.150	3.096	3.044	2.993	2.945	2.899	2.854	2.809
23	3.583	3.515	3.448	3.384	3.321	3.261	3.205	3.149	3.097	3.044	2.994	2.945	2.898	2.853	2.810
24	3.582	3.514	3.449	3.383	3.322	3.262	3.204	3.150	3.096	3.044	2.993	2.946	2.899	2.854	2.809
25	3.583	3.515	3.448	3.384	3.321	3.261	3.205	3.149	3.097	3.044	2.994	2.945	2.898	2.853	2.810
26	1.343	3.075	3.449	3.383	3.322	3.262	3.204	3.150	3.096	3.044	2.993	2.946	2.899	2.854	2.809
27			1.293	2.961	3.321	3.261	3.205	3.149	3.097	3.044	2.994	2.945	2.898	2.853	2.810
28					1.246	2.854	3.204	3.150	3.096	3.044	2.993	2.946	2.899	2.854	2.809
29							1.202	2.756	3.097	3.044	2.994	2.945	2.898	2.853	2.810
30									1.161	2.663	2.993	2.946	2.899	2.854	2.809
31											1.123	2.577	2.898	2.853	2.810
32													1.087	2.497	2.809
33															1.054

and the Recovery Period is:

the Depreciation Rate is:

If the Recovery Year is:	32.5	33.0	33.5	34.0	34.5	35.0	35.5	36.0	36.5	37.0	37.5	38.0	38.5	39.0	39.5
1	2.885	2.841	2.799	2.757	2.717	2.679	2.641	2.604	2.568	2.534	2.500	2.467	2.435	2.404	2.373
2	4.482	4.416	4.352	4.290	4.230	4.171	4.114	4.058	4.004	3.951	3.900	3.850	3.801	3.754	3.707
3	4.275	4.216	4.157	4.101	4.046	3.992	3.940	3.889	3.840	3.791	3.744	3.698	3.653	3.609	3.567
4	4.078	4.024	3.971	3.920	3.870	3.821	3.773	3.727	3.682	3.637	3.594	3.552	3.511	3.471	3.431
5	3.890	3.841	3.793	3.747	3.702	3.657	3.614	3.572	3.530	3.490	3.450	3.412	3.374	3.337	3.301
6	3.710	3.666	3.624	3.582	3.541	3.501	3.461	3.423	3.385	3.349	3.312	3.277	3.243	3.209	3.175
7	3.539	3.500	3.461	3.424	3.387	3.351	3.315	3.280	3.246	3.213	3.180	3.148	3.116	3.085	3.055
8	3.376	3.341	3.306	3.273	3.239	3.207	3.175	3.144	3.113	3.083	3.053	3.024	2.995	2.967	2.939
9	3.220	3.189	3.158	3.128	3.099	3.069	3.041	3.013	2.985	2.958	2.931	2.904	2.878	2.852	2.827
10	3.071	3.044	3.017	2.990	2.964	2.938	2.912	2.887	2.862	2.838	2.813	2.790	2.766	2.743	2.720
11	2.930	2.906	2.882	2.858	2.835	2.812	2.789	2.767	2.745	2.723	2.701	2.679	2.658	2.637	2.617
12	2.794	2.773	2.753	2.732	2.712	2.692	2.671	2.651	2.632	2.612	2.593	2.574	2.555	2.536	2.517
13	2.766	2.725	2.685	2.646	2.608	2.576	2.559	2.541	2.524	2.506	2.489	2.472	2.455	2.438	2.422
14	2.767	2.725	2.685	2.646	2.608	2.571	2.535	2.500	2.466	2.433	2.402	2.374	2.359	2.345	2.330
15	2.766	2.725	2.685	2.646	2.608	2.571	2.535	2.500	2.466	2.433	2.402	2.370	2.340	2.310	2.281
16	2.767	2.725	2.685	2.646	2.608	2.571	2.535	2.500	2.466	2.433	2.402	2.370	2.340	2.310	2.281
17	2.767	2.725	2.685	2.646	2.608	2.571	2.535	2.500	2.466	2.433	2.402	2.370	2.340	2.310	2.281
18	2.766	2.725	2.685	2.646	2.608	2.571	2.535	2.500	2.466	2.434	2.402	2.370	2.340	2.310	2.281
19	2.766	2.725	2.685	2.646	2.608	2.571	2.535	2.500	2.466	2.433	2.402	2.370	2.340	2.310	2.281
20	2.766	2.725	2.685	2.646	2.608	2.571	2.535	2.500	2.466	2.434	2.401	2.370	2.340	2.310	2.281
21	2.767	2.725	2.685	2.646	2.608	2.572	2.535	2.500	2.466	2.433	2.402	2.371	2.340	2.310	2.281
22	2.766	2.725	2.684	2.646	2.608	2.571	2.535	2.500	2.466	2.434	2.401	2.370	2.340	2.310	2.281
23	2.767	2.725	2.685	2.645	2.608	2.572	2.535	2.500	2.466	2.433	2.402	2.371	2.340	2.310	2.281
24	2.767	2.725	2.684	2.646	2.608	2.571	2.535	2.500	2.466	2.434	2.401	2.370	2.340	2.310	2.281
25	2.767	2.725	2.685	2.645	2.608	2.572	2.535	2.501	2.466	2.433	2.402	2.371	2.340	2.310	2.281
26	2.766	2.725	2.685	2.646	2.608	2.571	2.536	2.500	2.466	2.434	2.401	2.370	2.339	2.310	2.281
27	2.767	2.725	2.684	2.646	2.608	2.572	2.535	2.501	2.467	2.433	2.402	2.371	2.340	2.310	2.281
28	2.766	2.724	2.685	2.645	2.608	2.571	2.536	2.500	2.466	2.434	2.401	2.370	2.339	2.310	2.281
29	2.767	2.725	2.684	2.646	2.608	2.572	2.535	2.501	2.467	2.433	2.402	2.371	2.340	2.310	2.281
30	2.766	2.724	2.685	2.645	2.608	2.571	2.536	2.500	2.466	2.434	2.401	2.371	2.339	2.310	2.281
31	2.767	2.724	2.684	2.646	2.608	2.572	2.535	2.501	2.467	2.433	2.402	2.370	2.340	2.310	2.281
32	2.766	2.725	2.685	2.645	2.608	2.571	2.536	2.500	2.466	2.434	2.401	2.371	2.339	2.310	2.281
33	2.421	2.724	2.684	2.646	2.608	2.572	2.535	2.501	2.466	2.433	2.402	2.370	2.340	2.310	2.281
34		1.022	2.349	0.992	2.282	2.572	2.535	2.500	2.467	2.434	2.401	2.370	2.339	2.310	2.281
35						0.964	2.219	2.500	2.466	2.433	2.402	2.371	2.340	2.309	2.281
36								0.938	2.158	2.434	2.401	2.370	2.339	2.310	2.281
37										0.913	2.402	2.371	2.340	2.309	2.281
38											2.101	2.370	2.339	2.309	2.281
39												0.889	2.340	2.310	2.280
40													2.047	0.866	1.995

and the Recovery Period is:

the Depreciation Rate is:

If the Recovery Year is:	40.0	40.5	41.0	41.5	42.0	42.5	43.0	43.5	44.0	44.5	45.0	45.5	46.0	46.5	47.0
1	2.344	2.315	2.287	2.259	2.232	2.206	2.180	2.155	2.131	2.107	2.083	2.060	2.038	2.016	1.995
2	3.662	3.618	3.575	3.533	3.492	3.452	3.412	3.374	3.336	3.300	3.264	3.229	3.194	3.161	3.128
3	3.525	3.484	3.444	3.405	3.367	3.330	3.293	3.258	3.223	3.189	3.155	3.122	3.090	3.059	3.028
4	3.393	3.355	3.318	3.282	3.247	3.212	3.178	3.145	3.113	3.081	3.050	3.019	2.990	2.960	2.931
5	3.265	3.231	3.197	3.163	3.131	3.099	3.068	3.037	3.007	2.977	2.948	2.920	2.892	2.865	2.838
6	3.143	3.111	3.080	3.049	3.019	2.990	2.961	2.932	2.904	2.877	2.850	2.824	2.798	2.772	2.747
7	3.025	2.996	2.967	2.939	2.911	2.884	2.857	2.831	2.805	2.780	2.755	2.731	2.706	2.683	2.660
8	2.912	2.885	2.858	2.833	2.807	2.784	2.758	2.734	2.710	2.686	2.663	2.640	2.618	2.596	2.575
9	2.802	2.778	2.754	2.730	2.707	2.684	2.661	2.639	2.617	2.596	2.574	2.553	2.533	2.513	2.492
10	2.697	2.675	2.653	2.630	2.610	2.589	2.569	2.548	2.528	2.508	2.489	2.469	2.450	2.431	2.413
11	2.596	2.576	2.556	2.536	2.517	2.498	2.479	2.460	2.442	2.424	2.406	2.388	2.370	2.353	2.336
12	2.499	2.481	2.463	2.445	2.427	2.410	2.392	2.375	2.359	2.342	2.325	2.309	2.293	2.277	2.261
13	2.405	2.389	2.372	2.356	2.340	2.325	2.309	2.294	2.278	2.263	2.248	2.233	2.218	2.204	2.189
14	2.315	2.300	2.286	2.271	2.257	2.243	2.228	2.214	2.200	2.187	2.173	2.159	2.146	2.133	2.119
15	2.253	2.225	2.202	2.189	2.175	2.163	2.151	2.138	2.125	2.113	2.101	2.088	2.076	2.064	2.052
16	2.253	2.225	2.199	2.172	2.146	2.121	2.097	2.073	2.053	2.042	2.031	2.019	2.008	1.997	1.986
17	2.253	2.225	2.199	2.172	2.146	2.121	2.097	2.073	2.050	2.027	2.005	1.983	1.961	1.941	1.923
18	2.253	2.225	2.199	2.172	2.146	2.121	2.097	2.073	2.050	2.027	2.005	1.983	1.962	1.941	1.920
19	2.253	2.225	2.199	2.172	2.146	2.121	2.097	2.073	2.050	2.027	2.005	1.983	1.961	1.941	1.920
20	2.253	2.225	2.199	2.172	2.146	2.121	2.097	2.073	2.050	2.027	2.005	1.983	1.962	1.941	1.920
21	2.253	2.225	2.199	2.172	2.146	2.121	2.097	2.073	2.050	2.027	2.005	1.983	1.961	1.941	1.920
22	2.253	2.225	2.198	2.172	2.147	2.121	2.097	2.073	2.050	2.027	2.004	1.983	1.961	1.941	1.920
23	2.253	2.225	2.199	2.172	2.146	2.122	2.097	2.073	2.050	2.027	2.005	1.983	1.962	1.940	1.920
24	2.253	2.225	2.199	2.172	2.146	2.121	2.097	2.073	2.050	2.027	2.005	1.983	1.961	1.941	1.920
25	2.253	2.225	2.199	2.172	2.146	2.121	2.097	2.073	2.050	2.027	2.005	1.983	1.962	1.941	1.920
26	2.253	2.225	2.199	2.172	2.147	2.122	2.097	2.074	2.050	2.027	2.005	1.983	1.961	1.941	1.920
27	2.253	2.225	2.198	2.172	2.146	2.122	2.097	2.073	2.050	2.027	2.004	1.983	1.961	1.941	1.920
28	2.253	2.225	2.198	2.172	2.146	2.121	2.097	2.073	2.050	2.027	2.004	1.983	1.962	1.941	1.920
29	2.253	2.225	2.199	2.172	2.146	2.121	2.097	2.074	2.050	2.027	2.004	1.983	1.961	1.940	1.920
30	2.253	2.225	2.198	2.172	2.147	2.122	2.097	2.074	2.050	2.027	2.005	1.983	1.962	1.941	1.920
31	2.252	2.225	2.198	2.172	2.146	2.122	2.097	2.074	2.050	2.027	2.004	1.983	1.961	1.941	1.920
32	2.252	2.226	2.198	2.172	2.147	2.121	2.097	2.073	2.050	2.027	2.005	1.983	1.962	1.941	1.920
33	2.252	2.226	2.199	2.172	2.146	2.122	2.097	2.074	2.050	2.027	2.005	1.983	1.961	1.940	1.920
34	2.252	2.225	2.198	2.172	2.146	2.121	2.097	2.073	2.050	2.027	2.005	1.983	1.961	1.941	1.920
35	2.253	2.225	2.199	2.173	2.147	2.122	2.097	2.074	2.050	2.027	2.004	1.983	1.962	1.940	1.920
36	2.252	2.226	2.198	2.172	2.146	2.121	2.097	2.073	2.050	2.027	2.004	1.983	1.962	1.940	1.921
37	2.253	2.226	2.199	2.173	2.147	2.122	2.097	2.074	2.050	2.027	2.004	1.983	1.961	1.941	1.921
38	2.252	2.225	2.199	2.172	2.146	2.121	2.097	2.073	2.050	2.027	2.005	1.982	1.962	1.940	1.921
39	2.252	2.226	2.198	2.172	2.146	2.122	2.097	2.074	2.050	2.027	2.004	1.983	1.961	1.940	1.920
40	2.252	2.225	2.199	2.173	2.146	2.121	2.097	2.074	2.050	2.027	2.004	1.982	1.962	1.940	1.921
41	2.253	2.226	2.199	2.173	2.147	2.121	2.097	2.073	2.050	2.027	2.005	1.983	1.962	1.941	1.921
42	2.253	2.226	2.198	2.172	2.146	2.122	2.098	2.073	2.050	2.027	2.004	1.982	1.961	1.941	1.921
43	2.252	2.225	2.199	2.173	2.146	2.121	2.097	2.074	2.050	2.027	2.005	1.983	1.961	1.940	1.920
44	2.252	2.226	2.198	2.173	2.146	2.121	2.097	2.073	2.050	2.027	2.004	1.982	1.962	1.941	1.920
45	2.253	2.225	2.198	2.173	2.147	2.122	2.097	2.074	2.050	2.026	2.005	1.983	1.961	1.940	1.921
46	2.252	2.226	2.199	2.172	2.146	2.121	2.097	2.073	2.050	2.027	2.004	1.982	1.962	1.940	1.921
47	2.252	2.225	2.199	2.173	2.146	2.122	2.098	2.074	2.050	1.773	2.005	1.983	1.961	1.941	1.920
48	0.845	1.947	0.824	1.901	0.835	1.856	0.787	1.814	0.769		0.752	1.735	0.736	1.698	0.720

and the Recovery Period is:

the Depreciation Rate is:

If the Recovery Year is:	47.5	48.0	48.5	49.0	49.5	50.0
1	1.974	1.953	1.933	1.913	1.894	1.875
2	3.096	3.064	3.033	3.003	2.973	2.944
3	2.998	2.968	2.939	2.911	2.883	2.855
4	2.903	2.875	2.848	2.822	2.795	2.770
5	2.811	2.786	2.760	2.735	2.711	2.687
6	2.723	2.699	2.675	2.652	2.629	2.606
7	2.637	2.614	2.592	2.570	2.549	2.528
8	2.553	2.533	2.512	2.492	2.472	2.452
9	2.473	2.453	2.434	2.415	2.397	2.378
10	2.395	2.377	2.359	2.341	2.324	2.307
11	2.319	2.302	2.286	2.270	2.254	2.238
12	2.246	2.230	2.215	2.200	2.185	2.171
13	2.175	2.161	2.147	2.133	2.119	2.106
14	2.106	2.093	2.080	2.068	2.055	2.042
15	2.040	2.028	2.016	2.004	1.993	1.981
16	1.975	1.964	1.954	1.943	1.932	1.922
17	1.913	1.903	1.893	1.884	1.874	1.864
18	1.900	1.880	1.861	1.842	1.824	1.808
19	1.900	1.880	1.861	1.842	1.824	1.806
20	1.900	1.880	1.861	1.842	1.824	1.806
21	1.900	1.880	1.861	1.842	1.824	1.806
22	1.900	1.880	1.861	1.842	1.824	1.806
23	1.900	1.880	1.861	1.842	1.824	1.806
24	1.900	1.880	1.861	1.842	1.824	1.806
25	1.900	1.880	1.861	1.842	1.824	1.806
26	1.900	1.881	1.861	1.842	1.824	1.806
27	1.900	1.880	1.861	1.842	1.824	1.806
28	1.900	1.881	1.861	1.842	1.824	1.806
29	1.900	1.880	1.861	1.842	1.824	1.806
30	1.900	1.881	1.861	1.843	1.824	1.806
31	1.900	1.880	1.861	1.842	1.824	1.806
32	1.900	1.881	1.861	1.843	1.824	1.806
33	1.900	1.880	1.861	1.842	1.824	1.806
34	1.900	1.881	1.861	1.843	1.824	1.806
35	1.900	1.880	1.861	1.842	1.824	1.806
36	1.900	1.881	1.861	1.843	1.824	1.806
37	1.900	1.880	1.861	1.842	1.824	1.806
38	1.900	1.881	1.861	1.843	1.824	1.806
39	1.900	1.880	1.861	1.842	1.824	1.806
40	1.900	1.881	1.861	1.843	1.824	1.806
41	1.900	1.880	1.862	1.842	1.824	1.806
42	1.900	1.881	1.861	1.843	1.824	1.806
43	1.900	1.880	1.862	1.842	1.824	1.806
44	1.900	1.881	1.861	1.843	1.824	1.806
45	1.900	1.880	1.862	1.842	1.824	1.805
46	1.900	1.881	1.861	1.843	1.824	1.806
47	1.900	1.880	1.862	1.842	1.824	1.805
48	1.900	1.881	1.861	1.843	1.823	1.806
49	1.663	1.880	1.861	1.842	1.824	1.805
50		0.705	1.629	1.842	1.823	1.806
51				0.691	1.596	0.677

TABLE 17   Alternative Minimum Tax (see section 7 of this revenue procedure)
Applicable Depreciation Method: 150 Percent Declining Balance Switching to Straight Line
Applicable Recovery Periods: 2.5 – 50 years
Applicable Convention: Mid-quarter (property placed in service in third quarter)

and the Recovery Period is:

If the Recovery Year is:	2.5	3.0	3.5	4.0	4.5	5.0	5.5	6.0	6.5	7.0	7.5	8.0	8.5	9.0	9.5
				the Depreciation Rate is:											
1	22.50	18.75	16.07	14.06	12.50	11.25	10.23	9.38	8.65	8.04	7.50	7.03	6.62	6.25	5.92
2	46.50	40.63	35.97	32.23	29.17	26.63	24.48	22.65	21.08	19.71	18.50	17.43	16.48	15.63	14.85
3	27.56	25.00	22.57	20.46	19.44	18.64	17.81	16.99	16.22	15.48	14.80	14.16	13.57	13.02	12.51
4	3.44	15.62	22.57	20.46	18.30	16.56	15.19	14.05	13.10	12.28	11.84	11.51	11.18	10.85	10.53
5		2.82	2.82	12.79	18.30	16.57	15.20	14.05	13.10	12.27	11.48	10.78	10.18	9.64	9.17
6					2.29	10.35	15.19	14.05	13.11	12.28	11.48	10.78	10.17	9.65	9.18
7							1.90	8.79	13.10	12.28	11.48	10.78	10.18	9.64	9.17
8									1.64	7.67	11.48	10.79	10.17	9.65	9.17
9											1.44	6.74	10.18	9.64	9.18
10													1.27	6.03	9.17
11															1.15

and the Recovery Period is:

If the Recovery Year is:	10.0	10.5	11.0	11.5	12.0	12.5	13.0	13.5	14.0	14.5	15.0	15.5	16.0	16.5	17.0
				the Depreciation Rate is:											
1	5.63	5.36	5.11	4.89	4.69	4.50	4.33	4.17	4.02	3.88	3.75	3.63	3.52	3.41	3.31
2	14.16	13.52	12.94	12.41	11.91	11.46	11.04	10.65	10.28	9.94	9.63	9.33	9.05	8.78	8.53
3	12.03	11.59	11.18	10.79	10.43	10.08	9.77	9.46	9.18	8.92	8.66	8.42	8.20	7.98	7.78
4	10.23	9.93	9.65	9.38	9.12	8.88	8.64	8.41	8.20	7.99	7.80	7.61	7.43	7.26	7.09
5	8.75	8.51	8.33	8.16	7.98	7.81	7.64	7.48	7.32	7.17	7.02	6.87	6.73	6.60	6.47
6	8.75	8.34	7.97	7.63	7.33	7.05	6.79	6.65	6.54	6.42	6.31	6.21	6.10	6.00	5.90
7	8.75	8.34	7.97	7.63	7.33	7.05	6.79	6.55	6.31	6.10	5.90	5.72	5.55	5.45	5.38
8	8.74	8.34	7.97	7.63	7.33	7.05	6.79	6.54	6.32	6.10	5.90	5.72	5.55	5.38	5.23
9	8.75	8.34	7.97	7.63	7.33	7.05	6.79	6.55	6.31	6.10	5.91	5.72	5.55	5.39	5.23
10	8.74	8.35	7.96	7.63	7.33	7.05	6.79	6.55	6.32	6.10	5.90	5.72	5.55	5.38	5.23
11	5.47	1.04	4.98	7.64	7.32	7.04	6.80	6.54	6.31	6.10	5.91	5.72	5.55	5.39	5.22
12				0.95	4.58	7.05	6.79	6.55	6.32	6.10	5.90	5.72	5.55	5.38	5.23
13						0.88	4.25	6.54	6.31	6.11	5.91	5.72	5.55	5.39	5.22
14								0.82	3.95	6.10	5.91	5.72	5.55	5.38	5.23
15										0.76	3.69	5.72	5.55	5.39	5.23
16												0.72	3.47	5.39	5.22
17														0.67	5.22
18															1.27

and the Recovery Period is:

the Depreciation Rate is:

If the Recovery Year is:	17.5	18.0	18.5	19.0	19.5	20.0	20.5	21.0	21.5	22.0	22.5	23.0	23.5	24.0	24.5
1	3.21	3.13	3.04	2.96	2.88	2.813	2.744	2.679	2.616	2.557	2.500	2.446	2.394	2.344	2.296
2	8.30	8.07	7.86	7.66	7.47	7.289	7.116	6.952	6.794	6.644	6.500	6.362	6.230	6.104	5.982
3	7.58	7.40	7.22	7.06	6.90	6.742	6.596	6.455	6.320	6.191	6.067	5.947	5.833	5.722	5.616
4	6.94	6.78	6.64	6.50	6.37	6.237	6.113	5.994	5.879	5.769	5.662	5.559	5.460	5.364	5.272
5	6.34	6.22	6.10	5.99	5.88	5.769	5.666	5.566	5.469	5.375	5.285	5.197	5.112	5.029	4.949
6	5.80	5.70	5.61	5.51	5.42	5.336	5.251	5.168	5.088	5.009	4.932	4.858	4.785	4.715	4.646
7	5.30	5.23	5.15	5.08	5.01	4.936	4.867	4.799	4.733	4.667	4.604	4.541	4.480	4.420	4.362
8	5.08	4.94	4.81	4.69	4.62	4.566	4.511	4.456	4.402	4.349	4.297	4.245	4.194	4.144	4.095
9	5.08	4.94	4.82	4.69	4.57	4.460	4.353	4.252	4.156	4.064	4.010	3.968	3.926	3.885	3.844
10	5.08	4.94	4.81	4.69	4.57	4.460	4.353	4.252	4.156	4.064	3.975	3.889	3.807	3.729	3.655
11	5.08	4.94	4.82	4.69	4.57	4.460	4.353	4.252	4.156	4.064	3.975	3.889	3.807	3.730	3.655
12	5.08	4.95	4.81	4.69	4.57	4.460	4.353	4.252	4.156	4.064	3.975	3.889	3.807	3.729	3.655
13	5.08	4.94	4.82	4.69	4.58	4.461	4.353	4.252	4.156	4.064	3.975	3.889	3.807	3.730	3.655
14	5.08	4.95	4.81	4.70	4.57	4.460	4.353	4.252	4.156	4.064	3.975	3.889	3.808	3.729	3.655
15	5.08	4.94	4.82	4.69	4.58	4.461	4.353	4.252	4.155	4.064	3.975	3.889	3.807	3.730	3.655
16	5.08	4.95	4.81	4.69	4.57	4.460	4.353	4.252	4.156	4.064	3.975	3.889	3.808	3.729	3.655
17	5.08	4.94	4.82	4.70	4.58	4.461	4.354	4.252	4.156	4.064	3.974	3.889	3.807	3.730	3.655
18	5.09	4.94	4.81	4.69	4.57	4.460	4.353	4.251	4.155	4.064	3.975	3.889	3.808	3.729	3.655
19	5.08	4.95	4.82	4.70	4.57	4.461	4.354	4.252	4.155	4.065	3.974	3.889	3.807	3.730	3.655
20	0.64	3.09	0.60	2.93	4.58	4.460	4.353	4.251	4.156	4.064	3.975	3.889	3.808	3.729	3.655
21					0.57	2.788	4.354	4.252	4.155	4.065	3.974	3.889	3.807	3.730	3.655
22							0.544	2.657	4.156	4.064	3.975	3.889	3.808	3.729	3.655
23									0.519	4.065	3.974	3.889	3.807	3.730	3.655
24										2.540	0.497	2.431	0.476	2.331	3.656
25															3.655
26															0.457

and the Recovery Period is:

the Depreciation Rate is:

If the Recovery Year is:	25.0	25.5	26.0	26.5	27.0	27.5	28.0	28.5	29.0	29.5	30.0	30.5	31.0	31.5	32.0
1	2.250	2.206	2.153	2.123	2.083	2.045	2.009	1.974	1.940	1.907	1.875	1.844	1.815	1.786	1.758
2	5.865	5.753	5.644	5.540	5.440	5.343	5.250	5.159	5.072	4.988	4.906	4.827	4.751	4.677	4.605
3	5.513	5.414	5.319	5.227	5.138	5.052	4.968	4.888	4.810	4.734	4.661	4.590	4.521	4.454	4.389
4	5.182	5.096	5.012	4.931	4.852	4.776	4.702	4.630	4.561	4.493	4.428	4.364	4.302	4.242	4.184
5	4.871	4.796	4.723	4.652	4.583	4.515	4.450	4.387	4.325	4.265	4.207	4.150	4.094	4.040	3.987
6	4.579	4.514	4.450	4.388	4.328	4.269	4.212	4.156	4.101	4.048	3.996	3.945	3.896	3.848	3.800
7	4.304	4.248	4.194	4.140	4.088	4.036	3.986	3.937	3.889	3.842	3.796	3.751	3.707	3.664	3.622
8	4.046	3.998	3.952	3.906	3.860	3.816	3.773	3.730	3.688	3.647	3.607	3.567	3.528	3.490	3.453
9	3.803	3.763	3.724	3.685	3.646	3.608	3.571	3.534	3.497	3.461	3.426	3.392	3.357	3.324	3.291
10	3.584	3.542	3.509	3.476	3.443	3.411	3.379	3.348	3.316	3.286	3.255	3.225	3.195	3.165	3.136
11	3.584	3.514	3.447	3.383	3.321	3.262	3.205	3.171	3.145	3.118	3.092	3.066	3.040	3.015	2.989
12	3.584	3.514	3.447	3.383	3.321	3.262	3.205	3.150	3.096	3.044	2.994	2.946	2.899	2.871	2.849
13	3.584	3.514	3.447	3.383	3.321	3.262	3.205	3.150	3.096	3.044	2.994	2.946	2.899	2.853	2.809
14	3.584	3.514	3.447	3.383	3.321	3.262	3.205	3.149	3.096	3.044	2.994	2.945	2.899	2.853	2.809
15	3.584	3.514	3.447	3.383	3.321	3.262	3.205	3.150	3.096	3.044	2.994	2.946	2.899	2.853	2.809
16	3.584	3.515	3.447	3.383	3.322	3.262	3.206	3.150	3.096	3.044	2.994	2.945	2.899	2.853	2.809
17	3.584	3.514	3.447	3.383	3.321	3.262	3.205	3.149	3.096	3.044	2.994	2.946	2.899	2.853	2.809
18	3.584	3.515	3.447	3.383	3.322	3.262	3.205	3.150	3.095	3.044	2.994	2.945	2.899	2.853	2.809
19	3.584	3.514	3.447	3.383	3.321	3.263	3.206	3.149	3.096	3.044	2.993	2.946	2.899	2.854	2.809
20	3.584	3.515	3.447	3.383	3.322	3.262	3.205	3.150	3.095	3.044	2.994	2.945	2.899	2.853	2.809
21	3.585	3.514	3.448	3.383	3.321	3.263	3.206	3.149	3.096	3.043	2.993	2.946	2.899	2.853	2.809
22	3.584	3.515	3.447	3.383	3.322	3.262	3.205	3.150	3.095	3.044	2.994	2.945	2.899	2.854	2.809
23	3.585	3.514	3.448	3.383	3.321	3.262	3.206	3.149	3.096	3.043	2.993	2.946	2.899	2.853	2.809
24	3.584	3.515	3.448	3.382	3.322	3.262	3.205	3.150	3.096	3.044	2.994	2.945	2.899	2.853	2.809
25	3.585	3.514	3.447	3.383	3.321	3.261	3.206	3.149	3.095	3.043	2.993	2.946	2.899	2.853	2.809
26	2.240	3.515	3.447	3.382	3.322	3.262	3.205	3.150	3.096	3.044	2.994	2.945	2.899	2.853	2.809
27		0.439	2.155	3.383	3.321	3.262	3.206	3.149	3.095	3.043	2.993	2.946	2.899	2.854	2.809
28				0.423	2.076	3.262	3.205	3.150	3.096	3.044	2.993	2.945	2.899	2.854	2.809
29						0.408	2.003	3.149	3.095	3.043	2.994	2.946	2.900	2.853	2.809
30								0.394	1.935	3.044	2.993	2.945	2.899	2.853	2.809
31										0.380	1.871	2.946	2.900	2.854	2.809
32												0.368	1.812	2.853	2.810
33														0.357	1.756

and the Recovery Period is:

the Depreciation Rate is:

If the Recovery Year is:	32.5	33.0	33.5	34.0	34.5	35.0	35.5	36.0	36.5	37.0	37.5	38.0	38.5	39.0	39.5
1	1.731	1.705	1.679	1.654	1.630	1.607	1.585	1.563	1.541	1.520	1.500	1.480	1.461	1.442	1.424
2	4.535	4.468	4.402	4.339	4.277	4.217	4.158	4.102	4.046	3.992	3.940	3.889	3.839	3.791	3.743
3	4.326	4.265	4.205	4.147	4.091	4.036	3.983	3.931	3.880	3.831	3.782	3.735	3.690	3.645	3.601
4	4.127	4.071	4.017	3.964	3.913	3.863	3.814	3.767	3.721	3.675	3.631	3.588	3.546	3.505	3.465
5	3.936	3.886	3.837	3.790	3.743	3.698	3.653	3.610	3.568	3.526	3.486	3.446	3.408	3.370	3.333
6	3.754	3.709	3.665	3.622	3.580	3.539	3.499	3.459	3.421	3.383	3.346	3.310	3.275	3.240	3.206
7	3.581	3.541	3.501	3.463	3.425	3.387	3.351	3.315	3.280	3.246	3.213	3.180	3.147	3.116	3.085
8	3.416	3.380	3.345	3.310	3.276	3.242	3.209	3.177	3.146	3.115	3.084	3.054	3.025	2.996	2.967
9	3.258	3.226	3.195	3.164	3.133	3.103	3.074	3.045	3.016	2.988	2.961	2.934	2.907	2.881	2.855
10	3.108	3.080	3.052	3.024	2.997	2.970	2.944	2.918	2.892	2.867	2.842	2.818	2.794	2.770	2.746
11	2.964	2.940	2.915	2.891	2.867	2.843	2.820	2.796	2.774	2.751	2.729	2.707	2.685	2.663	2.642
12	2.828	2.806	2.784	2.763	2.742	2.721	2.700	2.680	2.660	2.639	2.619	2.600	2.580	2.561	2.542
13	2.766	2.725	2.685	2.646	2.623	2.605	2.586	2.568	2.550	2.532	2.515	2.497	2.480	2.462	2.445
14	2.766	2.725	2.685	2.646	2.608	2.571	2.535	2.500	2.467	2.434	2.414	2.399	2.383	2.368	2.352
15	2.766	2.725	2.685	2.646	2.608	2.571	2.535	2.500	2.466	2.434	2.402	2.370	2.340	2.310	2.281
16	2.766	2.725	2.685	2.646	2.608	2.571	2.535	2.500	2.467	2.434	2.402	2.370	2.339	2.310	2.281
17	2.766	2.725	2.685	2.646	2.608	2.571	2.535	2.500	2.466	2.434	2.402	2.370	2.340	2.310	2.281
18	2.766	2.725	2.685	2.646	2.608	2.571	2.535	2.500	2.467	2.434	2.402	2.370	2.339	2.310	2.281
19	2.766	2.725	2.685	2.646	2.608	2.571	2.535	2.500	2.466	2.434	2.402	2.370	2.340	2.310	2.281
20	2.766	2.725	2.685	2.646	2.608	2.571	2.535	2.500	2.467	2.434	2.401	2.370	2.339	2.310	2.281
21	2.766	2.725	2.685	2.646	2.608	2.571	2.535	2.500	2.466	2.434	2.402	2.370	2.340	2.310	2.281
22	2.766	2.725	2.685	2.646	2.608	2.571	2.535	2.500	2.467	2.434	2.402	2.370	2.340	2.310	2.281
23	2.766	2.725	2.685	2.646	2.608	2.571	2.535	2.500	2.466	2.434	2.401	2.370	2.339	2.310	2.281
24	2.766	2.725	2.685	2.646	2.608	2.571	2.535	2.500	2.467	2.434	2.402	2.370	2.340	2.310	2.281
25	2.766	2.725	2.685	2.646	2.608	2.571	2.535	2.500	2.467	2.434	2.401	2.370	2.340	2.310	2.281
26	2.766	2.725	2.685	2.646	2.608	2.571	2.535	2.500	2.466	2.434	2.402	2.370	2.339	2.310	2.281
27	2.767	2.724	2.685	2.646	2.608	2.571	2.535	2.501	2.467	2.434	2.401	2.370	2.340	2.310	2.281
28	2.767	2.725	2.685	2.646	2.608	2.571	2.535	2.500	2.466	2.434	2.402	2.370	2.339	2.310	2.281
29	2.766	2.724	2.685	2.646	2.608	2.571	2.535	2.500	2.467	2.434	2.401	2.370	2.340	2.310	2.281
30	2.767	2.725	2.685	2.647	2.608	2.571	2.535	2.500	2.466	2.434	2.402	2.370	2.339	2.310	2.281
31	2.766	2.724	2.685	2.646	2.608	2.571	2.535	2.501	2.467	2.434	2.401	2.370	2.340	2.310	2.281
32	2.766	2.725	2.684	2.647	2.608	2.571	2.535	2.500	2.467	2.434	2.402	2.370	2.339	2.310	2.281
33	2.766	2.724	2.685	2.646	2.608	2.571	2.536	2.500	2.466	2.434	2.401	2.370	2.340	2.310	2.281
34	2.766	2.725	2.684	2.647	2.608	2.571	2.535	2.501	2.467	2.434	2.402	2.370	2.339	2.310	2.281
35	2.766	1.703	2.685	2.646	2.608	2.571	2.535	2.500	2.466	2.434	2.401	2.370	2.340	2.310	2.281
36	2.766		2.684	2.647	2.608	2.571	2.535	2.500	2.467	2.433	2.402	2.370	2.339	2.310	2.282
37	2.767		2.685	2.646	2.608	2.571	2.536	2.501	2.467	2.434	2.402	2.371	2.340	2.310	2.282
38	2.766		0.336	2.647	2.608	2.571	2.535	2.500	2.466	2.433	2.402	2.370	2.340	2.310	2.281
39	2.766			2.647	2.609	2.571	0.317	2.500	2.467	1.521	0.300	1.482	0.292	2.309	2.282
40	2.766			1.654		1.607		2.500	0.308					1.443	2.281
41	0.346				0.326			1.563							0.285

and the Recovery Period is:

the Depreciation Rate is:

If the Recovery Year is:	40.0	40.5	41.0	41.5	42.0	42.5	43.0	43.5	44.0	44.5	45.0	45.5	46.0	46.5	47.0
1	1.406	1.389	1.372	1.355	1.339	1.324	1.308	1.293	1.278	1.264	1.250	1.236	1.223	1.210	1.197
2	3.697	3.652	3.608	3.565	3.524	3.483	3.443	3.404	3.366	3.328	3.292	3.256	3.221	3.187	3.153
3	3.559	3.517	3.476	3.437	3.398	3.360	3.323	3.286	3.251	3.216	3.182	3.149	3.116	3.084	3.053
4	3.425	3.387	3.349	3.312	3.276	3.241	3.207	3.173	3.140	3.108	3.076	3.045	3.014	2.984	2.955
5	3.297	3.261	3.227	3.193	3.159	3.127	3.095	3.064	3.033	3.003	2.973	2.944	2.916	2.888	2.861
6	3.173	3.141	3.109	3.077	3.047	3.016	2.987	2.958	2.929	2.902	2.874	2.847	2.821	2.795	2.770
7	3.054	3.024	2.995	2.966	2.938	2.910	2.883	2.856	2.830	2.804	2.778	2.754	2.729	2.705	2.681
8	2.940	2.912	2.885	2.859	2.833	2.807	2.782	2.757	2.733	2.709	2.686	2.663	2.640	2.618	2.596
9	2.829	2.804	2.780	2.756	2.732	2.708	2.685	2.662	2.640	2.618	2.596	2.575	2.554	2.533	2.513
10	2.723	2.700	2.678	2.656	2.634	2.613	2.591	2.571	2.550	2.530	2.510	2.490	2.471	2.451	2.433
11	2.621	2.600	2.580	2.560	2.540	2.520	2.501	2.482	2.463	2.444	2.426	2.408	2.390	2.372	2.355
12	2.523	2.504	2.486	2.467	2.449	2.431	2.414	2.396	2.379	2.362	2.345	2.329	2.312	2.296	2.280
13	2.428	2.411	2.395	2.378	2.362	2.346	2.330	2.314	2.298	2.282	2.267	2.252	2.237	2.222	2.207
14	2.337	2.322	2.307	2.292	2.277	2.263	2.248	2.234	2.220	2.206	2.192	2.178	2.164	2.150	2.137
15	2.253	2.236	2.223	2.209	2.196	2.183	2.170	2.157	2.144	2.131	2.118	2.106	2.093	2.081	2.068
16	2.253	2.225	2.198	2.172	2.146	2.122	2.097	2.083	2.071	2.059	2.048	2.036	2.025	2.014	2.002
17	2.253	2.225	2.198	2.172	2.146	2.122	2.097	2.073	2.050	2.027	2.005	1.983	1.962	1.949	1.938
18	2.253	2.225	2.198	2.172	2.146	2.121	2.097	2.073	2.050	2.027	2.005	1.983	1.962	1.941	1.920
19	2.253	2.225	2.198	2.172	2.146	2.122	2.097	2.073	2.050	2.027	2.005	1.983	1.962	1.941	1.920
20	2.253	2.225	2.198	2.172	2.147	2.121	2.097	2.073	2.050	2.027	2.005	1.983	1.962	1.941	1.920
21	2.253	2.225	2.198	2.172	2.146	2.121	2.097	2.073	2.050	2.027	2.005	1.983	1.962	1.941	1.920
22	2.253	2.225	2.198	2.172	2.147	2.122	2.097	2.073	2.050	2.027	2.005	1.983	1.962	1.941	1.920
23	2.253	2.226	2.198	2.172	2.146	2.122	2.097	2.073	2.050	2.027	2.005	1.983	1.962	1.941	1.920
24	2.253	2.225	2.198	2.172	2.147	2.121	2.097	2.073	2.050	2.027	2.005	1.983	1.962	1.941	1.920
25	2.253	2.226	2.198	2.172	2.146	2.121	2.097	2.073	2.050	2.027	2.005	1.983	1.962	1.941	1.920
26	2.253	2.225	2.198	2.172	2.147	2.122	2.097	2.073	2.050	2.027	2.005	1.983	1.961	1.941	1.920
27	2.253	2.226	2.199	2.172	2.146	2.121	2.097	2.073	2.050	2.027	2.004	1.983	1.962	1.941	1.920
28	2.253	2.225	2.198	2.172	2.146	2.122	2.097	2.073	2.050	2.027	2.005	1.983	1.962	1.940	1.920
29	2.253	2.226	2.199	2.172	2.147	2.121	2.097	2.073	2.050	2.027	2.004	1.983	1.961	1.941	1.920
30	2.253	2.225	2.198	2.172	2.146	2.121	2.097	2.073	2.050	2.027	2.004	1.983	1.961	1.941	1.920
31	2.253	2.226	2.199	2.172	2.147	2.122	2.097	2.073	2.050	2.027	2.005	1.983	1.961	1.941	1.920
32	2.253	2.225	2.198	2.172	2.146	2.122	2.097	2.073	2.050	2.027	2.004	1.983	1.962	1.941	1.920
33	2.253	2.226	2.199	2.172	2.147	2.121	2.097	2.073	2.050	2.027	2.004	1.983	1.961	1.941	1.920
34	2.253	2.225	2.198	2.172	2.146	2.122	2.098	2.074	2.050	2.027	2.005	1.983	1.962	1.940	1.920
35	2.253	2.226	2.199	2.172	2.147	2.121	2.097	2.073	2.050	2.027	2.004	1.983	1.962	1.940	1.920
36	2.253	2.225	2.198	2.172	2.146	2.121	2.097	2.073	2.049	2.027	2.004	1.983	1.962	1.941	1.920
37	2.253	2.225	2.198	2.172	2.147	2.122	2.098	2.074	2.050	2.027	2.005	1.982	1.961	1.941	1.920
38	2.253	2.226	2.199	2.172	2.146	2.121	2.097	2.073	2.049	2.027	2.004	1.983	1.962	1.941	1.920
39	2.254	2.225	2.199	2.172	2.147	2.122	2.097	2.074	2.049	2.027	2.004	1.982	1.961	1.940	1.920
40	2.254	2.226	2.198	2.172	2.146	2.121	2.093	2.074	2.050	2.027	2.005	1.983	1.961	1.940	1.920
41	2.254	2.225	2.199	2.172	2.147	2.121	2.097	2.073	2.049	2.027	2.004	1.983	1.962	1.941	1.920
42	2.254	2.225	2.198	2.173	2.146	2.122	2.093	2.074	2.049	2.026	2.004	1.983	1.962	1.941	1.920
43	2.253	2.226	2.199	2.172	2.147	2.121	2.097	2.073	2.050	2.027	2.004	1.983	1.961	1.941	1.920
44	2.253	2.225	2.198	2.173	2.146	2.122	2.093	2.074	2.049	2.026	2.005	1.982	1.961	1.941	1.920
45	2.254	2.225	2.199	2.172	2.147	2.121	2.097	2.073	2.050	2.027	2.004	1.983	1.962	1.940	1.920
46	2.253	2.225	2.198	2.173	2.146	2.121	2.093	2.074	2.050	2.026	2.004	1.982	1.961	1.940	1.920
47	2.254	2.225	2.199	2.172	2.147	2.122	2.097	2.074	2.049	2.027	2.005	1.982	1.961	1.941	1.921
48	1.408	0.278	1.374	0.272	1.342	0.265	1.311	0.259	1.281	0.253	1.253	0.248	1.226	0.243	1.200

and the Recovery Period is:

the Depreciation Rate is:

If the Recovery Year is:	47.5	48.0	48.5	49.0	49.5	50.0
1	1.184	1.172	1.160	1.148	1.136	1.125
2	3.121	3.088	3.057	3.026	2.996	2.966
3	3.022	2.992	2.962	2.933	2.905	2.877
4	2.927	2.898	2.871	2.844	2.817	2.791
5	2.834	2.808	2.782	2.757	2.732	2.707
6	2.745	2.720	2.696	2.672	2.649	2.626
7	2.658	2.635	2.613	2.590	2.569	2.547
8	2.574	2.553	2.532	2.511	2.491	2.471
9	2.493	2.473	2.453	2.434	2.415	2.397
10	2.414	2.396	2.378	2.360	2.342	2.325
11	2.338	2.321	2.304	2.288	2.271	2.255
12	2.264	2.248	2.233	2.217	2.202	2.187
13	2.192	2.178	2.164	2.150	2.136	2.122
14	2.123	2.110	2.097	2.084	2.071	2.058
15	2.056	2.044	2.032	2.020	2.008	1.996
16	1.991	1.980	1.969	1.958	1.947	1.937
17	1.928	1.918	1.908	1.898	1.888	1.878
18	1.900	1.880	1.861	1.842	1.831	1.822
19	1.900	1.880	1.861	1.842	1.824	1.806
20	1.900	1.880	1.861	1.842	1.824	1.806
21	1.900	1.880	1.861	1.842	1.824	1.806
22	1.900	1.880	1.861	1.843	1.824	1.806
23	1.900	1.880	1.861	1.842	1.824	1.806
24	1.900	1.880	1.861	1.843	1.824	1.806
25	1.900	1.880	1.861	1.842	1.824	1.806
26	1.900	1.880	1.861	1.843	1.824	1.806
27	1.900	1.880	1.861	1.842	1.824	1.806
28	1.900	1.881	1.861	1.843	1.824	1.806
29	1.900	1.880	1.861	1.842	1.824	1.806
30	1.900	1.881	1.861	1.843	1.824	1.806
31	1.900	1.880	1.861	1.842	1.824	1.806
32	1.900	1.881	1.861	1.843	1.824	1.806
33	1.900	1.880	1.861	1.842	1.824	1.806
34	1.900	1.881	1.861	1.843	1.824	1.806
35	1.900	1.880	1.861	1.842	1.824	1.806
36	1.900	1.881	1.861	1.843	1.824	1.806
37	1.900	1.880	1.861	1.842	1.824	1.805
38	1.900	1.881	1.861	1.843	1.824	1.806
39	1.900	1.880	1.861	1.842	1.824	1.805
40	1.900	1.881	1.861	1.843	1.824	1.806
41	1.900	1.880	1.861	1.842	1.824	1.805
42	1.900	1.881	1.862	1.843	1.824	1.806
43	1.900	1.880	1.861	1.842	1.824	1.805
44	1.900	1.881	1.862	1.843	1.824	1.806
45	1.900	1.880	1.861	1.842	1.824	1.805
46	1.900	1.881	1.862	1.843	1.824	1.806
47	1.899	1.880	1.861	1.842	1.824	1.805
48	1.900	1.881	1.862	1.843	1.823	1.806
49	0.237	1.880	1.861	1.843	1.824	1.805
50		1.175	0.233	1.152	1.823	1.806
51					0.228	1.128

TABLE 18   Alternative Minimum Tax (see section 7 of this revenue procedure)
Applicable Depreciation Method: 150 Percent Declining Balance Switching to Straight Line
Applicable Recovery Periods: 2.5 - 50 years
Applicable Convention: Mid-quarter (property placed in service in fourth quarter)

and the Recovery Period is:

the Depreciation Rate is:

If the Recovery Year is:	2.5	3.0	3.5	4.0	4.5	5.0	5.5	6.0	6.5	7.0	7.5	8.0	8.5	9.0	9.5
1	7.50	6.25	5.36	4.69	4.17	3.75	3.41	3.13	2.88	2.68	2.50	2.34	2.21	2.08	1.97
2	55.50	46.88	40.56	35.74	31.94	28.88	26.34	24.22	22.41	20.85	19.50	18.31	17.26	16.32	15.48
3	26.91	25.00	23.18	22.34	21.30	20.21	19.16	18.16	17.24	16.39	15.60	14.88	14.21	13.60	13.03
4	10.09	21.87	22.47	19.85	17.93	16.40	15.14	14.06	13.26	12.87	12.48	12.09	11.70	11.33	10.98
5		8.43	8.43	17.37	17.93	16.41	15.14	14.06	13.10	12.18	11.41	10.74	10.16	9.65	9.24
6					6.73	14.35	15.13	14.06	13.10	12.18	11.41	10.75	10.16	9.64	9.17
7							5.68	12.31	13.10	12.19	11.41	10.74	10.16	9.65	9.17
8									4.91	10.56	11.41	10.75	10.17	9.64	9.17
9											4.28	9.40	3.81	8.44	9.18
10															3.44
11															

and the Recovery Period is:

the Depreciation Rate is:

If the Recovery Year is:	10.0	10.5	11.0	11.5	12.0	12.5	13.0	13.5	14.0	14.5	15.0	15.5	16.0	16.5	17.0
1	1.88	1.79	1.70	1.63	1.56	1.50	1.44	1.39	1.34	1.29	1.25	1.21	1.17	1.14	1.10
2	14.72	14.03	13.40	12.83	12.31	11.82	11.37	10.96	10.57	10.21	9.88	9.56	9.27	8.99	8.73
3	12.51	12.03	11.58	11.16	10.77	10.40	10.06	9.74	9.44	9.16	8.89	8.64	8.40	8.17	7.96
4	10.63	10.31	10.00	9.70	9.42	9.15	8.90	8.66	8.43	8.21	8.00	7.80	7.61	7.43	7.25
5	9.04	8.83	8.63	8.44	8.24	8.06	7.87	7.69	7.52	7.36	7.20	7.04	6.90	6.75	6.61
6	8.72	8.32	7.95	7.63	7.33	7.09	6.96	6.84	6.72	6.60	6.48	6.36	6.25	6.14	6.03
7	8.72	8.31	7.96	7.63	7.33	7.05	6.78	6.53	6.31	6.10	5.90	5.75	5.66	5.58	5.50
8	8.72	8.32	7.95	7.63	7.33	7.05	6.78	6.53	6.31	6.10	5.90	5.72	5.54	5.38	5.22
9	8.72	8.31	7.96	7.63	7.33	7.05	6.78	6.53	6.31	6.10	5.90	5.72	5.54	5.38	5.23
10	8.71	8.32	7.95	7.63	7.33	7.05	6.78	6.53	6.31	6.10	5.91	5.72	5.54	5.38	5.22
11	7.63	8.31	7.96	7.63	7.32	7.05	6.78	6.53	6.31	6.10	5.90	5.72	5.55	5.38	5.23
12		3.12	6.96	7.62	7.33	7.05	6.78	6.53	6.31	6.09	5.91	5.72	5.54	5.38	5.22
13				2.86	6.41	7.04	6.78	6.54	6.30	6.10	5.90	5.73	5.55	5.38	5.22
14						2.64	5.94	6.53	6.31	6.09	5.91	5.72	5.54	5.38	5.23
15								2.45	5.52	6.10	5.90	5.72	5.55	5.37	5.22
16										2.29	5.17	5.72	5.54	5.38	5.23
17												2.15	4.85	5.38	5.22
18														2.02	4.57

and the Recovery Period is:

the Depreciation Rate is:

If the Recovery Year is:	17.5	18.0	18.5	19.0	19.5	20.0	20.5	21.0	21.5	22.0	22.5	23.0	23.5	24.0	24.5
1	1.07	1.04	1.01	0.99	0.96	0.938	0.915	0.893	0.872	0.852	0.833	0.815	0.798	0.781	0.765
2	8.48	8.25	8.03	7.82	7.62	7.430	7.250	7.079	6.916	6.760	6.611	6.469	6.332	6.201	6.076
3	7.75	7.56	7.38	7.20	7.03	6.872	6.720	6.573	6.433	6.299	6.170	6.047	5.928	5.814	5.704
4	7.09	6.93	6.78	6.63	6.49	6.357	6.228	6.104	5.985	5.870	5.759	5.652	5.549	5.450	5.354
5	6.48	6.35	6.23	6.11	5.99	5.880	5.772	5.668	5.567	5.469	5.375	5.284	5.195	5.110	5.027
6	5.93	5.82	5.72	5.63	5.53	5.439	5.350	5.263	5.179	5.097	5.017	4.939	4.864	4.790	4.719
7	5.42	5.34	5.26	5.18	5.11	5.031	4.958	4.887	4.817	4.749	4.682	4.617	4.553	4.491	4.430
8	5.08	4.94	4.83	4.77	4.71	4.654	4.596	4.538	4.481	4.425	4.370	4.316	4.263	4.210	4.159
9	5.08	4.94	4.81	4.69	4.57	4.458	4.352	4.252	4.169	4.124	4.079	4.034	3.991	3.947	3.904
10	5.08	4.94	4.81	4.69	4.57	4.458	4.352	4.252	4.156	4.062	3.972	3.888	3.807	3.730	3.665
11	5.08	4.95	4.81	4.69	4.57	4.458	4.352	4.252	4.156	4.062	3.972	3.887	3.807	3.730	3.655
12	5.08	4.94	4.82	4.69	4.57	4.458	4.352	4.252	4.155	4.062	3.973	3.888	3.807	3.729	3.655
13	5.08	4.95	4.81	4.69	4.57	4.458	4.352	4.252	4.156	4.061	3.972	3.887	3.807	3.730	3.655
14	5.08	4.94	4.82	4.69	4.57	4.458	4.352	4.252	4.155	4.062	3.973	3.888	3.807	3.729	3.655
15	5.08	4.95	4.81	4.69	4.57	4.458	4.352	4.252	4.156	4.061	3.972	3.887	3.807	3.730	3.655
16	5.08	4.94	4.82	4.69	4.57	4.458	4.352	4.252	4.155	4.062	3.973	3.888	3.807	3.730	3.655
17	5.08	4.95	4.81	4.68	4.57	4.458	4.353	4.252	4.156	4.061	3.972	3.887	3.806	3.729	3.655
18	5.08	4.94	4.82	4.69	4.57	4.458	4.352	4.252	4.155	4.062	3.973	3.888	3.807	3.730	3.655
19	1.90	4.33	4.81	4.68	4.57	4.459	4.353	4.252	4.156	4.061	3.972	3.887	3.806	3.729	3.655
20			1.81	4.10	4.57	4.458	4.352	4.251	4.155	4.062	3.973	3.888	3.807	3.730	3.655
21					1.72	4.459	4.353	4.252	4.156	4.061	3.972	3.887	3.806	3.729	3.655
22						3.901	1.632	3.720	1.558	4.062	3.973	3.888	3.807	3.730	3.655
23										3.554	3.972	3.887	3.806	3.729	3.655
24											1.490	3.402	3.807	3.730	3.656
25													1.427	3.263	3.655
26															1.371

and the Recovery Period is:

the Depreciation Rate is:

If the Recovery Year is:	25.0	25.5	26.0	26.5	27.0	27.5	28.0	28.5	29.0	29.5	30.0	30.5	31.0	31.5	32.0
1	0.750	0.735	0.721	0.708	0.694	0.682	0.670	0.658	0.647	0.536	0.625	0.615	0.605	0.595	0.586
2	5.955	5.839	5.728	5.620	5.517	5.417	5.321	5.229	5.139	5.052	4.969	4.888	4.809	4.734	4.660
3	5.598	5.496	5.397	5.302	5.211	5.122	5.036	4.953	4.873	4.796	4.720	4.647	4.577	4.508	4.442
4	5.262	5.172	5.086	5.002	4.921	4.842	4.766	4.693	4.621	4.552	4.484	4.419	4.355	4.293	4.233
5	4.946	4.868	4.792	4.719	4.648	4.578	4.511	4.446	4.382	4.320	4.260	4.202	4.145	4.089	4.035
6	4.649	4.582	4.516	4.452	4.389	4.329	4.269	4.212	4.155	4.101	4.047	3.995	3.944	3.894	3.846
7	4.370	4.312	4.255	4.200	4.146	4.093	4.041	3.990	3.940	3.892	3.845	3.798	3.753	3.709	3.666
8	4.108	4.059	4.010	3.962	3.915	3.869	3.824	3.780	3.737	3.694	3.653	3.612	3.572	3.532	3.494
9	3.862	3.820	3.779	3.738	3.698	3.658	3.619	3.581	3.543	3.506	3.470	3.434	3.399	3.364	3.330
10	3.630	3.595	3.561	3.526	3.492	3.459	3.426	3.393	3.360	3.328	3.296	3.265	3.234	3.204	3.174
11	3.582	3.513	3.446	3.383	3.321	3.270	3.242	3.214	3.186	3.159	3.132	3.105	3.078	3.051	3.025
12	3.582	3.513	3.446	3.382	3.321	3.262	3.204	3.148	3.095	3.043	2.994	2.952	2.929	2.906	2.883
13	3.582	3.513	3.446	3.383	3.321	3.262	3.204	3.148	3.095	3.043	2.994	2.945	2.898	2.853	2.808
14	3.582	3.513	3.446	3.382	3.321	3.262	3.204	3.148	3.095	3.043	2.994	2.945	2.898	2.853	2.808
15	3.582	3.513	3.446	3.383	3.321	3.262	3.204	3.148	3.095	3.043	2.994	2.945	2.898	2.853	2.808
16	3.583	3.513	3.446	3.382	3.322	3.262	3.204	3.148	3.095	3.043	2.994	2.946	2.898	2.852	2.809
17	3.582	3.513	3.446	3.383	3.321	3.262	3.204	3.148	3.095	3.043	2.994	2.945	2.898	2.853	2.808
18	3.583	3.513	3.446	3.382	3.322	3.262	3.204	3.149	3.095	3.043	2.993	2.946	2.898	2.852	2.809
19	3.582	3.513	3.446	3.383	3.321	3.262	3.204	3.148	3.095	3.043	2.994	2.945	2.898	2.853	2.808
20	3.583	3.513	3.446	3.382	3.321	3.262	3.204	3.149	3.095	3.044	2.994	2.946	2.898	2.852	2.809
21	3.582	3.512	3.447	3.383	3.322	3.262	3.204	3.148	3.095	3.043	2.993	2.945	2.898	2.853	2.808
22	3.583	3.513	3.446	3.382	3.321	3.263	3.204	3.149	3.095	3.044	2.994	2.946	2.898	2.853	2.808
23	3.582	3.512	3.447	3.383	3.322	3.262	3.205	3.148	3.095	3.043	2.993	2.945	2.898	2.852	2.808
24	3.583	3.513	3.446	3.382	3.321	3.263	3.204	3.149	3.095	3.044	2.994	2.946	2.898	2.853	2.809
25	3.582	3.512	3.447	3.383	3.322	3.262	3.205	3.148	3.095	3.043	2.993	2.945	2.898	2.853	2.808
26	3.135	3.513	3.446	3.382	3.321	3.263	3.204	3.149	3.095	3.044	2.994	2.946	2.898	2.853	2.809
27		1.317	3.016	3.383	3.322	3.262	3.204	3.148	3.095	3.043	2.993	2.945	2.898	2.853	2.808
28				1.268	3.321	3.263	3.205	3.149	3.095	3.044	2.994	2.946	2.898	2.852	2.809
29					3.322	3.262	3.204	3.148	3.095	3.043	2.993	2.945	2.899	2.853	2.808
30					2.906	3.263	3.205	3.149	3.095	3.044	2.994	2.946	2.898	2.852	2.809
31						1.223	3.204	3.148	3.094	3.044	2.519	2.945	2.899	2.852	2.808
32							2.804	3.148	2.708	1.141		1.105	2.536	2.852	2.809
33								1.181						1.070	2.457

and the Recovery Period is:

the Depreciation Rate is:

If the Recovery Year is:	32.5	33.0	33.5	34.0	34.5	35.0	35.5	36.0	36.5	37.0	37.5	38.0	38.5	39.0	39.5
1	0.577	0.568	0.560	0.551	0.543	0.536	0.528	0.521	0.514	0.507	0.500	0.493	0.487	0.481	0.475
2	4.589	4.520	4.453	4.387	4.324	4.263	4.203	4.145	4.088	4.034	3.980	3.928	3.877	3.828	3.779
3	4.377	4.314	4.253	4.194	4.136	4.080	4.025	3.972	3.920	3.870	3.821	3.773	3.726	3.680	3.636
4	4.175	4.118	4.063	4.009	3.956	3.905	3.855	3.807	3.759	3.713	3.668	3.624	3.581	3.539	3.498
5	3.982	3.931	3.881	3.832	3.784	3.738	3.692	3.648	3.605	3.563	3.521	3.481	3.441	3.403	3.365
6	3.798	3.752	3.707	3.663	3.620	3.578	3.536	3.496	3.457	3.418	3.380	3.343	3.307	3.272	3.237
7	3.623	3.582	3.541	3.501	3.462	3.424	3.387	3.350	3.315	3.280	3.245	3.212	3.178	3.146	3.114
8	3.456	3.419	3.382	3.347	3.312	3.278	3.244	3.211	3.178	3.147	3.115	3.085	3.055	3.025	2.996
9	3.296	3.263	3.231	3.199	3.168	3.137	3.107	3.077	3.048	3.019	2.991	2.963	2.936	2.909	2.882
10	3.144	3.115	3.086	3.058	3.030	3.003	2.976	2.949	2.923	2.897	2.871	2.846	2.821	2.797	2.773
11	2.999	2.974	2.948	2.923	2.898	2.874	2.850	2.826	2.802	2.779	2.756	2.734	2.711	2.689	2.668
12	2.861	2.838	2.816	2.794	2.772	2.751	2.729	2.708	2.687	2.666	2.646	2.626	2.606	2.586	2.566
13	2.766	2.725	2.690	2.671	2.652	2.633	2.614	2.595	2.577	2.558	2.540	2.522	2.504	2.486	2.469
14	2.766	2.725	2.685	2.646	2.608	2.570	2.535	2.500	2.471	2.455	2.439	2.423	2.407	2.391	2.375
15	2.766	2.725	2.685	2.646	2.607	2.571	2.535	2.500	2.467	2.433	2.401	2.370	2.339	2.310	2.285
16	2.766	2.725	2.685	2.646	2.608	2.571	2.535	2.500	2.467	2.433	2.401	2.370	2.339	2.310	2.281
17	2.766	2.725	2.685	2.645	2.607	2.570	2.535	2.500	2.467	2.433	2.401	2.370	2.339	2.310	2.281
18	2.766	2.725	2.685	2.646	2.608	2.571	2.535	2.500	2.467	2.433	2.401	2.370	2.339	2.310	2.281
19	2.766	2.725	2.685	2.646	2.607	2.570	2.535	2.500	2.466	2.433	2.401	2.370	2.340	2.310	2.281
20	2.766	2.725	2.685	2.645	2.608	2.570	2.535	2.500	2.467	2.433	2.401	2.370	2.339	2.310	2.281
21	2.766	2.725	2.685	2.646	2.607	2.571	2.535	2.500	2.466	2.433	2.401	2.370	2.340	2.310	2.281
22	2.766	2.725	2.685	2.646	2.608	2.571	2.535	2.500	2.467	2.433	2.401	2.370	2.339	2.310	2.281
23	2.766	2.725	2.685	2.645	2.608	2.570	2.535	2.500	2.466	2.433	2.401	2.370	2.340	2.310	2.281
24	2.766	2.725	2.685	2.645	2.607	2.570	2.535	2.500	2.467	2.433	2.401	2.370	2.339	2.310	2.281
25	2.766	2.725	2.685	2.646	2.608	2.571	2.535	2.501	2.466	2.433	2.401	2.370	2.340	2.310	2.281
26	2.766	2.725	2.685	2.646	2.607	2.570	2.535	2.500	2.467	2.433	2.401	2.370	2.339	2.310	2.281
27	2.766	2.725	2.685	2.645	2.607	2.571	2.535	2.500	2.466	2.434	2.401	2.370	2.340	2.310	2.281
28	2.766	2.725	2.685	2.646	2.608	2.570	2.535	2.501	2.467	2.433	2.401	2.369	2.339	2.310	2.281
29	2.766	2.724	2.685	2.646	2.607	2.571	2.535	2.500	2.466	2.434	2.401	2.370	2.339	2.310	2.281
30	2.766	2.725	2.685	2.645	2.608	2.570	2.535	2.500	2.467	2.433	2.401	2.370	2.339	2.310	2.281
31	2.766	2.724	2.685	2.646	2.607	2.570	2.535	2.501	2.466	2.434	2.401	2.369	2.340	2.310	2.281
32	2.766	2.724	2.684	2.646	2.608	2.570	2.535	2.500	2.467	2.433	2.401	2.370	2.339	2.310	2.281
33	2.766	2.725	2.684	2.645	2.607	2.571	2.535	2.500	2.467	2.433	2.401	2.369	2.340	2.310	2.281
34	1.037	2.724	2.685	2.646	2.608	2.570	2.535	2.501	2.466	2.434	2.402	2.370	2.339	2.310	2.282
35		2.384	1.007	2.645	2.607	2.571	2.534	2.500	2.467	2.433	2.401	2.369	2.340	2.309	2.281
36				2.315	0.978	2.570	2.535	2.501	2.466	2.434	2.402	2.370	2.339	2.310	2.282
37						2.249	0.950	2.500	2.467	2.433	2.401	2.369	2.340	2.309	2.281
38								2.188	0.925	2.434	2.402	2.370	2.339	2.310	2.281
39										2.129	0.901	2.369	2.340	2.309	2.281
40												2.073	0.877	2.310	2.282
41														2.021	0.856

and the Recovery Period is:

the Depreciation Rate is:

If the Recovery Year is:	40.0	40.5	41.0	41.5	42.0	42.5	43.0	43.5	44.0	44.5	45.0	45.5	46.0	46.5	47.0
1	0.469	0.463	0.457	0.452	0.446	0.441	0.436	0.431	0.426	0.421	0.417	0.412	0.408	0.403	0.399
2	3.732	3.587	3.642	3.558	3.556	3.514	3.473	3.433	3.395	3.357	3.319	3.283	3.248	3.213	3.179
3	3.592	3.550	3.509	3.468	3.429	3.390	3.352	3.315	3.279	3.243	3.209	3.175	3.142	3.109	3.077
4	3.458	3.419	3.380	3.343	3.306	3.270	3.235	3.201	3.167	3.134	3.102	3.070	3.039	3.009	2.979
5	3.328	3.292	3.257	3.222	3.188	3.155	3.122	3.090	3.059	3.028	2.998	2.969	2.940	2.912	2.884
6	3.203	3.170	3.137	3.105	3.074	3.043	3.013	2.984	2.955	2.926	2.898	2.871	2.844	2.818	2.792
7	3.083	3.053	3.023	2.993	2.964	2.936	2.908	2.881	2.854	2.828	2.802	2.776	2.751	2.727	2.703
8	2.968	2.939	2.912	2.885	2.858	2.832	2.807	2.782	2.757	2.732	2.708	2.685	2.662	2.639	2.617
9	2.856	2.831	2.805	2.781	2.756	2.732	2.709	2.686	2.663	2.640	2.618	2.596	2.575	2.554	2.533
10	2.749	2.726	2.703	2.680	2.658	2.636	2.614	2.593	2.572	2.551	2.531	2.511	2.491	2.471	2.452
11	2.646	2.625	2.604	2.583	2.563	2.543	2.523	2.504	2.484	2.465	2.447	2.428	2.410	2.392	2.374
12	2.547	2.528	2.509	2.490	2.472	2.453	2.435	2.417	2.400	2.382	2.365	2.348	2.331	2.315	2.298
13	2.451	2.434	2.417	2.400	2.383	2.367	2.350	2.334	2.318	2.302	2.286	2.271	2.255	2.240	2.225
14	2.359	2.344	2.328	2.313	2.298	2.283	2.268	2.253	2.239	2.224	2.210	2.196	2.182	2.168	2.154
15	2.271	2.257	2.243	2.230	2.216	2.203	2.189	2.176	2.162	2.149	2.136	2.123	2.110	2.098	2.085
16	2.253	2.225	2.198	2.172	2.146	2.125	2.113	2.101	2.089	2.077	2.065	2.053	2.042	2.030	2.019
17	2.253	2.225	2.198	2.172	2.146	2.122	2.097	2.073	2.050	2.027	2.005	1.986	1.975	1.965	1.954
18	2.253	2.225	2.198	2.172	2.147	2.122	2.097	2.073	2.050	2.027	2.005	1.983	1.961	1.940	1.920
19	2.253	2.225	2.198	2.172	2.146	2.121	2.097	2.073	2.049	2.027	2.005	1.983	1.961	1.940	1.920
20	2.253	2.225	2.198	2.172	2.147	2.122	2.097	2.073	2.050	2.027	2.005	1.983	1.961	1.940	1.920
21	2.253	2.225	2.198	2.172	2.146	2.121	2.097	2.073	2.049	2.027	2.005	1.983	1.961	1.940	1.920
22	2.253	2.225	2.198	2.172	2.147	2.122	2.097	2.073	2.050	2.027	2.005	1.983	1.961	1.940	1.920
23	2.253	2.225	2.198	2.172	2.146	2.121	2.097	2.073	2.049	2.027	2.005	1.983	1.961	1.940	1.920
24	2.253	2.225	2.198	2.172	2.147	2.122	2.097	2.073	2.050	2.027	2.005	1.983	1.961	1.940	1.920
25	2.253	2.225	2.198	2.172	2.146	2.121	2.097	2.073	2.049	2.027	2.005	1.983	1.961	1.940	1.920
26	2.253	2.225	2.198	2.172	2.147	2.122	2.097	2.073	2.050	2.027	2.005	1.983	1.961	1.940	1.920
27	2.252	2.225	2.198	2.172	2.146	2.122	2.097	2.073	2.049	2.027	2.005	1.983	1.961	1.940	1.920
28	2.253	2.225	2.198	2.172	2.147	2.121	2.097	2.073	2.050	2.027	2.005	1.983	1.962	1.940	1.920
29	2.252	2.225	2.198	2.172	2.146	2.122	2.097	2.073	2.049	2.027	2.004	1.983	1.961	1.940	1.920
30	2.253	2.225	2.198	2.172	2.147	2.121	2.097	2.073	2.050	2.027	2.005	1.983	1.962	1.941	1.920
31	2.252	2.225	2.198	2.172	2.147	2.122	2.097	2.073	2.049	2.027	2.004	1.983	1.961	1.941	1.920
32	2.253	2.225	2.198	2.172	2.146	2.121	2.097	2.073	2.050	2.027	2.005	1.983	1.962	1.940	1.920
33	2.252	2.225	2.198	2.172	2.147	2.122	2.097	2.073	2.049	2.027	2.004	1.983	1.961	1.941	1.920
34	2.253	2.225	2.198	2.172	2.146	2.121	2.097	2.073	2.050	2.027	2.005	1.983	1.962	1.940	1.920
35	2.252	2.225	2.198	2.172	2.147	2.122	2.097	2.073	2.049	2.027	2.004	1.983	1.961	1.941	1.920
36	2.253	2.225	2.198	2.172	2.146	2.121	2.097	2.073	2.050	2.027	2.005	1.983	1.962	1.940	1.920
37	2.253	2.225	2.198	2.172	2.147	2.122	2.097	2.073	2.049	2.027	2.004	1.983	1.961	1.941	1.920
38	2.253	2.225	2.198	2.172	2.146	2.121	2.097	2.073	2.050	2.027	2.005	1.983	1.962	1.940	1.920
39	2.253	2.225	2.198	2.172	2.147	2.122	2.097	2.073	2.049	2.027	2.004	1.983	1.961	1.941	1.920
40	2.252	2.225	2.198	2.172	2.146	2.122	2.097	2.072	2.050	2.027	2.005	1.983	1.962	1.941	1.920
41	2.253	2.224	2.199	2.172	2.147	2.121	2.097	2.072	2.049	2.026	2.004	1.982	1.961	1.941	1.920
42	2.252	2.225	2.198	2.172	2.147	2.121	2.097	2.072	2.050	2.027	2.005	1.983	1.962	1.940	1.919
43	2.252	2.224	2.199	2.171	2.146	2.122	2.097	2.073	2.049	2.026	2.004	1.982	1.961	1.940	1.919
44	1.971	2.225	2.198	2.172	2.147	2.121	2.097	2.073	2.050	2.026	2.005	1.982	1.962	1.940	1.919
45		0.834	1.924	0.811	1.878	0.796	1.834	0.777	2.050	2.027	2.005	1.983	1.961	1.941	1.920
46									2.049	2.027	2.004	1.982	1.962	1.940	1.919
47									2.050	2.026	2.005	1.983	1.961	1.940	1.919
48									1.793	0.750	1.754	0.743	1.716	0.728	1.680

and the Recovery Period is:

the Depreciation Rate is:

If the Recovery Year is:	47.5	48.0	48.5	49.0	49.5	50.0
1	0.395	0.391	0.387	0.383	0.379	0.375
2	3.145	3.113	3.081	3.050	3.019	2.989
3	3.046	3.016	2.986	2.956	2.927	2.899
4	2.950	2.921	2.893	2.866	2.839	2.812
5	2.857	2.830	2.804	2.778	2.753	2.728
6	2.767	2.742	2.717	2.693	2.669	2.646
7	2.679	2.656	2.633	2.610	2.588	2.567
8	2.595	2.573	2.552	2.531	2.510	2.490
9	2.513	2.492	2.473	2.453	2.434	2.415
10	2.433	2.415	2.396	2.378	2.360	2.342
11	2.356	2.339	2.322	2.305	2.289	2.272
12	2.282	2.266	2.250	2.235	2.219	2.204
13	2.210	2.195	2.181	2.166	2.152	2.138
14	2.140	2.127	2.113	2.100	2.087	2.074
15	2.073	2.060	2.048	2.036	2.023	2.011
16	2.007	1.996	1.984	1.973	1.962	1.951
17	1.944	1.933	1.923	1.913	1.903	1.893
18	1.900	1.880	1.864	1.854	1.845	1.836
19	1.900	1.880	1.861	1.842	1.824	1.806
20	1.900	1.880	1.861	1.842	1.824	1.806
21	1.900	1.880	1.861	1.842	1.824	1.806
22	1.900	1.880	1.861	1.842	1.824	1.806
23	1.900	1.880	1.861	1.842	1.824	1.806
24	1.900	1.880	1.861	1.842	1.824	1.806
25	1.900	1.880	1.861	1.842	1.824	1.806
26	1.900	1.880	1.861	1.842	1.824	1.805
27	1.900	1.880	1.861	1.842	1.824	1.806
28	1.900	1.880	1.861	1.842	1.824	1.805
29	1.900	1.880	1.861	1.842	1.824	1.806
30	1.900	1.881	1.861	1.842	1.824	1.805
31	1.900	1.880	1.861	1.842	1.824	1.806
32	1.900	1.881	1.861	1.842	1.823	1.805
33	1.900	1.880	1.861	1.842	1.824	1.806
34	1.900	1.881	1.861	1.842	1.823	1.806
35	1.900	1.880	1.861	1.842	1.824	1.805
36	1.900	1.881	1.861	1.842	1.823	1.806
37	1.900	1.880	1.861	1.842	1.824	1.805
38	1.900	1.881	1.861	1.843	1.823	1.806
39	1.900	1.880	1.861	1.842	1.824	1.805
40	1.900	1.881	1.861	1.843	1.823	1.806
41	1.899	1.880	1.861	1.843	1.824	1.806
42	1.900	1.881	1.861	1.842	1.823	1.805
43	1.899	1.880	1.862	1.843	1.824	1.806
44	1.900	1.881	1.861	1.842	1.823	1.805
45	1.899	1.881	1.862	1.843	1.824	1.806
46	1.900	1.881	1.861	1.842	1.823	1.806
47	1.899	1.880	1.862	1.843	1.824	1.805
48	1.900	1.881	1.861	1.842	1.824	1.806
49	0.712	1.645	1.862	1.843	1.823	1.805
50			0.698	1.612	1.824	1.806
51					0.684	1.580

Index

About the Author

Richard M. Contino is a practicing attorney and businessman in New York City. He is the chairman of the board and a co-founder of ELM Corporation, a company engaged in the origination and management of equipment leasing business opportunities. He is also a director and a co-founder of PC National Corporation, a publicly traded computer sales company.

From 1978 to 1985, Mr. Contino was the managing partner of Contino, Ross & Benedict, a New York City law firm which he founded and which represented major equipment lessors and lessees in all aspects of the leasing and financing of capital equipment. For a five-year period prior to founding the law firm, he held the positions of marketing vice president and eastern regional counsel for GATX Leasing Corporation, a major independent equipment leasing company.

Mr. Contino is the author of numerous articles on equipment leasing and has lectured extensively throughout the United States to private corporations, business groups, law associations, and other professional organizations on the legal, financial, business, and marketing aspects of equipment leasing.

The author is a member of the bars of the states of New York and Maryland and also the District of Columbia. He is also a member of the American Bar Association. Mr. Contino holds an LL.M. in corporate law from the New York University Graduate School of Law, a juris doctorate from the University of Maryland School of Law and a bachelor of aeronautical engineering from Rensselaer Polytechnic Institute. He is listed in *Who's Who of American Law, The International Who's Who of Contemporary Achievement,* and *Who's Who of Emerging Leaders in America.*